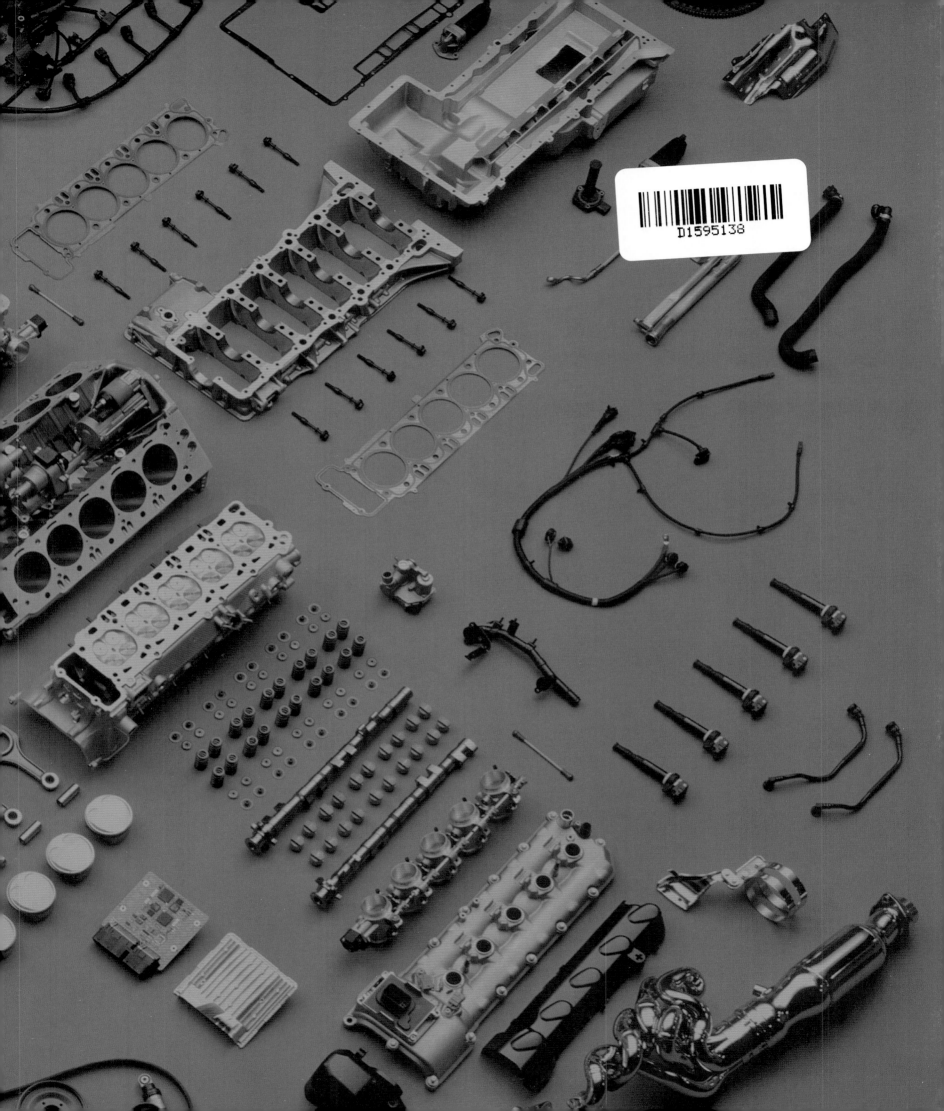

THE COMPLETE BOOK OF

BMW

EVERY MODEL SINCE 1950

First published in 2004 by Motorbooks, an imprint of MBI Publishing
Company, Galtier Plaza, Suite 200, 380 Jackson Street, St. Paul, MN
55101-3885 USA

The information in this book is true and complete to the best of our
knowledge. All recommendations are made without any guarantee
on the part of the author or Publisher, who also disclaim any liability
incurred in connection with the use of this data or specific details.

This publication has been prepared solely by MBI Publishing
Company and is not approved or licensed by any other entity.
We recognize that some words, model names, and designations
mentioned herein are the property of the trademark holder.
We use them for identification purposes only.
This is not an official publication.

Motorbooks titles are also available at discounts in bulk quantity for
industrial or sales-promotional use. For details write to Special Sales
Manager at MBI Publishing Company, Galtier Plaza, Suite 200, 380
Jackson Street, St. Paul, MN 55101-3885 USA

ISBN 0-7603-1951-0

Printed in China

Designed by Mark Roberts at Talking Design Ltd,
www.talkingdesign.net

Front cover: BMW Concept M5, March 2004
Back cover (l to r): BMW 2002 tii, BMW M5, BMW Z4,
Mini, BMW 1 Series

To my dear wife Christian, the cappuccino queen

BMW

MOTORBOOKS

··→ Contents

01 ⟶ Rebuilding a shattered heritage

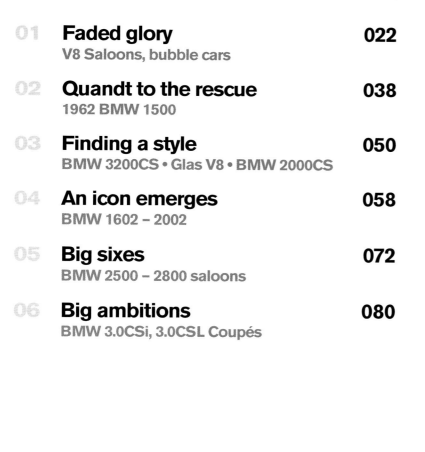

02 ⟶ Series to success: von Kuenheim's brilliant template

03 ⋯⋯▸ Technology leadership

04 ⋯⋯▸ Diversification and disaster

05 → The global grand plan

06 → Appendices

introduction

BMW is one of the most admired companies in the world. The surveys repeatedly show it, the corporate finance analysts regularly remind us of it, and the branding experts seem to chant it as something of a professional mantra.

By common consent BMW is a company that can do no wrong. It is one of the most consistent performers on the global business scene. For an unbroken and unprecedented run of 44 years it has seen increasing turnover, improving margins and, with only the very rare exception, steadily swelling profits. In today's stormy sea of corporate collapses, redundancies and rebates BMW is the gyro-stabilised ship that thrusts unflustered through the waves and which charts a smooth and constant course towards its port of destination. Not surprisingly, everyone now wants to climb aboard.

Yet if BMW were a finance house, a producer of farm machinery, fish-cakes or pharmaceuticals, would we care about it? The business gurus might get just as excited about it and the city would still take the same shine to the stock, but the likelihood is that the rest of us just wouldn't be bothered – or we wouldn't even know.

For BMW isn't about investments or earnings, capital or profitability – it's about products.

Whether it is cars or motorcycles or even aero engines, the products are what makes us care about BMW. The only reason BMW is the great presence it is today is that its products are good and people – more and more people – want to buy them.

Building cars that people desire is in BMW's blood, an article of faith in its corporate constitution. Only by pushing the boundaries of design and engineering did the company save itself from certain death in 1960; only by listening in to what its fanatical and often critical customers wanted could it stay one step ahead of everyone else and continue to create cars to intrigue, inspire and thrill. While car makers struggled and suffered, BMW couldn't make cars fast enough.

In researching this book I have become even more acutely aware of the strength and the continuity of the corporate culture at BMW, how the sense of mission and excitement permeates everything the company does – be it the

screaming 19,000 rpm engine for a Formula One car or the ergonomically optimised steering wheel for the new 1 Series. Whether it's a car or the whole company, BMW is like a stick of seaside rock: crack it open anywhere along its length and the driving pleasure message always reads through just as clearly.

Of course over the 50-plus years covered by this book the definition of driving pleasure has expanded enormously: at the beginning of the 1950s it might have simply meant getting to your destination safely and without breaking down; in the 1960s, with the advent of BMW's signature sports saloons such as the iconic 2002 tii, it meant agile handling and a potent engine. Today, in the early 21st century, driving pleasure could equally well be off-roading up a steep hillside in an X3, swishing along an Autobahn in high-speed silence in the 760i, or tackling twisty mountain passes in an open-topped Z4 roadster.

But perhaps the single thing that struck me most forcibly in my research was the sheer scale

> **"memorable models include the 2002tii for exuberance, the 507 for beauty and current M3 for being just about as complete a car as anyone could possibly wish for. The X5 and the Z4 count as highs, too – and can be set against disappointments, such as the 850 and the Z1"**

of BMW's expansion – how it grew from a bombed-out wreck in the late 1940s with no products at all to a company the world knows and admires. BMW's output in 1959 was 37,000 cars across four model lines: today, it has 10 main model lines and 18 variations and is a million-car company. That kind of growth doesn't happen by chance: it can come in one of two ways – by buying up other companies (which BMW tried once, with Rover, and failed) or, as has been BMW's overriding instinct, by coming up with an unstoppable flow of exciting products and systematically drawing in more and more customers each year. And that requires not just rare talent but the vision of a manager as inspirational as Eberhard von Kuenheim, who steered BMW with exceptional insight for 24 years to make it the company it is today.

Doubters might argue that expansion this far and this fast cannot be good, that the brand will become diluted and that a BMW will no longer be special once there's one in everybody's garage. It's a legitimate enough concern – or at least it would be for a marque whose attractiveness depended solely on its exclusivity. BMW's appeal, I believe, goes much deeper than mere rarity: in every BMW engineer is a deep-down understanding of what makes a car good to drive

and a pleasure to own. Americans call them car guys – as opposed to the money men, who tend to spoil the fun – and at BMW it is the car guys with their creative ideas who call the shots.

Above all, this book is a celebration of all those creative ideas turned into moving metal, an appreciation of how BMW's designers and engineers could capture the mood of the times and transform it into something alive and entertaining; the kind of car that people buy to enjoy and treasure rather than just utilise and discard. Sometimes the designs can themselves become the Zeitgeist: what better symbol of liberation in 1969 than the dynamic 2002 tii? The newly stylish 5 Series, heralding equality of opportunity in the '90s, the X5's expression of turn-of-the-millennium upward mobility, the born-again MINI's funky sense of fun – all are icons of their individual eras. With the new 1 Series – unique among small cars with its rear wheel drive – we could be on course for a welcome revival of the rebellious tii spirit, while Rolls-Royce under BMW stewardship is set to redefine the meaning of true luxury in a 21st century context.

I have been fortunate enough to experience almost all of the cars in this book from the driving seat and to have had quite a few of them parked outside my house, if only for the frustratingly

short periods allocated to automotive reviewers. Only a tiny fraction have I had the privilege of calling my own.

From a company where expectations always run very high, several especially memorable models nevertheless stand out: the 2002tii for its sheer exuberance, the 507 for its timeless beauty and current M3 for being just about as complete a car as anyone could possibly wish for. The X5, which rewrote the rules of the SUV game, and the subtly balanced Z4 count as highs, too – and can be set against the notably few disappointments, such as the 850 and the original but misguided Z1, that BMW has generated over the years.

Yet now, after having spent many months researching and writing, collating data and tracking down the photographs for this book, I am more than ever resolved to make amends and to re-live my mis-spent BMW youth – for which a tii-sized extension to my garage might just be needed. And if the many thousands of facts, figures, revelations and reminiscences I have assembled here do the same for you, then my efforts will not have been in vain.

Tony Lewin *August 2004*

von Kuenheim
The man who built BMW

One man has done more than any other to shape the prestigious, world-class BMW company we know today. Eberhard von Kuenheim laid the foundation for BMW to become a leading multi-national manufacturer, a company whose products inspire and delight car owners on every continent. If anyone deserves the title of Mr. BMW, it is this outstanding manager from an aristocratic East Prussian family.

Von Kuenheim had the strategic insight to foresee a prosperous future for a company selling high-quality high-performance cars to a discerning worldwide customer base: with uncanny perception he realised that top-level engineering and great driving dynamics did not have to be exclusively reserved for the rich and powerful but that smaller, more affordable cars could be just as fun and that they would appeal to enthusiastic drivers of all classes and on all continents. But von Kuenheim did not just devise the 3, 5 and 7 Series strategy that is still so successful today: he was instrumental in major BMW business decisions such as manufacturing in the USA, selling in Japan and developing the

V12 engines that would put BMW on a level technological footing to traditional status leaders Mercedes-Benz.

Like Volkswagen, BMW arose from the ashes of Germany's manufacturing base, ravaged by bombing in World War II. It took the battered BMW many years – and many crises – to regain its status as a serious car producer: only in 1962 did it launch the car which set the company truly back on its feet. It was in 1969 that von Kuenheim began his unprecedented 24 years at the head of the organisation in what he calls "the pioneering phase", when the engineering culture that was to drive BMW began to take hold.

He talks with affection about his beloved

BMW: "What we have done at BMW and still are doing at BMW … I think other people cannot imitate it, though they try."

He speaks with modesty about his own considerable achievements, though no one can match the impact of his reign, which lasted from 1969 to 1993. Von Kuenheim had been spotted as a talented young manager in the late 1960s by the Quandt family, who rescued BMW from certain bankruptcy in 1959. He was an East Prussian aristocrat who had been orphaned in World War II, worked for Bosch and then studied engineering in Stuttgart before joining – and turning round – one of Quandt's underperforming engineering companies.

"What we have done at BMW and still are doing at BMW ... I think other people cannot imitate it, though they try"

Taking the controls of BMW as chief executive officer (CEO) at the age of 41, von Kuenheim was quick to see the opportunities presented in the hitherto unexploited market for high-quality, high-performance saloon cars which could be sold at premium prices. His strategic template of the compact 2002, mid-sized 2000 and luxury 2500 proved a powerful engine for the growth of the once-small company, and can still be seen in the 3 Series, 5 Series and 7 Series which continue to be BMW's core products today.

He left the chairman's seat in 1993 with a remarkable record of corporate growth and consistent profits increase, but remains deeply connected to BMW and now runs the Eberhard von Kuenheim Stiftung, a foundation dedicated to providing educational opportunities to disadvantaged children.

Talking about the BMW of 1969, von Kuenheim says: "I went to the Frankfurt motor show and one of my future colleagues – Wilhelm Gieschen – was there. He announced that BMW didn't have new models but that it did have a new CEO. He said it as a bit of a joke.

"I think that in those days Herbert Quandt had an important influence with the board. They were questioning whether they could have the courage to choose somebody who was not an expert in the field to run the company and develop it.

"In the years leading up to this, I had been the chairman and CEO of one of the machinery companies of the Quandt group – Industriewerke Karlsruhe, or IWK. It was a smaller company – at that time it was the size of BMW; today it would only be one 10th or one 20th of that size."

IWK had been in bad shape but von Kuenheim turned it around, and when he left at the end of 1969 it was doing much better. IWK survived to become a respected company on the stock market.

Herbert Quandt had given von Kuenheim responsibility for BMW because of his endeavours at IWK, but the two did not know each other personally to any great extent.

BMW caused a sensation at the 1961 Frankfurt show with the Neue Klasse 1500. In the background is the big 3200 CS coupé, last of the old-era BMWs

The Quandt family hired him as a consultant and co-ordinator in 1965, though for the first two or three years he never saw Herbert Quandt.

Yet von Kuenheim already had a keen sense of BMW's history and how as a company which was primarily a manufacturer of aero engines it had seen its lifeblood taken away from it when, directly after WWII, the Allies stopped aircraft engine manufacture in Germany, forcing BMW to end its production.

"The only reminder of this phase of our history is our trademark of the propeller against the blue sky," says von Kuenheim. "Is that not a fine story? BMW was without any question the aircraft engine manufacturer here on the continent, the first in the world to produce jet engines in line manufacture."

BMW engineers had started jet engine production about a year earlier than Rolls-Royce,

he explains: its engine is the grandmother of the jet engines of General Electric, of SNECMA and of the Russians because its engineers were dispersed to many different countries at the end of the war.

"Car production had been in Eisenach, which was in Thuringia, by that time part of the Russian zone," explains von Kuenheim. "A few BMW people managed to get hold of the drawings of the cars and smuggle them into a rucksack: they succeeded in escaping in what we call 'black over the green border' in the middle of the night back to Munich because the Russians did not approve. For 10 to 15 years BMW struggled to find a direction: when it came to car production they hadn't the money or the factories, and with aircraft engines there was simply no market at that time.

"BMW had got more or less to the edge of bankruptcy by 1959. It all came to a head for the

BMW people at the famous shareholders meeting in December of that year. That is when Herbert Quandt made the decision to take the risk, or as we know it today, the chance.

"In those days it was seen as a risk to do that. The name of the company was there, the engineers were still there, the quality workers were still there. But there was no product there, no management either, nor was there any money. Yet Quandt said 'let's try'. When I came to BMW it was 10 years later. Those years of rebuilding and revitalising were still in full swing. We were still in what we would now see as the pioneering phase. The BMW spirit it was not yet fully formed at that stage and the identification with the company and the model range was all still not really there. The calibre and the behaviour of the different people in different positions were very different then too. Without any question, the single biggest

Herbert Quandt: "you must go for the higher price because you need to show people it is a car with real value"

task was how to survive – because we were a late starter, we were small, we had only a limited number of products, a limited number of good sales people and a limited sales organisation. And, let us not forget, we only had a limited amount of money."

Asked in an interview for this book what was the key to BMW's remarkable success, von Kuenheim makes it clear that the foundations were laid as early as the 1970s – perhaps before any external commentators had yet woken up to the true potential of the premium product formula.

Which products were being built when you arrived at BMW in 1969? Had the newer models been well received?
The so-called Neue Klasse was already established. In those days it was the 1500 and later on 1600, 1800 and 2000 – the equivalent model range to today's 5 Series. They were well accepted at the time, even though they were very expensive cars. The price of the Volkswagen Beetle in those days was between 4,000 and 5,000 Marks. Therefore, BMW said "OK now we have a very big crunch: we will introduce the car at 6,000 D-Marks".

Herbert Quandt was already a very influential shareholder, and he said: "You are wrong: you

must go for 8,000 D-Marks because you have to show people it is a car with [real] value."

That was before my time, but it shows BMW going against market research and "feeling with its fingertips" again. In those days it was a lot of money.

Did people complain it was too expensive?
Yes, they did – but it was accepted by people who said "I can afford that: I won't drive a Beetle any more – everybody has a Beetle." The effect of this was that BMWs became the cars for *"Aufsteigers"* – the social climbers of the era, rising up the ladder of social status. That car was doing well, and there was also the small two-door car 1600, 1800, and then the 2002, which I think only came out once I was already there.

Very new on the market then was the 2500: out of this car we later developed our 7 Series. We now have more versions and more variations, but even today we have more or less the same core models: the 3 Series, now with four doors, corresponds to the 1602-2002, we have the 5 Series and we have the 7 Series – and these three lines are still the core of our business today.

How were those products from a technical standpoint when you arrived?
The reliability of the cars was a bit limited in those days. So we needed to raise the quality, improve

the reliability and bring up the productivity. And don't forget that we had to build the factory, too. Until then the factory had worked in old halls here there and everywhere: what we did was to build a new hall on top of the old one. During the works holiday the old hall was pulled out and the new one was put in.

Those moves helped bring the product quality up: the next task we had was to upgrade the sales organisation, which was very limited at that time. The core was already there, but we had to go out into the international market. We were simply a company in upper Bavaria, and we had to go out into the world – and that is not only Austria but Holland and France and the UK, too, and also overseas to the USA. These were [perhaps] only details: I think most important thing for us was to build up the human beings – to find the right people, to find the right spirit and to bring them here. We asked ourselves "what is BMW? What do we require from people in lower positions, middle positions and higher positions?" We realised that the most important thing they could bring was the right attitude.

How effective was this?
At first we insisted that everybody knew his function. If he was on the Board and a member of the Vorstand (executive) or if he was in a little department he of course had to know the full depth of his function. In the same way, they would

"You need to follow the red line towards the target: it's like a lighthouse, and on your way towards the lighthouse the waves sometimes come from the left, other times from the right. You have to steer against the waves but you know where you want to go"

be expected to be capable of solving short-term problems. What we did was encourage them to find the right solution for the long-term task and the long-term problems. Today we would call this a sustainability approach: 30 years ago we didn't have that kind of vocabulary.

As an example, because we were still building up the company we had to sell as many cars as possible as we needed the cashflow to support a lot of investment and our investment range was very high. But it was more than just selling cars: we had to build up the right sales organisation – we needed to draw in the people with the right way of thinking to our dealers and to our subsidiaries around the world. We had already formed our subsidiary in the US, but we had to make it clear that the attitude of the people from Detroit was not for us. Instead, we made sure we hired the right people to suit our needs, to suit our culture. Of course we were duty-bound to deal with day-to-day problems, but we also had to be mindful of what would come after that to make sure that in 10 years' time we would not find ourselves in such a critical situation again.

Were you able to form a clear picture of where you wanted to see the company to go in the longer term?

It took a few days, months or years but I think what we really did was to make everyone realise that the company now has a reputation. We had

one question in those days: we were very small. The year before I joined BMW in 1969 was the first time BMW had a turnover in sales of over 1 billion DM. Today, as you know, BMW is a 42 billion euro company – that's equivalent to 80 billion DM.

So though we are quite a different company today, the success we have had has been built on the way we formed that company in the 1970s and 1980s. This meant that by the time the 90s came the company was very stable. We are now in the lucky position where we have people in Singapore or Tokyo and New York or Toronto, people who have exactly the right idea what BMW is and has to be – and we know these people will make the right decisions should a crisis come. And in a crisis you are able to see the best qualities of a man.

Who were the people, the key players in the company when you arrived? Was Paul Hahnemann influential?

Hahnemann left us in 1971 so I was only with him for one and a half years. The public thought he was the CEO but he never was. Hahnemann had done a great deal for BMW and he was an excellent salesman. He had the nose for sales: he could always instantly sniff out what the atmosphere in a particular room or situation was – he was excellent at that. But, though he helped a lot in BMW's development, his problem was that BMW

developed to higher levels and he didn't keep pace with the company.

He was an excellent guy for this pioneering time and an excellent man for the size of the company when everybody knows everyone else – because it was still very small. But to lead a company where you, for practical reasons, are no longer able to know all the people but have to make clear to all the people where the direction is – that's different. BMW has to be very thankful to him, but the company had begun to outgrow him. He was an aggressive salesman who knew every dealer. It works if you have 100 dealers: if you have 4,000 dealers and everybody expects the board member for sales to know every dealer, you're bound to get lost. For instance, he would know the birthday of every dealer's wife and send them flowers – that was fine at the beginning, but not right for a larger, more professional company.

How did you get on with the Quandt family? Were they very hands-on in influencing the company, or were you left to your own devices?

In the beginning, the contact with Herbert Quandt was closer but he had some real problems with his eyes and couldn't read. He was chairman of the supervisory board for a only short while. The first few years there were other people on the board and he took part in the meetings only as a guest: for a few years he was chairman, but

BMW chairman Eberhard von Kuenheim (left), Herbert Quandt (centre) and sales director Paul Hahnemann alongside an '02 Cabrio in March 1971

Count Goertz had the active role and was the man who represented the house of Quandt – so I had more contact with him than with the Quandt family. Much more, in fact, as he was chairman of the supervisory board for 15 years.

Would you say Herbert Quandt influenced the way the company was run, the direction it went in, or was he simply a shareholder?
It depends on the year – whether it was '65 or '70 or '75 or '80. He died in 1982. At the beginning he was more involved: later, when the company had found its own way – and he was getting older – he was very interested but his direct influence became less and less. We met every three months or so and very often he

invited us for dinner at his house, and then we spoke in a very relaxed way. But he didn't influence us, or let us say he didn't get into detailed decisions. He was always interested and would ask things like "do you think you are all right?" or "do you think we should go there or not?" I can remember a long discussion one evening. Some friends of his had said "you have to go to Brazil". So we discussed Brazil intensively, but we said that the USA and Japan were more important. He said "but my friends said it was a blossoming market... and so on." We argued we had to be realistic, Brazil is further away, it's a huge country and most of it consists of tropical rainforest.

So he asked questions rather than questioning your policies?
Yes, because he was intellectually interested. He was always asking about competitors, what they were doing, why weren't we doing it, and so on.

Were you usually able to satisfy him that you were doing the right thing?
Yes, because he had this limited ability to take part in normal life, one was always very polite and gave him information so that he would know things were going in the right direction or not. The real time for Herbert Quandt was in the beginning, in the 1960s when the whole situation was very risky – that was his time.

BMW headquarters tower has been an imposing sight in Munich since 1982

Was it because he understood the idea of BMW and what it symbolised?
Yes, and he also had a little problem in those early days: he was also on the supervisory board of Mercedes up to 1973 or 1974, when he sold his shares to Kuwait. We had great trust in him and his background, not just the money or looking after the products, but the man who stands behind the company. We knew that he stood behind BMW and that there wouldn't be any risk of a hostile takeover.

Was BMW often approached in that era?
Yes – there were a lot of approaches in our direction. GM, Ford and Chrysler in those days wanted to buy BMW: Fiat at one point wanted to take over BMW. I am speaking of the 70s and 80s – and there was also a Japanese company interested: I cannot remember which one. In the 90s Ferdinand Piëch from VW said he wanted to buy BMW shares. It was plainly ridiculous, but for BMW it helped a lot that we knew and still know that we can rely on the shareholder family to stay with BMW.

And that continues to this day?
More than ever. There was a gap, of course, after he [Quandt] died, and it was filled by Count Goertz and myself. But now both his children, Susanne and Stefan, are on the supervisory board where we have 20 members. So the family has two seats, and Stefan Quandt is vice-chairman.

Would you say that the stability that you gained from this shareholding has been one of the key factors that has allowed you to stay true to your ideals, perhaps to take risks that other companies might be too cautious to accept?
You need to follow the red line towards the target: it's like a lighthouse, and on your way towards the lighthouse the waves sometimes come from the left, other times from the right. You have to steer against the waves but you know where you want to go.

How would you explain the fantastic success of BMW, from 40,000 cars to over a million cars in a space of 40 years? What other secret is there to it?
There are no secrets at all.

"In the motor industry you need board people who have the feeling for design and for styling, for example. And even if they are not engineers they must have an understanding of, for instance, what acceleration means"

Well, other companies haven't done it, but BMW has.

No, at the end of the day, the first secret is not a secret, it is very open. These are human beings, and to find the right human beings and to integrate them you need a *Vorbild* – a role model, an example. That is very important – it's always a secret of leadership.

Something to aspire to?

Yes: if you are to be a role model you cannot ask your people to do something you are not doing yourself. You cannot ask for overtime work if you aren't prepared to do it. The higher you are as a role model, the more prepared you must be to stay on the ground as a work partner, but without being equal.

And as I mentioned before, we also expected the CEO and the members of the management board to know their functions. That is quite different to what you will find on a British or American board. Nowadays in England or America a CEO can be at a company which produces cornflakes and two years later you will find him at a shipyard; another three years later you will find him in investment banking. This means they can never go into things in depth – they can't identify themselves [with the company] and, as a result, these people at the top are not always experts. In the motor industry you need board people who have the feeling for design

and for styling, for example. And even if they are not engineers they must have an understanding of, for instance, what acceleration means, to have the feeling for the product and to identify themselves with that product. You can't do this if you jump between different companies with different products. I think that is one of the advantages we have here in Germany.

Is this common to all German companies, this knowledge of everything, or was it your management style?

In companies some more, some less: it's there in a lot of companies. It is more common in Germany than it is in Britain. This is why we are more industrialised in this country, but within Germany and this industry, I think BMW is one of the most advanced. I am a little bit reluctant to say in the lead, but we do this in greater detail than the others. We expect senior executives below the board level to know literally every detail of their business area without special preparation – not just if he or she is giving a presentation to the board. What we have done at BMW and still are doing at BMW … I think other people cannot imitate it, though they try.

Were there any points in your long time at the helm of the company where the Quandt family would ask whether you were sure something was going in the right direction? Did they ever express doubts? Questioned you, saying are you sure, trying to influence you?

No, they didn't. Let me make it quite clear the Quandts are very important and we are all to be very thankful that they stood behind the company, but they did not lead the company. They said "you have the responsibility and now do it." So their highest interest was who were the people at the top; they then said "we believe in them and we'll rely on them", and that was it. They didn't make their own policy, they didn't lead the company. Also by law it would not have been possible because we are still a public company, the Quandts are only one shareholder, and all the rest together have more shares than the Quandts.

How did your management style change over the years? Did you keep to the style you had identified at the beginning? After all, you were in charge for over 23 years.

Yes I was in my 24th year when I left. At the beginning we had to look after the details rather more; then as we were in the build-up phase and got more and more good people in the second and third tiers of management we were able to

"Yes, we did our duty – in the manner of Admiral Nelson when, just before the battle of Trafalgar, he gave a flag signal to the whole fleet which said 'England expects every man to do his duty'"

take views on the more fundamental questions. BMW was small in the beginning but later became an international sales organisation with our own companies rather than importers that did not belong to us: it was a tough job in those days. We started in Belgium and then in France and so on, and then to the USA, in Japan, in South Africa and in the UK and so on. Our aim was always to achieve a sustainable policy for sales; we didn't want to have to constantly monitor individual importers. We were more or less the first Europeans in Japan, for instance: in those days Japan was seen as a very exotic country and it was not easy to establish ourselves there."

When asked about his greatest achievement at BMW, von Kuenheim's modesty takes over and he declines to answer. However, an aide recalls his response a few years earlier:

"When I am travelling through lower Bavaria, which was a poor area, and I see how it is now blossoming, and when I travel through the Steyr area of Austria, the area where we have another factory, and I again see how it flowers, then I realise if it had been Toyota, for instance, they would have 10 factories around Munich in the middle of nowhere near the new airport."

Von Kuenheim also sidesteps an invitation to express pride in BMW achieving its high world ranking in automotive brands, saying instead: "Yes, we did our duty – in the manner of Admiral Nelson when, just before the battle of Trafalgar,

he gave a flag signal to the whole fleet which said 'England expects every man to do his duty.'"

Asked about what was the most difficult moment in his tenure, the former chairman of BMW is again reluctant to answer – but for the very different reason that, as far as he is concerned, such moments are simply water under the bridge: "After two or three decades, you can't really say any more. Difficult situations are in front of you, but they're no longer a big challenge once they are behind you.

"However," he continues, " there were without doubt some risky situations. One was in the autumn of '73, as a result of one of the Israeli wars with the Arabs. We had an energy crisis here in Germany, and all motor traffic was forbidden every weekend. We had just opened our new plant at Dingolfing in Bavaria in the month of November – and in that month we got 200 orders. Journalists declared that this would be the last new car factory ever built, and that the era of the motor car would soon be over. We had to keep our nerve. When you've just opened a new factory that morning you have to show to your own people that when it comes to the crunch you can make it, you can pull through.

"During that period, BMW increased sales and market share, while Opel, VW and other companies fired a lot of their people with compensation. They paid a lot of compensation, but we had to find another way to get through

the situation as we did not have enough money to pay compensation. It was therefore better that we didn't fire anybody."

"BMW is the only car company which has for the past 44 years been able each year to say that its results are better than last year's," says von Kuenheim. "We were able to say it in 1965 and 1966, we were able to say in 1972, 1978 and 1979 – and we can still say it today if you take BMW alone and strip out the few years of the Rover disaster. For BMW itself, the big question I have is how long will the gods allow it to continue."

"When I look at it all, I have to ask myself whether I took all the available opportunities. Other people tell me I took 80 or 90 per cent of all possible chances. A lot of people only end up taking 40 to 50 per cent of the chances."

One opportunity he was pleased to have taken was the key strategic move which would eventually see BMW developing a 12-cylinder engine and seizing the technological initiative to draw alongside Mercedes-Benz in the sophistication and ambitiousness of its engineering.

"Towards the middle of the 1980s, the 7 Series was doing very well. We were convinced that our six-cylinder engine was the best thing in world at that time, and every wisdom in those days said we should progress upwards to a V8, which was seen as the state-of-the-art engine for

The FIZ research and engineering centre resulted from von Kuenheim's big technology push in the early 1980s

an elite car. All the market research said we should go to the V8, too – but I disappointed a lot of people and I said 'no I am against this, full stop'. Instead, I said we should go straight to the V12. That was a very important decision for BMW: it was absolutely against the conventional rules but it meant we that we jumped over the competitors. We launched the engine and went on to make two thirds of all 12-cylinder products in the world. This gave us such a high ranking, and ever since that time we have been on the same level of status as Mercedes.

"Herbert Quandt had said that Mercedes was the finest company in Germany and in Europe and that we would never match them in our lifetime. I had always said to Mr Quandt that he was right – but now, for the first time, I was able to say 'I think I'm the one that's right'.

When von Kuenheim joined BMW in 1969 he

could not have envisaged that the company would reach the same level as Mercedes and one day even outsell it.

However, in an internal briefing in 1982, he did reveal how far ahead he had already begun to think. In a speech to senior managers, circulated internally, he set an ambitious goal for BMW that each area of activity was to interpret in its own way: this had a dramatic effect in boosting the company's self-confidence and focusing its efforts in all disciplines.

"We want to become number one" was the seemingly simple goal that von Kuenheim set for his senior executives and their divisions. Deliberately, he avoided saying the biggest: instead, he said BMW needed to set itself the task if becoming number one, in the premium league.

"The sales people interpreted this as 'overtake Mercedes'," recalls an aide. "The quality people

took it as 'be the best in quality'. The marketing people took it as 'make our brand world famous'."

The effect on the organisation was electric. The decision to go with the V12 was an intensely symbolic one, signalling BMW's entry into the big league of top-status players and technological hard-hitters. And, looking at BMW's powerful position today, it is clear that those few words ended up being a far more powerful motivation for everybody than anyone, even Eberhard von Kuenheim, could ever have imagined.

01

Rebuilding a shattered heritage

Faded glory

From its present privileged position as the world's leading producer of premium cars, a quality manufacturer on four continents and the custodian of Rolls-Royce, the most revered car marque of all, it is hard to believe that a company of BMW's great standing once teetered dangerously on the brink of bankruptcy. But that, astonishingly, was the position at the very end of the 1950s.

Once-powerful BMW had been hit hard after the War, forbidden to build the aero engines which had been its most famous and most important business, its Munich factory in ruins and its Eisenach plant seized by the Russians. Uneasily, the company wobbled between production of small motorcycles – the Allies would only allow BMW to make bikes of less than 250cc – and the large luxury saloons which the company's directors had stipulated should be the firm's calling card on its return to the car market. In the end, however, it was to be a lethal combination of rapid market changes and an ill-advised return to the aero engine business that would draw BMW perilously close to the abyss – and almost into the hands of its long-standing rival, Mercedes-Benz.

Surveying the bombed-out wreckage of their Milbertshofen factory in Munich in late 1945, BMW's surviving directors had much cause for alarm. The plant had been scheduled for demolition by the American occupying forces, the machine tools were irreparably damaged, raw materials were near-impossible to obtain, and in the post-war chaos there was little prospect of ready markets for BMW's staple products of aero engines, expensive luxury cars and quality motorcycles.

Nevertheless, the plant and its rag-bag workforce eked out enough of a hand-to-mouth existence making humdrum domestic items such as pots and pans and even bicycles that the Americans were persuaded to rescind the demolition order and, eventually, agreed to allow the manufacture of light motorcycles.

The first post-war BMW motorcycle, the R24, bore an uncanny resemblance to its more powerful predecessors of the 1930. It still had BMW's trademark shaft drive and black

Large and heavy 501 series relaunched BMW cars in the early 1950s. The models were expensive and never sold as well as expected, despite the introduction of innovative V8 engines

"While the public was wowed by the 507's glamorous design and the critics praised the much-improved handling of the shortened chassis, the expected payback in terms of sales failed to materialise"

paintwork with white coachlining, but its upright single-cylinder engine of just 247cc and its lowly price tag placed it in a very different and much more accessible market category than its aristocratic forebears. The R24 soon found a ready market in mobility-hungry Germany and – along with many German manufactured products – received an extra boost when currency reforms in the middle of 1950 stabilised the financial markets and marked the start of what was to become the Wirtschaftswunder or West German economic miracle. By 1951 the company was building over 18,000 of these single-cylinder machines a year, feeding useful cashflow into the system and allowing the development of a new, flat-twin boxer model, the R51, that BMW had been given permission to make.

On the car side things were less straightforward. Almost everything to do with BMW's car operations had been located in Eisenach, in the zone which fell under the control of the Russians. Not only were all the skilled craftsmen and engineering equipment inaccessible to the Munich rump of the company; to add insult to injury, the Eisenach operation had

restarted production of some models using stored spare parts, the surviving tooling and much of the former workforce. The cars were used by officials in what had become East Germany, already aligned with Moscow and economically cut off from the West. The concern at BMW's Munich headquarters turned to outright alarm when the eastern BMW began exporting its wares into Western Europe in the search for foreign exchange.

By this time, according to one account, there were many thousands of these cars in stock in Scandinavia, Switzerland and the Netherlands: BMW's only real remaining automotive asset, its trademark, was clearly being undermined by the inferior quality of the eastern-build models. BMW formally disowned its Eisenach facility and successfully sued its managers. As a result of the court decision, the factory had to rename itself EMW (for Eisenacher Motoren Werke), use of the BMW roundel was forbidden and, astonishingly, Western dealers with cars in stock were obliged to file off the two loops of the B on the BMW badges and paint the blue quadrants red in order to rebrand the cars as EMWs. Even the B cast on

501/2

Specifications	501 (1952)	502 (1954)
Cylinders/capacity	6/1971	V8/2580
Max power @ rpm	65@4400	100@4800
Manual transmission	4-speed	4-speed
Wheels/tyres	5.5 x 16	4.5 x 15
Kerb weight, kg	1340	1440
Max speed, km/h	135	160
0-100 km/h, sec	27.0	17.5
Fuel consumption, lit/100km	12.5	14.5
Launch date	10/52	7/54
Pricing, DM	15,150	17,800

503

Specifications	503
Cylinders/capacity	V8/3168
Max power, bhp @ rpm	140@4800
Manual transmission	4-speed
Automatic	Not available
Wheels/tyres	4.5 x 16
Kerb weight, kg	1500
Max speed, km/h	190
Fuel consumption, lit/100km	16.0
Launch date	5/56
Pricing, DM	29,500

Above:
**507 gained in handling and
agility by moving to a
shortened version of the
tubular chassis underpinning
the 501 and 502**

the engine blocks had to be filed into an E.

All these traumas occurred well before BMW directors in Munich had managed to agree on a suitable strategy for the restart of car production. Not least of the difficulties faced by the BMW managers was the fact that, because everything to do with cars had fallen into the hands of the Russians, any new products would have to be completely fresh designs starting from blank sheets of paper. As Eberhard von Kuenheim, chairman throughout BMW's years of most spectacular growth in the 1970s and 1980s, recalls:

"A few BMW people managed to get hold of the drawings of the cars and smuggle them into a rucksack: they succeeded in escaping 'black over the green border' as we call it in the middle of the night back to Munich because the Russians did not approve. For 10 to 15 years BMW struggled to find a direction: when it came to car production they hadn't the money or the factories."

The dilemma was entirely understandable. The identity BMW had painstakingly built up in the pre-war years was solidly welded to sleek and exciting sports cars and elegant, subtle sports

coupés, an intelligent use of power and engineering rather than the grandiose excess of Mercedes-Benz and its ilk. Yes, BMW had begun life on four wheels with licence-built versions of Austin's humble Seven in 1922, but it had long since outgrown those roots with its trademark six cylinder engines and decent brakes, steering and suspension: to relaunch after the war with a cheap, austerity car would put that uniquely classy, sporting reputation at risk — even though the centre of gravity of the post-war market was certain to lie with simpler and less resource-hungry designs.

Though historians with the useful advantage of hindsight now regard it as a near-fatal mistake, BMW's decision to embark on the development of voluminous luxury saloons in the late 1940s did have a certain business logic at the time. By re-establishing the BMW name at a high level, argued the company's directors, subsequent models in lower size and price categories could benefit from what in modern marketing terms would now be labelled the halo effect of the

prestigious big models and thus enjoy enhanced status and, hopefully, margins.

The only problem was that the design that eventually resulted, the 501, was not strong enough. Unveiled at the Frankfurt show in September 1951 but not delivered to customers until at least a year later, the 501 proved to be a bulky, curvaceous saloon, high on comfort and equipment and steeply priced at over DM 15,000. Innovations on the engineering front were confined to double-wishbone independent front suspension by torsion bars — not always a routine feature at that time — and a centrally-mounted gearbox, placed under the front seats in the interests of weight distribution. Unfortunately, with a hefty tubular chassis and a substantial separate body there was far too much weight to distribute, especially as the 501's engine was a barely warmed-over pre-war unit developing just 65 horsepower from its two litres. At least it had the advantage of six cylinders for a certain smoothness, though the tortuous linkage from the central gearbox to the column mounted lever

Above:
Contemporary poster did its best to explain the complexities of BMW's six- and eight-cylinder ranges

Left:
Baroque Angel of the 1950s and a modern 3 Series Compact

Right:
First deliveries of the BMW 501 from the Munich plant took place in 1952

Below right:
The separate chassis construction of the 501/502 allowed coachbuilders considerable scope, but the two-door coupé by Baur did not enjoy the best of proportions

"It was not long before the 501 acquired the not entirely complimentary nickname of Baroque Angel: sales had been falling well below BMW's expectations"

made shifts ponderous, further exacerbating the car's feeling of inertia.

It was not long before the 501 acquired the not entirely complimentary nickname of Baroque Angel: sales had been falling well below BMW's expectations, though the bottleneck of coachbuilder Baur's painfully slow production of 501 bodies was soon bypassed when BMW brought manufacture in-house and output speeded up. Just 49 left the factory in 1952, with 1,645 the following year – hopelessly low numbers in relation to the money and the expectations invested in the model. BMW's response was a succession of power hikes, price reductions and equipment adjustments, which saw a doubling of output in 1954.

Everyone had known for some while, however, that this was nowhere near enough to keep the company afloat, and engineers had started work on an engine which was remarkably advanced for its time – an all-aluminium V8, designed by Leonhard Ischinger in just eight weeks and destined to be Germany's first. The 502, looking just like the 501 but with more chrome

embellishments, was announced at the Geneva show in spring 1954 and went on sale in July at the pretty intimidating price of DM 17,800: with 100 horsepower from its 2.6 litres and 'substantial' torque it was clearly better to drive than its six-cylinder companion, but its main advantage lay in what was judged to be outstanding smoothness and refinement.

The Baroque Angel was systematically developed over the years, V8 versions rising in capacity and power to the 3.2 litres and 160 horsepower of the final 3200 S of September 1961. By this time its flamboyantly rounded style, which had gained a fashionable wraparound rear screen in 1955, was looking decidedly out of place against the finned Mercedes 220 series. Not so its technical specification, where it had been the first German car with disc brakes as standard (1960) and had offered power steering from the previous year: the final model became Germany's fastest production car at 190 km/h, at which speed, according to reports, it emitted a characteristic whistle to announce its rapid approach behind slower traffic on the Autobahn.

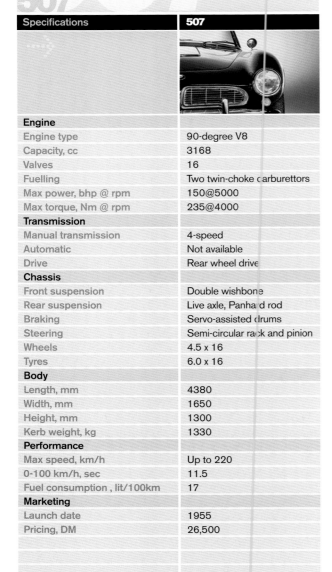

Specifications	507
Engine	
Engine type	90-degree V8
Capacity, cc	3168
Valves	16
Fuelling	Two twin-choke carburettors
Max power, bhp @ rpm	150@5000
Max torque, Nm @ rpm	235@4000
Transmission	
Manual transmission	4-speed
Automatic	Not available
Drive	Rear wheel drive
Chassis	
Front suspension	Double wishbone
Rear suspension	Live axle, Panhard rod
Braking	Servo-assisted drums
Steering	Semi-circular rack and pinion
Wheels	4.5 x 16
Tyres	6.0 x 16
Body	
Length, mm	4380
Width, mm	1650
Height, mm	1300
Kerb weight, kg	1330
Performance	
Max speed, km/h	Up to 220
0-100 km/h, sec	11.5
Fuel consumption , lit/100km	17
Marketing	
Launch date	1955
Pricing, DM	26,500

Though it had a high profile in the public imagination, the Baroque Angel had been a financial headache for BMW throughout its long life and only sold one sixth of its originally target amount. Assembled largely by costly hand labour, the Szimanowski design was notoriously expensive to build: the voluminous wings, for instance, had such a deep profile that they required three separate pressing operations to make. One estimate puts the total loss on the programme at DM 76 million: in 1956, when BMW overall lost DM 60 million on car manufacturing – 38 per cent of its total turnover – it was calculated that the company was subsidising each car to the tune of DM 4,000 or 5,000.

For over 10 years BMW's white-coated engineers had been busy fine-tuning the big baroque machine into something that would better the competition to draw in the customers and generate profit: the model was finally pensioned off in 1963, when it was viewed as something of an antique and no longer fitted with BMW's thrusting new image. Long before this, however, BMW had had its eye on the affluent United States market and the company's

enterprising US agent, Max Hoffman, had been pressing for a more sporting derivative to capitalise on BMW's reputation in motorsport and, quite naturally, the Americans' perceived eagerness for the impulse purchase of expensive and attractive cars.

Hoffman even went to the lengths of finding a designer to come up with a concept for his proposed grand touring sports car. The man in question, who had been working under the legendary industrial designer Raymond Loewy in New York and had contributed to several shapes for Studebaker, was an exceptionally lucky find. Not only did Count Albrecht Goertz come up with a dignified and elegant style for a big 2+2 seater luxury coupé on the standard 502 chassis, he also suggested – and drew – a much smaller and much more racy sports roadster based on a cut-down version of the same chassis.

Thus was born the enduring legend of the BMW 507. Count Goertz's design for a compact, V8-powered two-seater roadster was near-perfect from any angle and has gone on to inspire many generations of designers and designs. It even provided unmistakeable cues for BMW's own Z07 design study shown at the

Left:
The inspiration of Count Albrecht Goertz's classic 507 is clearly evident in the modern Z8

Right:
Goertz also had a hand in the more dignified 503 coupé. It was luxurious, with an electric hood on the open version

Though very expensive and produced in small numbers, the 507 soon became an emblem of the growing international jet-set, as this 1955 brochure suggests

1999 Tokyo show and the Z8 sports car which followed in 2000.

But while the public was wowed by the 507's glamorous design and the critics praised the much-improved handling and performance of the shortened chassis tweaked by Alex von Falkenhausen, the expected payback in terms of sales failed to materialise. A steep price of over DM 26,000 – more, even, than the extremely prestigious Mercedes 300SL – put it out of reach of all but the wealthiest of buyers, and by the time its three-year production run ended in 1959 just 253 examples had been sold.

A similar fate befell the less overtly glamorous 503 coupé and cabriolet, unique in Europe at that time with its electrically operated hood. Priced closer to DM 30,000, combined sales amounted to 412 in four years, despite an engineering update which saw the separate gearbox moved forward to a more conventional position bolted directly onto the engine, permitting a much more satisfying floor mounted gear shift.

The Baroque Angels, the 503 and the instant-classic 507, were unquestionably the most famous BMWs of the 1950s. Yet, in hindsight, they can be seen as nothing more than an

507 roadster remains the iconic BMW design if the 1950s, even though it was expensive and sold poorly

unfortunate side-show to what was really going on at the company, an ill-timed distraction for managers whose attention could have been more usefully focused on the broader strategic direction of the company in an unpredictable but nevertheless opportunity-rich market.

Fuelled by Germany's accelerating Wirtschaftswunder, the booming market for motorcycles had kept BMW's cashflow going through the early 1950s, the revenue disguising the continuing losses on the underperforming large luxury cars. What BMW had failed to anticipate about the continuing economic miracle, however, was that in a sustained boom consumers would soon begin to look beyond motorcycles and their associations with basic transportation and hanker after the warmth, comfort and practicality of four wheels, a roof and a boot. One-time motorcyclists switched in their droves to low-cost cars such as the Volkswagen Beetle as well as early midgets such as the Messerschmitt and the Goggomobil, produced not far away from Munich by Glas at Dingolfing.

Not for the first time in its history, BMW would find itself in a serious position, and by 1956 Deutsche Bank was in virtual control of the company. It installed the Prussian Heinrich Richter-Brohm in the MD's seat: Richter-Brohm quickly drew up plans – again, not for the first time in the company's history – to build a 1.6 litre mid-range car with 80 horsepower and set to go into production in 1959 at the rate of 24,000 a year (significantly more than BMW was producing in 1956). Inevitably, however, the entry-ticket into this survival route was too high for BMW's limited liquidity and the plans only materialised after the near-collapse and subsequent restructuring in 1959-60.

Back in 1954 BMW's two-wheeler sales were about to plunge from over 30,000 to little more than 5,000 three years later, but with rare foresight an open-minded BMW engineer by the name of Eberhard Wolff, checking out the company's exhibits at that 1954 Geneva motor show, had stumbled across what he described as an 'egg on wheels' at the stand of a small Italian producer, Iso Rivolta. With a keen eye for the clever engineering involved and for the likely low cost of building the tiny 2.3 metre bubble, Wolff

ISETTA 600

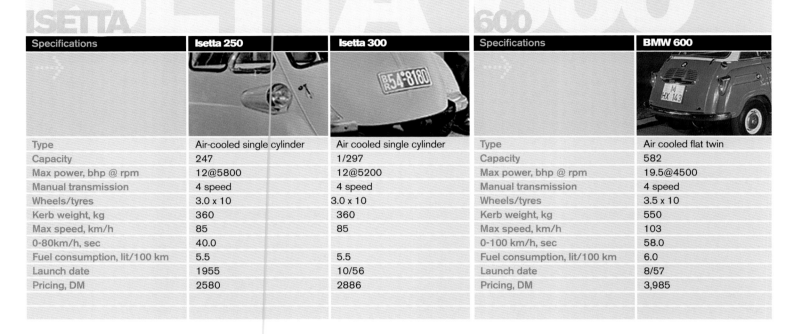

Specifications	Isetta 250	Isetta 300	Specifications	BMW 600
Type	Air-cooled single cylinder	Air cooled single cylinder	Type	Air cooled flat twin
Capacity	247	1/297	Capacity	582
Max power, bhp @ rpm	12@5800	12@5200	Max power, bhp @ rpm	19.5@4500
Manual transmission	4 speed	4 speed	Manual transmission	4 speed
Wheels/tyres	3.0 x 10	3.0 x 10	Wheels/tyres	3.5 x 10
Kerb weight, kg	360	360	Kerb weight, kg	550
Max speed, km/h	85	85	Max speed, km/h	103
0-80km/h, sec	40.0		0-100 km/h, sec	58.0
Fuel consumption, lit/100 km	5.5	5.5	Fuel consumption, lit/100 km	6.0
Launch date	1955	10/56	Launch date	8/57
Pricing, DM	2580	2886	Pricing, DM	3,985

Tiny Isetta was a bought-in design from Italy but saved BMW's finances in the mid 1950s when it could not afford to develop its own mid-sized car

figured the car would be a lot better with BMW's single-cylinder four-stroke motorcycle engine than Iso's noisy, smoky two-stroke. Expecting a hostile reception, he took his ideas back to his bosses and, much to everyone's surprise, they responded with enthusiasm.

Almost before anyone had had time to consider the consequences too deeply, BMW had signed with Iso to build the so-called Isetta Motocoupé under licence, with BMW power, and had even bought the production facilities for a quick start-up. The effect was electric: aided by a price little higher than that of a motorcycle, BMW sold almost 13,000 of the tiny, front-doored two-seaters. The following two years, with the benefit of a 300cc option and an attractive facelift, saw sales of well over 30,000 units; Britain was quick to take up bubble mania, too, a factory behind the railway station in the fashionable south coast resort of Brighton turning out special versions with a single rear wheel to qualify the car as a

Four-seater 600 was an extension of Isetta bubble-car thinking but failed to catch on with buyers, who objected to its 'microbus' looks

motorcycle for taxation and licence purposes. Mainland European Isettas had twin rear wheels for stability, but set sufficiently close together that the designers did not have to go to the expense of fitting a differential.

Soon, with total production passing the 100,000 mark, the Isetta became the most successful BMW to date, but by 1958, with fuel shortages easing off and another upward twist of the economic miracle encouraging buyers to aim for 'real', four-seater cars, interest in the Isetta began to tail off and the rising sales graph started to flatten. Once again, BMW was faced with the dilemma of how to respond to the trend in the market, and once again the lack of investment resources led to a half-hearted solution. Ever since the company had reassembled its automotive operations after the War there had been regular proposals for a medium-class car; each time it came up for

EARLY MODELS PRODUCTION

Production History:	In production: 1952-1965		Total produced 219,661			
model	501-507/ 3200CS	chassis	Isetta	600	total for year	SKD
1952	49				49	
1953	1,645				1,645	
1954	3,463	8			3,471	
1955	4,554	13	12,911		17,478	
1956	3,718	18	31,700		35,436	
1957	1,691	10	33,708	332	35,741	4,630
1958	1,868	3	21,198	27,187	50,256	825
1959	1,801	2	17,536	6,799	26,138	7,809
1960	656	5	9,007		9,668	7,540
1961	1,514	4	7,629		9,147	4,252
1962	1,007	2	2,678		3,687	800
1963	692				692	
1964	282				282	
1965	115				115	
totals	**23,055**	**65**	**136,367**	**34,318**		
				grand total	**193,805**	**25,856**
			grand total inc SKD		**219,661**	

"The BMW 700 was a sharply-styled two-door coupé with its twin-cylinder motorcycle engine in the rear. The public response was immediate and enthusiastic"

Compact 700 was designed as a stepping stone to the planned medium car: its rear suspension layout was used on BMWs until the 1990s

discussion it was once again put on hold because of insufficient funds; instead, interim fixes such as the isetta were chosen. Unfortunately, though the Isetta was popular and did sell well, its thin profit margins were not enough to offset the big losses on the V8 saloons and coupés. This meant that the much-touted medium-sized car was ruled out yet again, this time in favour of a new design, also in-house, which represented bubble-car philosophy extrapolated to convey four passengers and provide better comfort and performance.

Sadly, the BMW 600 which resulted from this thinking proved a major sales disaster. Just when BMW could afford it least, the 600 flopped, selling 27,000 in its debut year but under 7,000 in 1959, when production was abandoned after less than two years. Powered by BMW's well-

respected 600cc flat twin motorcycle engine, the 600 was well made and roomy, but consumers objected to the bubble-car associations of its shape, its front-entry door and its single side door giving access to the back seat. Nevertheless, the 600 did make one very positive contribution to the BMW story: it pioneered the semi-trailing arm rear suspension arrangement for precise handling and stable cornering. The layout went on to become a key feature of every BMW right into the 1990s, giving BMW a competitive advantage in handling for several model generations and being widely copied throughout the industry.

But while the failure of the microbus-shaped 600 helped bring the uncertainties of the 1950s to a frustratingly downbeat close, the chassis structure of the model was at the same time

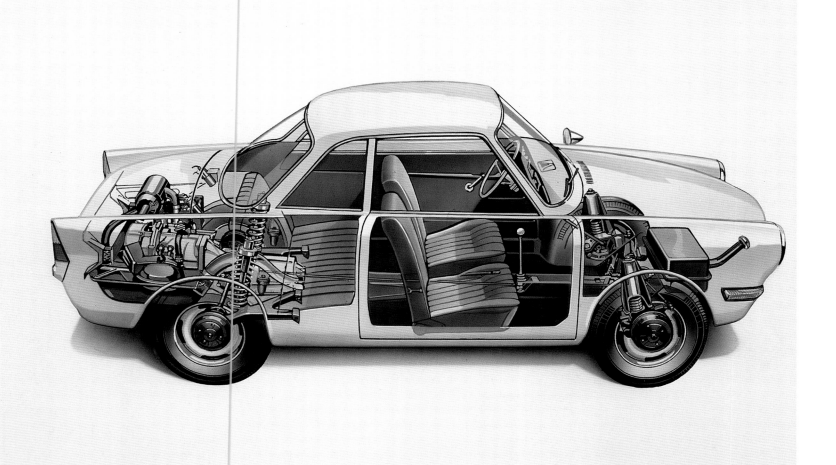

BMW's 507 is highly prized among enthusiasts and collectors

being honed to produce a very different model, as chic and as stylish as the BMW bus was dull and dowdy, a model which would relaunch BMW's fortunes, re-establish its sporting reputation and recapture the public imagination.

Penned by the Italian Michelotti, very much the designer of the moment in the late 1950s thanks to fashionable small cars such as the Triumph Herald, the BMW 700 was a sharply-styled two-door coupé with its twin-cylinder motorcycle engine in the rear, just as in the 600. Oddly enough, the 700 had begun its existence as a semi-private initiative by BMW's entrepreneurial Austrian importer, Wolfgang Denzel. With the tacit approval of BMW's top management Denzel had been operating a works design studio in Vienna, his underlying mission being to use the already developed chassis of the 600 to underpin a more conventional small car that would sell well and generate enough profit to fund the development of the medium-sized car that would, in turn, bring BMW the volume breakthrough that had so long eluded it.

September 1959's Frankfurt show saw the debut of both saloon and coupé editions of the 700; the public response was immediate and enthusiastic, with over 15,000 domestic and 10,000 US orders flooding in. This was to be the car that would save BMW, that would at last

begin bringing in the profits, that despite its tiny engine would prove an unexpected success on the racetracks and rally stages of Europe. But more important than any of those achievements was to be its first, accidental, role as the model which through an accounting error would save BMW from being swallowed up by a greedy and acquisitive Daimler Benz.

The scene was the tumultuous and now legendary meeting of BMW shareholders, held in December 1959. A mixture of small private shareholders, many of them BMW dealers, and representatives of banks owning larger chunks of stock, the investors had one thing in common: they were concerned about the company's inconsistent, often lacklustre financial performance and feared it would slide into insolvency. In a rowdy meeting the directors' insistence that the 700 series would save the company was rejected as too risky by the institutional investors, who suggested a restructuring of the company and a share issue, open only to the banks and Daimler-Benz, which would effectively halve the value of the existing shares. Recounted by Horst Mönnich in great detail as a theatrical event where power swung first one way and/ then the next, the meeting saw dramatic clashes between the different shareholder groups, with neither able to

700/700 SPORT

Specifications	700	700 sport

Engine		
Type	Air cooled flat twin, rear mounted	Air cooled flat twin, rear mounted
Cylinders	2	2
Capacity, cc	697	697
Valves	Ohv 4	Ohv 4
Fuelling	Single Solex carburettor	Twin Solex carburettors
Max power, bhp @ rpm	32@5000	40@5700
Max torque, Nm @ rpm	30@3400	51@4500
Transmission		
Manual transmission	4-speed	4-speed
Optional transmission	Saxomat	
Drive	Rear wheels	Rear wheels
Chassis		
Front suspension	Leading links, coil springs	Leading links, coil springs, anti-roll bar
Rear suspension	Semi trailing arms, coil springs	Semi trailing arms, coil springs
Braking	Drums	Drums
Steering	Rack and pinion	Rack and pinion
Wheels	3.5 x 12	5.2 x 12
Body		
Length, mm	3540	3450
Width, mm	1480	1480
Height, mm	1270	1290 (cabrio)
Kerb weight, kg	640	685 (cabrio)
Performance		
Max speed, km/h	120/125 (coupé)	135
0-100 km/h, sec	26.5	20.0
Fuel consumption , lit/100km	7.0	7.5
Marketing		
Launch date	8/59 (Coupé)	1963
Pricing, DM	4,760 (sedan)	5,850 (Coupé)

command a majority. Eventually, however, the dealer bloc was able to force an adjournment during which lawyers discovered accounting anomalies in the documentation presented by the board to the meeting. In particular, the development costs for the 700 series were all written down against a single year rather than spread across several, making the present position seem worse.

This revelation forced the resignation of the chairman, and with him the Deutsche Bank delegation, which also sat on the board of Daimler-Benz. The threat of being absorbed by Daimler-Benz had gone and, right on cue, a hitherto unknown white knight stepped forward to snap up the stake sold by a disgruntled investor and ensure the vote went in favour of continuing as an independent company.

That white knight was Herbert Quandt who, together with his brother Harald and, later, his two children, were the family dynasty which would provide the long-term financial vision and security for BMW and become inextricably bound up with its gathering global success over the next four decades.

Right:
Despite its small, motorcycle-derived engine, the pretty 700 was eminently tuneable and won much respect in competition

Left:
Stormy shareholders' meeting in December 1959 proved a turning point in BMW history when moves to allow Mercedes to absorb the struggling company were blocked by Herbert Quandt, who went on to become a central figure in BMW's resurgence

700 PRODUCTION

Production History:	In production: 1959-64				Total produced 188,121					
model	700	700 Lux	700 LS	700 LS Lux	700 Coupé	700 CS	700 LS C	700 Cabrio	total for year	SKD
1959	14				2,648				2,662	
1960	24,500				9,040	757			34,297	2,383
1961	6,879	16,872			2,344	4,269		16	30,380	9,164
1962	221	961	538	31,537	1,551	2,111		1,214	38,133	9,170
1963			4,021	13,521	1,083	1,196		1,013	20,834	8,367
1964			417	15,096	141	311	353	349	16,667	6,994
1965				4,872			1,377		6,249	2,821
totals	31,614	17,833	4,976	65,026	16,807	8,644	1,730	2,592		
								grand total	149,222	38,899
								grand total inc SKD	188,121	

02

BMW 1500 Die neue Klasse

1962 BMW 1500

→ Turning point in BMW's history
→ First BMW of the modern era
→ "Neue Klasse" marks return to genuine BMW sporting values
→ Outstanding engine and handling for its time
→ Crisp, modern good looks
→ Fore-runner of today's 5-series
→ Developed into 1600, 1800 and 2000
→ 2000 tii model first with fuel injection
→ Desirable TiSA competition models

Quandt to the rescue

Smart "Neue Klasse" 1500 is an immediate hit

Saved from the threat of being swallowed up by Daimler-Benz and becoming just another overflow plant to build Mercedes components, BMW at last found stability and direction under the guidance of Herbert Quandt. Not before time, the medium-sized car was finally designed and built. It proved an instant success – despite a high price, rushed development and troublesome transmissions. The "Neue Klasse" 1500, with its outstanding engine, smart looks and keen handling, set the template for all future BMWs as compact, quality cars that were fun to drive, attractive to look at and an exciting alternative to the stodgy, patrician products of Mercedes-Benz.

Reaching the showrooms in 1962, the 1500 was the genuine BMW that people had been waiting for for so long. Recalling the sporty, enthusiastic temperament of the coupés and roadsters that had made BMW famous in the 1920s and 1930s, the 1500 can nevertheless be seen as the first truly modern BMW, the car that set BMW onto the path that has seen it become a powerful worldwide force.

Following the tumultuous shareholders' revolt of December 9th 1959, BMW entered the 1960s with no discernable improvement to its dismal financial position and, on paper at least, its model range was just as illogical as it had been

throughout the decade. Tiny bubble cars sold only to a dwindling bunch of buyers seeking minimalist transport, while overweight luxury sedans sought to lure rich business types – all the while, there was nothing in between for the vast majority of buyers, large numbers of them suddenly affluent on the strength of the Wirtschaftswunder economic boom and thirsting for something more youthful and more dynamic than a Mercedes.

But while little about BMW's hard-numbers business position had changed, the company that emerged from the aftermath of that historic meeting was a dramatically different one. Thanks to the obvious confidence shown in BMW by new

BMW's fresh, modern and attractive 1500 saloon was appropriately christened 'The New Class" when it appeared in 1962. Its success astonished even BMW

Four-door Neue Klasse 1500 immediately won praise for its performance and keen handling. Its success led BMW out of its crisis and paved the way for the future 3, 5 and 7 Series strategy

"The 1500 can be seen as the first truly modern BMW, the car that set BMW on the path that has seen it become a powerful worldwide force"

investor Herbert Quandt, morale had suddenly shot sky-high and people at all levels gained a sense of direction – something which had been painfully absent throughout the previous decade of muddle-along management and sticking-plaster solutions that could hardly be called model policies.

What Quandt provided was a clear vision of BMW's ambitions for the future, where the company aimed be in terms of image and products in five or 10 years' time. His stewardship provided the stability that allowed BMW's pent-up engineering talent to blossom once more, as Alex von Falkenhausen, ex-racing driver turned engine design genius, testified in Eric Dymock's *BMW: a Celebration*:

"I think the main problem was that every year we seemed to have a new board of directors,"

explained von Falkenhausen. "They changed very quickly. It was difficult to come into contact with a new director – they were all in despair. But the people under the directors wanted to do something, so they tried very hard."

Herbert Quandt had known all along that the most important priority for BMW was to develop and launch the much talked about mid-sized car; the lack of long-term planning under previous management regimes had made this impossible, and in any case the necessary funds would never have been available.

But Quandt had two key advantages: as well as being (or perhaps because he was) a member of the German elite of super-rich families, he was trusted by German banks who had refused previous BMW regimes loans to fund running costs. Secondly, he was someone who had the

knack of finding the right person for the job, something which again reassured both backers and BMW staff.

One such person was Gerhard Wilcke, who had been Quandt's legal adviser for several years. Quandt ensured he was placed on the supervisory board of BMW early in 1960, gradually strengthening the influence of the new thinkers. Wilcke was particularly skilful in handling the relationship with Daimler-Benz, where Herbert Quandt still had a stake and where many believed that a hostile takeover was still a threat. Wilcke was also able to deal with approaches for BMW from companies such as American Motors, which had hoped to build its Rambler in Munich, Chrysler, Simca, Britain's Rootes Group, Fiat and Ford.

"There was always a change of heart when we declared that no participation in the BMW share capital could be tolerated if it exceeded 50 per cent." Wilcke later commented.

Yet the combination of Quandt's influence, the new confidence in BMW's revised structure, and the growing success of the small, stylish 700 saloon, convertible and, soon, Baur-built

Interior of 1500 looks sparse by modern standards but counted as a class act in 1962

1500
NEUE KALSSE

Specifications	1500	1600
Engine		
Enginr type	Inline 4-cylinder	Inline 4-cylinder
Bore & stroke, mm	82x71	84x71
Capacity, cc	1499	1573
Valves	8	8
Valve actuation	sohc	sohc
Compression ratio	8.8:1	8.8:1
Fuelling	Single Solex carburettor	Single Solex carburettor
Max power, bhp @ rpm	80@5700	83@5500
Max torque, Nm @ rpm	118@3000	123@3000
Transmission		
Manual transmission	4-speed	4-speed
Drive	Rear wheels	Rear wheels
Chassis		
Front suspension	MacPherson strut	MacPherson strut
Rear suspension	Semi-trailing arms, coil springs	Semi-trailing arms, coil springs
Braking	Drums	Drums
Steering	Worm and roller	Worm and roller
Wheels, in	4.5 x 14	4.5 x 14
Tyres, in	6.0 x 14	6.0 x 14
Body		
Structure	Steel monocoque	Steel monocoque
Wheelbase, mm	2550	2550
Track F/R, mm	1320/1366	1320/1366
Length, mm	4500	4500
Width, mm	1710	1710
Height, mm	1450	1450
Kerb weight, kg	1060	1070
Fuel tank capacity, lit	53	53
Performance		
Max speed, km/h	148	155
0-100 km/h, sec	16.0	14.0
Fuel consumption , lit/100km	11.0	12.0
Marketing		
Launch date	10/62	4/64
Pricing, DM	9,485	9,485

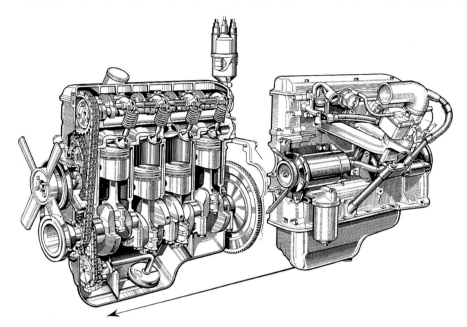

Above left
Von Falkenhausen's design for the 1500 engine was thoroughly modern and deliberately left room for expansion to two litres and much high power outputs

Above
Key figures clustered around this award-winning 1500 in 1963: engine designer and racing driver Alexander von Falkenhausen (second from left), styling chief Wilhelm Hofmeister (fourth from right) and sales director Paul Hahnemann (right)

convertible, was able to bring BMW much easier access to investment funds. Almost all of these were channelled into the development of the Neue Klasse mid-range car, for which BMW had set itself almost impossibly tight development programme timing.

Here, others' misfortune miraculously played into BMW's hands at precisely the right moment. Borgward, the Bremen-based carmaker run by its founder Carl Borgward, had gone into liquidation, unable to pay its substantial debts. Carl Borgward, now 70, was a better engineer than businessman, building sophisticated and complex cars on a whim and, according to those who knew him, delegating little, avoiding business decisions and carrying most of the vital information in his head. Borgward's cars, typified by the Isabella, were compact sports saloons that had been successful in competition and among a sporting clientele. It was only when he branched out into the fiendishly complex, six-cylinder 2.3 litre luxury saloon, with air suspension and numerous technical innovations, that Borgward swam out of his depth and, ultimately, sank.

Some contend that it was the collapse of Borgward that allowed BMW to rise again: indeed, BMW's Neue Klasse cars would be competing for many of the same customers as Borgward's Isabella. Nevertheless, the two events were unconnected: in the same economic climate BMW, now well managed, succeeded in growing:

poorly-run Borgward went to the wall, a victim of its own inept planning rather than any outside circumstance. BMW directors, including Quandt, went to Bremen to inspect the stricken Borgward company: they declined to buy the operation but instead purchased some much-needed machinery for volume production. Quandt returned with some very useful contacts, too: from Borgward he hired chief engineer Wilhelm Heinrich Gieschen, who would soon become chairman of the BMW Board of Management, and also managed to poach sales manager Paul Hahnemann, who had been just about to leave Auto Union (then part of Mercedes-Benz) to go to Borgward to clear the stock of 15,000 unsold Arabellas.

So BMW did certainly benefit indirectly from Borgward's collapse: not only was a key (if small) competitor eliminated from the car market, a large number of talented engineers were suddenly released onto the jobs market – and were eagerly snapped up by short-staffed BMW.

It was thus that, astonishingly, the combined talents of BMW and ex-Borgward engineers succeeded in completing a prototype in time for the Frankfurt show in September 1961: the car was unveiled as the BMW 1500. The newcomer, a four-door saloon 4.5 metres in length, was fresh and attractive in its looks and immediately won praise for its style and modern image; the engine, meanwhile, impressed technical

commentators with its overhead camshaft and claimed output of 75 horsepower – at that time a very good figure for a 1.5 litre.

BMW, too, was conscious of the significance of this comeback model. The company's press material for the 1500's debut described the event in almost Churchillian terms: "In the history of automobile construction there are few models which have been the subject of so much public interest and discussion as the new medium-sized BMW," said the release. Warming to its theme, it went on to laud the 1500's "sportiness, refinement, genuine comfort and timeless elegance," noting that the mission of the 1500 was to bring the qualities of BMW's big V8s into a smaller-capacity car, and that BMWs in general had a tradition of being ahead of their time.

The 1500 weighed in at just 900 kg, claimed BMW, which allowed the company to get away with no servo assistance for the disc front, drum rear brakes; likewise, power assistance for

steering was unknown except on top luxury cars. The interior, though stark by today's standards, was seen as stylish and attractive, and safety features included mounting points for seat belts for all four occupants, a padded steering wheel boss and recessed instruments – just speedometer, clock, temperature and fuel level – to avoid reflections.

BMW's claim that the M10 engine "would be up to the minute for the next 10 years" was not just an idle boast. Alex von Falkenhausen's design, which married an iron block with the aluminium head containing the chain-driven overhead camshaft, was deliberately conceived to be capable of expansion up to two litres in capacity. This did of course soon happen, and the M10 remained in production until 1988, with over 3.2 million made: it powered not just the Neue Klasse cars but also the '02 series, including the infamous Turbo, two generations of 3 series and 5 series and, most remarkably of all, BMW's first

"Everyone agreed that the 1500 was worth the wait – and the occasional gremlin – as the engine, now boosted to 80 horsepower, gave lively performance on the road and the suspension provided responsive handling"

Neue Klasse BMWs rapidly won a strong reputation in racing: the 1800, shown here, was soon made available to competition licence holders as the 130 bhp TISA production racer. The 2000 version later offered the innovation of fuel injection

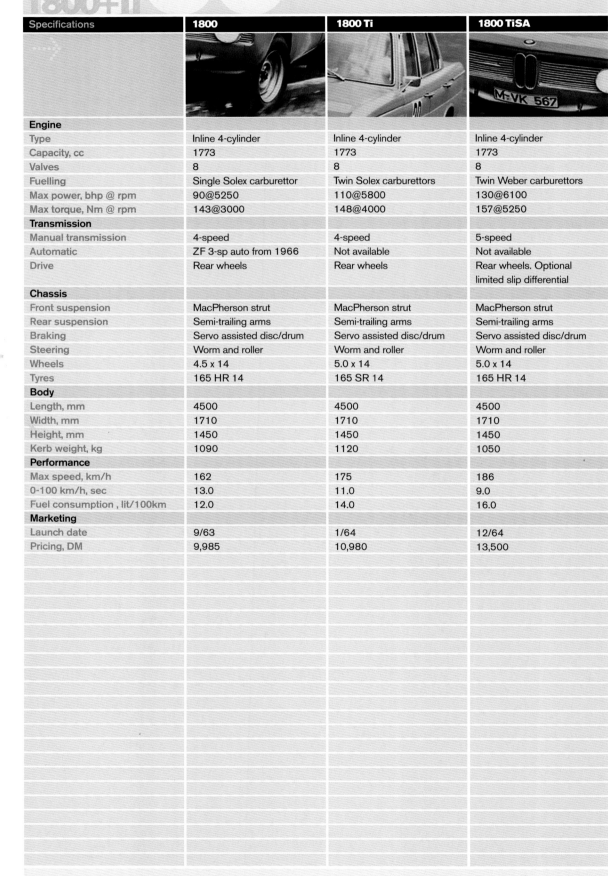

Specifications	1800	1800 Ti	1800 TiSA
Engine			
Type	Inline 4-cylinder	Inline 4-cylinder	Inline 4-cylinder
Capacity, cc	1773	1773	1773
Valves	8	8	8
Fuelling	Single Solex carburettor	Twin Solex carburettors	Twin Weber carburettors
Max power, bhp @ rpm	90@5250	110@5800	130@6100
Max torque, Nm @ rpm	143@3000	148@4000	157@5250
Transmission			
Manual transmission	4-speed	4-speed	5-speed
Automatic	ZF 3-sp auto from 1966	Not available	Not available
Drive	Rear wheels	Rear wheels	Rear wheels. Optional limited slip differential
Chassis			
Front suspension	MacPherson strut	MacPherson strut	MacPherson strut
Rear suspension	Semi-trailing arms	Semi-trailing arms	Semi-trailing arms
Braking	Servo assisted disc/drum	Servo assisted disc/drum	Servo assisted disc/drum
Steering	Worm and roller	Worm and roller	Worm and roller
Wheels	4.5 x 14	5.0 x 14	5.0 x 14
Tyres	165 HR 14	165 SR 14	165 HR 14
Body			
Length, mm	4500	4500	4500
Width, mm	1710	1710	1710
Height, mm	1450	1450	1450
Kerb weight, kg	1090	1120	1050
Performance			
Max speed, km/h	162	175	186
0-100 km/h, sec	13.0	11.0	9.0
Fuel consumption , lit/100km	12.0	14.0	16.0
Marketing			
Launch date	9/63	1/64	12/64
Pricing, DM	9,985	10,980	13,500

Formula One effort, where it yielded up to 1300 horsepower in highly turbocharged qualifying trim.

The company had high expectations of the 1500, but even the most optimistic of its managers were taken aback by the enthusiasm with which the public took to the new car. Even the high price of DM 9485 appeared acceptable to the customers who eagerly signed up for the waiting list: sales manager Paul Hahnemann declared at the show that that price included all necessary equipment, such as disc brakes, heater, two-speed wipers and screen washer, and that it left "little room for profit." Only higher volumes could boost profits, predicted Hahnemann.

He must have been one of the first auto industry figures to come up with the idea of niche marketing: priced at DM 9,5000 the 1500 was, he said, specially targeted at the rising market of middle class buyers. He went on to list its competitors as the Opel Rekord, Peugeot 4o4, Taunus 17M TS and Volvo Amazon at the lower end, and the Mercedes 180 and 190, plus the Citroen ID19 and Opel Kapitän in the more expensive class.

In the event, those who had signed up for the born-again BMW had to wait rather longer for their cars than they had expected: it was October of the following year before the first customer cars were delivered, and even then there were enough teething troubles to suggest that development had been somewhat rushed; at one point 124 defects were recorded. Everyone was agreed, however, that the 1500 was worth the wait – and the occasional gremlin – as the engine, now boosted to 80 horsepower in production trim, gave lively performance on the road, and the independent semi-trailing arm rear suspension, developed from that of the 700 Coupé, provided responsive handling and a good ride. Quickly, the 1500 gained a reputation as the car for the sporting driver to have – though today its vital statistics of 0-100 km/h acceleration in 16.8 seconds and a top speed of 148 km/h seem positively pedestrian.

The unexpected scale of the 1500's success did however present BMW managers with some awkward problems. The most acute of these was the inability of the company's new production

Earliest 2000 models were sold with the round headlights of the 1800. Again, sport successes soon followed

NEUE KLASSE PRODUCTION

Production History:	In production: 1962-71			Total produced 198,039			
model	1500	1600	1800	1800 Ti	1800 TiSA	total for year	SKD
1962	1,737					1,737	
1963		19,634		8,346	7	27,987	
1964	2,436	2,131	25,063	8,191		37,821	
1965		6,395	38,048	12,427	200	57,070	
1966		1,202	13,393	4		14,599	1,397
1967			8,893	419		9,312	1,089
1968			7,777	67		7,844	264
1969			11,273	1		11,274	2,561
1970			14,367			14,367	1,576
1971			7,654			7,654	1,347
1972						0	140
totals	23,807	9,728	134,814	21,116	200		
					grand total	189,665	8,374
					grand total inc SKD	198,039	

Launched in 1966, the 2000
version had rectangular lights
and more décor, though
earliest examples retained
familiar round lights

facilities to keep up with demand for the new car – an unaccustomed problem as, with the exception of the small 700 and certain periods of intense Isetta activity, BMW had not had such a popular model for a generation or more.

It was thus that in order to free up more production capacity for the Neue Klasse car, the tough decision was taken to axe two models of great sentimental importance but only marginal profitability. The Isetta, known at BMW as the Motocoupé, was phased out at the end of 1962 with almost 140,000 having been built since 1955, when as the 'egg on wheels' it had saved the company from another of its periodic crises; the second casualty was something of a sacred cow – the big Baroque Angel, first made in 1951 but now only surviving in V8 form. In its 11-year run just 23,000 had left the production lines – and only BMW's accountants know the true size of the red stain it left in the company's profit and loss account.

In contrast to those two extremes of the range, the small 700 saloon and coupé, with their rear-mounted air-cooled motorcycle engines, were still selling well and achieving remarkable successes in motorsport, despite the design only being intended as a bridge between the old models and the new-era 1500 family. There was no question of dropping the 700 in any case as an elegant convertible had just been launched, built by Baur, and demand had strengthened with the launch earlier in the year of the LS versions with their lengthened wheelbase and much-improved interior space.

It was as much a sign of the times as of corporate good planning that the Neue Klasse 1500 sold more units in two years than the whole Baroque Angel and big coupé range had done in over a decade; with the new class BMW had clearly hit upon a fresh and lucrative market sector where buyers were prepared to pay a premium for the experience of driving a sporty, responsive car – and not just for a star on the bonnet.

Eberhard von Kuenheim, yet to begin his astonishing 24 year tenure at the helm of BMW, recounts how Herbert Quandt deliberately encouraged the premium price policy at that time. "Yes, the price was high but it was accepted by people who said 'I can afford that: I won't drive a Beetle any more – everybody has a Beetle.' The effect of this was that BMWs became the cars for "Aufsteigers" – the social climbers of the era, rising up the ladder of social status. The 1500 series was doing well, and there was also the small 2-door car, the 1600, 1800, and then the 2002."

Two years after the 1500 had hit the stage it gave way to the 1600, visually identical but with a 2 mm bore increase to boost and torque; the price remained as unchanged as the car's appearance, and both performance and economy showed gains, too. A year earlier, however, BMW had already gone one better with the 1800 – again very similar externally, though with the distinguishing feature of chromed rocker panels.

"Thousands of tests by top writers in Germany and abroad," announced BMW prophetically at the 1963 show, "and the verdicts of thousands of BMW 1500 drivers have confirmed the first impressions of over two years ago, that the 1500 has created a new class in the market." Now, clearly, was the ideal opportunity to further exploit the market it had just created.

The 1800 offered a substantial power hike to 90 horsepower, lifting top speed to 162 km/h or exactly 100 mph – but more importantly it also provided the basis for the 1800 Ti, first in a long line of derivatives designed to appeal to enthusiastic and sporty drivers.

"The 1800 Ti is a car for exacting people who drive it for the sake of driving," noted BMW. But soon, in its turn, the already special Ti prompted an even more special edition still. The 1800 Ti/SA, standing for SportAusfuhrung, or sports version, was a short run of 200 cars sold only to drivers in possession of a racing licence: the compression ratio rose to 10.5 to one, Weber carburettors replaced the Solexes and the result was 130 bhp with full inlet and exhaust silencing in place. This power was fed through a five-speed gearbox and a split propshaft into a chassis tautened up by the addition of a limited slip differential and anti roll bars front and rear. Inside, there were hip-hugging racing bucket seats and a real icon of the age – a woodrim steering wheel.

Despite its intimidating price of DM 13,500 ex-works, the 180-plus km/h TiSA quickly

"No car did more than the Neue Klasse saloons to help turn BMW's fortunes from bankrupt basket case to confident challenger for the top honours in the car business"

2000/2000Ti/2000Tii

Specifications	2000 CS	2000 Ti	2000 Tii
Engine			
Type	Inline 4-cylinder	Inline 4-cylinder	Inline 4-cylinder
Capacity, cc	1990	1990	1990
Valves	Sohc 8	Sohc 8	8. sohc
Fuelling	Single Solex carburettor	Twin Solex carburettors	Kugelfischer fuel injection
Max power, bhp @ rpm	100@5500	120@5500	130@5800
Max torque, Nm @ rpm	157@3000	167@3600	165@4500
Transmission			
Manual transmission	4-speed	4-speed	5-speed
Automatic	3-sp ZF optional		
Drive	Rear wheels	Rear wheels	Rear wheels
Chassis			
Front suspension	MacPherson struts	MacPherson struts	MacPherson struts
Rear suspension	Semi-trailing arms, coil springs	Semi-trailing arms, coil springs	Semi-trailing arms, coil springs
Braking	Servo-assisted disc/drum	Servo-assisted disc/drum	Servo-assisted disc/drum
Steering	Worm and roller	Worm and roller	Worm and roller
Wheels	5 x 14	5.5 x 14	5.5 x 14
Tyres	6.45 165 S 14	6.75 175 H 14	175 HR 14
Body			
Length, mm	4500	4500	4500
Width, mm	1710	1710	1710
Height, mm	1450	1450	1450
Kerb weight, kg	1170	1150	1170
Performance			
Max speed, km/h	168	181	185
0-100 km/h, sec	13.0	12.0	11.0
Fuel consumption , lit/100km	13.0	13.5	13.5
Marketing			
Launch date	2/66	1/66	1/70
Pricing, DM	11,475	12,750	14,290

2000 SERIES: PRODUCTION

Production History:	In production: 1966-1972			Total produced 150,642		
model	2000	2000 Ti	2000 Ti Lux	2000 tii	total for year	SKD
1966	28,654	4,100	3,485		36,239	1494
1967	22,019	2,026	6,573		30,618	1078
1968	20,404	356	3,949		24,709	1184
1969	17,126		3,339	5	20,470	1846
1970	16,414		94	542	17,050	2180
1971	8,330			1,405	9,735	1593
1972	127				127	899
1973					0	1048
1974					0	372
totals	113,074	6,482	17,440	1,952		
			grand total		138,948	11,694
			grand total inc SKD		150,642	

became must-have equipment for saloon car racers in Germany and across Europe. Available only in authentically German racing silver, it was the first of many high-performance BMW saloons to set both race and road driving alight.

The standard two-litre version of the M10 engine had appeared in summer 1965 in the 2000CS coupé (see chapter 3); it was not long before BMW applied it to the four-door saloon to move the range still further up the price and performance scale. Single and twin-carburettor (TI) versions were offered, as on the 1800, with 100 and 120 bhp respectively, giving top speeds of 168 and 180 km/h. Very early 2000 models had the same round headlights and upright rear lights as the smaller-engined cars, but within a matter of months BMW had introduced the 2000 tilux which brought in a revised front and rear look incorporating large, rectangular headlights and larger, horizontal taillights with the rear BMW badge between the licence plate and the right hand rear light. In something of a departure for BMW, the tilux boasted its designation on the front grille and, inside, wooden door trims, a parcels drawer on the transmission tunnel and, in the boot, full carpeting. Mechanically, the rear suspension mounts were revised to improve ride comfort.

Stressing its sporting credentials, BMW claimed the 2000 TI was the "absolute fastest production car at the Nurburgring", with a lap speed of 137.2 km/h in the hands of saloon race ace Hubert Hahne. Already, this model was the hotshot sports saloon to be seen in. Yet towards the end of 1969 BMW went one better and fitted fuel injection – the first time BMW had employed it on a road car – to the 2000, creating the tii model, a designation which was to become even more famous on the compact 2002 model, launched 18 months later.

Explaining its decision to go the fuel injection route, BMW said that it had used the system in racing for some while and that it was now natural to use it in a sports road car for a gradual increase in power.

The injection mechanism employed was Kugelfischer's mechanical system, which used a sophisticated three-dimensional cam to provide the equivalent of a modern electronic map and

deliver different fuel/air mixtures in relation to engine load, engine speed and temperature. The fuel injection – at that time an exotic novelty fitted only to a few top sports and luxury cars – gave the two-litre an extra 10 horsepower over the twin-carburettor Ti, boosting top speed to 185 km/h and making for something that had no real competition in the car market. Its only close equivalents were the Rover 2000, Triumph 2000 – both less sporty – and the somewhat smaller Alfa Romeo Giulia; buyers had to pay quite a significant premium for the tii version, ensuring that sales only ran at a small fraction of those of the standard 2000. The biggest seller of all was the 1800, which appeared to have just the right blend of ingredients for the late-1960s customer – especially in its revised form after June 1968.

Distinguishable from the outside by matt chrome wheel covers and a black-finish grille with two horizontal bars picked out in chrome, the revised model also featured a much-improved dashboard. More modern in style, incorporating a central fresh air diffuser and with the bold, clear

instruments set in a raised hood directly in front of the driver, it set the pattern for BMW interior design which was to last until the major upheaval after 2001 when the i-Drive monitor became a major feature of new-look BMW interiors.

But as far as the driver was concerned the most welcome improvements were dual-circuit brakes and a much better engine. By using the block and pistons of the two-litre together with the short-throw crankshaft of the 1600 model, BMW achieved a very similar swept volume but with a much shorter stroke: this made the engine much happier to be driven hard and revved high, something close to the heart of BMW drivers.

In 1971, towards the end of its life and a grand total of 160,000 examples produced, the 1800 took on the rectangular headlights and horizontal strip rear lights of the 2000. The 2000 finished in the same year, replaced after a short interregnum by the first of the 5 Series, the first BMW with a direct bloodline to today's models.

The Neue Klasse saloons may look somewhat quaint and simple by our extravagant

modern standards, and even in their hottest forms their performance is insignificant in comparison with quite modest modern models. But in their day and in their turn the 1500, the 1600, the 1800 and then the 2000 tii were the smartest things on the road, the equivalent of an M5 today. No car did more than the Neue Klasse saloons to help turn BMW's fortunes from bankrupt basket case to confident challenger for the top honours in the car business. And, as was to happen so many more times in the decades to come, BMW proved itself able to not only read the market and judge its mood and movements, but also to build precisely the right car at the right time – and reap the rewards.

Finding a style

Elegant coupés become an essential element in the BMW mix

Coupés have always been favoured by BMW's product planners but their was little discipline in the mid '60s when no fewer than four different coupé types were in production at the same time – in addition to the tiny and always popular rear-engined 700 Coupé.

Each of the four had its own story to tell. The elegant 3200 CS, clothed elegantly in Turin by Bertone, was a throwback to the 1950s with its separate chassis and old V8 engine; the Glas V8 Coupé arrived by accident when BMW bought the company and decided to tack it on to the main range. Only the 2000 CS was a properly planned programme: it served as the coupé version of the super-successful Neue Klasse saloon line and was the first BMW to use the two-litre M10 engine.

2000 coupé was directly related to four-door saloon (left) but its styling theme would last well into the 1970s

The four-cylinder 2000 CS in turn led directly to that most famous coupé series of all, the big six-cylinder CSi and CSL of racetrack legend, a lengthened nose accommodating the longer engines and improving the styling.

You could be forgiven for thinking it was a large classic Italian coupé and indeed there are many genes in common. The BMW 3200 CS, though launched in 1961 alongside the Neue Klasse 1500 saloon, had absolutely no

connection with the smart new saloons: while the 1500 represented everything that was new about born-again BMW, the big 3200 CS was very much the last gasp of the old BMW.

Technically, it was a throwback to the earlier era of separate chassis construction, where it was comparatively easy to ask a design house to come up with a one-off special body concept or even a limited production run. So BMW supplied master craftsmen Bertone in Turin with its full-

length chassis and aluminium V8 – elements which went back to the early 1950s – with the request to build a high-class four-seat grand touring coupé. To its great credit Bertone – the Italian connection, having been responsible for many Alfas – produced a body of remarkable grace and elegance on this awkwardly long chassis.

A single cabriolet prototype was built, too: it became the personal transport of Herbert Quandt and had a unique electrically-operated roof, but BMW decided only to build the fixed-head model. The all-steel bodies were made by Bertone in Turin and shipped to Munich where

BMW painted them, married them up with the chassis and completed final assembly almost entirely by hand.

The V8 engine had by this time risen to 160 horsepower in output (10 more than in the exotic 507), but even this was not enough to endow the heavy four-seater with GT-like performance; the live rear axle brought a similarly dampening effect on any pretensions to sporting handling. The 3200 CS was BMW's most expensive car, at a snatch under DM 30,000 – a price which would have bought three 1500 saloons. Unusually, as with the big V8 saloons, the CS's four-speed gearbox migrated forwards during the short

lifetime of the car: initially, it was sited under the front seats and controlled by a column shift which was reluctant to be hurried; later, it became a much better floor shift with the box bolted in conventional fashion to the back of the engine. No automatic was offered.

Billed on its launch as "a car of the international extra-class", BMW claimed the 3200 CS was completely noiseless at 20 km/h and would storm within a minute to its top speed, with the "needle hovering close to 200 km/h." A steady stream of the "cream of European society" kept Bertone's and BMW's craftsmen busy until September 1965, when the last of 603 units was completed.

The 3200 CS may not have contributed much to BMW's profits – in fact its cash flow was probably negative – but it did perform the valuable task of keeping the company's name alive in high society and outside the most exclusive hotels and resorts in Europe. And, probably most importantly of all, it provided the style template for later generations of BMW coupés: the low waistline, the slender roofline, the frameless doors and pillarless side windows (all seen on the 2000 CS and the 2800 CSi series), the round rear lights that were later to feature on the 2002, and the reverse kink on the rear pillar that has become a design signature on almost every BMW product since.

Something of a diversion was provided by the Glas V8, not a true member of the BMW family but an in-law by marriage or, strictly speaking, takeover.

Hans Glas's company was based at Dingolfingen in a very poor and rural part of Lower Bavaria, not far from BMW in Munich. Glas, a resolutely family firm which never took on debt, had been a producer of agricultural machinery since the turn of the century and had

made a light motorcycle – the Goggo – with some success after the War. Sensing, just as BMW had done, that the market was beginning to shift from two-wheelers to small cars in the mid-1950s, Glas went to BMW to request supplies of the 250 cc engine to power his proposed small car. Summarily dismissed by BMW, he vowed to build his own – which he duly did, creating the tiny Goggomobil. This proved to be a big success, selling twice as many as the BMW Isetta and the Lloyd from Borgward.

Again sensing a shift in the market as the 1950s became the 1960s, Glas branched out into larger cars, prompting the complaint from BMW that he was copying everything the Munich company did. However, Glas went one further and vowed to challenge not just BMW but Porsche, too: remarkably, he proposed to do this from above, with a V8 coupé.

Glas's cars were full of technical innovation. He pioneered the toothed belt drive to an overhead camshaft (on the stylish 1700), for instance, and the 2.6 litre V8 originally designed for the Coupé had this arrangement for each of its cylinder banks and was the first engine in

Germany to use transistorised ignition. Smart styling from Frua in Turin gave Glas's products an exotic, Italian air, and his loyal customers enjoyed the company's personal service, even if the quality and reliability of the models was disappointing.

But by the middle of the 1960s Glas was finding it hard to keep pace with product development without breaking his 'never borrow' rule. At the same time, thanks to the success of the Neue Klasse saloons, BMW was bursting at the seams trying to produce 400 or 450 cars a day at Milbertshofen when in reality demand was running at 500 or 600 a day. Clearly, BMW would have to expand somewhere else, and it was not long before the Bavarian grapevine brought Glas's difficulties to BMW's notice. Negotiations – mainly within BMW, for many regarded this as a risky move – followed, and in 1966 Glas was bought for DM 9.1 million, along with a promise to integrate its dealers into the BMW network and keep its range of cars in production.

It was a risky promise, for many believed the Glas cars would drag down BMW's high image and engineers had already found quality

Opposite & left:
Long and low 2000 CS coupé of 1965 drew some of its inspiration from Bertone's 3200 CS (see page 56). The odd frontal treatment was rethought on later six-cylinder models to create a timeless classic

"Paul Hahnemann, BMW's powerful sales director, decided the attractive Glas sports coupés would be re-engineered to accept the BMW 1600 Ti engine and transmission, and that they would carry the BMW badge"

problems which needed immediate fixing – to the extent that BMW formed roving hit squads which swooped on dealers to update the many cars held in stock. For 1967-68 the advertised Glas range comprised nine models ranging from the 250 cc Goggomobil at DM 3450 to the three-litre V8 Coupé at 23,850, and in a speech explaining the takeover in May 1967 Glas MD Helmut Werner Bönsch said that BMW would formally take ownership in January of the following year. "There will be a three-point programme to improve quality, rationalise the ranges and revise Glas models to fit them into the BMW range," he stated. Munich insiders joked ruefully about BMW kidney grilles on the Goggomobil, but the reality proved thankfully different. Before long Paul Hahnemann, BMW's powerful sales director, had managed to sell off the surplus Glas stock, had identified the Glas models which clashed with BMW products, and had decided that the attractive 1300 GT and

1700 GT sports coupés would be re-engineered to accept the engine, transmission and rear axle of the BMW 1600 Ti saloon, and that they would carry the BMW badge.

Thus was born the inevitably short-lived BMW 1600 GT, with 1259 made over an 11-month period before BMW shipped out all the Glas production machinery to South Africa and installed its own lines to make pure BMW cars. BMW was now set to embark on its most important stride forward since the restructuring in 1960, to make the former Glas plant at Dingolfing its main manufacturing site, doubling its manufacturing capacity to allow it to become a serious player on the world stage.

Of the Glas range only the Goggomobil remained, destined to last one more year before renegotiated supply contracts threatened to raise its price to unsustainable levels. The big V8 Coupé, meanwhile, had quietly slipped away amid a certain feeling of sadness and missed

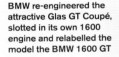

BMW re-engineered the attractive Glas GT Coupé, slotted in its own 1600 engine and relabelled the model the BMW 1600 GT

BMW bought the Glas company in 1966 and took over selected designs, including the Frua-styled 2.6 litre V8. BMW expanded the innovative engine to three litres brought quality up to scratch

2000
2000C/2000CS

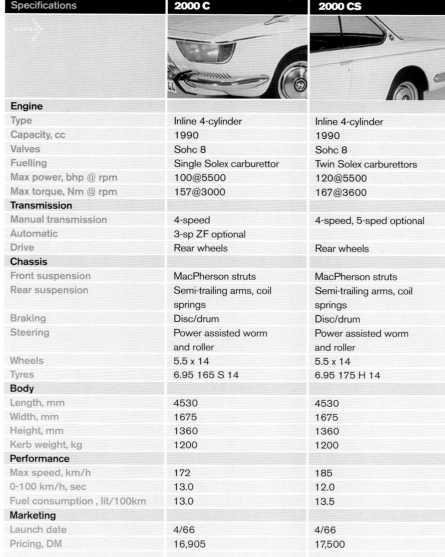

Specifications	2000 C	2000 CS
Engine		
Type	Inline 4-cylinder	Inline 4-cylinder
Capacity, cc	1990	1990
Valves	Sohc 8	Sohc 8
Fuelling	Single Solex carburettor	Twin Solex carburettors
Max power, bhp @ rpm	100@5500	120@5500
Max torque, Nm @ rpm	157@3000	167@3600
Transmission		
Manual transmission	4-speed	4-speed, 5-sped optional
Automatic	3-sp ZF optional	
Drive	Rear wheels	Rear wheels
Chassis		
Front suspension	MacPherson struts	MacPherson struts
Rear suspension	Semi-trailing arms, coil springs	Semi-trailing arms, coil springs
Braking	Disc/drum	Disc/drum
Steering	Power assisted worm and roller	Power assisted worm and roller
Wheels	5.5 x 14	5.5 x 14
Tyres	6.95 165 S 14	6.95 175 H 14
Body		
Length, mm	4530	4530
Width, mm	1675	1675
Height, mm	1360	1360
Kerb weight, kg	1200	1200
Performance		
Max speed, km/h	172	185
0-100 km/h, sec	13.0	12.0
Fuel consumption , lit/100km	13.0	13.5
Marketing		
Launch date	4/66	4/66
Pricing, DM	16,905	17,500

opportunity: there was a clear clash with BMW's own, ageing 3200 CS Coupé (though Glas boasted its car was just two-thirds the price and had better performance) but the technical specification of the Glas was superior, with its advanced overhead camshaft V8 engine giving more development potential than BMW's ancient pushrod device, and its self-levelling de Dion rear axle and inboard rear brakes offering a higher standard of road behaviour. Uncertain as to which way to proceed, BMW compromised by enlarging the engine to three litres and placing BMW badges on the bonnet, boot and wheels; even so,

the V8 lived out its final eight months in production as a Glas, never entering the official BMW portfolio. Just 666 were built.

Mainstream BMW had in any case already placed a big bet in the coupé stakes with the 2000 C, derived directly from the Neue Klasse saloon. Marking the first use of the two-litre version of the already-successful M10 engine, the new Coupé had obvious echoes of Bertone's 3200 CS at the rear and in its rear window shape, but was strikingly styled in-house by Wilhelm Hofmeister at the front with huge, high-mounted rectangular headlights set in a flat

sheet-metal nose broken up only by the small BMW double-kidney grille and a full-width row of vertical slats punched through the metal at just above bumper height. The bodies were to be built by Karmann at Osnabrück, with final assembly in BMW's Milbertshofen plant in Munich. The two-litre engine would be available in two different versions, said BMW at the Coupé's 1965 Frankfurt show presentation: a single carburettor, 100 bhp edition offering the alternative of automatic transmission, and a manual-only twin carburettor with 20 bhp more.

Admitting that it had not had an affordable

3200 1600

3200 CS

1600GT/GLAS V8

Specifications	3200 CS Coupé
Cylinders/capacity	V8/3168
Max power, bhp @ rpm	160@5600
Max torque, Nm @ rpm	240@3600
Manual transmission	4-speed
Wheels/tyres	5 x 15; 185 HR 15
Kerb weight, kg	1500
Max speed, km/h	200
0-100 km/h, sec	14.0
Fuel consumption, lit/100km	16.0
Launch date	1962
Pricing, DM	29,850
Units built	602

Specifications	1600 GT	Glas 3000 V8
Cylinders/capacity	4/1573	V8/2982
Max power, bhp @ rpm	105@6000	160@5100
Max torque, Nm @ rpm	131@4500	235@3900
Manual transmission	4-speed; 5-sp optional	4-speed
Wheels/tyres	4.5 x 14; 155HR14	5.5 x 14; 185H14
Kerb weight, kg	970	1350
Max speed, km/h	185	195
0-100 km/h, sec	11.0	10.0
Fuel consumption, lit/100km	12.5	16.0
Launch date	9/67	9/67
Pricing, DM	15,850	23,850
Units built	1259	389

Above and right:
BMW went to Turin's Bertone for the style of its luxurious 3200 CS coupé. The modern exterior design proved highly influential and did well to disguise a chassis and drivetrain which dated back to the mid 1950s

coupé for some while, BMW said the 2000 Coupé was designed to "hark back to the legendary 327 – the model which more than any other has become the Leitmotiv for the concept of BMW."

"The 2000 CS is the rebirth of the 327," continued the statement. "It is built using all the experience we have gained in the last five years in high performance engines: it represents a harmonious balance between the performance of a rakish sports car and the comfort of a luxurious cruiser."

Explaining the car in more detail, BMW referred to the Coupé's massive headlights as 'Asiatic eyes', claiming there were not "an extravagant fashion game but a completely new development which aligns a four-light system with European conditions."

Changes to the engine included a 5mm increase in bore, larger valves, a crankshaft with eight counterweights, as well as a move to 18,000 km oil change intervals – something of a novelty in the industry at the time – and there was a belated graduation to 12-volt electrics, something BMW's larger cars had failed to adopt for several years.

However, the one commodity that was absent was real performance. The coupés weighed 1200 kg, at least 30 more than the equivalent saloon would, and acceleration was correspondingly blunted – though superior aerodynamics still gave a respectable 185 km/h top speed to the twin-carb CS, which proved to be much the stronger seller.

While the strange looks of the 2000 Coupés certainly counted against them in a market stuffed with ravishingly good-looking Alfa Romeos and Lancias, what ultimately limited the model's appeal was the realisation that it was not only expensive but had more show than go. However, to BMW the swift tail-off of sales after 1966 was of little concern: company managers knew that , waiting in the wings, was the six-cylinder version of the large coupé which, as the CSi and CSL, would banish forever any notions that big BMWs didn't perform.

"The new coupé had obvious echoes of Bertone's 3200 CS at the rear but was strikingly styled in-house by Wilhelm Hofmeister at the front with huge high-mounted rectangular headlights set in a flat sheet-metal nose"

04

An icon emerges

Compact '02 Series is BMW's first big hit worldwide

BMW 1602-2002

→ Produced from 1966 to 1977
→ Massive success for BMW
→ Over 860,000 built
→ Took America by storm, building up a fanatical fan base
→ Declared "World's best $2500 automobile" by *Car and Driver*
→ Used components from larger 4-door
→ Iconic 2002 tii still a great driver's car
→ Potent 170 horsepower 2002 turbo rare but desirable
→ Touring hatchback a sales failure but now sought after
→ All models fun to drive, affordable

It was early in 1965 when BMW's product strategists first gathered around the boardroom table to plan their next move to make the most of the unexpectedly big success they had just created with the Neue Klasse saloons. They decided on two moves, not one. The first, and most daring, was to begin development of a big six-cylinder luxury car to challenge the dominance of the mighty Mercedes SE: the second programme was much more cautious – and few within BMW at the time could have had any inkling that the car they were planning would be a massive worldwide hit that would put BMW on the map, especially in the USA.

Indeed, there must have been those inside the company who feared that the idea of removing content from the successful four-door sedan to create a smaller, lighter and cheaper lead-in model would be a non-starter, that buyers would turn their noses up at a simplified, stripped-out economy model – after all, the policy seemed to go directly counter to the BMW brand ethos of classy, premium-priced sports sedans offering high performance and a pedigree driving experience.

Any such doubters were proved completely and utterly wrong when the unlikely recipe of a cut-down two-door with skimpy equipment, plain looks and BMW's smallest engine instantly caught the public imagination – despite its clumsy 1600-2 title, dreamed up at the last minute to differentiate it from the existing four-door 1600. This was the car that would spawn the legendary 2002 tii and the fearsome turbo – and bring the BMW experience to an eager universal audience.

Right from the start, buyers couldn't get enough of these beginners' BMWs. In its first full year on sale the two-door straight away matched its bigger brother in the showroom: year two saw it sell twice as many, while after three years, at almost 85,000 units, it more than quadrupled the bigger car's sales performance.

By this stage BMW had had to build a second

Derived from the already successful four-door 1500, the shorter, two-door '02 Series became the icon which introduced BMW to a global audience

Left:
George Bertram's 1965 design drawing for the proposed smaller car shows simplicity and elegance

Below:
The first '02 model, launched in 1966, was labelled 1600-2 to distinguish it from the 1600 four-door

factory to cope with demand: clearly, in devising this implausible mix, the company had by happy chance created a small car set for big success. BMW was simply not accustomed to sales figures like these: it was barely eight years since the company had so narrowly escaped collapse. Yet even greater heights were still to come. By 1972, what was now universally known as the 02 series smashed triumphantly through the 100,000-unit barrier, going on to record its best-ever sales year in 1974 with over 111,000 finding eager buyers.

Americans took to the baby BMW with particular relish. In an era when Detroit's products were still overweight, oversized and dull to drive, the quick and accurate responses and the fresh, energetic powertrain of this modest machine came across as an absolute revelation. Suddenly,

Americans discovered that driving could be fun and not cost the earth, that German products with quality and integrity were more affordable than they had imagined. *Car and Driver* splashed the 1600-2 on its front cover, loudly proclaiming it "the world's best $2,500 automobile."

All this appears to have taken the BMW planners by surprise. At the 1600-2's low-key unveiling at the Geneva motor show in March 1966, the company described it as "exactly like the 1800, but produced in response to requests for a more economical solution."

To this end BMW chopped 50mm out of the four-door's wheelbase, deleted the rear passenger doors, dropped the wheel size down to 13 inches, and installed the 1600 cc engine from the larger car – though with one difference in the shape of the larger inlet valves of the 1800 version.

The result was an engine which gave 85 horsepower at 5700rpm, installed in a somewhat awkward-looking two-door body where the boot seemed almost as long as the bonnet, the shortening operation appearing to have taken place entirely in the rear half of the passenger compartment. Inside was a simple but well made dashboard modelled on that of the revised four-door, a good driving position, generous seating for the driver and front passenger, and a less generous bench for those clambering into the back. Underneath – and here lay the newcomer's real secret – were concealed the steering, suspension and complete driveline taken from the larger car, which had won copious plaudits for its handling and roadholding.

Best of all, however, the whole ensemble was very light, tipping the scales at just 940 kg ready for the road. Even with only 85 horsepower on tap this made for very lively performance, with 0-100 km/h acceleration claimed in 13.3 seconds and a top speed of 160 km/h – just short of the magic 100 mph mark.

BMW's press information, which in that era swung happily from cool technical detail to grandiose and often exaggerated proclamations of superiority, waxed enthusiastically about the "exhilarating acceleration" that this combination produced: this car, said the company, provided the ideal justification to dust off the old corporate publicity catchline of Freude am Fahren, or fun to drive.

What was then labelled the 1600-2 went into production soon after its Geneva debut: over 13,000 were built in the remaining months of that year and no fewer than 38,566 in 1967 when the plain 1600 was joined by a spiced-up Ti edition complete with twin carburettors (boosting power to 105 bhp), anti-roll bars, much-needed servo assistance for the brakes, and a rev-counter.

The Ti produced another wave of excited press reports but, at DM 9,950, it was DM 1,300 more expensive than the original and only sold in small quantities, principally to the United States: this derivative would in any case not remain in production for long as it was replaced in November by the 2002 ti.

The two-litre version, which was the first to be given an official 02 label, appeared in BMW dealerships at the beginning of 1968. Surprisingly, its larger engine offered less power – 100 bhp at 5500 rpm – than the 1600 Ti, but BMW already had its explanation prepared. "The 2002 is not designed as a sports car," read the announcement, "Instead it is [intended as] a touring saloon to meet exacting regulations under all present traffic conditions."

Stripped of the coded language, BMW was saying that it was easier to make the two-litre engine comply with upcoming US emissions laws. Fortunately, what was BMW's gain was the car enthusiast's gain, too, for though the 2002 has slightly less power at peak engine speeds than the revvy 1600 Ti, it had much more low-end torque and felt more gutsy to drive. BMW may not have intentionally set out to create a sports car: instead, by putting a large engine in a small, light body, it created the template for a whole dynasty of dynamic greats leading directly to today's M3.

The autumn of 1968 saw further delights for the enthusiast when the 2002 gained an extra carburettor – and, in the process 20 horsepower and 20 km/h in top speed – to become the 2002 ti. At the same time all models gained dual circuit brake lines, with a grille badge distinguishing the new ti edition. Surprisingly, the faster ti was never as strong a seller as the mainstream 2002, despite a very modest price difference. Perhaps all those keen drivers had been waiting for the next logical move expected from BMW: to give the 2002 the 130 horsepower fuel injection engine first employed in the 2000 tii sedan in late 1969.

It was February 1971 when the eagerly awaited 2002 tii burst onto the scene, generating superlatives in the press and waiting lists at BMW dealerships in equal measure. The Kugelfischer fuel injection, though considered tricky to set up, turned the '02 into a veritable bombshell: in particular, there was "instant pick-up as soon as the throttle is opened – the car leaps forward" in dramatic contrast to the hesitation and flatspots often experienced with carburettor set-ups.

Suddenly, BMW had hit the big time. The 2002 tii was unquestionably the most thrilling

Wo sich die Geister scheiden.

Variation

This is where opinions differ – BMW advertising was already original and provocative in the 1960s (top); Variations on a theme: BMW's more practical Touring derivative of the '02 Series failed to catch on with buyers – a rare marketing mistake for the company

1502·2002

1502/1602/1600 Ti/1802/2002/2002Ti

Specifications	1502	1602	1600 Ti	1802	2002
Engine					
Type	Inline 4-cylinder	Inline 4-cylinder	Inline 4-cylinder	Inline 4-cylinder	Inline 4-cylinder
Bore & stroke	84 x 71	84 x 71	84 x 71	89 x 71	89 x 80
Capacity	1573	1573	1573	1766	1990
Valves	8	8	8	8	8
Valve actuation	Sohc	Sohc	Sohc	Sohc	Sohc
Compression ratio	8.o:1	8.6:1	9.5:1	8.6:1	8.5:1
Fuelling	Single Solex carburettor	Single Solex carburettor	Twin Solex carburettors	Single Solex carburettor	Single Solex carburettor
Emission control					
Max power, bhp @ rpm	75@5800	85@5700	105@6000	90@5250	100@5500
Max torque, Nm @ rpm	118@3700	123@3000	131@4500	143@3000	157@3500
Transmission					
Manual transmission	4-speed	4-speed	4-speed; 5-speed optional	4-speed	4-speed; 5-speed optional
Automatic					3-speed ZF optional
Drive	Rear wheels	Rear wheels	Rear wheels	Rear wheels	Rear wheels
Chassis					
Front suspension	MacPherson struts	MacPherson struts	MacPherson struts	MacPherson struts	MacPherson struts
Rear suspension	Semi-trailing arms, coil springs	Semi-trailing arms, coil springs	Semi-trailing arms, coil springs	Semi-trailing arms, coil springs	Semi-trailing arms, coil springs
Braking	Servo-assisted disc/drum	Disc/drum	Servo-assisted disc/drum	Servo-assisted disc/drum	Servo-assisted disc/drum
Steering	Worm and roller	Worm and roller	Worm and roller	Worm and roller	Worm and roller
Wheels	4.5 x 13	4.5 x 13	4.5 x 13	4.5 x 13	4.5 x 13
Tyres	165 SR 13	165 SR 13	165 SR 13	165 SR 13	165 HR 13
Body					
Structure	Steel monocoque	Steel monocoque	Steel monocoque	Steel monocoque	Steel monocoque
Wheelbase, mm	2500	2500	2500	2500	2500
Track F/R, mm	1330/1330	1330/1330	1330/1330	1330/1330	1330/1330
Length, mm	4230	4230	4230	4230	4230
Width, mm	1590	1590	1590	1590	1590
Height, mm	1410	1410	1410	1410	1410
Kerb weight, kg	980	940	960	980	990
Fuel tank capacity, lit	50	50	50	50	50
Performance					
Max speed, km/h	157	162	175	167	173
0-100 km/h, sec	14.5	13.5	11.0	12.0	12.0
Fuel consumption , lit/100km	12.0	11.5	12.5	12.0	12.5
Marketing					
Launch date	1/75	3/66	9/67	4/71	1/68
Pricing, DM	11,390	8,650	9,950	10,435	8,680

2002 ti

Inline 4-cylinder
89 x 80
1990
8
Sohc
9.3:1
Twin Solex carburettors

120@5500
178@3600

4-speed; 5-speed optional

Rear wheels

MacPherson struts
Semi-trailing arms, coil
springs
Servo-assisted disc/drum
Worm and roller
5.00 x 13
165 HR 13

Steel monocoque
2500
1330/1330
4230
1590
1410
990
50

185
10.0
13.0

9/68
8,760

small car on sale anywhere, and the world soon sat up and took notice. Among car enthusiasts the buzz was no longer Alfa or Porsche or Jaguar: the car for the quick driver to have – even the very rich quick driver who could afford to park a Porsche alongside the Mercedes in his garage – was a tii. The tii had become an emblem of everything that was fast and fun about driving. Square and boxy and basic it might be, but it appealed to the playful – and competitive – instinct in people of all ages and occupations; fun was the main ingredient in the mix, with snob value at that stage counting for little or nothing.

The tii, more by coincidence than design, came as part of a big wave of changes

expanding the 02 model line. There had been a 1600 Cabrio, converted by Baur, since 1967: with a fully retracting hood it looked attractive but was poor on torsional rigidity and, as was later discovered, prone to rusting. Fewer than 2000 were made, most of them with the 1600 engine, until the all-change month in early 1971 when a new cabriolet appeared with a strong and safe – but also unattractive – thick rollover structure. This made the car stiffer, safer and better to drive, but again sales take-up was modest.

At the same time the whole range received a visual makeover. Larger bumpers, the rear ones now wrapping right round to reach the rear wheel arch cut-out, carried black rubber strips, and a

The 2002 was an absolute natural on the racetrack and even found its way on to the rally stages, scoring a single international victory

Above:
BMW 2002s were a force to be reckoned with in touring car races throughout the 1970s

bumper-height rubbing strip ran the length of each side. On the mechanical side a third engine size appeared, in the shape of the 1802 with the short-stroke unit that had been such a favourite in the four-door; however, spring 1971 is best remembered as the point where BMW launched one of its few self-confessed marketing failures.

There was unquestionable logic behind the idea of expanding the appeal of the 02 series by adding a more practical variant – a version which would retain the model's universally celebrated fun-to-drive character but which would acknowledge the emerging trend in the volume car market for versatile hatchbacks which, with their folding seats and opening tailgates, combined the advantages of both saloons and estate cars.

But, for some reason, the car which BMW so carefully developed never caught on. Clearly already becoming aware of some sensitivity in this area, BMW wanted to distance it from both estates and hatchbacks and called the new car the Touring: initially, it was available as either a 1600, 2000 or 2000 Tii, though within 18 months the 1600 had been replaced by an 1800. Confusingly, too, it was only after two years later these models officially gained '02 on their designations. However, this confusion was

nothing compared to the muddle in the minds of the buyers, who did not know what to make of the new model.

The two-door saloon could never be thought pretty, but the public had come to accept and even aspire to its blocky shape, its odd proportions and details like its round rear lights. Yet the shape of the Touring, with its 'fastback' tailgate and its droopy rear deck-line just didn't click with BMW's clientele.

The failure of the Touring remains one of the auto industry's great debating points, and there are probably as many different opinions on the subject as the number of Tourings (just 29,330, or 3 per cent of all '02s) produced in its truncated three-year existence. All sorts of theories have been advanced for the disaster, the consensus perhaps being that, though the Touring was a logical BMW, it might not have fitted the perception of a BMW that people wanted to have at that time. For, with the ultra-sporty 2002 Tii riding high in the charts, buyers wanted their BMWs to look sporty and untainted by considerations of utility: any hint or suggestion of a utilitarian mission or an association with the world of prosaic and practical family hatchbacks detracted from the perceived purity of the BMW's purpose.

Just one final chapter remained to be written in the 2002 saga. The 2002 turbo came in with a bang at a triumphant time for BMW, but went out with something of a whimper, a casualty of political correctness and a panic among buyers in the first fuel crisis of 1973-4.

The 1972 Olympic Games, held in BMW's home city of Munich, were a high point for BMW – a chance to demonstrate its new-found status, to show off its technical expertise, to build a distinctive new headquarters tower block that could be seen from all over the city. But most pointedly of all, the Olympics allowed BMW to upstage its long-standing rival Mercedes-Benz: it provided the official cars, making a perfect debut for the shiny new 5 Series, it made special electric versions of some models for silent, emission-free operation within the stadiums, and it designed and constructed a highly futuristic concept car – the BMW Turbo.

This dramatically wide and low-set mid-engined supercar, designed by BMW studio head Paul Braque, had a feeling of Lamborghini to its flat, angular surfaces and gull-wing doors; the cockpit was pure space-age, with headline features such as radar and an electronic speedometer display. Powered by a 200 horsepower turbocharged version of the 2002 tii's two-litre engine, it was used to lead parades at the

Olympics and gained widespread media exposure. Only two were built – but the lasting value to BMW was in the turbo engine it gave to the volume production 2002 series, making it the first turbocharged saloon car offered on general sale.

Little more than a year after the athletes had packed up and left what turned out to be a tragic and terrorism-struck Olympic festival, BMW unveiled the 2002 turbo at the September 1973 Frankfurt show. But while the super-fast derivative generated great excitement among speed-hungry magazine editors who lusted after its 170 tyre-smoking horsepower and 210 km/h top speed, there were others who asked serious questions about the aggressive style.

Road testers loved and were intimidated by the turbo in equal measure. The main change in the two-litre engine was a drop in compression ratio to 6.9 to one in order to allow for the KKK turbocharger's boost higher up the scale; the Kugelfischer fuel injection was carried over with few alterations, while modifications to the chassis included wider 6J wheels (though still 13 inches in diameter) and, in expectation of higher fuel consumption, a larger 70 litre tank. The result was a Jekyll and Hyde motor car which would be docile, not to say lethargic, most of the time, but which would burst into explosive action once the turbo boost came in at 4000 rpm. At that point,

> "There was unquestionable logic behind the idea of expanding the appeal of the '02 series by adding a more practical variant – but for some reason the car which BMW so carefully developed never caught on"

1602-2002 PRODUCTION

Production History:	In production: 1966-1977		Total produced 827,533							
model	1502	1602	1600 Ti	1802	2002	2002 Ti	2002 Tii	2002 turbo	total for year	SKD
1966		13,244							13,244	219
1967		34,842	3,712		12				38,566	3,916
1968		28,749	4,958		27,721	952			62,380	3,970
1969		25,686			34,948	4,899			65,533	4,787
1970		30,520			44,327	8,630			83,477	5,755
1971		22,837		14,675	46,306	1,967	8,266		94,051	6,200
1972		23,280		25,420	47,505		12,343		108,548	5,369
1973		20,051		21,022	42,987		10,337		94,404	2,570
1974	18	35,960		19,353	47,697		6,425	7	110,930	3,048
1975	41,133	8,947		2,881	24,333		1,330	1,477	78,812	396
1976	21,530				10,081			188	31,611	504
1977	8,883								8,883	360
totals	71,564	244,116	8,670	83,351	325,917	16,448	38,701	1,672		
								grand total	790,439	37,094
								grand total inc SKD	827,533	

1602·2002
1502/1602/1600 ti/1802/2002/2002ti

Specifications	1600 Cabrio	1600 Touring	1802 Touring	2002 Cabrio	2002 Touring
Engine					
Type	Inline 4-cylinder	Inline 4-cylinder	Inline 4-cylinder	Inline 4-cylinder	Inline 4-cylinder
Bore & stroke, mm	84 x 71	84 x 71	89 x 71	89 x 80	89 x 80
Capacity, cc	1573	1573	1766	1990	1990
Valves	8	8	8	8	8
Valve actuation	Sohc	Sohc	Sohc	Sohc	Sohc
Compression ratio	8.0:1	8.6:1	8.6:1	8.5:1	9.3:1
Fuelling	Single Solex carburettor	Single Solex carburettor	Single Solex carburettor	Single Solex carburettor	single Solex carburettors
Max power, bhp @ rpm	85@5700	85@5700	90@5250	100@5500	100@5500
Max torque, Nm @ rpm	123@3000	123@3000	143@3000	157@3500	157@3500
Transmission					
Manual transmission	4-speed	4-speed	4-speed	4-speed; 5-speed optional	4-speed; 5-speed optional
Automatic				3-speed ZF optional	3-speed ZF optional
Drive	Rear wheels	Rear wheels	Rear wheels	Rear wheels	Rear wheels
Chassis					
Front suspension	MacPherson struts	MacPherson struts	MacPherson struts	MacPherson struts	MacPherson struts
Rear suspension	Semi-trailing arms, coil springs	Semi-trailing arms, coil springs	Semi-trailing arms, coil springs	Semi-trailing arms, coil springs	Semi-trailing arms, coil springs
Braking	Servo-assisted disc/drum	Servo-assisted disc/drum	Servo-assisted disc/drum	Servo-assisted disc/drum	Servo-assisted disc/drum
Steering	Worm and roller	Worm and roller	Worm and roller	Worm and roller	Worm and roller
Wheels	4.5 x 13	4.5 x 13	4.5 x 13	4.5 x 13	4.5 x 13
Tyres	165 SR 13	165 SR 13	165 SR 13	165 SR 13	165 SR 13
Body					
Structure	Steel monocoque	Steel monocoque	Steel monocoque	Steel monocoque	Steel monocoque
Wheelbase, mm	2500	2500	2500	2500	2500
Track F/R, mm	1330/1330	1330/1330	1330/1330	1330/1330	1330/1330
Length, mm	4230	4110	4110	4230	4110
Width, mm	1590	1590	1590	1590	1590
Height, mm	1410	1380	1380	1410	1380
Kerb weight, kg	940	1030	1030	1040	1030
Fuel tank capacity, lit	50	52	52	50	52
Performance					
Max speed, km/h	162	162	167	173	173
0-100 km/h, sec	13.5	13.5	12.0	12.0	12.0
Fuel consumption , lit/100km	11.5	11.5	12.0	12.5	13.0
Marketing					
Launch date	9/67	4/71	10/71	4/71	4/71
Pricing, DM	11,980	11,320	11,870	14,985	11,545

2002 Tii Touring

Inline 4-cylinder
89 x 80
1990
8
Sohc
9.5:1
Kugelfischer fuel injection
130@5800
176@4500

4-speed; 5-speed optional

Rear wheels

MacPherson struts
Semi-trailing arms, coil
springs
Servo-assisted disc/drum
Worm and roller
5.0 x 13
165 HR 13

Steel monocoque
2500
1330/1330
4110
1590
1380
1050
52

190
10.0
13.0

4/71

Left:
Hatchback Touring was one of BMW's rare marketing failures: buyers appeared to have little interest in practicality

Above:
Original Baur Cabrio with fully retracting hood (left) was elegant but lacked rigidity; later Cabrio with rollover hoop sacrificed beauty for safety and tauter handling

all hell was let loose.

The suddenness of this personality switch could take even highly experienced drivers by surprise – especially on wet roads. Even the standard 2002 could be tricky on damp bends, but with the turbo the driver stood little chance of preventing a spin if the engine came onto boost unexpectedly – as it was prone to do.

The turbo was expensive; indeed, its price was even raised by DM 2,000 during its mere ten months of production. In the end, however, what killed the turbo off – after just 1672 had been made, all of them left hand drive – was not adverse comment in the specialist magazines but

the global fuel crisis which had plunged western economies and, especially, car companies into something of a panic.

Yet even BMW, which had by now been under the leadership of Eberhard von Kuenheim for four stable, successful years, was not immune to the effects of the crisis: as a producer of premium, performance cars it should in theory have been hit harder than its mainstream competitors by the crisis gripping Germany, a crisis which had seen widespread fuel shortages as a result of the Arab oil embargo, and the unprecedented imposition of timetabled driving bans. Everywhere, experts were predicting doom for the auto industry as

"There was unquestionable logic behind the idea of expanding the appeal of the '02 series by adding a more practical variant – but for some reason the car which BMW so carefully developed never caught on"

Brochure for 2002 turbo was scarcely credible in claiming 'moderate performance characteristics' for an engine whose explosive power delivery earned the model a reputation as an unpredictable but thrilling drive. Fears of fuel shortages in 1974 killed the model off after only 1672 were made

Germany's famed car economy imploded.

To make matters worse, BMW was about to go live on the second phase of its big expansion, the opening of sophisticated modern facilities to build the new 5 Series at the Dingolfing plant, once the site of Hans Glas GmbH. All around, companies were laying off workers, putting factories on to short-time working or mothballing them altogether. Yet, buoyed by consistent demand for BMW models, von Kuenheim kept his nerve:-

"One of the toughest decisions I had to make was in the autumn of '73," he said in an interview for this book. "As a result of one of the Israeli wars with the Arabs we had an energy crisis here in Germany, and all motor traffic was forbidden every weekend. We had just opened our new plant at Dingolfing in Bavaria in the month of November – and in that month we got 200 orders. Journalists declared that this would be the last new car factory ever built, and that the era of the motor car would soon be over. We had to keep our nerve. When you've just opened a new factory that morning you have to show to your own people that when it comes to the crunch you can make it, you can pull through.

And we did improve sales. Opel, VW and other companies fired a lot of their people with compensation. They paid a lot of compensation, but we had to find another way to get through the situation as we did not have enough money to pay compensation. It was therefore better that we didn't fire anybody."

BMW's confidence in its own abilities was

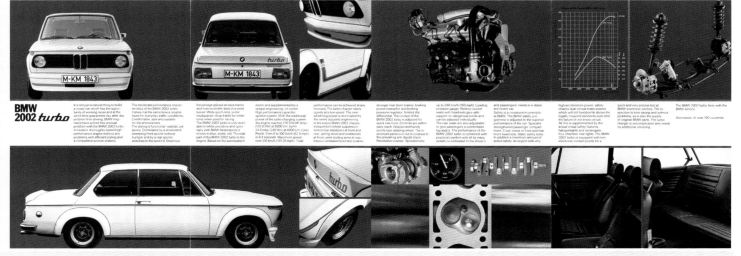

2002 Tii + TURBO

Specifications	2002 Tii	2002 Turbo
Engine		
Type	Inline 4-cylinder	Inline 4-cylinder
Bore & stroke, mm	89 x 80	89 x 80
Capacity, cc	1990	1990
Valves	8	8
Valve actuation	Sohc	Sohc
Compression ratio	9.5:1	6.9:1
Fuelling	Kugelfischer fuel injection	Kugelfischer fuel injection; KKK turbocharger
Max power, bhp @ rpm	130@5800	170@5800
Max torque, Nm @ rpm	176@4500	240@4000
Transmission		
Manual transmission	4-speed; 5-speed optional	4-speed; 5-speed optional
Drive	Rear wheels	Rear wheels
Chassis		
Front suspension	MacPherson struts	MacPherson struts
Rear suspension	Semi-trailing arms, coil springs	Semi-trailing arms, coil springs
Braking	Disc/drum	Disc/drum
Steering	Worm and roller	Worm and roller
Wheels	5.0 x 13	5.5 x 13
Tyres	165 HR 13	185/70 HR 13
Body		
Structure	Steel monocoque	Steel monocoque
Wheelbase, mm	2500	2500
Track F/R, mm	1330/1330	1330/1330
Length, mm	4230	4230
Width, mm	1590	1620
Height, mm	1410	1410
Kerb weight, kg	1010	1080
Fuel tank capacity, lit	46	70
Performance		
Max speed, km/h	190	211
0-100 km/h, sec	10.0	8.0
Fuel consumption , lit/100km	13.0	14.5
Marketing		
Launch date	10/68	9/73
Pricing, DM	10,990	18,720

evident. Since its restructuring at the beginning of the previous decade its mistakes had been few – the rushed development and troublesome gearboxes of the Neue Klasse, soon rectified by increasingly perfectionist engineers; the failure of the Touring, readily conceded as diversion from the true BMW path; and the 2002 turbo, perhaps an over-ambitious bid to be first with a turbo passenger car but also without question a victim of outside circumstance. The modest costs involved in developing the '02 series had paid dividends hundredfold, with a design that had put BMW on the map.

The first 3 series was about to be launched, the economy-special 1502 with its detuned, regular-fuel engine was an unexpected success and was destined to stay in production until 1977. The cash tills were rolling, the engineers were inventing, Mercedes was getting frightened and the buyers could not get their new BMWs soon enough. Things looked good indeed.

Gaudy mirror-script slogan on 2002 turbo's front spoiler was universally condemned and swiftly dropped

1602-2002 series bowed out
in 1977 after 860,000 had
been built, making it the
biggest hit in BMW's history

02 CABRIO + TOURING PRODUCTION

Production History:		In production: 1967-1975		Total produced 33,529			
model	1600 Cabrio	2002 Cabrio	1602 touring	1802 touring	2002 touring	2002 Tii touring	total for year
1967							0
1968	6						6
1969	548						548
1970	650						650
1971	454	433	1,998	269	5,466	2,428	11,048
1972	24	662	2,341	1,633	4,700	1,867	11,227
1973		843	40	1,197	4,808	1,269	8,157
1974		309			1,095	219	1,623
1975		270					270
totals	1,682	2,517	4,379	3,099	16,069	5,783	
						grand total	33,529
						grand total inc SKD	33,529

05

Big sixes

Large six-cylinder saloons take the fight to Mercedes-Benz

BMW 2500-2800

→ BMW returns to the prestige class
→ 2500 and 2800 favour sportiness over luxury
→ Six-cylinder enginesdeveloped from M10 two-litre
→ Engines set new standards for smoothness
→ Later engines with 3.0 and 3.3 litres
→ Bavaria value version succeeds in US
→ Injection model is first BMW over 200 bhp
→ Forerunner of first 7 Series

The science of market research was in its infancy – at least in Europe – when BMW began planning its three-pronged expansion strategy in the early 1960s. Already, the instant success of the Neue Klasse 1500 and its derivatives had revealed an unexpectedly rich groundswell of demand for a quality, high-performance medium-sized car, and at a premium price, too; now BMW sought to introduce model series both below and above the mid-sized car, putting itself into direct competition with Alfa Romeo in the small car class and the august Mercedes-Benz in the luxury sector.

First, however, BMW had to make room for its new model lines by moving motorcycle production to Berlin and clearing out the scarcely profitable old-era ranges still in production – and it was here that Paul Hahnemann, BMW's sales director (who enjoyed such a high profile that most people thought him the managing director) began to make use of market psychology techniques to decide what to get rid of and what to introduce in its place. It was these methods, highly innovative at the time, which told BMW that its image was still a very sporting one and which led it to make its new large car deliberately very sporty – and deliberately less comfortable than its Mercedes counterpart.

Hahnemann believed fervently in the then-novel concept of niche marketing – after all, hadn't the 1500 succeeded largely because it appealed to a narrow (but rich) band of enthusiasts whose demands had been overlooked by every other manufacturer? Surely, he reasoned, there could be equal opportunities for BMW in other market sectors if the underlying desires of consumers could be explored and those tallying with BMW brand values exploited.

Anonymous research carried out with consumer panels selected for their impartiality had uncovered some useful facts about both BMW and its potential rival, Mercedes-Benz. Particularly surprising was the finding that many thought Mercedes was owned by the German

Large six-cylinder 2500 and 2800 were developed from experience gained with four-cylinder models

The 2500 and 2800 were aimed directly at Mercedes, even if BMW denied it. The focus was deliberately kept sporty, even though some customers complained about ride and equipment

"Early press reviews of the new series were guardedly complimentary: lavish praise for the smoothness of the engine and the responsiveness of the handling were tempered with criticisms of what was judged to be a too-firm ride for a luxury car"

state, whereas it has always been resolutely private and it was in fact BMW that had been applying for state aid from Bavaria for the expansion of its manufacturing facilities.

On a model level the research revealed that models such as the Isetta and 600 'minibus' had not actually stigmatised the BMW image simply because they were not often linked with the mainstream BMW products; the pretty 700 saloon and coupé, on the other hand, were accepted as appropriate to the BMW image as they were sporty and powerful for their size. The big V8 cars, revered as symbols of corporate prestige by senior company managers, were not seen as doing any harm to BMW even though they were clearly a hangover from the previous decade – they had little that was typically BMW in them, the survey said. However, one clear-cut finding stood out from all the rest: those surveyed repeatedly cited the 326, 327 and 328 as being central models in the public image of BMW.

For Hahnemann this was an absolute gift. The 326, 327 and 328 were elegant sporting saloons, coupés and sports cars from the 1930s: fast, exclusive and highly regarded, they represented the very peak of BMW's automotive achievements in the pre-war period. To translate those values into the language of a top-technology contemporary product for the late 1960s would allow BMW once again to annexe

the high-image, high-performance market and provide a product which, while equivalent in price to a medium-to-top Mercedes, would attract a different and more sporting type of customer.

Against the background of such high perceived potential, it was only natural that BMW set its sights high when establishing the parameters for the new big saloon. It would be considerably larger than the Neue Klasse cars, and its six-cylinder engines would be developed from the fours of the mid-sized models. While the all-independent suspension would follow the pattern of the mid-sized cars, too, the front end would employ innovative geometry to sharpen up steering response and, at the rear, a shallower angle for the semi-trailing arms would minimise camber change on bumps so as to reduce the likelihood of tail-end breakaway under extreme cornering loads.

The car that was presented to the international media in Rottach-Egern in September 1968 was all those things and more. Describing the 2500 and 2800 as "a new chapter in the programme", BMW said how the success of the Neue Klasse had made it clear to any doubters that "we have grown in business terms".

The publicity material laid great stress on the emergence of a new type of driver, a type of driver who must be provided with the optimal car.

"Our role model for this new type of buyer is neither the muscle-bound body builder nor the portly gentleman", explained BMW. "Instead, we correspond to a light athlete, who is young and quick on his feet."

True to form, the six-cylinder cars did indeed prove innovative, quick and, for their size, agile. Developed by von Falkenstein from his own highly successful four-cylinder, two litre, the 2.5 and 2.8 litre engines gave keen power, the all-up weight of 1360 kg was usefully less than the hefty Mercedes equivalents, and advanced chassis features such as all-disc brakes, optional power steering and automatic transmission, and a limited slip differential on the larger-capacity model emphasised the BMW's advanced and sporting make-up.

Mercedes complained, not for the first time, that BMW was trying to challenge it by copying its exact engine sizes; BMW contended, perhaps tongue in cheek, that this was simply the optimum size of engine and that earlier suggestions for a 2.2 and 2.6 litre combination had been rejected precisely because Mercedes had a successful 220. One point where BMW did put its hand up and admit noblesse oblige was in the matter of the new car's ignition key. "We have copied the ignition key of the Mercedes 600," confessed BMW with mock humility. "It has 12,000 combinations instead of the 140 we had before."

Other novel features of the new series included an oil cooler, a side-flow radiator with a thermostat which reacted to both engine load and temperature, a thermostatic cooling fan which reduced noise and saved 6 bhp at maximum speed and, on the safety front, a two-piece steering column with a shear section incorporated, and extensive padding on the dashboard. No quarterlights were provided, BMW claiming its ventilation system could produce 100 litres of fresh air per second – though to today's

In their design and engineering BMW's six-cylinder models closely paralleled the smaller cars, with semi-trailing arm rear suspension and innovative front end geometry. Von Falkenhausen's smooth and vigorous six-cylinder engine was lavishly praised and eventually grew to 3.3 litres

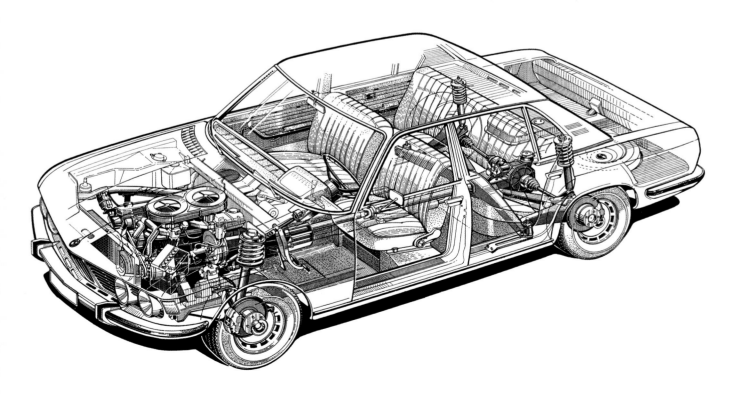

1602-2002

1502/1602/1600 ti/1802/2002/2002ti

Specifications	2500	2800/2.8/Bavaria	3.0 S/L	3.0 Si	3.3 L
Engine					
Type	Inline 6-cylinder	Inline 6-cylinder	Inline 6-cylinder	Inline 6-cylinder	Inline 6-cylinder
Bore & stroke, mm	86 x 71.6	86 x 80	89 x 80	89 x 80	89 x 88.4
Capacity, cc	2494	2788	2985	2985	3295
Valves	12	12	12	12	12
Valve actuation	Sohc	Sohc	Sohc	Sohc	Sohc
Compression ratio	9.0:1	9.0:1	9.0:1	9.5:1	9.0:1
Fuelling	Twin Zenith carburettors	Twin Zenith carburettors	Twin Zenith carburettors	Bosch D-Jetronic electronic fuel injection	Twin Zenith carburettors
Max power, bhp @ rpm	150@6000	170@6000	180@6000	200@5500 (195 after 1976)	190@5500
Max torque, Nm @ rpm	211@3700	235@3700	255@3700	272@4300 (267 after 1976)	289@3500
Transmission					
Manual transmission	4-speed	4-speed	4-speed	4-speed	4-speed
Automatic	3-speed ZF optional	3-speed ZF optional	3-speed Borg Warner optional	3-speed Borg Warner optional	3-speed Borg Warner optional
Drive	Rear wheels	Rear wheels	Rear wheels	Rear wheels	Rear wheels
Chassis					
Front suspension	MacPherson struts	MacPherson struts	MacPherson struts	MacPherson struts	MacPherson struts
Rear suspension	Semi-trailing arms, coil springs	Semi-trailing arms, coil springs	Semi-trailing arms, coil springs	Semi-trailing arms, coil springs	Semi-trailing arms, coil springs
Braking	Servo-assisted discs	Servo-assisted discs	Servo-assisted discs	Servo-assisted discs	Servo-assisted discs
Steering assistance optional	ZF worm and roller, power	Power assisted ZF worm and roller	Power assisted ZF worm and roller	Power assisted ZF worm and roller	Power assisted ZF worm and roller
Wheels	6.0 x 14	6.0 x 14	6.0 x 14	6.0 x 14	6.0 x 14
Tyres	175 HR 14	195/70 HR 14	195/70 HR 14	195/70 VR 14	195/70 VR 14
Body					
Structure	Steel monocoque	Steel monocoque	Steel monocoque	Steel monocoque	Steel monocoque
Wheelbase, mm	2692	2692 (L: 2792)	2692	2692	2792
Track F/R, mm	1446/1464	1446/1464	1446/1464	1446/1464	1446/1464
Length, mm	4700	4700 (L:4800)	4700	4700	4800
Width, mm	1750	1750	1750	1750	1750
Height, mm	1450	1450	1450	1450	1450
Kerb weight, kg	1360	1360 (L: 1440)	1470	1440	1520
Fuel tank capacity, lit	75	75	75	75	75
Performance					
Max speed, km/h	190	200	205	210	205
0-100 km/h, sec	11.0	10.0	9.0	8.5	9.0
Fuel consumption , lit/100km	16.0	16.5	17.5	17.5	17.5
Marketing					
Launch date	10/68	10/68	4/71	8/71	8/73
Pricing, DM	15,485	17,250	19,980	22,960	35,600

3.3 Li

Inline 6-cylinder
89 x 86
3205
12
Sohc
9.0:1
Bosch L-Jetronic electronic
fuel injection
197@5500
280@4300

4-speed
3-speed Borg Warner
optional
Rear wheels

MacPherson struts
Semi-trailing arms, coil
springs
Servo-assisted discs
Power assisted ZF worm
and roller
6 x 14
195/70 VR 14

Steel monocoque
2792
1446/1464
4800
1750
1450
1520
75

205
9.0
17.5

12/76
43,320

eyes even the higher-specified 2800 looks astonishingly simple for a top of the line car. The dashboard is extremely sparse, the gearchange is a four speed manual, and the windows are hand operated.

The 2500/2800 was the first to introduce – albeit initially as an option – a BMW feature which has since become a brand trademark: the neat toolkit hinging down from the boot lid. Reputedly, this was at the suggestion of Max Hoffman, BMW's influential US importer.

Early press reviews of the new series were guardedly complimentary: lavish praise for the smoothness of the engine and the responsiveness of the performance and handling were tempered with criticisms of the interior fixtures and fittings and what was judged to be a too-firm ride for a luxury car. The price – at DM 15,485 for the 2500 and DM 17,250 for the

2800 – was judged to be high, too. Criticisms these may have been, but in many ways they were just what Hahnemann wanted: to be sporty and expensive suited the brand image he was trying to build for BMW, it was relatively easy to improve the interior equipment, and he had no intention of making his BMWs as comfortable as Mercedes models as this would undermine their sportiness, the most important differentiation they enjoyed over the three-pointed star brand.

Nevertheless, though the model got off to a quick start and had built up an 18-month waiting list (the same as that for a Mercedes 280) within a year, it soon became clear it would not sell as well as BMW had hoped. Despite various moves to improve the specification and, later, to raise the power of the engines, the big car was a slow mover off the showroom floor and BMW's concept of 'unpretentious exclusivity' was

3.3 litre long wheelbase version of 1974 was edging uncomfortably close to Mercedes in price; cost had been a problem throughout the models' life

BMW had only its Munich plant until Dingolfing opened for the 5 Series in 1972. Here, Munich workers put the finishing touches to 1970 2800 saloon

beginning to look shaky. The notion was based on circumventing the appeal of Mercedes' blue-chip status, the company arguing that "if a businessman has made something of his life in Germany and has to show his neighbour he is something, he can only drive a Mercedes. If, however, he has made something of his life but feels not the slightest need to show off, then he can buy himself a BMW."

Slow sales were not helped by adverse currency movements on the principal export markets, either. France devalued the Franc twice, Sweden imposed new safety and emission requirements, and the Mark/Dollar relationship swung against BMW at just the wrong time. Before long BMW found itself with 5,000 six-

cylinder cars stockpiled – two months' production – and resolved to reduce its costs in order to be able to offer better prices.

This policy helped produce the 1971 Bavaria, a version of the big six specially aimed at kick-starting sales in the USA. Once again the inspiration of the US importer, Max Hoffman, the Bavaria was in effect a hybrid of the 2500, with its lower equipment and price, and the 2800, with its more powerful engine: it did the trick in the US and soon became so sought after that owners of other models attached Bavaria badges to the backs of their cars.

Compared with other BMW model series, the evolution of the first big sixes is a relatively straightforward one. The 2500 and 2800

launched in 1968 continued with few changes until the crunch time of 1971 when the 2800's previously standard limited slip differential was made optional; power steering remained an option on both models. The 2.8 engine grew to three litres and 180 bhp in April 1971 and was sufficiently clean-running on its twin carburettors to fulfil the first US emissions requirements without additional equipment; later, Bosch D-Jetronic fuel injection was added to produce the first BMW engine to hit the 200 horsepower mark, though this was wound back to 195 in 1995 in deference to emissions rules. Nevertheless, the 3.0i – again, Bavaria in the US – was by now a convincing high performance saloon for its time, with a top speed of 130 mph or 210 km/h.

As a running change the original ZF automatic gearbox, which had proved unpopular with customers, gave way to a Borg Warner box, also three-speed, and the ZF manual four-speed with its weak second gear synchromesh was replaced by a much better Getrag transmission.

1974 saw the first long wheelbase 'L' version, 100 mm longer and available initially with the three-litre engine (the 2.8 had meanwhile been dropped) and in 1976 with the expanded 3.3 litre unit – either as a twin-carburettor giving 190 bhp or a L-Jetronic fuel-injected unit with seven horsepower more. The final change was the switch to a shorter stroke engine displacing 3205 cc in the 3.3, though the same designation was retained.

Few changes were made visually: in 1971 the air vents on the rear pillar moved from horizontal to a more subtle vertical, and in September 1973 a bigger facelift saw a tidier, black grille, new wheel design and, inside, the provision of head restraints, seat height adjusters and standard inertia reel belts.

'L' versions initially cost some DM3500 more than their standard-wheelbase equivalents, but by the time the model was run out in February 1977 the top 3.3 L cost as much as a Mercedes 450 SE – complete with V8 engine and prestigious badge.

That, in a way, was the BMW six's problem all along: overly ambitious pricing. At points in the model's 11-year history this led to crisis and uncertainty; in brighter years it helped bring in a healthy cash flow. Though far from perfect initially and looking decidedly dated towards the end of their 222,000 unit production run, BMW's first big sixes performed a valuable function in establishing the brand at a higher level, providing a next step up the ladder for owners of the first 5 Series and for teaching BMW the most important lessons it needed to make the sixes' successor – the E23 7 Series – a much bigger success.

2500-2800 PRODUCTION

Production History:		In production: 1968-78		Total produced 221,991							
model	2500	2800 Bavaria	2.8 L	3.0 L	3.0 S	Bavaria 3.0	3.0 Si	3.3 L	3.3 Li	total for year	SKD S. Africa
1968	2,560	2								2,562	
1969	20,004	13,211								33,215	
1970	17,210	13,210	194							30,614	613
1971	10,242	4,817	1,718			8,414	2,446	1,944		29,581	695
1972	13,652	2,571				8,206	5,670	5,747		35,846	987
1973	12,822	2,371				8,286	5,200	6,356	3	35,038	693
1974	4,654	948				4,506	2,308	2,363	1,131	15,910	216
1975	5,065	14		2,441	2,606	2,548	2,209	488	397	15,768	204
1976	5,249			2,359	2,618	2,578	3,447		927	17,178	696
1977	957			226	297	122		244	77	1,923	252
totals	92,415	37,144	1,912	5,026	5,521	34,660	15,624	22,310	1,622	1,401	
									grand total	217,635	4,356
									grand total inc SKD	221,991	

06

BMW 3.0 CSi, 3.0 CSL

→ 1968 – 1975
→ Big six-cylinder coupés
→ Benchmark for style and
  power
→ Legendary 3.0 CSL
  'Batmobile'
→ Dominated endurance racing
→ Established BMW in top
  performance league
→ An all-time great
  collector's BMW

Big ambitions

Mighty six-cylinder coupés signal BMW's power

No car is more evocative of hard fought, high speed, long distance racing than the BMW 3.0 CSL. For almost a decade the legendary Batmobile coupés – so called because of their outrageously large rear wings on massive fin-like supports – engaged in epic wheel-to-wheel 24-hour battles at Spa, the Nurburgring, Le Mans and other venues, creating heroes out of their drivers and classic icons out of their insane shapes, in the process helping sell svelte luxury GTs to Europe's jet-set and promote entry-level 3 Series to the man in the modest housing estate.

The move to six-cylinder engines in 1968 allowed BMW to graft a much more attractive front onto its coupé body, making the most of an elegant shape

It was the classic exercise in halo marketing, the use of a glamorous race winner, based on an exclusive and expensive product, to project high-powered glory over the lower-ranking, big-selling models. Fewer than 30,000 of these elegant six-cylinder machines were built, yet their effect on the BMW psyche – and on the perception of the marque at street level – was electric. After the CSL, no-one could doubt that BMW meant business, and at the very highest level too.

In terms of production numbers the CSL is only a small part of the Coupé story: fewer than 1100 of these highly specialised, lightweight racers-for-the-road came off the production lines, and of these the overwhelming majority were made in 1972 and 1973 – precisely the years

when the track models were staking their first claims to chequered-flag glory. Regular production Coupés bridged two distinct eras of BMW products: the first examples were derived directly from the original Neue Klasse sedans, which kicked off BMW's revival in 1962, while the final editions led directly to the first 6 Series, itself largely derived from the 5 Series of 1972.

The 2800 CS took over more or less seamlessly from the 2000 CS in December 1968, having been shown publicly three months previously. Like the 2000, it had its all-steel body built by Karmann in Osnabrück, but BMW styling chief Wilhelm Hofmeister had taken the opportunity of the new six-cylinder engine and the longer nose it required to restyle the car's

The move to three litres and
fuel injection in the 3.0 CSi
(above) brought BMW's
coupé into the league of big
performers

Final fling of the CL series was the 2.5, a more economical version brought out amid the 1974 fuel shortages

ungainly front end. In place of the large 'Asiatic' rectangular headlamps and plain metal front panel came a full-width grille carrying the BMW double kidneys in the centre and paired round headlights either side; wisely, Hofmeister kept the elegant glasshouse of the 2000, together with its discreet rear end, itself inspired by Bertone's design for the 3200 CS.

But while the 3200 CS had been respected for its dignity and craftsmanship, albeit at a high price, the 170 horsepower 2800 CS made an immediate impact not just with its looks but also its performance – a top speed of 206 km/h – and its price, which was a clear 25 per cent below the 3200's, at less than DM 23,000. The value for the buyer was clear – a coupé with abundant style, the very latest engineering of the 2500-2800 sedans (running to independent suspension front and rear) and impressive performance through the gears. More than 9,000 2.8 litre coupés were sold before it was replaced by a three-litre edition, the 3.0 CS, in April 1971. However, neither car was as strongly priced in the USA market where, at $9,000, the BMW was pricier than its rivals.

The CS had gained 10 horsepower and 9 km/h thanks to its extra capacity, but buyers

would have to wait a further six months for what was to become the definitive luxury coupé of the era, the 3.0 CSi. Bosch D-Jetronic fuel injection added spice to the engine's top-end performance and improved tractability in the lower ranges; with power now at 200 bhp and maximum speed at 220 km/h, BMW at last saw fit to give the coupé the rear disc brakes unaccountably omitted.

Throughout, the CS series had been earning rave reviews in the media, with near-universal praise for its smooth and eager yet immensely powerful engine, and many testers pronouncing it the world's best grand tourer; some reservations were expressed by Europeans about the predictability of the CS's handling on the limit, but that was about the extent of any criticism.

The first of the now-legendary CSLs arrived in May 1971, equipped with a three-litre, twin carburettor engine giving 180 bhp, and with its special aluminium doors, bonnet and boot lid saving some 200 kg over the standard version. That, together with some aerodynamic tweaks (the big wings had yet to appear) was enough to shave a full second off the 0-100 km/h time.

Further improvements were recorded in August 1972 by the second CSL, which marked the switch to fuel injection. With 200 bhp now

aboard and only a negligible gain in weight, it was half a second quicker to 100 km/h and now hit a top speed of 220 km/h. Yet more was still to come: the third incarnation of the CSL, in August 1973, saw engine capacity taken out to 3153 cc, raising power to 206 bhp and improving subjective performance still further, though BMW's official factory claims remained.

The most dramatic difference, however, was in the CSL's appearance. Reflecting the experience of the Touring Car championship winning teams, the final CSL had sprouted perhaps the most extreme aerodynamic package ever seen on a road car, a set of add-ons that soon earned it the enduring nickname of 'Batmobile'. Under the front bumper a deep airdam ensured as much of the air flowed over the smooth top half of the body rather than underneath, where it would create both lift and drag; the front wings sported long black splitters, extending back as far as the wheel centres, to separate out the turbulent air flow, while chromed wheel arch extensions protected the wider tyres on their cross-spoke alloy rims. Further back, a subtle full width aerofoil at the rear of the roof further tidied up the flow of air over the rear screen and boot – and atop the boot itself was

"Atop the boot was the CSL's most distinctive feature of all – its huge wing mounted high on what looked like an aircraft's twin tail fins; full-length M stripes ran along the CSL's waistline to ram the message home to anyone who had failed to recognise the significance of all the other signals"

Mighty 3.0 CSL became a legend on the endurance racing tracks and in popular imagination, with competition developments being incorporated into successive road versions. This is the final 1973 iteration which gave rise to the Batmobile tag

BMW 3.0 CSL: technical details.

The CSL power unit is a modification of the 3 l CSi unit. This modification was necessary to enable the car to compete with group 2 racing cars between 3 and 5 l. The capacity of 3153 cc is the result of the optimum combination of output and torque.

The chassis of the BMW 3.0 CSL, the springs and shock absorbers, are carefully coordinated to the high performance of the car and its low weight. The bodywork was lowered by 20 mm. This achieved a lower centre of gravity and reduced rolling tendencies. The camber was increased by 1°, which correspondingly increased the

The CSL power unit develops an output of 206 BHP (152 kW) at 5600 rpm, a maximum torque of 29.2 mkp (292 Nm) at 4000 rpm and accelerates from 0 to 100 in 7.1 sec. The maximum speed is 220 km/h.

stability and further improved handling on bends.

The BMW 3.0 CSL is fitted in series production with Bilstein gas pressure shock absorbers, specially developed for motor sport use. Even under the greatest stress these shock absorbers have an unaltered effect, where hydraulic shock absorbers can be affected by foam

caused from a mixture of air and oil. For rigorous sports driving, progressive and stronger coil springs were chosen to match the shock absorbers. This new spring/ shock absorber coordination and the reduction in pitching means that the front and rear stabilisers can be dispensed with.

To complement this careful

coordination, the BMW 3.0 CSL is fitted with a limited slip differential with 25% locking action, 7 J x 14 H2 light alloy sports wheels and Michelin 195/70 VR 14 XWX sports tyres.

---

the CSL's most distinctive feature of all, its huge wing mounted high on what looked like an aircraft's twin tail fins. As if this was not extrovert enough, full-length multi-coloured 'M' stripes ran along the CSL's waistline to ram the message home to anyone who had failed to recognise the significance of all the other signals.

The CSL was another BMW to instantly grab the public's attention, more as an object of fantasy and desire than a serious proposition; the last few units were sold by 1974, but in racing the Batmobile continued to break records for several years more. It won a total of six European Touring Car championships between 1973 and 1979 (long after the whole model range had been replaced by the 6 Series), it was home to the first 24-valve engine that would later become BMW's legendary M1 and M5 power unit, and it even helped develop anti-lock braking systems on the racetrack before they appearing on the 7 Series.

Ultimate racing developments of the CSL saw

single and twin-turbo racing engines go to 750 or 800 horsepower and beyond – yet, ironically, the last of the six-cylinder CS coupés for the road was also the mildest and quietest. Concerned in the autumn of 1973 that the Arab oil embargo would sound the death-knell for aggressive, extrovert sports coupés such as the CSi, BMW hedged its bets by developing and launching a fuel crisis edition to suit the prevailing climate of restraint and economy. Powered by the 150 bhp 2.5 litre six of the sedan, the 2.5 CS had reduced equipment levels (power steering, for instance, was relegated to the options list, as were alloy wheels), more discreet performance and a price trimmed back to DM 28, 550, or a full DM 10,000 less than the CSL. It sold just 844 units in the two years before the whole range disappeared at the end of 1975 – to the regret of many who believe that there will never be a car as sensational as the CSL.

3.0cs
3.0csi 3.0csL
2.5cs

200-2800CS

2.5CS/2800CS/3.0CS/3.0CSL/3.0CSi/3.0 CSL (1973 ON)

Specifications	2.5CS	2800 CS	3.0 CS	3.0 CSL	3.0 CSI
Engine					
Type	Inline 6-cylinder	Inline 6-cylinder	Inline 6-cylinder	Inline 6-cylinder	Inline 6-cylinder
Bore & stroke, mm	86 x 71.6	86 x 80	89 x 80	89 x 80	89 x 80 (1973 on: 89.3 x 80)
Capacity, cc	2494	2788	2985	2985	2985 (1973 on: 3003)
Valves	12	12	12	12	12
Valve actuation	Sohc	Sohc	Sohc	Sohc	Sohc
Compression ratio	9.0:1	9.0:1	9.0:1	9.0:1	9.5:1
Fuelling	Twin Zenith carburettors	Twin Zenith carburettors	Twin Zenith carburettors	Twin Zenith carburettors	Bosch D-Jetronic electronic fuel injection
Max power, bhp @ rpm	150@6000	170@6000	180@6000	180@6000	200@5500
Max torque, Nm @ rpm	210@3700	234@3700	255@3700	255@3700	272@4300
Transmission					
Manual transmission	4-speed	4-speed	4-speed	4-speed	4-speed
Automatic	3-speed ZF optional	3-speed ZF optional	3-speed Borg Warner optional	Not available	Not available
Drive	Rear wheels	Rear wheels	Rear wheels	Rear wheels	Rear wheels
Chassis					
Front suspension	MacPherson struts	MacPherson strut	MacPherson strut	MacPherson strut	MacPherson strut
Rear suspension	Semi-trailing arms, coil springs	Semi-trailing arms, coil springs	Semi-trailing arms, coil springs	Semi-trailing arms, coil springs	Semi-trailing arms, coil springs
Braking	Servo-assisted disc/drum	Servo-assisted disc/drum	Servo-assisted disc/drum	Servo-assisted discs	Servo-assisted discs
Steering	ZF worm and roller, power assistance optional	Power-assisted ZF worm and roller	Power-assisted ZF worm and roller	Power-assisted ZF worm and roller	Power-assisted ZF worm and roller
Wheels	6.0 x 14	6.0 x 14	6.0 x 14 aluminium	7.0 x 14 aluminium	7.0 x 14 aluminium
Tyres	175 HR 14	195/70 HR 14	195/70 VR 14	195/70 VR 14	195/70 VR 14
Body					
Structure	Steel monocoque	Steel monocoque	Steel monocoque	Steel monocoque, light alloy doors, bonnet, boot	Steel monocoque, light alloy doors, bonnet, boot
Wheelbase, mm	2625	2625	2625	2625	2625
Track F/R, mm	1446/1402	1446/1402	1446/1402	1446/1402	1446/1426
Length, mm	4660	4660	4660	4660	4630
Width, mm	1670	1670	1670	1670	1730
Height, mm	1370	1370	1370	1370	1370
Kerb weight, kg	1400	1355	1400	1200	1270 (1973 on)
Fuel tank capacity, lit	70	70	70	70	70
Performance					
Max speed, km/h	201	206	215	215	220
0-100 km/h, sec	10.5	10.0	9.0	8.0	7.5 (1973 on)
Fuel consumption , lit/100km	16.0	16.5	17.5	17.5	17.5
Marketing					
Launch date	6/74	12/68	4/71	7/71	7/71
Pricing, DM	28,550	22,980	26,975	31,950	30,650

3.0 CSL (1973 ON)

Inline 6-cylinder
89.3 x 84
3153
12
Sohc
9.5:1
Bosch D-Jetronic electronic
fuel injection
206@5600
286@4200

4-speed
Not available

Rear wheels

MacPherson strut
Semi-trailing arms,
coil springs
Servo-assisted discs
Power-assisted ZF worm
and roller
7.0 x 14 aluminium
195/70 VR 14

Steel monocoque, light alloy
doors, bonnet, boot
2625
1446/1426
4630
1730
1370
1270
70

220
7.5
17.5

9/73
35,700

BMW's first art cars were 3.0
CSL racers: this is Frank
Stella's 1976 contribution

2000-2800CS PRODUCTION

Production History:	In production: 1965-1975			Total produced 44,237			
model	2000 CS	2.5 CS	2800 CS	3.0 CS	3.0 CSi	3.0 CSL/ CSiL	total for year
1965	57						57
1966	7,192						7,192
1967	3,800						3,800
1968	1,641		138				1,779
1969	936		3,400				4,336
1970	65		5,242				5,307
1971			619	2,855	1,061		4,535
1972				3,175	3,001	601	6,777
1973				2,781	2,807	438	6,026
1974		373		1,574	707	40	2,694
1975		471		678	568	17	1,734
totals	13,691	844	9,399	11,063	8,144	1,096	
						grand total	44,237
						grand total inc SKD	44,237

Series to success: von Kuenheim's brilliant template

Young man with bold vision

First 5 Series shows von Kuenheim's strategy

First 5 Series (E12)

→ 1972 – 1981
→ Launched BMW's Series model policy
→ Highly successful 9-year production run
→ Almost 700,000 made
→ Innovative design by Paul Bracq
→ Astute marketing brought in mainstream buyers
→ Powerful 528i became enthusiasts' favourite
→ First car manufactured at Dingolfing plant

Launched in the autumn of 1973, the first 5 Series is the car that marked BMW's coming of age – in more ways than one. Perhaps most importantly, it was the first model to be part of new CEO Eberhard von Kuenheim's ambitious plan for three co-ordinated ranges – the press soon named them Series – that would turn BMWs into the must-have cars for the up-and-coming generation of fast-moving business executives.

First-generation 525i launched the era of six-cylinder sophistication in a sports saloon. Introduced a year after the original 520, it answered calls for a faster, sportier car.

It was launched just as the company was on the crest of a wave. BMW's three main model lines were unstoppably successful, it had shot to international notice as the futuristic Turbo concept car led the athletes' parade at the 1972 Olympic Games in its home city of Munich, and the shiny, just-completed 'four cylinder' company headquarters tower reached symbolically skyward, its top floor just two metres shorter than the famous Frauenkirche cathedral in the town centre.

To the glare of this international spotlight was added the closely-focused attention of both industry commentators and BMW enthusiasts worldwide. To the business contingent the launch was a highly significant event, for the 5 Series was the car which would replace the Neue Klasse 1500-2000, the range which had saved BMW from the financial abyss in 1962 and

which had led it to prosperity and global respect in the years that followed. The reception given to the new car would be critical to BMW's future growth prospects, predicted the analysts. There was also considerable interest surrounding the new production facilities at Dingolfing which, after having been acquired when BMW bought Glas, had been remodelled to become the company's largest and most modern factory.

To the growing band of BMW enthusiasts on both sides of the Atlantic the launch was awaited with especial eagerness. How would BMW follow up the car that had created the brand's shiny new identity, the car that had established a whole new genre of classy sports saloon?

The answer came soon enough as the first Five revealed itself as a noticeably larger but also much more stylish four-door saloon with a

Opposite and left:
Eberhard von Kuenheim's vision for BMW's future started with the 5 Series as the core model. Fresh, light design gave more space and comfort than earlier, sportier BMW saloons: ergonomic interior and toolkit in bootlid became BMW trademarks

gentler, more rounded theme to its lines. The interior was notably more adventurous, the centre portion of the dashboard being drawn rearwards to bring the heater and radio controls into easier reach of the driver, and the main instruments being housed in a single clear array directly behind the steering wheel. The design represented a major step forward in ergonomics and would lead directly to the driver-oriented 'cockpit' interiors which became a key BMW trademark a few years later.

In engineering terms the 5 Series' body structure was innovative too. A reinforced safety cell surrounded the passenger compartment, the sills were reinforced and strengthened frontal structures provided extra energy absorption in a head-on crash. The four-spoke steering wheel had a very large boss, the column itself was

jointed and the interior surfaces were carefully padded. BMW was clearly taking safety very seriously.

The smooth body shape might have marked a change of style, but underneath it the mechanical elements were pretty familiar. Front and rear suspensions followed the successful pattern of the previous model, and the initial engine choices – the 520 with the twin carburettor version of the 1990 cc M10 giving 115 horsepower and the 130 bhp 520i with its Kugelfischer fuel injection – paralleled those of the old car. Automatic transmission was available on the 520 only.

The 520 immediately sold well, thanks partly to a relatively modest price jump from the outgoing 2000. Take-up of the more expensive 520i was slower, the perception being that the extra cost was not reflected in significant extra

performance. This underlined what many enthusiasts had begun to fear – that BMW was allowing its cars to become larger and heavier, and that sporty, responsive driving characteristics were becoming less of a priority.

Nevertheless, the formula proved a big hit with the broader public and in its first full year on sale the 520/520i combination sold almost as many as the 2000 in its best year, and the expanded line up later went on into six-figure annual production numbers.

BMW had in any case anticipated the hard-driving enthusiasts' worries and within a year the first six-cylinder 5 Series had appeared. Using the much-praised 2.5 litre unit from the large 2500 line, the 525 tactfully dropped the power from 150 to 145 bhp; even so, this was enough to push top speed past 190 km/h and trim two seconds from the 0-100 km/h acceleration time.

The 525 was well received, but its initial success was short-lived as by the end of 1973 Germany – and many other European countries – were in the grip of the first fuel crisis, the panic that killed off the BMW 2002 turbo among other models. To address the sudden energy awareness that had hit the market, BMW responded with the 518, a low-power derivative

which, with its 90 bhp, 1280 kg and automatic option, led some sceptics to ask whether BMW was still a maker of sporty cars. But again BMW had judged the market shrewdly and the 518 was the biggest seller in the 5 Series palette in 1975. By the end of the year the hot-shot 528, which had been waiting patiently in the wings until the fuel panic had subsided, had appeared in the catalogue – much to the delight of keen drivers who relished its 165 horsepower (later to rise to 170), sharpened handling and top speed nudging the psychologically important 200 km/h barrier.

In the United States, meanwhile, BMW had decided to move up market and provide only larger-engined six-cylinder versions of the new 5 Series. These were something of a mixed blessing, for with the mandatory de-smogging equipment the 530i – which was in fact assembled in South Africa – performed well when driven hard but had inconsistent performance at low speeds, along with high fuel consumption and a tendency to problems with the cylinder heads. This was blamed on the thermal reactor system BMW had chosen in order to allow the 530i to run on leaded fuel: as soon as the US cars switched to a proper catalyst

"The smooth body shape might have marked a change of style, but underneath it the mechanical elements were pretty familiar. Front and rear suspensions followed the successful pattern of the previous model"

E12: 5 SERIES: SPECIFICATION

Specifications	518	520	520i	520-6	525
Engine					
Engine type	Inline 4-cylinder	Inline 4-cylinder	Inline 4-cylinder	Inline 6-cylinder	Inline 6-cylinder
Bore & stroke, mm	89 x 71	89 x 80	89 x 80	80 x 66	86 x 71.6
Capacity, cc	1766	1990	1990	1990	2494
Valves	8	8	8	12	12
Valve actuation	Sohc	Sohc	Sohc	Sohc	Sohc
Compression ratio	8.6:1 (1980 on: 9.5:1)	9.0:1	9.5:1	9.2:1	9.0:1
Fuelling	Single Solex/Pierburg carburettor	Single Stromberg carburettor	Kugelfischer mechanical fuel injection (1975 on: Bosch electronic)	Single Solex carburettor	Twin Zenith carburettors (1976 on: single Solex)
Max power, bhp @ rpm	90@5500	115@5800	130@5800 (1975 on: 125@5700)	122@6000	145@6000 (1976 on: 150@5800)
Max torque, Nm @ rpm	142@3500	162@3700	176@4500 (1975 on: 172@4350)	160@4000	208@4000
Transmission					
Manual transmission	4-speed (1979 on: 5-speed)	4-speed	4-speed	4-speed (1979 on: 5-speed)	4-speed (1979 on: 5-speed)
Automatic	3-speed auto optional	3-speed auto optional	Not available	3-speed auto optional	3-speed auto optional
Drive	Rear wheels	Rear wheels	Rear wheels	Rear wheels	Rear wheels
Chassis					
Front suspension	MacPherson strut	MacPherson struts	MacPherson struts	MacPherson struts	MacPherson struts
Rear suspension	Semi-trailing arms, coil springs	Semi-trailing arms, coil springs	Semi-trailing arms, coil springs	Semi-trailing arms, coil springs	Semi-trailing arms, coil springs
Braking	Discs/drums, power assisted	Discs/drums, power assisted	Discs/drums, power assisted	Discs/drums, power assisted	Discs/drums, power assisted
Steering	ZF worm and roller, power-assistance optional	ZF worm and roller, power assistance optional	ZF worm and roller, power assistance optional	ZF worm and roller, power assistance optional	ZF worm and roller, power assistance optional
Wheels	5.5 x 14	5.5 x 14	5.5 x 14	5.5 x 14	5.5 x 14
Tyres	175 SR 14	175 SR 14	175 HR 14	175 SR 14	175 HR 14
Body					
Structure	Steel monocoque	Steel monocoque	Steel monocoque	Steel monocoque	Steel monocoque
Wheelbase, mm	2636	2636	2636	2636	2636
Track F/R, mm	1406/1442	1406/1466	1406/1465	1406/1465	1406/1470
Length, mm	4620	4620	4620	4620	4620
Width, mm	1690	1690	1690	1690	1690
Height, mm	1425	1425	1425	1425	1425
Kerb weight, kg	1260	1275	1280	1350	1380
Fuel tank capacity, lit	56	56	56	70	70
Performance					
Max speed, km/h	163	175	184	181	192
0-100km/h	15.0	13.0	12.0	12.5	10.5
Fuel consumption , lit/100km	12.5	13.5	13.5	13.5	15.5
Marketing					
Launch date	6/74	6/72	10/72	8/77	10/73
Pricing, DM	14,870	14,490	15,670	20,200	17,505

Inline 6-cylinder
86 x 80
2788
12
Sohc
9.0:1
Twin Zenith carburettors
(1976 on: single Solex)

165@5800 (1976 on:
170@5800)
233@4000

4-speed
3-speed auto optional
Rear wheels

MacPherson struts
Semi-trailing arms, coil
springs
Discs/drums,
power assisted
ZF worm and roller, power
assisted
6.0 x 14
195/70 HR 14

Steel monocoque
2636
1406/1470
4620
1690
1425
1415
70

198
10.0
16.0

1/75
22,530

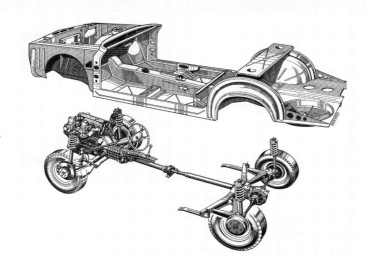

Ultra-smooth six-cylinder engine and all-independent suspension gave top 5 Series models a key advantage. Safety was by now an important factor in structural design

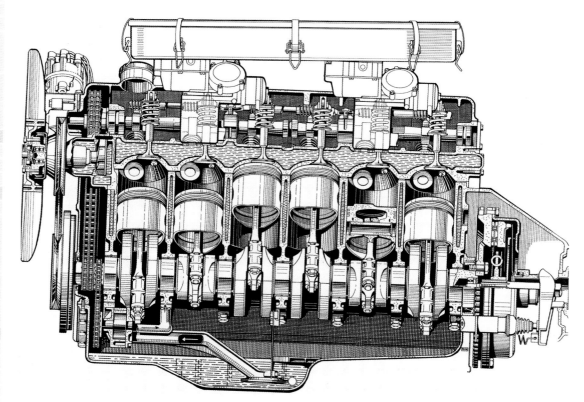

system in 1977 the problem was solved. The 528i which resulted from this process became something of a classic sports saloon, hitting almost 210 km/h in its final 184 bhp European tune.

Big things had been happening at the lower end of the range, too. All models, beginning with the US 530i in late 1977, saw a change in style, with a taller grille at the front, broader rear lights displacing the fuel filler from the back panel to the right-hand rear flank, and the driver's mirror repositioned from the door surface to the front lower edge of the window frame. At the same time the 520 became a six-cylinder, taking on the

brand new M20 small six rated at 122 bhp – though critics frowned at a simultaneous weight increase of almost 100 kg. The six-cylinder proved to be pleasingly refined, but its performance, especially in flexibility, fell short of that of its four-cylinder, fuel injection counterpart. Nevertheless, the new model soon assumed the mantle of best seller in the 5 line, setting a pattern for future generations of the car.

The 5 series continued to sell strongly – and bring in the dollars and Deutschmarks – until 1980, going out in June 1981 after a final high-performance flourish in the shape of the M535i. Sold through BMW Motorsport GmbH, this

E12: 5 SERIES

Specifications	528i	530i (US)	M535i
Engine			
Engine type	Inline 6-cylinder	Inline 6-cylinder	Inline 6-cylinder
Bore & stroke, mm	86 x 80	89 x 80	93.4 x 84
Capacity, cc	2788	2985	3453
Valves	12	12	12
Valve actuation	Sohc	Sohc	Sohc
Compression ratio	9.0:1	9.0:1	9.3:1
Fuelling	Bosch L-Jetronic electronic fuel injection	Bosch L-Jetronic electronic fuel injection	Bosch L-Jetronic electronic fuel injection
Max power, bhp @ rpm	176@5800 (1978 on: 184@5800)	176@5500	218@5200
Max torque, Nm @ rpm	240@4300	233@4000	310@4000
Transmission			
Manual transmission	4-speed (1979 on: 5-speed)	5-speed	5-speed
Automatic	3-speed auto optional	3-speed auto optional	
Drive	Rear wheels	Rear wheels	Rear wheels
Chassis			
Front suspension	MacPherson struts	MacPherson struts	MacPherson struts
Rear suspension	Semi-trailing arms, coil springs	Semi-trailing arms, coil springs	Semi-trailing arms, coil springs
Braking	Discs/drums, power assisted	Discs/drums, power assisted	Discs/drums, power assisted
Steering	ZF worm and roller, power-assistance optional	ZF worm and roller, power assistedl	ZF worm and roller, power assistedl
Wheels	6.0 x 14	6.0 x 14	6.0 x 14
Tyres	195/70 HR 14	195/70 HR 14	195/70 HR 14
Body			
Structure	Steel monocoque	Steel monocoque	Steel monocoque
Wheelbase, mm	2636	2636	2636
Track F/R, mm	1422/1470	1422/1470	1422/1470
Length, mm	4620	4823	4620
Width, mm	1690	1707	1690
Height, mm	1425	1422	1425
Kerb weight, kg	1450	1505	1465
Fuel tank capacity, lit	70	70	70
Performance			
Max speed, km/h	208	194	222
0-100km/h, sec	9.5	–	8.0
Fuel consumption , lit/100km	16	–	17.5
Marketing			
Launch date	3/77	10/74	4/80
Pricing, DM	22,800	$9,097 (US only)	43,535

unashamedly sporting model married an upgraded version of the big M30 six-cylinder engine, now with 218 bhp, a five-speed overdrive or close-ratio gearbox, a deep air dam under the front bumper and a none-too-neat black spoiler on the boot lid. It was a storming performer, capable of 140 mph or 225 km/h. To match the performance the suspension was stiffened, the solid front discs were swapped to ventilated ones and a limited slip differential was fitted. Yet despite its tremendous performance the M535i was smooth, comfortable and – apart from the dog-leg gear pattern on the close-ratio gearbox – easy to drive. Though the idea of specially-built 'M' cars had yet to emerge, the M535i embodied many of the qualities that would mark out later generations of M5 as truly special saloons. Just 1410 were made, and today they are highly sought after.

The South African plant continued assembling the E12 5 Series for some while after the model had been replaced by the E28 in the summer of 1981. The final South African build models were a curious hybrid as they featured the smartened-up driver-oriented interior of the E28 but still looked like the older model externally; the were even a limited number of 3.3 litre engined 533i models commissioned.

As would so often become the pattern with successive BMW model generations, the E12 5 Series of 1972-1981 was the most successful so far, with almost 700,000 examples leaving the assembly lines in Dingolfing and Midrand/Rosslyn

Far left:
Large impact-absorbing bumpers became a legal requirement in the US in the early 1970s: even BMW's designers had not yet learnt how to integrate them neatly

Left:
1980 M535i was the hotshot of the 5 Series line and pioneered the concept which later became the M5

Below:
Five generations of 5 Series: from 1972 (left) to 2003. Each raised the bar in the sports saloon sector

in South Africa. Though this first 5 Series was criticised in its earliest incarnations for sacrificing speed and sportiness for comfort and status, BMW soon regained favour with those hard-driving customers with the memorable 528i. Nevertheless, this model series will still go down in history as the car that steered BMW from the enthusiasts-only area of the market into the premium centre-ground where the real prizes were to be won.

E12: FIRST 5 SERIES PRODUCTION

Production History:	In production: 1972-1981				Total produced 697,400							
model	518	518i	520	520i	520-six	525	528	528i	530i	535i	total for year	SKD CKD
1972			10,697	2,198							12,895	
1973			34,817	9,168		3,668					47,653	754
1974	9,848		16,130	2,456		18,356	19		2,000		48,809	4,662
1975	20,290		18,622	3,196		15,919	9,885		5,202		73,114	4,140
1976	18,484		19,836	3,980		17,946	13,638		7,353		81,237	8,040
1977	19,099		13,512	2,553	5,973	18,792	7,023	5,102	7,648		79,702	6,612
1978	17,025		147	1,021	35,072	15,125		13,628	5,667		87,685	8,448
1979	15,983	557	21	584	39,828	18,477		22,387			97,837	8,484
1980	13,184	1,820			37,199	11,602		17,813		919	82,537	10,332
1981	2,970	638			11,675	2,387		8,606		491	26,767	7,692
total	116,883	3,015	113,782	25,156	129,747	122,272	30,565	67,536	27,870	1,410		59,164
									grand total		638,236	
									grand total inc SKD		697,400	

08

A new icon

The 3 Series becomes the BMW everybody wants

First 3 Series (E21)

→ 1975 – 1983
→ Eagerly-awaited replacement for '02 Series
→ Broadened appeal of BMW to mainstream buyers
→ First BMW to sell over a million
→ 323i became the new performance icon
→ Introduced small six-cylinder engine

The first 3 Series was another critically important car for BMW. Taking over from the ultra-successful and much-loved 1602-2002 line it had, like most BMW introductions, a lot to live up to. In this role it performed admirably, yet, in contrast to its predecessor, it was not so much a turning point as a powerful affirmation of BMW's ability to come up with appealing designs and sophisticated engineering to draw in not just the performance enthusiast but also the more mainstream buyers in search of a convincing quality product.

The 3 Series was the first BMW to sell over a million: in fact, more than 1,366,000 were made, offering ample proof that the company's policy of high quality and even higher prices was as popular with the public as it was good for profits.

The 1975 3 Series faced much the same task as its bigger-brother 5 Series had done three years before: it had to take over from a very familiar car which had not just put BMW back onto the road to prosperity but which had so captured the public imagination that it had become something of an icon, especially to keen drivers.

The 5 Series was widely thought to have gone soft on BMW's hardline performance ethos when it appeared in 1972, so there was

understandable apprehension that the upcoming 3 Series could follow suit. The new 3, it was feared, could emerge fatter and feebler than its lean and mean predecessor and thus betray the memory of the cherished '02, especially the near-sacred 2002 Tii.

In the event those anxious BMW fans did have to wait for a further two and a half years for what they were prepared to accept as a true substitute for the 2002 Tii – but in the meantime a third of a million more mainstream customers had responded to BMW's broader, more luxurious offering and bought into the new, more inclusive 3 Series thinking.

The compact, two-door BMW that emerged in May 1975 was clearly from the same Paul Bracq

Six-cylinder 323i with its silky-smooth engine turned the first 3 Series into a classy small car as well as a performance icon as the '70s drew to a close

"With the benefit of hindsight it would seem that BMW's buyer pattern had shifted: many buyers were pleased to be able to get onto the BMW ladder with the basic 316"

Above left and above:
Neat exterior styling, smooth-running engines and ground-breaking ergonomics in cockpit-style cabin were established as BMW brand values with the 3 Series

pen as the 5 series: however, it had more of a wedge feeling, with the front noticeably lower and the blacked-out panel between the high-set rear lights accentuating the car's width. The quad-headlight set-up of the top-end models (initially the 320 and 320i) provided another link with the 5 Series, whereas the humbler 316 and 318 made do with larger, single lamps each side.

Inside, Bracq's team scored another advance in the art of interior design and ergonomics with a further landmark dashboard configuration. Extending the thinking premiered in the 5 Series, the 3 introduced an asymmetric centre console curved towards the driver, creating the feeling of a very convenient cockpit with all controls within fingertip reach. The instrument pack was again a model of clarity and good graphic design, and at night the whole was illuminated with a classy orange glow, again setting the benchmark for other carmakers to emulate.

Everything about the 3 Series was bigger: it

was longer and wider than the '02 and had usefully more room in the rear seat and the boot; what were basically the same engines as in the outgoing models had been re-tuned to run on regular grade fuel yet produce more power. The only thing that did not seem to have grown was performance – for the simple reason that weight had risen in direct proportion to the improvement in comfort, safety and sophistication. As a result, the new models were hard pushed to match the on-the-road responsiveness of their predecessors, despite a switch to a more precise rack and pinion steering system. There was mumbled criticism of the 3 Series' prices, too: BMW seemed to be making the most of its good name among buyers to increase margins on the new car, though the general consensus was that it was exceptionally solid and well made for a car of its size.

Of the original line-up the entry-level 90 bhp 316 and the 109 bhp carburettor-fed 320 were

the runaway best sellers; there was less interest in the intermediate 318 (with 98 bhp) and top, fuel-injected 320i, even though it offered a tempting 125 bhp. With the benefit of hindsight it would seem that BMW's buyer pattern had shifted: many buyers were pleased to be able to get onto the BMW ladder with the basic 316, while for the next step up image-conscious customers not especially concerned with maximising performance were happy to pay the extra over the 318 for the smarter-looking four-headlamp 320.

Still, however, there was a certain sense of disappointment: the 3 Series might have propelled BMW upwards in quality, status and snob-appeal, but in the process – just as with the 5 Series – it had gone soft on the sporting

E21: BAUR CABRIO

Specifications	320 Baur Cabriolet	323i Baur Cabriolet
Type		
Type	Inline 6-cylinder	Inline 6-cylinder
Capacity, cc	1990	2315
Max power, bhp @ rpm	122@6000	143@6000
Max torque, Nm @ rpm	160@4000	190@4500
Transmission		
Manual transmission	4-speed	4-speed
Automatic	3-speed auto optional	3-speed auto optional
Chassis		
Wheels/tyres	185/70 HR 13	185/70 HR 13
Body		
Kerb weight, kg	1090	1110
Performance		
Max speed, km/h	180	200
0-100km/h, sec	10.0	8.3
Marketing		
Launch date	12/77	12/77
Pricing, DM	25,000	27,500
Units Built	3,000 (total for both models)	

Left:
Coachbuilder Baur provided this open-topped version of the 3 Series: the rear roof folded down, while the rigid roof panel stowed in the boot. Twin exhaust pipes identify this car as a 323i

E21: 3 SERIES

Specifications	315	316	318	320	320i
Engine					
Engine type	Inline 4-cylinder	Inline 4-cylinder	Inline 4-cylinder	Inline 4-cylinder	Inline 4-cylinder
Bore & stroke, mm	84 x 71	84 x 71	89 x 71	89 x 80	89 x 80
Capacity, cc	1573	1573	1754	1977	1977
Valves	8	8	8	8	8
Valve actuation	sohc	Sohc	Sohc	Sohc	Sohc
Compression ratio	8.3:1	8.3:1	8.3:1	8.1:1	9.3:1
Fuelling	Single Solex carburettor	Single Solex carburettor	Single Solex carburettor	Single Solex carburettor	Bosch K-Jetronic mechanical fuel injection
Emmision Control					
Max power, bhp @ rpm	75@6000	90@6000	98@5800	109@5800	125@5700
Max torque, Nm @ rpm	110@3000	123@3000	142@4000	157@3700	172@4350
Transmission					
Manual transmission	4-speed	4-speed	4-speed	4-speed	4-speed
Automatic	3-speed auto optional	3-speed automatic optional	3-speed automatic optional	3-speed automatic optional	Not available
Drive	Rear wheels	Rear wheels	Rear wheels	Rear wheels	Rear wheels
Chassis					
Front suspension	MacPherson strut	MacPherson struts	MacPherson struts	MacPherson struts	MacPherson struts
Rear suspension	Semi-trailing arms, coil springs	Semi-trailing arms, coil springs	Semi-trailing arms, coil springs	Semi-trailing arms, coil springs	Semi-trailing arms, coil springs
Braking	Disc/drum. Servo assisted	Disc/drum. Servo assisted	Disc/drum. Servo assisted	Disc/drum. Servo assisted	Disc/drum. Servo assisted
Steering	ZF rack and pinion	ZF rack and pinion	ZF rack and pinion	ZF rack and pinion	ZF rack and pinion
Wheels	5.0 x 13	5.0 x 13	5.0 x 13	5.0 x 13	5.0 x 13
Tyres	165 SR 13	165 SR 13	165 SR 13	165 SR 13	185/70 HR 13
Body					
Structure	Steel monocoque	Steel monocoque	Steel monocoque	Steel monocoque	Steel monocoque
Wheelbase, mm	2563	2563	2563	2563	2563
Track F/R, mm	1364/1399	1364/1377	1364/1377	1364/1377	1364/1377
Length, mm	4355	4355	4355	4355	4355
Width, mm	1610	1610	1610	1610	1610
Height, mm	1380	1380	1380	1380	1380
Kerb weight, kg	1040	1040	1040	1060	1080
Fuel tank capacity, lit	52	52	52	52	52
Performance					
Max speed, km/h	160	161	168	173	182
0-100km/h	13.0	14.0	12.0	11.5	10.0
Fuel consumption , lit/100km	11.0	11.5	12.0	12.5	13.0
Marketing					
Launch date	4/81	6/75	6/75	6/75	10/75
Pricing, DM	15,850	13,980	14,850	15,880	17,980

320-six	323i
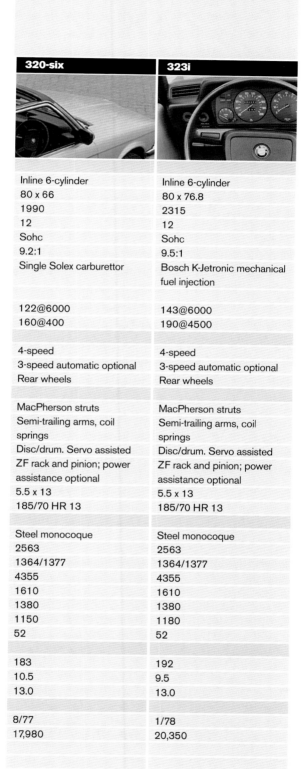	
Inline 6-cylinder	Inline 6-cylinder
80 x 66	80 x 76.8
1990	2315
12	12
Sohc	Sohc
9.2:1	9.5:1
Single Solex carburettor	Bosch K-Jetronic mechanical fuel injection
122@6000	143@6000
160@400	190@4500
4-speed	4-speed
3-speed automatic optional	3-speed automatic optional
Rear wheels	Rear wheels
MacPherson struts	MacPherson struts
Semi-trailing arms, coil springs	Semi-trailing arms, coil springs
Disc/drum. Servo assisted	Disc/drum. Servo assisted
ZF rack and pinion; power assistance optional	ZF rack and pinion; power assistance optional
5.5 x 13	5.5 x 13
185/70 HR 13	185/70 HR 13
Steel monocoque	Steel monocoque
2563	2563
1364/1377	1364/1377
4355	4355
1610	1610
1380	1380
1150	1180
52	52
183	192
10.5	9.5
13.0	13.0
8/77	1/78
17,980	20,350

3 Series in action: six-cylinder models and 320i were distinguished by four-headlight grille. Lesser models made do with two headlamps

expectations associated with the marque. In the US the situation was worse still. Just one model, labelled 320i, was imported: thanks to emission controls it gave just 110 bhp in its 49-state guise, whereas for California's more stringent air quality regulations it was further stifled to 105. To make matters more depressing still, US models had to wear the mandatory safety bumpers which not only spoiled the 3's appearance but added a distinctly unwelcome extra 70 kg to the car's weight. Later, the sole US model was de-stroked to just 1.8 litres, but the fitment of a proper catalyst in place of the two-litre's thermal reactor system improved both consumption and driveability at low speeds and resulted in a more pleasant car than the temperamental original.

The six-cylinder models which brought about such a brilliant transformation in the European range were never exported to the US, much to the chagrin of Stateside BMW enthusiasts. In Europe, a six-cylinder engine of just two litres counted as something of a novelty in early 1978, and there was much interest in the 320 six on its debut. Commentators were full of praise for its refinement and astonishing smoothness but disappointed that its performance was no better than the outgoing four's: some even felt it

"**While the 320 six made a quantum jump on the scale of sophistication, its companion 323i managed the impossible – to boost performance too**"

subjectively less potent than the old 320i, whose price the new, carburettor 320 six exactly matched.

While the 320 six showed BMW making a clear quantum jump on the scale of sophistication and refinement, its companion 323i managed the impossible – to combine this with a simultaneous leap in performance as well. No one was quite prepared for the amazing blend of razor-sharp potency and silken smoothness the fuel-injected 323i suddenly presented: this car went like an absolute rocket, yet its turbine-smooth engine would rev with addictive eagerness and a total absence of vibration. Instantly, the 323i was the classiest hotshot in town, the perfect vehicle for the ambitious 30-something professional who needed to be smart but also wanted to have serious fun.

With no less than 143 bhp on tap the 323i – distinguished by its dual line exhausts terminating in a prominent tailpipe either side – was slick, quick and exciting; sometimes all too exciting. Quite often, drivers graduating from predictable hot-hatches like the Golf GTi and enjoying the free-revving extra energy of the BMW would unexpectedly learn the meaning of oversteer as they accelerated round a damp roundabout or

through a tight turn. Such heart-stopping moments were part of the experience of driving this belated inheritor of the 2002 tii's crown.

The E21 3 Series underwent remarkably few external changes over its eight years in the BMW catalogue, and the only stylistically different version was the Baur TopCabrio, so called because it had a strong fixed rollover hoop behind the doors, acting as the fixing point for the folding rear window section and the rigid roof panel which stowed in the boot when not in position. The penalty for this complex arrangement was three fold: the car looked awkward, it was expensive and it was heavy, blunting the performance of even the more powerful derivatives. Some 3000 – mainly 320s – were completed by the time production of all 3 Series ended in late 1982.

All in all, 1.36 million had been sold, a remarkable achievement for a company which had been facing total financial meltdown just 20 years previously. Over half that total was exported, and one third the pricier six-cylinder versions. BMW had become a byword for quick, responsive quality cars that drove with both precision and refinement – and the first 3 Series was the model that cemented that reputation.

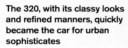

The 320, with its classy looks and refined manners, quickly became the car for urban sophisticates

Left:
With 143 bhp from 2.3 litres, the 323i brought new levels of performance for the time

FIRST E SERIES: E21 PRODUCTION

Production History:		In production: 1975-83			Total produced 1,364,039					
model	315	316	318	318i	320	320i	320-six	323i	total for year	SKD/CKD
1975		10,629	10,446		20,423	1,851			43,349	540
1976		42,166	14,618		53,560	20,477			130,821	1,164
1977		52,834	20,369		42,453	32,322	18,203	37	166,218	1,836
1978		53,513	20,897		1,159	26,775	61,402	18,467	182,213	1,968
1979		45,914	16,388	9,901	804	17,474	65,369	31,123	186,973	1,872
1980	2	54,794	10,491	43,264			59,383	36,424	204,358	756
1981	33,115	44,019		71,739			44,882	33,205	226,960	408
1982	47,112	28,727		66,358			21,206	17,851	181,254	
1983	27,609	4,438		1,302					33,349	
total	107,838	337,034	93,209	192,564	118,399	98,899	270,445	137,107		8,544
							grand total		1,355,495	
							grand total inc SKD		1,364,039	

09

First 6 Series (E24)

→ 1976 – 1987
→ Classy, elegant coupé style by Paul Bracq
→ 86,000 built
→ Focused on refinement rather than raciness
→ 6-cylinder engines
→ All models desirable
→ M635CSi used 24-valve engine from M1

First 7 Series (E23)

→ 1977 – 1986
→ Final piece in BMW's series strategy
→ Six-cylinder engines parallel those in 6 Series
→ 732i first car with electronic engine management
→ Rare 745i turbo had 252 bhp
→ 285,000 built

Moving on up

6 Series Coupé and 7 Series saloon move into luxury territory

By the middle of the 1970s BMW had become a mature, stable company. It had kept its nerve through several crises since its restructuring in the early 1960s and had emerged stronger and fitter each time. By now a respectable member of the automotive establishment, it had left its wild years behind and the focus was no longer on survival, but to find the best strategy for sustainable, long-term growth.

The classy, elegant 6 Series coupé, unveiled in the spring of 1976, provided the perfect illustration of BMW's transition. Aimed unashamedly at affluent and discerning individuals in high society, its discreet and elegant lines contrasted markedly with the outrageous racetrack wings and gaudy paint jobs of the CS coupés which it succeeded; its ultra-smooth six-cylinder engines were developed in the cool of the scientific laboratory rather than the late-night heat of the competition department workshop. In short, BMW had been enjoying an extremely good party, a party in which it had been the undisputed belle of the ball — and now it was time to sober up and face the realities of everyday life as lived by normal people.

The energy crisis of 1973-74 was a testing time for most car companies, but BMW held its nerve better than most. Yet even the outwardly self-effacing but quietly confident Eberhard von Kuenheim must have had occasion to question the way things were going in the broader industry, even if for BMW itself business was continuing to expand. In particular, concerns must have been raised at the prospects for the upcoming 6 and 7 Series designed to mark new high-points on BMW luxury and prestige, and being readied for production just as the fuel crisis was reaching its height.

Paul Bracq's in-house BMW design for 6 Series coupé was chosen in preference to Giugiaro proposal; the classy shape lasted well and marked a departure from the previous CSL's aggressive aerodynamic add-ons

Above:
Motorsport-developed 24-valve 3.5 litre six came straight from M1 supercar to become one of the classic engines of the '80s and '90s. In the M635CSi it gave a storming 286 bhp to produce the most desirable of the big BMW coupés

> "If these large and expensive cars were to remain socially acceptable they would have to become more efficient, more intelligent and, if possible, more discreet. This played straight into the hands of BMW with its expertise in engine design"

All around, carmakers were cancelling plans to invest in large and thirsty cars for rich customers. Suddenly, it had become unacceptable to be seen as a conspicuous consumer in a prestige car, and business leaders were openly talking of downsizing their own personal transport as well as their firms' products. But BMW, under von Kuenheim, was accustomed to looking beyond the immediate panic and taking the long view – and here, they reasoned, large and expensive cars would continue to be an essential part of the picture.

The only difference was that if those large and expensive cars were to remain socially acceptable they would have to become much more efficient, more intelligent and, if possible, more discreet. This of course played straight into the hands of BMW with its expertise in engine design and its position as the challenger to the grandiose, bourgeois establishment of Mercedes-Benz.

So the 630 and 633CSi coupés presented at the Geneva show in March 1976 emerged as an airy, glassy design with a low waist, predominantly straight lines and flat, expansive surfaces: the dominant impression was of classy, clean elegance, and the four-seater cabin reflected

Right:
No other carmaker could match the appeal of BMW's interior design in the 1970s; 6 Series had decent rear space despite coupé roofline

Specifications	628CSi	630CS	633CSi	635CSi	M635CSi
Engine					
Engine type	Inline 6-cylinder	Inline 6-cylinder	Inline 6-cylinder	Inline 6-cylinder	Inline 6-cylinder
Capacity, cc	2788	2985	3210	3453 (1987 on: 3430)	3453
Valves	Sohc 12	Sohc 12	Sohc 12	Sohc 12	Dohc 24
Fuelling	Bosch L-Jetronic fuel injection	Single Pierburg carburettor	Bosch L-Jetronic fuel injection	Bosch L-Jetronic fuel injection (1987 on: Motronic)	Bosch Motronic fuel injection
Max power, bhp @ rpm	184@5800	185@5800	197@5800	218@5200	286@6500
Max torque, Nm @ rpm	240@4200	255@3500	289@4300	310@4000	340@4500
Transmission					
Manual transmission	4-speed (1982 on: 5-speed optional	4-speed (1977 on: 5-speed optional	4-speed (1977 on: 5-speed optional	5-speed	5-speed
Automatic	3-speed ZF optional (4-speed from 1982)	3-speed ZF optional	Not available	ZF auto optional	Not available
Drive	Rear wheels	Rear wheels	Rear wheels	Rear wheels	Rear wheels
Chassis					
Front suspension	MacPherson strut	MacPherson struts	MacPherson struts	MacPherson struts	MacPherson struts
Rear suspension	Semi-trailing arms, coil springs	Semi-trailing arms, coil springs	Semi-trailing arms, coil springs	Semi-trailing arms, coil springs	Semi-trailing arms, coil springs
Braking	Discs, servo assisted	Discs, servo assisted	Discs, servo assisted	Discs, servo assisted	Discs, servo assisted
Steering	ZF recirculating ball, power assisted	ZF recirculating ball, power assisted	ZF recirculating ball, power assisted	ZF recirculating ball, power assisted	ZF recirculating ball, power assisted
Tyres	195/70 VR 14	195/70 VR 14	195/70 VR 14	195/70 VR 14	195/70 VR 14
Body					
Length, mm	4755	4755	4755	4755	4755
Width, mm	1725	1725	1725	1725	1725
Height, mm	1365	1365	1365	1365	1365
Kerb weight, kg	1475	1475	1495	1475	1510
Performance					
Max speed, km/h	210	210	215	222	255
0-100km/h	9.5	9.0	8.5	8.0	6.5
Fuel consumption , lit/100km	15.5	16.5	16.5	17.0	18.0
Marketing					
Launch date	6/79	2/76	1/76	6/78	4/84
Pricing, DM	46,000	40,600	43,100	49,000	89,500

"Superlatives flowed about the M535i – except about the price, which , at almost double that of the 628CSi, was seen as excessive. In the US it was pegged at a terrifying $60,000"

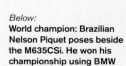

Below:
World champion: Brazilian Nelson Piquet poses beside the M635CSi. He won his championship using BMW turbo power

Left and far left:
CSi: (far left); in action lacks the deeper front air dam of the potent 24-valve M635CSi: left, is the first true M car

2985 cc 630CS were similar externally, with a pronounced forward slope to the front and a full-width grille in black carrying BMW's signature quadruple round headlights and the central double-kidneys with chrome surrounds. The wheels were at last standard light-alloy items with an attractive finned design, and the interior offered a choice of cloth or leather upholstery. The price was set at an initially intimidating DM 40,600, putting it right into Mercedes, Porsche and top Jaguar territory: later, the race-derived M635CSi was to cost more than double this figure.

Early reviews were predictable, balancing regret at the passing of the highly focused CS generation with praise for the 6's great refinement, elegance and dignity. But while the speed of the car – especially the 633CSi – impressed the reviewers, few were moved to describe the new line as exciting or thrilling. BMW, the magazines concluded, had grown up and become a responsible citizen.

The first few months of 6 Series production had been difficult ones for BMW as assembly at the Karmann works had failed to produce the

BMW's growing confidence in cockpit-like environments for the driver.

Under the skin – Paul Bracq's design, chosen over a rival proposal from Italy's fashionable Giorgio Giugiaro – lay familiar BMW engineering elements from the 5 Series updated to suit the new era. Among these were fuel injection for the larger of the two six-cylinder engines, the 3210 cc unit now giving 197 bhp; the ZF recirculating ball steering had a novel variable assistance mechanism which reduced the amount of assistance as road speed rose. Also newsworthy was the first appearance of BMW's check control, a centralised panel of warning lights for systems which continually monitored bulbs, fluid levels and brake pad wear.

The 633CSi and the 185 bhp carburettor-fed,

FIRST 6 SERIES PRODUCTION

Production History:	In production: 1975-89				Total produced 86,216
model	628CSi	630CS	633CSi	M635CSi	total for year
1976		2,075	2,858		
1977		2,518	3,258	5	
1978		924	3,387	1,286	
1979	286	249	2,439	3,755	
1980	1,018		2,043	3,567	
1981	785		1,781	3,086	
1982	1,111		2,334	4,148	
1983	972		3,325	3,668	5
1984	741		2,007	4,103	1,407
1985	593			7,270	1,763
1986	367			5,956	704
1987	77			4,128	1,487
1988				3,229	437
1989				1,012	52
total	5,950	5,766	23,432	45,213	5,855
				grand total	86,216

"Commentators of the era marvelled at the thought of an electronic system able to compute precise fuel mixtures and spark timing for each cylinder for every single revolution of the engine – even at its 6000 rpm red line"

Big 7 Series saloon had close parallels with 6 Series coupé. It drew BMW closer to the Mercedes customer but was still sportier and less comfort oriented

required levels of quality, prompting BMW to bring assembly in-house to the newly refurbished Dingolfing plant and just use Karmann for the supply of the unpainted bodies in white.

Two years into the production run BMW added a more powerful version in the shape of the 635CSi. This used the largest of the sixes, (3453 cc), again with Bosch L-Jetronic fuel injection. The higher 218 horsepower output pushed top speed to beyond 220 km/h, making the 635CSi – distinguished by a frontal airdam and a lip spoiler on the boot – one of the fastest four-seaters on the market. A year later the fuel-injected 628CSi replaced the 630CS, offering the same performance but lower consumption, while in March 1982 came the only real appearance change, the move to the full wraparound of the rear bumper. This coincided with internal changes to the 3.5 litre engine and the dropping of the 633CSi. Innovations from the second-generation 5 Series, launched in 1981, were added at the same time: these included changes to the front suspension, BMW's first trip computer, and its pioneering Service Interval Indicator. In the US, meanwhile, catalytic converters had replaced the troublesome thermal reactors as the 6 Series' emission control system.

Much the most charismatic of the 6 Series was the M635i, shown in the autumn of 1983 but only delivered to customers from the spring of the following year. Carrying the now-familiar M badge on its grille, it borrowed the potent 24-valve M88 engine from the M1 supercar. Displacing the same 3453 cc as the plain 635, the straight six's racing-derived cylinder head, raised compression ratio and higher rev limit boosted power to a heady 286 bhp; channelled

through a close-ratio five-speed gearbox and limited slip rear axle, the extra power gave the big coupé a top speed of well over 250 km/h and 0-100 km/h acceleration in under seven seconds, making it one of the fastest cars of its era.

Understandably, the superlatives flowed – except about the price, which, at almost double that of the 628CSi, was seen as excessive. In the US the M635i (which for a while was sold as the M6, to distinguish it from the lower powered, luxury-oriented L6) was pegged at a terrifying $60,000. Nevertheless, BMW had little difficulty finding buyers for a grand total of 5,855 M635i models around the world.

The large four-door 7 Series sedan, developed from the 2500/2800 models of the late 1960s to square up to Mercedes' top SE range, closely parallels the history of the 6 Series, whose engines and engineering it largely shared. First to appear – in May 1977 – was a three-model line-up comprising a 728 and 730, both with carburettor engines, and the range-topping 733i with fuel injection. Longer, wider and some 200 kg heavier than the outgoing car, all showed a clear family likeness to the 3 and 5 Series and an even clearer link with the 6 Series coupé. Equipment was much more comprehensive than on the outgoing big car, and BMW had learnt its lesson with troublesome dealer-fit air conditioning systems in the US, choosing now to fully integrate the mechanism and install a powerful compressor sourced from General Motors. Unusual, especially in the US, was the choice between manual and automatic transmissions, earning the new 7 considerable respect as a sporty big saloon that was a surprisingly adept handler for its size. Compared

E23: 7 SERIES

Specifications	728	728i	730	732i	733i
Engine					
Engine type	Inline 6-cylinder	Inline 6-cylinder	Inline 6-cylinder	Inline 6-cylinder	Inline 6-cylinder
Bore & stroke, mm	86 x 80	86 x 80	89 x 80	89 x 86	89 x 86
Capacity, cc	2788	2788	2985	3210	3210
Valves	12	12	12	12	12
Valve actuation	sohc	Sohc	Sohc	Sohc	Sohc
Compression ratio	9.0:1	9.3:1	9.0:1	9.3:1	9.3:1
Fuelling	Single Pierburg carburettor	Bosch Motronic electronic fuel injection	Single Pierburg carburettor	Bosch Motronic electronic fuel injection	Bosch electronic fuel injection
Emmision Control					
Max power, bhp @ rpm	170@5800	184@5800	184@5800	197@5500	197@5500
Max torque, Nm @ rpm	233@4000	240@4200	255@3500	285@4300	280@4300
Transmission					
Manual transmission	4-speed; 5-sp optional 1979	4-speed (1982: 5-speed)	4-speed; 5-sp optional 1979	5-speed, sport or economy	5-speed, sport or economy
Automatic	3-speed ZF auto optional	3-speed ZF auto optional	3-speed ZF auto optional	3-speed ZF auto optional	3-speed ZF auto optional
Drive	Rear wheels	Rear wheels	Rear wheels	Rear wheels	Rear wheels
Chassis					
Front suspension	MacPherson strut	MacPherson struts	MacPherson struts	MacPherson struts	MacPherson struts
Rear suspension	Semi-trailing arms, coil springs	Semi-trailing arms, coil springs	Semi-trailing arms, coil springs	Semi-trailing arms, coil springs	Semi-trailing arms, coil springs
Braking	Disc, servo assisted; ABS optional	Disc, servo assisted; ABS optional	Disc, servo assisted; ABS optional	Disc, servo assisted; ABS optional	Disc, servo assisted; ABS optional
Steering	ZF recirculating ball, power assisted	ZF recirculating ball, power assisted	ZF recirculating ball, power assisted	ZF recirculating ball, power assisted	ZF recirculating ball, power assisted
Wheels	6.0 x 14	6.0 x 14	6.5 x 14	6.5 x 14	6.5 x 14
Tyres	195/70 HR 14	195/70 HR 14	205/70 HR 14	205/70 HR 14	205/70 HR 14
Body					
Structure	Steel monocoque	Steel monocoque	Steel monocoque	Steel monocoque	Steel monocoque
Wheelbase, mm	2795	2795	2795	2795	2795
Track F/R, mm	1502/1516	1502/1516	1502/1516	1502/1516	1502/1516
Length, mm	4860	4860	4860	4860	4860
Width, mm	1800	1800	1800	1800	1800
Height, mm	1430	1430	1430	1430	1430
Kerb weight, kg	1550	1530	1600	1580	1660
Fuel tank capacity, lit	85	85 (1980 on: 100)	85	85 (1980 on: 100)	85
Performance					
Max speed, km/h	195	200	200	210	205
0-100km/h, sec	10.0	9.5	9.5	8.5	9.0
Fuel consumption , lit/100km	16.5	16.5	17.5	16.5	17.5
Marketing					
Launch date	5/77	6/79	7/77	5/79	4/77
Pricing, DM	29,300	33,700	33,600	37,700	38,600

735I

Inline 6-cylinder
93.4 x 84
3453
12
Sohc
9.3:1
Bosch Motronic electronic
fuel injection

218@5200
310@4000

5-speed, sport or economy
3-speed ZF auto optional
Rear wheels

MacPherson struts
Semi-trailing arms, coil
springs
Disc, servo assisted; ABS
optional
ZF recirculating ball, power
assisted
6.5 x 14
205/70 HR 14

Steel monocoque
2795
1502/1516
4860
1800
1430
1580
85 (1980 on: 100)

213
8.0
16.5

5/79
43,750

Angular 7 Series shape remained in production for a decade; high-grade interior introduced firsts such as electronic speedometer and Check Control which monitored vehicle fluid systems and brake pad wear

with its Mercedes equivalents it was judged to offer much more performance for the price.

Technical specification changes closely followed those of the 6 Series, a notable first coming with the introduction of an all-injection line-up in May 1979 when the 732i became the first car in the world with fully electronic management of the engine's fuelling and ignition systems, courtesy of Bosch's Motronic control unit. Commentators of the era marvelled at the thought of a system able to compute precise fuel mixtures and spark timing for each cylinder for every single revolution of the engine, even at its 6000 rpm red line. Shortly beforehand the 7 Series had become the first BMW and the second car in the world (after the Mercedes S-Class) to be offered with ABS anti-lock brakes.

Coinciding with this round of technical updates was a mild freshening-up of the 7's exterior detailing. The BMW kidney grilles became flatter and squarer and incorporated into the full width main grille rather than having body colour paint around them, and there was a deeper (but still subtle) airdam under the front bumper.

Something of a technical blind alley was represented by the 745i, first announced in summer 1979 as BMW's flagship model. Rather an embarrassment for BMW, the 745i took a long time to get into production and, uncharacteristically, was not well sorted out even then. The 745i designation was in any case misleading, for rather than develop a new, larger engine for its flagship BMW had opted to turbocharge its existing 3.2 litre six, reasoning that the driver did not need extra power or extra cylinder capacity all the time; the turbo, BMW believed, would supply the extra power when needed but would not give a weight or friction

E23: 745i

Specifications	745i
Type	
Type	Inline 6-cylinder
Capacity, cc	3210 (1983 on: 3430)
Valves	Sohc 12
Fuelling	Bosch Motronic fuel injection, KKK K 27 Turbocharger
Max power, bhp @ rpm	252@5200 (1983 on: 252@4900)
Max torque, Nm @ rpm	380@2200
Transmission	
Manual transmission	Not available
Automatic	3-speed (1983 on: 4-speed)
Drive	Rear wheels
Chassis	
Wheels/tyres	185/70 HR 13
Front suspension	MacPherson struts
Rear suspension	Semi-trailing arms, coil- spring/damper units, hydropneumatic self-levelling
Braking	Disc, servo assisted; ABS
Steering	ZF recirculating ball; power assisted
Wheels	6.5 x 14
Tyres	205/70 VR 14
Body	
Length, mm	4860
Width, mm	1800
Height, mm	1430
Kerb weight, kg	1670
Performance	
Max speed, km/h	222 (1983 on: 227)
0-100km/h	7.9
Fuel consumption, lit/100 km	19.5
Marketing	
Launch date	8/79
Pricing, DM	52,000

penalty under non maximum power conditions. The 745i designation was said to have come from an estimation of the size of a naturally aspirated engine that would match the turbo unit's 252 horsepower.

However, right from the start the 745i was flawed: the cars ran unevenly and though they were fast they were heavy on fuel; the prices were spectacularly high, especially for the later Executive versions, laden with every conceivable luxury gadget. Two engine iterations later, with a move to 3430 cc and a four-speed automatic, the 745i had become a more acceptable luxury vehicle: nevertheless, the damage had been done and BMW would never rush into petrol turbocharging again.

By the time the first 7 Series ceased production in May 1986 it had served BMW well, with 285,000 examples built and with steady sales of around 30,000 a year. Its success had put Mercedes on its guard – if not yet on the back foot – yet better was still to come: the stylish, brand new E32 7 Series for 1986 would make the old version look very dated indeed, and was destined to worry Mercedes even more.

Left and below:
BMW decided against a V12 in 1979 and launched turbocharged six-cylinder 745i to compete against Mercedes V8s. High consumption and fast but uneven performance from turbo engine (below) put BMW off turbocharging until the arrival of diesels in the late 1980s

FIRST 7 SERIES PRODUCTION

Production History:	In production: 1977-86								Total produced 285,029	
model	725i	728	728i	730	732i	733i	735i	745i	total for year	SKD
1977		7,069	100	4,669		7,225			19,063	912
1978		14,162	32	8,274		11,525			33,993	1,752
1979		9,486	5,949	3,905	3,035	7,803	3,692	4	33,874	1,248
1980			14,230		9,952	97	6,984	2,175	33,438	1,632
1981	25		9,972		8,124	439	5,777	2,504	26,841	3,000
1982	553		8,887		8,941	149	6,102	1,510	26,142	3,300
1983	248		8,866		11,845		5,355	2,541	28,855	2,424
1984	34		7,031		10,382		8,343	3,545	29,335	1,776
1985	48		5,763		1,994		15,381	2,831	26,017	432
1986	13		2,078		503		7,108	921	10,623	372
total	921	30,717	62,908	16,848	54,776	27,238	58,742	16,031		16,848
							grand total		268,181	
							grand total inc SKD		285,029	

10

An ambitious diversion

Failed bid to join supercar elite finally turns to BMW's advantage

M1 (E26)

→ 1978 – 1981
→ Mid-engined supercar co-developed with Lamborghini
→ 24-valve six gave 277 bhp and 260 km/h
→ 470 and 850 bhp racing versions
→ Starred in ProCar race series
→ 400 roadgoing versions built
→ Assembled by Baur, Stuttgart

M1's body design by Giugiaro was beautifully proportioned: Lamborghini was to have built the cars but fell into difficulties, forcing BMW to move construction to Baur in Stuttgart

For a car which was a commercial disaster and of which just 450 examples were made, the BMW M1 has occupied an enormous square footage of magazine pages and newspaper articles. Even by 2004, a quarter century after it first appeared, the M1 still commanded huge attention and is a shape that enjoys worldwide recognition.

The interest is hardly surprising given the ambitions BMW had for the M1 programme, the fact that Lamborghini was involved in its genesis and that it was to have been BMW's entry ticket into the world supercar elite and competition with Ferrari, Porsche and Lamborghini itself.

Only the still-confidential minutes of BMW's management board meetings of the early 1970s would be capable of supplying the real answer to one of the unexplained riddles of the automotive industry: what were BMW's true motives in embarking on the M1 programme around 1975 or 1976?

Some hold that BMW wanted to enter the glamorous arena of extravagant, high-powered exotic sports cars, a policy that would not tie in very well with BMW chief Eberhard von Kuenheim's strategy of carefully planned rather than reckless expansion into new segments; others suggest that BMW wanted to rival Porsche and Ferrari in Le Mans style endurance racing.

The two things that are clear, however, are that the programme went disastrously wrong almost as soon as it had begun, and that BMW was forced to push it in a different direction to save face – and to recoup what it could of the substantial losses it must have incurred.

The original plan had been for BMW to approach this exotic but notoriously quixotic segment by proxy, contracting out the design and engineering to other firms and using outside suppliers to provide the parts and undertake assembly. BMW would provide its race-bred 3.5 litre, 24-valve six-cylinder engine, ZF would offer its five-speed transaxle, Giugiaro's Italdesign would style the plastic composite body and

"So much time had been wasted that the racing regulations for which the M1 was designed had changed – and so many customers cancelled orders that BMW was in danger of not being able to produce and sell the 400 cars required for Group 4 homologation"

Lamborghini in Italy would design the car's tubular spaceframe chassis with a view to eventually undertaking series production.

The difficulties began when it became clear that Lamborghini was falling seriously behind schedule in developing the structure and running gear of the mid-engined two-seater. When prototypes failed to materialise by the appointed deadline BMW took the programme back in house to put its own people on the job. Unfortunately, so much time had been wasted that the racing regulations for which the M1 was designed had changed – and so many customers cancelled orders that BMW was in danger of not being able to produce and sell the 400 cars

required for Group 4 homologation.

Three versions had been envisaged: a 'basic' roadgoing version with the 277 bhp powerplant; a Group 4 racing version with suspension changes and a tuned 480 bhp engine, and, for Group 5 racing, a much more potent turbocharged 3.2 litre edition with some 850 bhp and extensive chassis and bodywork modifications.

In the event BMW decided on novel approach: it would create its own high-profile race series to promote the M1, in the hope that this would generate interest in the car and improve its sales prospects. The series, dubbed ProCar, would run on Grand Prix race days as a

M1 came at the height of BMW's Art Car boom: its broad, flat surfaces were the ideal canvas for artists' designs. Andy Warhol's brush-painted example (below) finished sixth at Le Mans in 1979, but the M1 made a tremendous road car too

support event, and Formula One drivers in factory-supported cars would be pitted against private owners.

The ProCar fields were large, the racing close and dramatic and with plenty of contact between the composite bodywork panels of the competing M1s. Yet even with the ongoing rubber-burning advertisement for the M1 in full swing the road car editions were failing to find buyers at their high price of DM 100,000; for a while the price rose to DM 113,000 but BMW was later forced into the ignominy of discounting the model to below DM 90,000 in order to shift the remaining

"Even if, ultimately, the M1 proved to be an embarrassing dead end for BMW, at least it was a highly attractive one"

Right:
The M1 with its front and rear bodywork removed, showing the spaceframe chassis made of square-section tubing, and the twin overhead cam 24-valve straight six. Giving 277 bhp in road trim, the engine became as much of a legend as the car itself

Above:
Roadgoing versions of M1 handled with ease as race car had almost twice the power

Left:
Art in action, from left to right: Roy Lichtenstein, BMW 320i, 1977; Robert Rauschenberg, BMW 633 CSi, 1986; Andy Warhol, BMW M1, 1979; Frank Stella, BMW 3.0 CSL, 1976; Alexander Calder, BMW 3.0 CSL, 1975

E26 M1

Specifications	M1
Type	
Engine type	Inline 6-cylinder
Bore & stroke, mm	93.4 x 84
Capacity, cc	3453
Valves	24
Valve actuation	Dohc
Compression ratio	9.0:1
Fuelling	Kugelfischer mechanical fuel injection
Max power, bhp@rpm	277@6500
Max torque, Nm@rpm	330@5000
Transmission	
Manual transmission	ZF 5-speed
Automatic	Not available
Drive	Rear wheels
Chassis	
Front suspension	Double wishbones, coil springs, gas dampers
Rear suspension	Double wishbones, coil springs, gas dampers
Braking	Disc, servo assisted
Steering	Rack and pinion
Wheels front + rear	7.0 x 16 + 8.0 x 16
Tyres front + rear	205/55 VR 16 + 225/50 VR 16
Body	
Structure	Steel tubular spaceframe, composite body panels
Wheelbase, mm	2560
Track F/R, mm	1550/1576
Length, mm	4360
Width, mm	1824
Height, mm	1140
Kerb weight, kg	1300
Fuel tank capacity, lit	2 x 58
Performance	
Max speed, km/h	250
0-100 km/h, sec	6.5
Fuel consumption, lit/100 km	17.0
Marketing	
Launch date	10/78
Pricing, DM	100,000

examples. The consensus was that would-be buyers wanted a more exotic brand name and more than six cylinders.

For all its faults the M1 was undeniably pretty, Giugiaro's sharply-cut lines giving it an elegance and pleasing proportions that are often difficult to achieve in a mid-engined design. Notable features were the twin BMW roundels on the rearmost edges of the extended rear pillars and the miniaturised BMW kidney grilles on a front end strongly reminiscent of the 1972 Turbo concept car from Paul Bracq.

The broad, flat surfaces of the M1 also found favour with a very different group of individuals – the international art set. In 1975 the American artist Alexander Calder had painted a BMW 3.0 CSL for an art collector friend; soon, other artists turned further BMWs into mobile galleries. Andy Warhol painted the most highly publicised M1, a racer which finished sixth overall at Le Mans in 1979: at the finish it became clear that some of

his brush-painted work had worn off during the course of the 24-hour epic.

As a road car the M1 was surprisingly civilised, with air conditioning, electric windows and good quality fittings – in contrast to many race-car derived GTs. Lacking assistance, the steering was heavy and the dog-leg first of the ZF transmission was awkward, but as the chassis was plainly capable of taking the racecar output of 480 horsepower, it had no difficulties with the 277 of the road version.

Commercial disaster it might have been, but the M1 was skilfully turned round by BMW into something of a public relations triumph. Even if, ultimately, it proved to be an embarrassing dead end for the company, at least it was a highly attractive one.

11

Second 5 Series (E28)

→ 1981 – 1987
→ Criticised for unchanged conservative styling
→ Smoother and more comfortable
→ Home to BMW's first diesel engines
→ Innovations include service interval indicator
→ First genuine M5
→ 722,000 built

Reinforcing the identity

Look-alike second-generation 5 Series homes in on Mercedes

The Olympic stadium in Munich has played host to many BMW new model launches since it was built for the 1972 games, but the atmosphere in June 1981 was subtly different to previous occasions.

BMW had been consistently successful throughout the 1970s. It had sailed through the 1974 energy crisis almost unscathed, investing a massive DM 300 million in new production facilities at Dingolfing. Turnover was DM 5 billion in 1977 (three times what it had been in 1969) on sales of 300,000 cars and 30,000 motorcycles: by the end of the decade BMW's fortunes were on a steeply rising curve, it was seen as the most inventive and most go-ahead car company and expectations were high.

Appearing in 1981, the second-generation 5 Series was widely criticised for conservative styling barely distinguishable from the outgoing model. The new car proved much better to drive

So the disappointment was clear to see when the wraps came off the sparkling new 5 Series – and it looked just like the outgoing 5 Series. Whichever way the assembled commentators squinted at the car, tried to imagine it on the open road or in the thick of Munich's traffic, they could not believe it was different: a mild mid-life facelift, perhaps, with a neater grille, smoother rear lights and fresh wheels – but not a new car. Yet BMW insisted every single panel – apart from the roof pressing – was new, and that this really was the next step forward for the 5 Series.

Coming from the company which had created the red-hot 2002 Tii, the silkily potent 323i and the mighty 3.0 CSL, enthusiasts had expected more. It was hard to accept that this thrusting, dynamic company had thrown its creativity into reverse and come up with something so cautious and conservative – so the second-generation 5 Series faced a sceptical, if not overtly hostile reaction from the press.

The public, on the other hand, did not seem as hungry for radical change as their peers on the newspapers and magazines. Under the seemingly unchanged skin of the 5 lay a whole host of directly beneficial and cleverly thought through innovations, and even the skin itself was a big improvement in terms of aerodynamic

"The public did not seem as hungry for radical change as their peers on the newspapers and magazines. The seemingly unchanged skin of the new car was a big improvement in terms of aerodynamics despite its boringly bluff façade"

BMW tried ambitious new engine technologies in the 1980s, including the efficient low-revving Eta petrol principle and the first genuine performance turbo diesel (above); the latter was better accepted by buyers

efficiency, despite its boringly bluff façade. Among the most interesting novelties developed by BMW's engineers were the energy control, which monitored fuel injection pulses to give a real-time read-out of actual fuel consumption, displayed via a needle in the base of the rev counter. The service interval indicator (SII) was hailed as an even more interesting step forward in using technology to save on ownership costs and raw materials. Linked to the engine management system, the SII logged the type of use the car received – the number of cold starts, the time spent at high revs, and so on – to calculate the degradation of the oil and thus when the next oil change or service was due. By careful driving, said BMW, the interval between services could be almost doubled from the previous fixed mileage-related figure.

There were more chassis changes than at first appeared, too. Double-pivot front suspension allowed improved geometry for better ride comfort and reduced nose-dive under braking, while a re-angling of the semi-trailing arm pivots at the rear reduced the car's tendency to

oversteer when lifting off the throttle on a bend. The three principal launch engines were all six-cylinder units familiar from the old model: however, they had been carefully reworked with fuel injection and close attention to emissions, though catalysts had yet to appear in Europe. Only the four-cylinder, 90 bhp 518 – very much a token entry-level model – relied on carburettor induction: the 520i, 525i and 528i offered 125, 150 and 184 bhp respectively, the latter upholding BMW's sporting honour with 0-100 km/h acceleration in under 8.5 seconds and a top speed of 210 km/h.

Once inside the new model – especially one of the larger sixes – any thoughts of it being an old model were soon banished. New, larger seats and an especially attractive, ergonomic dashboard gave the driver one of the most comfortable operating environments of any car, and on the move the revised suspension provided a noticeably smoother ride. The 528i, with its choice of overdrive or close-ratio five-speed gearbox, had tauter spring rates to suit its faster temperament, but it was the step-up in

refinement and quality across the range that was the most impressive difference.

The 520i quickly established itself as the runaway best seller of the range, finding 56,000 customers in 1983 alone, compared with 22,000 for the 528i; by the end of that year the US market was receiving the hotshot 533i which, at 134 mph, was the fastest saloon car in the country, and it was coming to grips with a new engine concept being advanced by BMW in the shape of the 528e. The e in the title stood for the Greek letter eta, which engineers use to represent efficiency, the central purpose of the Eta motor. BMW experts reasoned that as frictional losses rise with the square of engine speed, a lower-revving engine could be a more efficient one. At the same time a larger capacity and strong torque could help compensate for the

lack of top-end power: the Eta engine emerged as a 2.7 litre version of the BMW big six, using far more sophisticated electronic control of its key functions than had ever been seen before, and developing the same 125 bhp as the 520i but at the much lower engine speed of 4600 rpm. The Eta's torque output matched that of the potent 528i, giving the car a very gentle, easy-going nature with plenty of flexibility and a surprising turn of speed.

Commentators in the US – where the car was labelled 528e – were sceptical, but the buyers loved it: the low-revving model sold twice as well as the outgoing 528i, whose place in the range it took. Nevertheless, the car did not do well in Europe and the Eta idea was quietly dropped for the third generation 5 series in 1988.

The 5 Series was also the car which

Above:
The 5 Series introduced the Service Interval Indicator which calculated when maintenance was due

Left:
With 2.8 litres and 184 bhp, the 528i was a high-quality sports saloon which found broad appeal

introduced the BMW driver to diesel power, albeit a particularly BMW-like form of diesel power which insisted on smoothness, quietness and a decent level of performance – qualities woefully lacking in competing makes' diesel offerings. For a start, BMW insisted on six cylinders to minimise vibration, and a turbocharger to ensure decent power and torque. The 524td which resulted from this programme in 1982 earned glowing reports, even in the US where a sudden wave of unreliable and unpleasant diesels had given the fuel a very bad name. The BMW engine even had the honour of being fitted by Ford to its flagship Lincoln Continental Mk VII.

A round of interim changes to the 5 Series saw the 518 gain fuel injection and jump to 105 bhp, partly rectifying its performance deficit, the 520i rising to 129 bhp, and the 528i being complemented by the 3.5 litre 535i with a catalysed engine of similar power. In parallel, the automatic transmission option moved from three to four speeds and five-speeds became the standard manual fitment.

The 535i spawned a more sporting derivative in 1984, a model which continues to cause much confusion. The M535i was not a direct product of

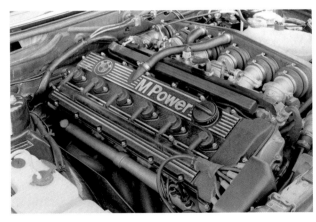

Above and right:
Genuine M5 built by BMW's Motorsport GmbH had 24-valve engine from M1 along with uprated suspension. Mixing ultra high performance with a discreet exterior, it set entirely new standards and became the first of a long line of M5s, each of which upped the ante

Specifications	520i	525i	528i	M535i	M5
Engine					
Engine Type	Inline 6-cylinder	Inline 6-cylinder	Inline 6-cylinder	Inline 6-cylinder	Inline 6-cylinder
Bore & stroke, mm	80 x 66	86 x 71.6	86 x 80	92 x 86	93.4 x 84
Capacity, cc	1990	2494	2788	3430	3452
Valves	12	12	12	12	24
Valves actuation	Sohc	Sohc	Sohc	Sohc	Dohc
Compression ratio	9.8:1	9.6:1	9.3:1	8.0:1	10.5:1
Fuelling	Bosch K-Jetronic mechanical fuel injection	Bosch L-Jetronic electronic fuel injection	Bosch L-Jetronic electronic fuel injection	Bosch ME-Motronic electronic fuel injection	Bosch Motronic electronic fuel injection
Max power, bhp @ rpm	125@5800 (from 1985: 129@6000)	150@5500	184@5800	185@5400	286@6500
Max torque, Nm @ rpm	162@4500	215@4000	240@4200	290@4000	340@4500
Transmission					
Manual transmission	4-speed (from 1982: 5-speed)	4-speed (from 1982: 5-speed)	5-speed standard or close ratio	5-speed standard or close ratio	5-speed
Automatic	ZF 3-speed optional (4-speed from 1983)	ZF 3-speed optional (4-speed from 1983)	ZF 3-speed optional (4-speed from 1983)	ZF 4-speed optional	
Drive	Rear wheels	Rear wheels	Rear wheels	Rear wheels	Rear wheels
Chassis					
Front suspension	MacPherson struts	MacPherson struts	MacPherson struts	MacPherson struts	MacPherson struts
Rear suspension	Semi-trailing arms, coil springs	Semi-trailing arms, coil springs	Semi-trailing arms, coil springs	Semi-trailing arms, coil springs	Semi-trailing arms, coil springs
Braking	Discs/drums, servo assisted; ABS optional from 1982, standard 1986	Discs, servo assisted; ABS optional, standard 1986	Discs, servo assisted; ABS optional, standard 1986	Discs, servo assisted; ABS	Discs, servo assisted; ABS
Steering	ZF recirculating ball, power assisted	ZF recirculating ball, power assisted	ZF recirculating ball, power assisted	ZF recirculating ball, power assisted	ZF recirculating ball, power assisted
Wheels	5.5 x 14	5.5 x 14	5.5 x 14	165 TR 390	165 TR 390
Tyres	175 SR 14	175 HR 14	175 HR 14	220/55 VR 390 TRX	220/55 VR 390 TRX
Body					
Structure	Steel monocoque	Steel monocoque	Steel monocoque	Steel monocoque	Steel monocoque
Wheelbase, mm	2625	2625	2625	2625	2625
Track F/R, mm	1430/1470	1430/1470	1430/1470	1430/1465	1430/1465
Length, mm	4620	4620	4620	4620	4620
Width, mm	1700	1700	1700	1700	1700
Height, mm	1415	1415	1415	1397	1397
Kerb weight, kg	1250	1330	1370	1450	1250
Fuel tank capacity, lit	70	70	70	70	70
Performance					
Max speed, km/h	185	200	210	215	245
0-100km/h, sec	12.0	10.0	8.5	8.5	7.0
Fuel consumption , lit/100km	12.5	13.0	13.5	15.0	15.0
Marketing					
Launch date	4/81	4/81	4/81	3/85	10/84
Pricing, DM	24,900	29,000	32,450	49,400	80,750

E28

E28 5 SERIES

Specifications	518	518i	525e	525d	524td
Engine					
Cylinders	Inline 4-cylinder	Inline 4-cylinder	Inline 6-cylinder	Inline 6-cylinder swirl chamber diesel	Inline 6-cylinder swirl chamber turbo diesel
Capacity, cc	1766	1766	2693	2443	2443
Valves	Sohc 8	Sohc 8	Sohc 12	Sohc 12	Sohc 12
Fuelling	Twin Zenith carburettors	Bosch L-Jetronic electronic fuel injection	Bosch Motronic fuel injection	Diesel injection pump	Diesel injection pump, Garrett turbocharger
Max power, bhp @ rpm	90@5500	105@5800	125@4600	86@4600	115@4800
Max torque, Nm @ rpm	140@4000	145@4500	149@3200	149@2500	210@2400
Transmission					
Manual transmission	4-speed; 5-speed optional	4-speed; 5-speed optional	5-speed	5-speed	5-speed
Automatic	Not available	Not available	4-speed auto optional	Not available	Not available
Drive	Rear wheels	Rear wheels	Rear wheels	Rear wheels	Rear wheels
Chassis					
Front suspension	MacPherson struts	MacPherson struts	MacPherson struts	MacPherson struts	MacPherson struts
Rear suspension	Semi-trailing arms, coil springs	Semi-trailing arms, coil springs	Semi-trailing arms, coil springs	Semi-trailing arms, coil springs	Semi-trailing arms, coil springs
Braking	Disc/drum, servo assisted	Disc/drum, servo assisted	Disc, servo assisted, ABS optional	Disc, servo assisted, ABS optional	Disc, servo assisted, ABS optional
Steering	ZF recirculating ball, power assistance optional	ZF recirculating ball, power assistance optional	ZF recirculating ball, power assisted	ZF recirculating ball, power assisted	ZF recirculating ball, power assisted
Wheels	5.5 x 14	6.0 x 14	6.0 x 14	5.5 x 14	5.5 x 14
Tyres	175 SR 14	175 HR 14	195/70 HR 14	175 HR 14	175 HR 14
Body					
Length, mm	4620	4620	4620	4620	4620
Width, mm	1700	1700	1700	1700	1700
Height, mm	1415	1415	1415	1415	1415
Kerb weight, kg	1160	1200	1280	1160	1160
Performance					
Max speed, km/h	165	180	190	165	180
0-100km/h	13.0	12.5	12.5	18.5	13.5
Fuel consumption , lit/100km	12.0	11.0	12.5	10.5	11.0
Marketing					
Launch date	4/81	12/84	3/83	9/86	11/82
Pricing, DM	20,950	25,800	30,164	31,400	32,300

BMW Motorsport GmbH, the organisation which was to produce the genuine M5 the following year; instead, it used the standard 218 bhp, 12-valve engine and suspension, but added lightweight alloy wheels, front and rear spoilers and M-style interior touches like the three-spoke steering wheel.

The pukka M5 which emerged, largely hand-built and at a very much higher price, from Motorsport GmbH in 1985 was the first in what has become an illustrious and highly desirable line. The 24-valve M-Power M88 engine had grown slightly in capacity to 3452 cc and a raised compression ratio pushed power to an impressive 286 bhp at 6500 rpm, and extensive chassis modifications ensured the power was easily handled. Externally the M5 was the very model of discretion, with little outward sign of its potent status (in contrast to the M535i there were no visible aerodynamic add-ons); it was rapid yet very easy to drive, making it the perfect vehicle for low-key, high-speed driving over long distances.

Enthusiasts in the United States, where the M5 was only offered in black with tan upholstery and at the tidy price of $43,500, took especially avidly to the exhilarating 250 km/h model, accounting for over half the 2,145 examples sold. *Car and Driver* was moved to declare the M5 "a no-compromises, foot-to-the-floor screamer built for those who demand the ultimate in speed and

refinement. The few who can afford it are going to have a ball."

Over the years, successive generations of M5 would prompt even greater floods of superlatives as the new version raised the dynamic bar that impossible bit higher each time. In creating an entirely new class of vehicle, a high-quality luxury sedan which could mix it with the best sports cars and often beat them hollow, the first M5 had really started something. It allowed the second-generation 5 Series to go out on a high note at the beginning of 1988 when, after that shaky 1982 start and uncertainty over BMW's softer, more middle of the road direction, the strategy had come good with almost three quarters of a million fives sold in six years.

Not to be confused with genuine M5, lower-priced M535i was built in main BMW plant using some Motorsport parts but 12-valve engine from standard 535i

SECOND 5 SERIES: E28 PRODUCTION

Production History:			In production: 1980-87				Total produced 722,348							
model	518	518i	520i	525e	528e	525i	528i	533i	M535i	M5	524d	524td	total for year	SKD
1980	7		7					9					23	23
1981	6,580	911	19,349		4,228	10,059	9,992						51,119	3,348
1982	18,265	2,233	56,226	41	11,904	17,563	22,412	1,924				100	130,668	13,476
1983	11,051	1,751	37,407	8,134	11,499	11,802	17,819	6,475				16,197	122,135	7,620
1984	5,003	5,186	30,418	7,772	12,977	6,537	13,458	4,398	3,371	25		15,407	104,552	2,944
1985		12,168	18,924	10,779	13,924	4,084	8,330		16,850	267		22,595	107,921	3,348
1986		7,847	15,789	8,970	16,255	2,834	5,830		15,247	478	2,775	13,139	89,164	2,520
1987		7,172	23,048	4,925	19,066	1,184	2,922		10,187	1,375	1,464	6,996	78,339	3,492
1988														1,656
total	40,906	37,268	201,168	40,621	89,853	54,063	80,772	12,797	45,655	2,145	4,239	74,434		38,427
												grand total	683,921	
												grand total inc SKD	722,348	

12

Second 3 Series (E30)

→ 1983 – 1994
→ Evolutionary design with stronger wedge profile
→ Cabrio and Touring estate versions
→ Expanded range of engines
→ Highly successful despite high prices
→ First BMW to pass two million sales
→ First M3 recreated magic of 2002 Tii
→ In production for 11 years

Popularising the message

Second-generation 3 Series is BMW's first mass seller

While the second generation of the larger 5 Series was taken to task in 1981 for being dull and unadventurous, the 3 Series follow-up in early 1983 had an easier ride with the critics. It, too, was a cautious update of the by now very familiar 3 Series theme, but its sharpened-up lines, its more wedge-like profile and its generally more harmonious proportions made it much more pleasing to look at. Whereas the 5 had begun to look staid and sleepy, the new 3 gave a fresher, more youthful impression.

Again, BMW seemed to have judged the mood of the times almost perfectly – and again the new car succeeded in skilfully shifting BMW's position in the market so that it was able to draw in a large number of new customers who might never before have considered a BMW.

So successful was the formula, in fact, that well over two million copies of the 3 Series saloon were produced over an eight-year span; a further quarter million customers chose the elegant convertible version and a very significant expansion of the 3 Series' remit, the Touring estate. Yet again, all sale records were shattered.

The car succeeded so well because it had dramatically expanded its role and its position in the market. No longer was a BMW 3 Series simply a compact, sporty high-quality two-door

saloon: now it had become a whole range of designs which appealed to many different buyer groups and the theme of sportiness was no longer central to its attraction – buyers were just as likely to choose it for the quality of its construction and finish, the refinement of its engineering or, increasingly and very significantly, the snob appeal of the blue and white badge on its bonnet.

The addition of a four-door version was an important step in drawing in a wider audience of older customers uncomfortable with what could have been seen as the slightly coupé-like awkwardness of the familiar two-door; this also made it more easily eligible as a company car for businesses. The Touring estate, which did not arrive until the basic car had been on sale for four

Second-generation 3 Series' styling was less criticised than conservative 5's; the move to four doors and, later, the Touring estate expanded the model's market beyond that of the sporting enthusiast

Pleasing proportions and an excellent interior brought in customers seeking quality and status

years, provided a further enlargement of BMW's market radius to pull in families, people with sporting hobbies, people with dogs – buyer groups the company had never before addressed. At the same time the first of a race-oriented ultra high performance line – the M3 – dramatically restored the credibility BMW had been losing with sports-minded drivers and won a lot of races too. Only the half-hearted venture into four wheel drive – which spectacularly failed to produce a fun-to-drive rally style car like the Lancia Integrale – could be seen as a misjudgement.

Production, initially of the two-door model, began in both the Milbertshofen 'mother' plant in Munich and at Dingolfingen in late 1982, with the first customer deliveries early the following year. The four-door followed, to great interest, in the autumn of 1983, sharing the same engine choices of the 1.8 litre four-cylinder (available in the carburettor-fed 316 with 90 bhp and the 318i, fuel-injected to produce 105 bhp), and the six-cylinder 320i and 323i, echoing the choice

"Immediately, the new 3 Series was a big success: everyone admired the very neat interior design, which brought the BMW cockpit concept to a new high"

Below:
Close to the end of the production run, the new M40 engine and a 16-valve head brought extra sparkle to the 318iS

presented by the outgoing range. Electronic innovations included the service interval indicator, the energy control and, on most models, the on-board computer already seen in the 5 Series; the check control was positioned above the interior mirror. On the mechanical front the brakes, steering and suspension were revised: changes in the rear geometry aimed at reducing the car's rear-end breakaway prompted the repositioning of the rear dampers away from the springs and further back, aiding much-needed rear seat space in the process.

Immediately, the new 3 Series was a big success. Perhaps predictably, the press complained it wasn't as much fun as the old one, but everyone admired the extremely neat interior design (bringing the BMW cockpit concept to a new high), the solid materials and the excellent fit and finish of the whole vehicle; customers flocked into BMW showrooms in such numbers that BMW was forced to work extra shifts to meet demand. In 1983 well over 200,000 examples were turned out, with the 318i the runaway favourite with over one-third of all sales, the pricier 320i slightly behind and the basic 316 and top 323i each accounting for in excess of 30,000 units.

These figures, for just one derivative of just

SECOND 3 SERIES E30 SEDANS PRODUCTION

Production History: In production: 1982-94 — Total produced 2,085,573

model	316 & 316i	318iS	320i	323i	325i	325iX	325e	324d	324td	320iS	M3		total for year	SKD
1982	1,199	2,339		7,133	4,909								15,580	
1983	37,536	76,387		64,766	32,611			872					212,172	6,029
1984	65,185	75,535		65,444	33,411			25,471					265,046	20,088
1985	59,053	82,369		46,010	18,538	13,636	677	59,832	10,853			1	290,969	10,980
1986	63,699	50,146		36,227	1,307	32,245	6,752	77,317	35,562			2,396	305,651	13,020
1987	46,888	48,889		61,606		52,958	10,327	22,393	17,800	7,261	11	6,396	274,529	14,856
1988	54,122	50,199		38,306		43,280	5,494	3,402	5,259	7,029	2,419	3,426	212,936	17,582
1989	75,181	36,855	9,442	33,949		30,035	4,047		3,729	4,251	624	2,541	200,654	17,582
1990	63,361	31,754	29,171	26,400		23,179	2,256		2,763	2,973	691	2,424	184,972	15,192
1991	1,337	2,391	2,621	901		1,603	36						8,889	16,428
total	467,561	456,864	41,234	380,742	90,776	196,936	29,589	189,287	75,966	21,514	3,745	17,184		114,175

grand total **1,971,398**
grand total inc SKD **2,085,573**

"The Touring, a discreetly stylish estate rear grafted onto the four-door saloon, must have been approached with some trepidation by BMW executives who remembered all too clearly the failure of the original 2002 Touring"

one model line, showed just how far BMW had come in the 20 years since its restructuring: twenty years ago, that kind of output would have been excellent for the entire company and all its ranges.

The 3 Series continued to gather pace in the market, breaking through the 300,000-unit mark in 1986, by which time the 316, now with the brand-new 1.6 litre, fuel-injected M40 engine instead of the detuned M10 1.8, had become the top seller. The very stylish in-house Cabrio was well established, having taken over from the ungainly Baur Topcabrio early on, and the Touring estate was beginning to filter through to the dealerships. The Cabrio sold best with the most powerful 325i engine (which had replaced the 323i in 1985) whereas Touring customers favoured the bottom-end engines (316i and 318i) throughout the production run of the model.

The Touring, a discreetly stylish estate rear grafted on to the four-door saloon body, must have been approached with some trepidation by BMW executives who remembered all too clearly the failure of the original 2002 Touring – but this time the surprise was in the opposite direction and the model was an unexpectedly big success. It was expensive and not high on practicality (hatchbacks such as the VW Golf had a bigger load space and easier access) but buyers were

drawn to its classy looks and its association with the affluent lifestyles led by BMW customers further up the social scale.

The 1985 Frankfurt show where BMW's Touring direction had first been revealed also marked the start of another fine tradition, much closer to the company's natural roots. BMW wanted to get back into top-level touring car racing, and chairman Eberhard von Kuenheim personally commissioned engine king Paul Rosche to produce a suitable power unit. This Rosche duly did by the unusual method of cutting off two cylinders from the 24-valve head of the legendary M-Power straight six and mating this to the block of the four-cylinder M10 – which, remember, was by now even being used in Formula One racing. The results were spectacular, with close on 200 bhp from a 2.3 litre engine that was little heavier than the standard item in the 316. The rest of the car was lightened, strengthened and adapted, always with the needs of racing as the top priority; wider wheelarches left space for hefty 205 series tyres on 15 inch rims, while a raised boot line carried a rear spoiler which grew as the model evolved.

A proper account of all the Evolutions of the M3 would occupy a book in its own right; suffice it to say that anyone who has experienced the spectacular 7500 rpm power delivery and the taut race-car like handling of the ultimate Sport

SECOND 3 SERIES: E30 CABRIO/TOURING PRODUCTION

Production History:			In production: 1985-94				Total produced 247,1297				
model	318i Cabrio	320i Cabrio	325i Cabrio	M3 Cabrio	316i Touring	318i Touring	320i Touring	324td Touring	325i Touring	325iX Touring	total for year
1985			11								11
1986		206	10,585								10,791
1987		2,425	24,249						16		26,690
1988		7,378	13,637	130			7,245	2,170	6,065	1,932	38,557
1989		7,704	12,863	180		8,280	5,913	1,695	3,173	1,653	41,461
1990	2,640	7,907	11,241	176		13,782	4,405	1,082	3,222	936	45,391
1991	11,406	4,519	7,454	300	3599	6,001	472	1,252	1,336	539	36,878
1992	8,500	2,544	5,189		5018	3,967		974	513	208	26,913
1993	2,160	4	17		10621	5,235		217	181	5	18,440
1994					1357	640					1,997
total	24,706	32,687	85,246	786	20,595	37,905	18,035	7,390	14,506	5,273	
										grand total	247,129

Evolution will be in no doubt that BMW had lost none of its expertise in producing cars to thrill and delight the most demanding of its sporting customers. The different versions of the M3 went by different names in each of the markets in which they were sold; however, another model, going by the innocent title of 320iS, is also an M3 offshoot – and a very interesting one at that. The 320iS was developed specially for the Italian and Portuguese markets where punitive taxes hampered sales of cars over two litres: BMW engineers were able to shrink the M3 engine to just under that limit and still squeeze well over 190 bhp from it – at a dizzy 6900 rpm – and maintain torque at 210 Nm, only marginally less than the standard M3's 230 Nm. With a top speed of 231 km/h the 320iS was one of the fastest two-litres around: it was available as a two or four-door (as the standard model would soon be) and came with the close ratio dog-leg five-speed gearbox. 3745 were produced between 1988 and 1990, compared with 17,184 saloon M3s and 786 M3 Cabrios.

By this time the mainstream 3 Series saloon

Touring estate version of E30 3 Series was unexpectedly successful: buyers seemed to be more concerned with style, status and performance than practicality, where the BMW compared poorly

Four wheel drive 325iX
used clever centre differential
and had noticeably higher
ride height. It built up a
following in Switzerland and
Austria but few other places

had been replaced by the completely new E36 model, though the Cabrio was to continue for three more highly profitable years and the Touring for a remarkable four and a half. At its peak, 3 Series production was running at more than 1,000 cars a day and even with both the Milbertshofen (Munich) and Dingolfing plants running flat out there was still not enough capacity. The opening of BMW's third big plant, at Regensburg, eased the pressure somewhat in 1987: the Cabrio, Touring and 325iX four wheel drive were built at both Dingolfing and Regensburg, the M3 at Milbertshofen only, whereas the rest of the models were built at all three plants. Milbertshofen also produced some 114,000 CKD sets to be assembled in BMW facilities all round the world, notably South Africa, India and Thailand.

The South Africans were particularly enterprising: they built their own idea of an M3. Using the 3.2 litre six from the 733i, they created the rapid 333i, which some owners even had

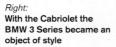

Right:
With the Cabriolet the
BMW 3 Series became an
object of style

Specifications	316i	318i	320i	323i	325i
Engine					
Engine type	Inline 4-cylinder	Inline 4-cylinder	Inline 6-cylinder	Inline 6-cylinder	Inline 6-cylinder
Bore & stroke, mm	89 x 71	89 x 71	80 x 66	80 x 76.8	84 x 75
Capacity, cc	1766	1766	1990	2316	2494
Valves	8	8	12	12	12
Valve actuation	Sohc	Sohc	Sohc	Sohc	Sohc
Compression ratio	9.5:1	9.5:1	9.8:1	9.8:1	9.7:1
Fuelling	Single Pierburg carburettor	Bosch L-Jetronic fuel injection	Bosch L-Jetronic fuel injection	Bosch Motronic electronic fuel injection	Bosch ME-Motronic electronic fuel injection
Max power, bhp @ rpm	90@5500	105@5800	125@5800; 9/95 on: 129@6000	139@5300; 9/93 on: 150@6000	171@5800
Max torque, Nm @ rpm	140@4000	145@4500	171@4000	205@4000	226@4000
Transmission					
Manual transmission	4-speed; 1984 on: 5-speed	4-speed; 1984 on: 5-speed	5-speed	5-speed; optional close ratio 5-speed	5-speed; optional close ratio 5-speed
Automatic	3-speed; 1984 on: 4-speed	3-speed; 1984 on: 4-speed	4-speed	4-speed	4-speed
Drive	Rear wheels	Rear wheels	Rear wheels	Rear wheels	Rear wheels
Chassis					
Front suspension	MacPherson struts	MacPherson struts	MacPherson struts	MacPherson struts	MacPherson struts
Rear suspension	Semi-trailing arms, minibloc coil springs	Semi-trailing arms, minibloc coil springs	Semi-trailing arms, minibloc coil springs	Semi-trailing arms, minibloc coil springs	Semi-trailing arms, minibloc coil springs
Braking	Disc/drum, servo assisted	Disc/drum, servo assisted	Disc, servo assisted; ABS optional	Disc, servo assisted; ABS optional	Disc, servo assisted, ABS optional
Steering	ZF rack and pinion, power assistance optional	ZF rack and pinion, power assistance optional	ZF rack and pinion, power assisted	ZF rack and pinion, power assisted	ZF rack and pinion, power assisted
Wheels	5.0 x 14; 9/85 on: 5.5 x 14	5.0 x 14; 9/85 on: 5.5 x 14	5.5 x 14	5.5 x 14	5.5 x 14
Tyres	175/70 TR14	175/70 HR14; 195/65 HR14	195/60 HR14	195/65 VR14	195/65 VR14
Body					
Structure	Steel monocoque	Steel monocoque	Steel monocoque	Steel monocoque	Steel monocoque
Wheelbase, mm	2570	2570	2570	2570	2570
Track F/R, mm	1407/1415	1407/1415	1407/1415	1407/1415	1407/1415
Length, mm	4325	4325	4325	4325	4325
Width, mm	1645	1645	1645	1645	1645
Height, mm	1380	1380	1380	1380	1380
Kerb weight, kg	1020	1020	1110	1140	1190
Fuel tank capacity, lit	55	55	55	55	55
Performance					
Max speed, km/h	175	185	200	205	220
0-100km/h	12.0	11.5	10.0	9.0	8.0
Fuel consumption , lit/100km	11.0	11.0	12.0	12.5	12.5
Marketing					
Launch date	11/82	11/82	11/82	11/82	9/85
Pricing, DM	19,250	21,550	24,550	27,400	33,000

E30: 3 SERIES DERIVATIVES

Specifications	324d	324td	318is	325iX
Engine				
Engine type	Inline 6-cylinder indirect injection diesel	Inline 6-cylinder indirect injection turbo diesel	Inline 4-cylinder	Inline 6-cylinder
Capacity, cc	2443	2443	1796	2494
Valves	Sohc 12	Sohc 12	Dohc 16	Sohc 12
Fuelling	Diesel injection pump	Electronic diesel injection, turbocharger	Bosch Motronic electronic fuel injection	Bosch ME Motronic fuel injection
Max power, bhp @ rpm	86@4600	115@4800	136@6000	171@5800
Max torque, Nm @ rpm	149@2500	210@2400	169@4600	226@4000
Transmission				
Manual transmission	5-speed	5-speed	5-speed	5-speed
Automatic	4-speed auto optional	4-speed auto optional		4-speed auto optional
Drive	Rear wheels	Rear wheels	Rear wheels	All 4 wheels: 37:63 front-rear torque split via centre differential
Chassis				
Front suspension	MacPherson struts	MacPherson strut	MacPherson strut	MacPherson strut
Rear suspension	Semi-trailing arms, minibloc coil springs	Semi-trailing arms, minibloc coil springs	Semi-trailing arms, minibloc coil springs	Semi-trailing arms, minibloc coil springs
Braking	Disc/drum, servo assisted	Disc/drum, servo assisted	Disc, servo assisted; ABS optional	Disc, servo assisted; ABS
Steering	ZF rack and pinion, power assistance optional	ZF rack and pinion, power assisted	ZF rack and pinion, power assistance optional	ZF rack and pinion, power assisted
Wheels	5.5 x 14	5.5 x 14	5.5 x 14	6.0 x 14
Tyres	175/70 TR 14	195/65 HR 14	196/65 HR 14	195/65 VR 14
Body				
Length, mm	4325	4325	4325	4325
Width, mm	1645	1645	1645	1662
Height, mm	1380	1380	1380	1400
Kerb weight, kg	1220	1270	1135	1270
Performance				
Max speed, km/h	170	185	205	210
0-100 km/h, sec	16.0	12.5	10.0	9.0
Fuel consumption , lit/100km	9.5	10.0	11.5	14.0
Marketing				
Launch date	9/85	10/87	9/89	10/85
Pricing, DM	27,450	35,700	32,700	43,900

Factory-built Cabriolet was pretty, practical and a huge commercial success. It stayed in production until 1993

E30: DERIVATIVES DIMENSIONS

Specifications	2-Door Sedan	4-Door Sedan	Cabriolet	Touring
Dimensions				
Wheelbase, mm	2570	2570	2570	2570
Track F/R, mm	1407/1415	1407/1415	1407/1415	1407/1415
Length, mm	4325	4325	4325	4325
Width, mm	1645	1645	1645	1645
Height, mm	1380	1380	1370	1380
Kerb weight, kg	–	2-door + 25kg	2-door + 130 kg	2-door + 100 kg
Fuel tank capacity	55 (1987 on: 64)	55 (1987 on: 62)	62	55
Marketing				
Launch date	10/82	10/82	3/86	8/87
Pricing, DM	–	2-door +DM 850	2-door +DM 8,500	2-door +DM 6,000

Below:
M3 evolved into a series of ever-faster derivatives, including the Sport Evolution. Each has its own aficionados, but all provide all-time driving thrills

turbocharged in the manner of BMW's own 745i. For their equivalent of the 745i, they used the M1's 24-valve engine, which many argue was a better (if less quiet) solution than BMW's troublesome turbocharging system.

The second-generation 3 Series demonstrated many important things about BMW. It showed how the company was prepared to shift its ground tactically away from narrowly focused sports models in order to draw in the customers it knew wanted BMW quality but not necessarily speed; it was able to diversify intelligently in order to do this, and it while it was not afraid of offering low-powered and low-specification cars it was never tempted to compromise on quality or engineering integrity. But most of all, this 3 Series showed the growing power of the BMW brand – how buyers desired a BMW first and foremost, and did not necessarily care too much about the technical specification or the fact that other makes might offer a more complex car at a lower price.

Much of this was attributable to highly inventive advertising and general brand-building, the image of the company sometimes running a higher level than many of the mainstream products truly justified. But at the end of the second 3 Series' astonishing run BMW had achieved the best of both worlds: it was a volume producer of mass-market models.

Designed from the outset around racing rules, the 16-valve M3 had prodigious speed and poise, and dispelled any doubts that BMW had gone soft

E30: M3 – A SELECTION OF THE 12 VARIATIONS

Specifications	M3 1986	M3 Evolution	M3 Sport Evolution	M3 Cabriolet
Engine				
Engine type	Inline 4-cylinder	Inline 4-cylinder	Inline 4-cylinder	Inline 4-cylinder
Capacity, cc	2302	2302	2467	2302
Valves	Dohc 16	Dohc 16	Dohc 16	Dohc 16
Fuelling	Bosch Motronic electronic fuel injection	Bosch Motronic electronic fuel injection		Bosch Motronic electronic fuel injection
Max power, bhp @ rpm	195@6750	215@7650	238@7000	215@7650
Max torque, Nm @ rpm	226@4600	230@4600	240@4750	230@4600
Transmission				
Manual transmission	5-speed	5-speed	5-speed	5-speed
Drive	Rear	Rear	Rear	Rear
Chassis				
Front suspension	MacPherson struts	MacPherson struts	MacPherson struts	MacPherson struts
Rear suspension	Semi-trailing arms, coil springs	Semi-trailing arms, coil springs	Semi-trailing arms, coil springs	Semi-trailing arms, coil springs
Braking	Disc, servo-assisted; ABS	Disc, servo-assisted; ABS	Disc, servo-assisted; ABS	Disc, servo-assisted; ABS
Steering	ZF rack and pinion, power assisted	ZF rack and pinion, power assisted	ZF rack and pinion, power assisted	ZF rack and pinion, power assisted
Wheels	7.0 x 15	7.0 x 16	7.5 x 16	7.0 x 15
Tyres	205/55 ZR15	225/45 ZR 16	225/45 ZR 16	205/55 VR15
Body				
Length, mm	4360	4360	4360	4360
Width, mm	1765	1765	1765	1765
Height, mm	1370	1370	1370	1370
Kerb weight, kg	1200	1200	1200	1360
Performance				
Max speed, km/h	235	241	248	239
0-100km/h, sec	7.0	6.7	6.5	7.3
Fuel consumption , lit/100km	13.0	8.8	8.8	8.9
Marketing				
Launch date	6/86	3/88	1/90	5/88
Price DM	59,800	–	93,000	93,250

The racing line

Competitive edge in the air and on the tracks

Motorsport on two wheels and four

→ High flying bi-plane
→ 700 Coupe goes rallying
→ Touring Car triumphs
→ Pivotal 1500
→ Endurance car success
→ Turbo F1 engines

For close to a century BMW has sought to excel in motorsport as well as in developing road cars with sporting appeal. Soon after the company was founded, it produced an engine which took a plane to a record height; from the 1930s until now, BMW has its attention on land, securing records and winning races on two wheels as well as four. BMW has made its mark in rallying, ProCar racing and Formula One with its engines, never missing an opportunity to use the investment in sport to improve the quality and enjoyment of its production models.

High-achieving, high-performance machinery has been part of the BMW ethos virtually since the company's foundation in 1917. Appropriately for a group whose corporate symbol represents a rotating propeller, it was a biplane powered by a Type IV BMW aero engine which in 1919 launched the record-setting tradition.

Flown by a Bavarian, Flight Lieutenant Zeno Diemer, the four-valve-per-cylinder, straight-six power unit carried the DFW airframe to a world altitude record of more than six miles (9,760 metres) in 89 minutes.

BMW's quest for speed and distance records first manifested itself in setting motorcycle land speed records between the wars, and endures into the 21st century. Ernst Henne, a BMW

dealer, played his part in this early form of motorsport brand-building when he established a benchmark of nearly 280 km/h in 1933 on a closed section of newly-completed autobahn in a streamlined, bullet-shaped 500cc motorcycle.

Another central element in BMW's early motorsport heritage involved using ostensibly humble production vehicles to establish street and track credibility. Thoroughly redeveloped 748cc versions of the Austin Seven, named Dixis by BMW, were built in Eisenach, eastern Germany, and won the team prize in the 2,500-kilometre 1929 Alpenpokal, predecessor to the classic Alpine Rally; from 1962 onwards, BMW repeated the same process with its genuinely legendary 700 Coupé. Featuring styling akin to

The 3.0 CSL scored some of its most famous triumphs at Spa. Here, Dieter Quester thunders through the legendary Eau Rouge at the beginning of another lap

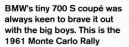

BMW's tiny 700 S coupé was always keen to brave it out with the big boys. This is the 1961 Monte Carlo Rally

The 2002 was an immediate sensation in touring car racing. Here a whole cluster do battle with Alfa GTVs and Porsche 911s in 1966

an upmarket Trabant, it was powered by a rear-mounted, flat-twin, motorcycle-derived engine, uprated to 65 horsepower; among the drivers were Hans Stuck senior and a young Belgian prospect, Jacky Ickx, who was to emerge as a leading Formula One driver of the late '60s and early '70s, and ultimately one of the world's greatest endurance sports car drivers.

He graduated through BMW-powered Formula 2 cars to the marque's large coupés; despite its lack of cubic capacity the 700 frequently upstaged 1-litre and 1.3-litre rivals, including Mini Coopers, Alfa Romeo Juniors and Fiat Abarths.

Soon to be BMW's motorsport manager, the aristocratic Alex von Falkenhausen drove the 'mighty atom' (also dubbed the 'poor man's Porsche'), while another 700 advocate was Burkard Bovensiepen, now head of the Alpina BMW tuning concern. Equally at home on the loose surfaces of rallying as tarmac, the 700 in 1961 finished fifth overall in the Monte Carlo

Rally and eighth on the Acropolis Rally. Like the Mini Cooper S and Porsche 911, the BMW 700 Coupé proved the merits of placing the engine over the driving wheels.

Hubbert Hahne, a BMW stalwart through most of his career, maintained this giant-killing routine in 1963 when he led the European Touring Car Championship round at Mallory Park, finishing a close second to the winning Saab, which benefited from an extra 300cc. The 700, a lightweight upstart, audaciously earned BMW a born-again motorsport reputation in the 1960s when a new generation of four-cylinder engines laid the foundations for an ultra successful series of touring and formula racing successes.

As BMW emerged from the financial mire of the late '50s, Alex von Falkenhausen's resources and budget were derisory. But youth, resourcefulness and enthusiasm – epitomised by Paul Rosche, the engine specialist recruited in 1957 – helped establish a racing line that earned 27 European Touring Car drivers and

manufacturers' titles between 1966 and 1988.

Unveiled in 1961, but not fully ready for market until mid 1962, the 1500 was pivotal for BMW's production and motorsport future. It also provided an access ticket to BMW for the fledgling Alpina performance and production house of founder Burkard Bovensiepen, who boosted the 1500's engine to 92 horsepower and its top speed to 156 km/h. When the new model made its works or factory-racing debut in early 1964, it had grown in engine size and muscle to the 1800ti. Typical of its road and track era, road-registered cars were often driven to and from the circuits.

BMW's emergence as a motorsport marque within the burgeoning European Touring Car series involved racing wheel-to-wheel with the

giant 7-litre US Ford Galaxies, Jaguar Mark IIs and Mercedes 300SEs.

Significant results in that debut season included outright victory in the Nurburgring 12 hours and second in the 24-hour Spa event where Hahne was partnered by Rauno Aaltonen, rallying's flying Finn. Hahne and the nimble BMW, with its independent rear suspension, also collected the domestic German championship.

BMW sustained its commitment to touring or sedan car racing in 1995 by homologating (building a stipulated number of street-legal versions) its track racer to qualify for Group 2 European championship competition. Badged the 1800ti/SA, with the SA denoting special equipment, the car inevitably was dubbed Tisa, and in racing form the evolving four-cylinder

Above:
Cleared for take-off: the legendary CSL 'Batmobile' in full flight at the Nurburgring in 1973

Left:
Prior to the arrival of the M3, 3 Series cars were successful in circuit racing; the M3 proved dominant on the tracks but had only one world rally victory, Bernard Beguin taking the Tour de Corse in 1987

M1s blast through an atmospheric Casino Square in the ProCar support race prior to the Monaco grand prix

engine produced nearly 160 horsepower.

Von Falkenhausen guided the motorsport programme which was nevertheless eclipsed by his British contemporary, Sir John Whitmore, who dominated with the Ford Lotus-Cortina. Particularly galling for BMW was Ford's victory on Germany's own and daunting 23 km Nurburgring, though pride was salvaged when the 1800Ti (shared by Pascal, Jacky Ickx's brother) averaged just under 160 km/h to win the Spa 24 hours endurance challenge. BMW went on to win more round-the-clock Spa races than all other manufacturers put together.

To keep pace with the Lotus Cortinas and the agile, lightweight Alfa GTAs, BMW's "new saloon" benefited from 2-litre power in the 2000ti in 1966. The latest in a series of Spa 24-hour triumphs involved Jacky Ickx and Hahne surrendering the lead and diverting into the pits where mechanics spent six minutes replacing the radiator. That year also marked the arrival of an Austrian driver, Dieter Quester, who had earlier campaigned his own off-the-shelf 1800 Tisa, winning the domestic Austrian road racing series. His name was synonymous with BMW over the course of 30 years, with success in Formula 2

single-seaters and touring cars (particularly the 635 coupé) and marriage to Julianna von Falkenhausen, the boss's daughter. Quester brought his 1966 Touring Car contract to a juddering halt by destroying a works 2000Ti at the Nurburgring in a test session, after attempting the Brunchen corner at 160 km/h, which by his admission was 50 too fast.

BMW's racing influence as an engine producer extended in 1966 from propelling largely British-built sports cars, like Elvas and Lotus 23s, to developing power units for the higher-profile F2 single-seater category, then the feeder formula for F1. BMW's continuing policy of deriving racing engines from production units was to provide a base line from which to launch the legendary four-cylinder turbo F1 engines of the early 1980s. BMW-powered F2 cars won six European titles between 1967 and 1984 and, although in the early '70s the department which developed and built them worked secretly within the company, most of the 500 M12 F2 engines built were sold profitably.

Instead of sub-contracting racing engine technology to specialised engineering firms outside the company, BMW's F2 programme remained mainly in-house, providing a rare profit centre within the sport. Drivers who gained

results in BMW-engined F2 cars provide an intriguing multi-national historical insight into an unequalled period of success; they included John Surtees, Hubert Hahne, Jo Siffert, Jacky Ickx, Jean-Pierre Jarier, Vittorio Brambilla, Hans Stuck, Jacques Laffite, Ronnie Peterson, Patrick Tambay, Eddie Cheever, Jochen Mass, Bruno Giacomelli, Riccardo Patrese and Marc Surer.

The term icon is over-used in describing significant automotive products but BMW's 2002 in general, and its turbocharged counterpart in particular, unquestionably qualify for the term. Debuting in early 1968, the two-door 2002 helped to complete BMW's renaissance as a producer of dynamic road cars, cars which appeared to make seamless transitions into racing and rallying contenders. Graduating through the 2002 Ti and 2002 Tii, the ultimate version of the compact saloon went racing seriously in 1969 as the turbocharged 2002, officially designated 2002 Tik (k for Kompressor).

Although the 2002 in normally-aspirated and turbocharged forms lasted only two seasons as a works racer, it won division three (the largest class) in the 1969 European Touring Car Championship, with BMW relishing a five-point margin over Porsche.

Turbocharging was banned from the class in

"Though ProCar racing was related to production cars, it cost BMW the equivalent of a contemporary F1 team's seasonal budget. Niki Lauda and Nelson Piquet were the 1979 and 1980 ProCar champions, but they were not challenged by the Ferrari drivers, whose team barred them from supporting the BMW enterprise"

The big 6 Series coupés did battle with Jaguars, Volvos and Rovers in the 1980s

Powered by a specially designed BMW V12, the McLaren F1 scored a historic debut when at Le Mans in 1995

1970. The ultimate road-going 2002 Turbo, with 170 horsepower, 'cowcatcher' front air dam and none-too-subtle turbo badging, coincided with the 1974 oil crisis, generated by the Yom Kippur War. Only 1,672 of the street legal high performer were produced. BMW justifiably laid claim to running the first turbocharged European touring car but, as a production road car, it marked a technical departure which the brand was only once to apply again to a petrol engine in Europe.

Between 1980 and 1986, a BMW with a turbocharged six-cylinder 3.2-litre engine was exported mainly to the US with 745i badging. In total 16,031 were made.

The Munich factory, and its motorsport offshoot, has never fully endorsed world rallying, an attitude reflected in the fragmented official approach to the 2002 family between 1969 and 1973. In fact Achim Warmbold, with limited works support, won the Portuguese Rally in 1972, testimony to its competitiveness on tarmac. Sporadic works or semi-works involvement threatened to produce results, even on loose gravel, and Sweden's Bjorn Waldegard – chasing the leading Ford Escort on the 1973 British RAC Rally – crashed off a forest track. The car was retrieved from the undergrowth to finish seventh.

BMW made a significant move upwards in terms of model and engine size during 1973 with the CSL series, and most notably the winged 'Batmobile' coupés, which command a place in touring car racing folklore. The earlier CSi was too heavy and aerodynamically inefficient to seriously challenge Ford and its Cologne purpose-built lightweight Capris in 1972. A rapid development programme driven by Jochen Neerpasch, who defected from Ford in 1972, helped generate a quantum leap in pace. This resulted in a 3.3-litre, straight-six CSL driven by Hans Stuck lapping the Nurburgring a full 10 seconds faster than the previously dominant Capri.

In a halcyon era when Grand Prix drivers competed with touring car specialists, the BMW and Ford ranks included Niki Lauda, Chris Amon, Jochen Mass, James Hunt, Jacky Ickx, Jackie Stewart and Emerson Fittipaldi; this was a line-up with nine F1 world titles between them. Lauda was particularly impressive in 1973 and at the Nurburgring reeled off three identical, metronomic consecutive laps of 8 minutes 23.8 seconds on a 23 km course through a myriad series of corners and race traffic. The tradition of using stellar drivers continued a year later at the same track when Sweden's Ronnie Peterson, who died after a start-line crash in the 1978

Italian Grand Prix, lopped 12 seconds off Lauda's time when taking pole position in a 400 horsepower 'Batmobile'.

The fuel crisis that year intervened and the Ford versus BMW struggle was terminated after just two races. The works CSLs moved on to the important American IMSA arena in 1975 with turbocharging pushing the power output up towards 850 horsepower. Pitched against the Porsche 935 turbo, temperatures generated from the CSL's engine compartment would make the floor glow and the rear wing was a necessity to keep the tail on the ground. Peterson took part in the final factory CSL outing at Dijon in September, 1976, but the suspension could not take the strain. That finale was in one of a series of BMW "art" racers. this time finished in a graph paper style by the artist Frank Stella.

BMW's two central motorsport constituents, production-related track racers and Formula Two racing powerplants, were brought together in 1977 with the new 3 Series and 320i. In the late '70s the specialist Schnitzer tuning operation and

BMW were jointly developing a 1.4-litre turbo, which ultimately heralded the early '80s Grand Prix engine. For most car makers keen to create or sustain a motorsport heritage, and create a halo effect for their road cars', excellence, a supercar in the portfolio often becomes an essential symbol of corporate virility.

For BMW, the two-seater, mid-engined M1 fulfilled that role for the first and last time in 1978, as the mid '90s McLaren F1 GT-BMW V12 road-racer was a McLaren-generated project. Conceived to challenge Porsche's 911, the M1 had serious birth pangs which included extracting production of the car from a then ailing Lamborghini and transferring it to Baur, the German coach builder. In racing terms the M1 was an alternative to F1 competition and, allegedly, a less expensive option. But due to delays in the project, plans to tackle the troubled Group 5 international category were abandoned and the logic of running one of the most exotic one-make series took root.

Max Mosley and Bernie Ecclestone, destined

Below:
The M3 GTR in the American Le Mans series, 2001

BMW X5s storm to success in the 2004 Dakar Rally, finishing 4th and 8th overall and winning the diesel class. Later it was revealed that the cars had been using the secret two-stage turbocharging system, since released for production in the 535d

"Masterminded by designer Gordon Murray, who had designed the BMW turbo powered Brabhams in the early 1980s, the McLaren F1 used a mid-mounted aluminium BMW V12 engine of 6 litres"

to be the future joint ringmasters of F1, became linked to BMW through the Brabham-BMW project and backed ProCar support races at eight Grands Prix.

With 470 horsepower, the straight-six powered sports coupés were driven by five leading Grand Prix drivers competing against 15 privateer cars for an impressive prize fund. There was a prize of $5,000 for a win, plus $50 a lap for each one that a non-F1 driver led a Grand Prix racer.

Though this form of racing was related to production cars, it cost BMW the equivalent of a contemporary F1 team's seasonal budget. Niki Lauda and Nelson Piquet were respective 1979 and 1980 ProCar champions but they were not challenged by Ferrari F1 drivers, whose team barred them from supporting the BMW enterprise.

M1s registered limited wider success including class wins at Le Mans between 1981 and 1985 and the "art car" movement applied the classic French endurance track layout and that of its Nurburgring counterpart as novel liveries. Another M1 appeared at Le Mans in 1979 as a high-speed piece of Andy Warhol art work. Out of a total production run of 456 M1s, 49 were racing machines.

The ultra successful CSL 'Batmobile' was always going to be a hard act to follow on international race tracks, particularly as privately-run cars continued to compete and win up until the end of 1979. Its farewell tour involved winning 12 of the 13 ETC rounds to grasp a sixth European title. During 1980 and 1981 BMW gave only tacit support to independent preparation houses running the 635CSi in the restricted Group 2 formula but the privately run cars managed a handful of wins, including the Tourist Trophy at Silverstone in 1980. In conjunction with Schnitzer, the big coupé was homologated for the technically less restrictive and well-supported Group A discipline in 1983. That European Touring Car series was a vintage battle between the Bavarian marque's Schnitzer-prepared cars and the Jaguars of Tom Walkinshaw, previously a successful driver, BMW entrant and UK championship mastermind. The climax was at the tawdry Zolder track in Belgium with the German and English factory teams on five wins apiece. BMW stalwart Dieter Quester won the race, bringing BMW's tally of ETC titles to 13 in 17 years.

BMW surrendered the championship to Jaguar in 1984 and Volvo the following year but

gained consolation from maintaining the institution of winning the Spa 24 hours with a 635 CSi.

The CSi's swansong came in 1986 with Roberto Ravaglia becoming champion by one point from the Rover V8 of Britain's Win Percy. With the M3 undergoing development, the 635 CSi was officially pensioned off after the smaller and lighter stablemate, with less than 300 horsepower, proved significantly faster in a comparative time trial. It may not have possessed the presence and spectacle of BMW's large racing coupés but the ubiquitous M3, which raced, rallied and hill-climbed to such effect between 1987 and 1992, became the marque's most successful touring car racer.

Requiring a 5,000-car production run to qualify for Group A and N competition, the E30 and later post-1992 E36 M3s, demonstrated BMW's thoroughness. Between 1985 and 1990 more than 22,300 production M3 saloons were built for Europe and the US. Some 330 motorsport "kits" were supplied by 1991. 1987 and 1988 netted the first and last world touring car championship, the European series and numerous national titles.

On paper rather than on tarmac, the M3's 360 horsepower left it breathless against the muscular turbocharged Ford Sierra Cosworths in 1987. In reality the BMWs could run nearer their optimum pace for longer, with lower fuel consumption, lower tyre wear and less drastic use of brake pads.

Rallying, always something of a Cinderella department within BMW Motorsport, gave BMW a single World Rally Championship victory on the 1987 Tour de Corse, with a UK Prodrive-operated M3 driven a Belgian, Bernard Beguin. Success for the M3 in Britain's frantically competitive touring car championship became almost institutionalised as BMW dealer and Alpina distributor Frank Sytner won the 1988 title. In 1991 an E30 M3 carried Will Hoy to the same championship, with Tim Harvey emulating him with an E36 Coupé version one year later, while a similar car maintained the record driven by Jo Winkelhock in 1993.

The E46 incarnation continues that M3 success in domestic championships, with mainly Group N 320iS ; BMW Team Deutschland captured yet another European touring car title in 2003.

Some things in racing never change, and the on-track battles (and showroom brand rivalry) between BMW and Alfa-Romeo since the 1960s endure. In 2003 BMW won the manufacturers' series by a comfortable margin but Alfa's Italian veteran Gabriele Tarquini took the drivers' crown by a single point from BMW's Jörg Muller of Germany.

BMW competitors, including British ETCC rookie Andy Priaulx, who finished third, took seven out of the top ten drivers' points places. History also repeated itself in the mid 1990s when BMW became involved in a second supercar road and racing car project, the McLaren F1 BMW V12.

Unlike the M1, this time round the project was not hatched in-house but came at the behest of McLaren, who had extensive experience of working with BMW on touring car racing projects.

Masterminded by designer Gordon Murray (who designed the BMW-powered turbo Brabhams in the early '80s) it used a mid-mounted, aluminium, 6-litre V12 BMW engine. In production form, three occupants sat abreast with the driver in the middle; home comforts included air conditioning and a powerful stereo sound system, but no power steering.

By winning on its debut at Le Mans in 1995, a feat only repeated by one other manufacturer (Ferrari with the 166MM in 1949) it added the French sports car classic to McLaren's Grand Prix triumphs and Indianapolis successes. It also provided useful experience to help BMW triumph four years later on the same event with its own pure-bred car in partnership with Williams.

14

Brand stretch

Technology leap helps stylish new 7 Series overtake Mercedes

Second 7 Series (E32)

→ 1986 – 1994
→ Major strides in style and engineering
→ Dramatically increased electronic content
→ Launched BMW's V12 engine
→ Outsold Mercedes S-Class for the first time
→ Advanced V8 engines in 1992
→ Put BMW on a level with Mercedes-Benz

It was not only in its engineering and its dynamics that the original BMW 7 Series, dating back to 1976, was beginning to feel its age: by the early 1980s its slab-sided body, pointedly aggressive nose and upright cabin had begun to look embarrassingly dated too. This was especially true in relation to its most important and most sensitive rival, the Mercedes S-Class, half a model generation younger but more aerodynamic and looking very much less old fashioned.

BMW knew it needed an ultra-modern luxury car to get itself noticed in this highly status-conscious class; it also knew that if it was to be considered in the same breath as the Mercedes S-Class it would have to score some notable technical advances. So that is precisely what BMW did, launching what became dubbed the "Wunderauto", or miracle car, in September 1986.

The company had not been idle: for some time it had been working on a large V12 engine for the luxury class and had been close to launching it in the then-current 7 Series in the summer of 1979 when concerns about fuel shortages led the company to hastily substitute the six-cylinder turbo. BMW knew Mercedes had shelved its plans for a V12, so there was every chance that the second-generation 7 Series

could score a big publicity coup over Mercedes and become the first German car to carry a 12-cylinder engine since the 1930s.

Yet even the 'standard' 7 Series caused gasps of wonderment when it appeared that September. Most strikingly, it had real style. Claus Luthe's shape ditched the angular lines and flat planes of recent BMWs and opted instead for softer, gently curving surfaces with a lower, friendlier version of the familiar BMW face at the front and a raised deckline at the rear, giving a dignified, but nevertheless modern profile with a hint of a wedge to it. At the rear, the stepped tail-lights were a distinctive feature that would become as much a BMW brand signature as the double-kidney grille.

Inside the 730i and 735i – the two versions

The E32 7 Series of 1986 marked the moment where BMW put real style into its flagship model. It was to prove a turning point for the company in its battle for equal status to Mercedes-Benz

155

Right and below:
Front or rear, inside or out,
fast or slow – the second-
generation 7 Series
presented a harmonious
picture

Specifications	730i	735i	730i V8	740i	750i
Engine					
Engine type	Inline 6-cylinder	Inline 6-cylinder	90-degree V8	90-degree V8	60-degree V12
Bore & stroke, mm	89 x 80	92 x 86	84 x 67.6	89 x 80	84 x 75
Capacity, cc	2986	3430	2997	3982	4988
Valves	12	12	32	32	24
Valve actuation	Sohc	Sohc	Dohc per bank	Dohc per bank	Sohc per bank
Compression ratio	9.0:1	9.0:1	10.5:1	10.0:1	8.8:1
Fuelling	Bosch Motronic electronic fuel injection	Bosch Motronic electronic fuel injection	Bosch Motronic M 3.3 electronic engine management	Bosch Motronic M 3.3 electronic engine management	Dual Bosch Motronic electronic fuel injection
Max power, bhp @ rpm	188@5800	211@5700	218@5800	286@5800	300@5200
Max torque, Nm @ rpm	260@4000	305@4000	290@4500	400@4500	450@4100
Transmission					
Manual transmission	5-speed	5-speed	5-speed	Not available	Not available
Automatic	ZF 4-speed optional	ZF 4-speed optional	ZF 5-speed optional	ZF 5-speed standard	ZF 4-speed standard
Drive	Rear wheels	Rear wheels	Rear wheels	Rear wheels	Rear wheels
Chassis					
Front suspension	MacPherson struts	MacPherson struts	MacPherson struts	MacPherson struts	MacPherson struts
Rear suspension	Semi-trailing arms, coil spring/damper units	Semi-trailing arms, coil spring/damper units	Semi-trailing arms, coil spring/damper units	Semi-trailing arms, coil spring/damper units; optional self-levelling	Semi-trailing arms, coil spring/damper units; self-levelling
Braking	Disc, servo assisted; ABS	Disc, servo assisted; ABS	Disc, servo assisted; ABS	Disc, servo assisted; ABS	Disc, servo assisted; ABS
Steering	ZF recirculating ball, power assisted	ZF recirculating ball, power assisted	ZF recirculating ball, power assisted	ZF recirculating ball, power assisted	ZF recirculating ball, power assisted
Wheels	6.5 x 15	7.0 x 15	7.0 x 15	7.0 x 15	7.0 x 15
Tyres	205/65 VR 15	225/60 ZR 15	225/60 ZR 15	225/60 ZR 15	225/60 ZR 15
Body					
Structure	Steel monocoque	Steel monocoque	Steel monocoque	Steel monocoque	Steel monocoque
Wheelbase, mm	2833	2833 (L version 2947)	2833 (L version 2947	2833 (L version 2947)	2833 (L version 2947)
Track F/R, mm	1530/1558	1530/1558	1530/1558	1530/1558	1530/1558
Length, mm	4910	4910 (L version 5024)	4910(L version 5024	4910 (L version 5024)	4910 (L version 5024)
Width, mm	1845	1845	1845	1845	1845
Height, mm	1411	1411	1411	1411	1411
Kerb weight, kg	1720	1720	1720	1810	1870
Fuel tank capacity, lit	90	90	90	90	102
Performance					
Max speed, km/h	222	230	233	240	250 (limited)
0-100 km/h	9.3	8.3	8.5	7.4	7.4
Fuel consumption , lit/100km	11.7	11.4	10.9	11.9	13.2
Marketing					
Launch date	2/86	9/86	9/91	11/91	5/87
Pricing, DM	60,570	72,570	86,000	100,000	98,000

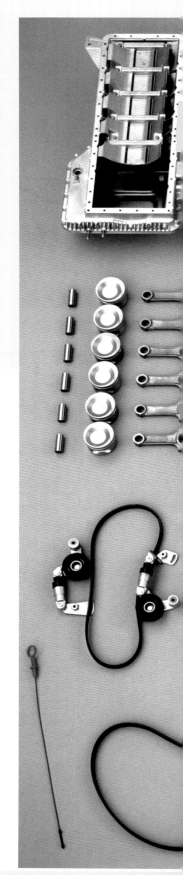

Left:
Straight six engine had reached a high level of development but competitors had V8s

Right:
Anatomy of an aristocratic engine: BMW's pivotal 1987 5-litre V12 taken apart

initially offered – BMW showed the world once again how cockpit design should be done, scoring further advances in ergonomics and introducing a whole raft of electrical and electronic systems never before seen on a car. Among these were position memories for the front seats and door mirrors: the nearside rear-view mirror even dipped to give a view of the kerb and the rear wheel to aid reversing, while the wipers automatically reduced in speed as the car slowed; the functions of the on-board computer were expanded massively, the air conditioning became full climate control, the automatic transmission offered four speeds and a choice of modes, and electronics regulated wheelspin under acceleration. In short, there was no car more advanced than the 735i, and even the Jaguar XJ40 launched at the same time looked positively simplistic by comparison.

But while BMW had made radical changes in the image the 7 Series presented to the outside world, its mechanical elements – certainly on the initial versions – were developed directly from the highly-regarded systems fitted to the previous generation cars. The 3.0 and 3.5 litre six-cylinder engines gave 188 and 211 bhp resectively, which against a respectable weight of 1720 kg provided top speeds of 222 and 230 km/h and 0-100 km/h acceleration in 9.3 and 8.3 seconds. On the road the most impressive aspect of the 7 Series was its ability to be driven quickly, handle tidily and enjoyably and yet maintain excellent ride comfort thanks to its adjustable dampers.

Buyers did not have to wait long for the technical highlight of this range, the car that would finally cement BMW's equality in status with Mercedes-Benz and which would play an important role in helping the top BMW surge past the top Mercedes in the sales charts. August 1987 was a psychologically memorable month for BMW, for it marked the first deliveries of the 750i, the first German car for half a century with a 12-cylinder engine.

As Eberhard von Kuenheim, BMW chairman throughout the era of rapid growth, recalls, the jump to the V12 was a deliberate strategic move

The all-aluminium V12 gave 300 bhp in its initial form for 750i: external identification points include broader grilles, flatter alloy wheels and twin square exhaust tailpipes; this is the long wheelbase version. Special Individual cabin treatment from Karl Lagerfeld is from 1992 and includes silver-grey leather and special wood finishes

designed to allow BMW to leapfrog over Mercedes and assume technical superiority:

"Towards the middle of the 1980s, the 7 Series was doing very well. We were convinced that our six-cylinder engine was the best thing in world at that time, and every wisdom in those days said we should progress upwards to a V8, which was seen as the state-of-the-art engine for an elite car. All the market research said we should go to the V8, too – but I disappointed a lot of people and I said 'no I am against this, full stop.' Instead, I said we should go straight to the V12. That was a very important decision for BMW: it was absolutely against the conventional rules but it meant we that we jumped over the competitors. We launched the engine and went on to make two thirds of all 12-cylinder products in the world. This gave us such a high ranking, and ever since that time we have been on the same level of status as Mercedes."

Technical commentators could only stare in astonished admiration when they examined the massive, all-aluminium five-litre engine. Developing an easy 300 bhp, the M70 V12 was in reality two six-cylinders joined together: each

bank of six had its own injection system, its own mapped ignition system and its own catalyst; in cases of emergency the engine could run on one bank only.

With its prodigious power the 750i became the first BMW to have its top speed electronically limited to 250 km/h, the company citing its sense of social responsibility for the move – though some insist it was because there were no tyres available which could withstand the stress of a two-tonne car travelling at perhaps 300 km/h for extended periods.

As well as an altogether new dimension in smoothness, silence and effortless performance, the 750i also provided many technical innovations that are now considered essential in any luxury car. It introduced ultrasonic park distance control, for instance, and it pioneered 'soft-close' doors and bootlid, and it was the first with xenon gas discharge headlights. Long wheelbase versions of the 750i – and indeed the 735i – even had electrically adjustable rear seats. The options list for the 750 ran to every conceivable business-executive gadget for the rear seat area. Externally, the V12 was distinguished by

"Buyers did not have to wait long for the technical highlight of this range, the car that would finally cement BMW's equality in status with Mercedes-Benz. August 1987 was a psychologically memorable month for BMW, for it marked the first deliveries of the 750i, the first German car with a 12-cylinder engine for half a century"

Left:
Poles apart: not since the 502 of the early 1950s had a BMW boasted a V8 engine

Opposite and opposite below:
BMW replaced its 3.5 litre six with 3.0 and 4.0 litre V8s in 1992. The extra cylinders brought greater smoothness, but initial versions lacked the six's torquey feel

"To the historian in touch with the era, the 7 Series will always be the model which scored that proud victory over Mercedes-Benz to put BMW back on top"

wider kidney grilles at the front and by dual square cross-section exhausts at the rear.

It was just two years before the E32 7 Series gave way to the 1994 E38 that BMW introduced a new generation of advanced, all-aluminium V8 engines to replace the familiar sixes. The M60 powerplants, BMW's first V8s since Ischinger's classic design of the 1950s, had four valves per cylinder and twin overhead camshafts per bank, an impeccable specification which gave the three litre unit in the new 730i 218 bhp and the four-litre 286 bhp for the 740i. These were impressive outputs and usefully higher than the figures for the sixes, and on the road the cars were supremely smooth and refined; nevertheless, some critics found that the V8s, especially the heavily oversquare three-litre, lacked torque and were less spirited in action than the sixes. Perhaps for this reason BMW continued to offer the six-cylinder 730i alongside the V8: the V8 was a clear DM 11,000 more expensive than the six and was identified, along with the 740i V8, by

the same wide kidney grilles as the 750i, though the exhaust outlets were oval, not square.

The 750i made a useful contribution to science when BMW engineers converted an example to run on hydrogen, stored in a pressurised tank in the boot and pumped through the V12 engine like conventional fuel. BMW chose the mighty V12 for this early zero-emissions vehicle because at that time an internal combustion engine running on hydrogen developed only half its normal power – and the 750i was one of the few cars which could run perfectly normally on half power.

The second-generation 7 Series ended its production run just when it appeared to have got into its stride – and certainly well before it had begun to seem dated. Company accountants may remember it as the car in which BMW invested more than the usual millions of Marks but to the historian more in tune with the era, it will always be the model which scored that proud victory over Mercedes to put BMW back on top.

E32
SECOND 7 SERIES E32 PRODUCTION

Production History:	In production: 1986-94			Total produced 311,015			
model	730i/730iL	735i/735iL	730iV8/730iV8L	740i/740iL	750i/750iL	total for year	SKD
1986	528	6,734			3	7,265	5
1987	15,304	34,446			4,860	54,610	996
1988	15,454	26,577			14,657	56,688	1,440
1989	14,619	20,840			9,064	44,523	1,033
1990	13,214	20,808			8,791	42,813	690
1991	11,913	16,375	114	44	6,527	34,973	810
1992	6,568	4,740	7,992	9,576	2,816	31,692	540
1993	3,156		5,558	15,260	1,418	25,392	588
1994	603		675	5,307	162	6,747	210
total	81,539	130,520	14,399	30,187	42,298		6,312
				grand total		304,703	
				grand total inc SKD		311,015	

163

15

Third 5 series (E34)

→ 1988 – 1996
→ Brought style to BMW's large car line
→ Shared engines with 7 Series and 3 Series
→ Big success with buyers
→ Touring estate broadened appeal
→ First electronically-injected diesel
→ M5 versions set new dynamic standards
→ First large BMW to sell over a million

On a level with Mercedes

Fresh 5 Series takes new 7's style to a broad audience and finds new friends

If the new 7 Series had been the car that gave BMW its big breakthrough in style, in image and in acceptability, then this, the third-generation 5 Series, was the car which took advantage of that breakthrough to win new friends and truly level the score with the arch-opponent Mercedes-Benz.

The previous 5 Series had looked old-fashioned even before it drove out of the garage. It was only once people knew how well it drove, how smooth it was, how exciting the M5 was, that they began to appreciate the shape and what the engineering underneath it could deliver. It was like fine chocolates in a dull cardboard box: boring on the surface but enjoyable inside.

The new, 1988-model 5 Series was different: very different. You could tell it was different even from a distance of 100 metres. This was no plain-paper wrapper, no anti-style statement intended to let the engineering do the talking: here, just as with the enthusiastically-received 7 Series a year earlier, was evidence in metal, glass, leather and every known automotive material that BMW was at last giving style equal billing to engineering.

To say that the 5 Series was a scaled-down version of the 7 was a compliment, not a criticism. The exterior design had very much the same gentle

wedge feel, with a low front rising to the raised, slightly coupé-like rear; it was subtly streamlined, but not an amorphous aerodynamic blob like some of its peers. Inside, passengers sat lower and more securely, less exposed to others' gazes than in the glassy, low-waisted previous model. If anything, the design of the 5 was better resolved than that of the 7, especially around the rear pillars and rear window: the proportions worked better than any mid-sized BMW since the 1930s.

It was not only in its appearance that the new model could count itself a smaller 7 Series: much of the chassis thinking was shared with the big sister, as were the two top engines – the M30 sixes of 2986 cc and 188 bhp and 3430 cc and 211 bhp for the 530i and 535i respectively. Thanks to the improved aerodynamics of the new body these models were able to post impressive top speeds of 215 and 230 km/h – an important selling point in the derestricted Autobahn

Three generations of 5 Series: the 1988 version took a radical rather than cautious tack in its design and became a major success

165

Above and right:
Both in its profile and in its interior, the new 5 Series came across as a scaled-down version of the already acclaimed 7 – a useful boost to its status

environment of their main market, Germany.

Lesser models ranged downwards from the M20-engined sixes with 170 bhp (525i) and 129 bhp (520i); also included was the 2.4 litre six-cylinder turbodiesel from the 3 Series, giving the same 115 bhp. BMW had originally intended the range to be six-cylinder only, but pressure from export markets prompted the introduction of the 1.8 litre 518i, on 118 bhp: this, along with the original diesel, was the only model not to be able to exceed the 200 km/h mark.

The positives came thick and fast as soon as the test drive reports began coming in: the six-cylinder engines were smooth and sweet, the steering was sporty and accurate, and the ride comfort was the equal of anything in the class. The contrast with the stodgy, underpowered Mercedes 200-300 range could not have been clearer: with the only real criticism of the 5 Series being the lack of feel of the new, optional, Servotronic power steering on the top 535i, BMW was at last getting on to buyers' shopping lists, if not yet gaining the upper hand.

The 535i was in any case a potent match for Mercedes' then-top 300E – but more was to come with the sensational M5 which arrived with surprising promptness before 1988 was out. With a new version of the famous 24-valve Motorsport S38 straight six it drew 315

"This was no plain-paper wrapper, no anti-style statement intended to let the engineering do the talking: here was evidence in metal, glass, leather and every known automotive material that BMW was at last giving style equal billing to engineering"

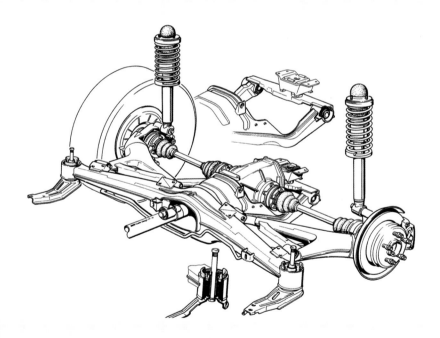

Above and left:
The principal mechanical elements for the new 45 Series were drawn from both the outgoing model and the larger 7 Series: engines were initially all straight sixes, but a four-cylinder and two V8s were added later

"The sophisticated diesel was smoother and more responsive than any other on the market and soon became a strong seller, accounting for more than one fifth of all models sold in 1992"

horsepower from its 3.6 litres: despite extensive suspension and braking upgrades the car's top speed was electronically limited to 250 km/h, while 100 km/h was reached in just 6.5 seconds. Following the example of the previous M5, the new model was again exemplary in its smoothness, in its ease of driving and in the discreetness of its exterior. It would be two years before Mercedes could respond with its V8-engined 500E.

In typical BMW fashion a significant upgrade was slipped in as a running change when the new twin overhead camshaft 24-valve M50 engines replaced the long-serving 12-valve sixes in the 520i and 525i: the power outputs were substantially higher at 150 and 192 bhp, leading to the dropping of the 530i, but some critics insisted that the new units were not as silky-

smooth as their predecessors.

One area where BMW had always trailed Mercedes was in the variety of body types offered: BMW was only present in the saloon sector, while Mercedes also had a coupé and an increasingly successful estate. BMW's response arrived at the 1991 Frankfurt show in the shape of the 5 Series Touring, a stylish BMW take on the estate theme: engineered with typical BMW originality, it had a novel tailgate with a separately hinged rear window, allowing users to post in smaller items without having to open the whole tailgate – and without any risk of items already in the cargo area falling out. The Touring also had an optional double sunroof of fiendish complexity, allowing owners endless combinations of opening which took intensive study of the handbook to master.

Right and opposite:
The major move on the third-generation 5 Series was the launch of a stylish Touring estate, broadening the model's market reach significantly. BMW had engineered a complex tailgate in which the rear window could be opened separately from the main cargo door

Also added (this time to counter the 4WD threat from the Mercedes 4-Matic) were four-wheel-drive versions of the both saloon and Touring, labelled 525iX and using the drivetrain from the smaller 3 Series, and the advanced 525tds which, as the world's first electronically controlled turbodiesel gave 143 bhp to become the only high-performance diesel on the market and the first to exceed 200 km/h.

The sophisticated diesel was smoother and more responsive than any other on the market and soon became a strong seller, accounting for more than one fifth of all models sold in 1992: with the Touring the proportion was even higher

at one third. The centre of gravity of the sales had always been between the 520i and 525i, but that year saw a step-up in the sales of the larger-capacity models as BMW brought in the powerful 3.0 and 4.0 V8 engines from the 7 Series. The resultant 540i was especially potent with its 286 bhp and 7.5-second surge to 100 km/h.

The early V8s, along with the equivalent 7 Series models, suffered well-publicised problems in the US when high sulphur-content fuel destroyed the Nikasil coating lining the aluminium cylinder bores: a switch to Alusil blocks in 1996 cured the problem. Americans had further cause to regret the 540i, however, for

E34: 5 SERIES

Specifications	520i	525i	530i	535i	M5 (1998-91)
Engine					
Engine type	Inline six cylinder,	Inline six cylinder,	Inline six cylinder,	Inline six cylinder,	Inline six cylinder,
Bore & stroke, mm	80 x 66	84 x 75	89 x 80	92 x 86	93.4 x 86
Capacity, cc	1991	2494	2986	3430	3535
Valves	12	12	12	12	24
Valve actuation	sohc	Sohc	Sohc	Sohc	dohc
Compression ratio	8.6:1 (1980 on: 9.5:1)	8.8:1	9.0:1	8.8:1	10.0:1
Fuelling	Bosch Motronic electronic fuel injection	Bosch Motronic electronic fuel injection	Bosch Motronic electronic fuel injection	Bosch Motronic electronic fuel injection	Bosch Motronic electronic fuel injection
Max power, bhp @ rpm	129@6000	170@5800	188@5800	211@5700	315@6900
Max torque, Nm @ rpm	164@4300	222@4300	290@4000	305@4000	360@4300
Transmission					
Manual transmission	5-speed	5-speed	5-speed	5-speed	5-speed
Automatic	ZF 4-speed optional	ZF 4-speed optional	ZF 4-speed optional	ZF 4-speed optional	
Drive	Rear wheels	Rear wheels	Rear wheels	Rear wheels	Rear wheels
Chassis					
Front suspension	MacPherson strut	MacPherson struts	MacPherson struts	MacPherson struts	MacPherson struts
Rear suspension	Semi-trailing arms, coil-spring/damper units	Semi-trailing arms, coil-spring/damper units	Semi-trailing arms, coil-spring/damper units, hydropneumatic self-levelling	Semi-trailing arms, coil-spring/damper units, hydropneumatic self-levelling	Semi-trailing arms, coil-spring/damper units, hydropneumatic self-levelling, electronic damper control
Braking	Disc, servo assisted; ABS optional	Disc, servo assisted; ABS	Disc, servo assisted; ABS	Disc, servo assisted; ABS	Disc, servo assisted; ABS
Steering	ZF recirculating ball, power assisted	ZF recirculating ball, power assisted	ZF recirculating ball, power assisted	ZF recirculating ball, power assisted	ZF recirculating ball, power assisted
Wheels	6.0 x 15	6.5 x 15	6.5 x 15	7.0 x 15	8.0 x 17 forged
Tyres	195/65 HR 15	195/65 VR 15	205/65 VR 15	225/60 VR 15	235/45 ZR 17
Body					
Structure	Steel monocoque	Steel monocoque	Steel monocoque	Steel monocoque	Steel monocoque
Wheelbase, mm	761	2761	2761	2761	2761
Track F/R, mm	1470/1495	1470/1495	1470/1495	1470/1495	1470/1495
Length, mm	4720	4720	4720	4720	4720
Width, mm	1751	1751	1751	1751	1751
Height, mm	1412	1412	1412	1412	1412
Kerb weight, kg	1480	1530	1590	1620	1720
Fuel tank capacity, lit	80	80	80	80	80
Performance					
Max speed, km/h	200	220	210	225	250 (limited)
0-100km/h	12.0	9.5	8.6	7.7	6.5
Fuel consumption , lit/100 km	11.0	11.0	12.0	13.5	15.5
Marketing					
Launch date	11/87	11/87	11/87	11/87	9/88
Pricing, DM	38,500	47,000	69,500	62,000	101,800

M5 (1992-95)

Inline six cylinder,
94.6 x 90
3795
24
Dohc
10.5:1
Bosch Motronic electronic
fuel injection
340@6900
400@4750

5-speed (1994 on: 6-speed)

Rear wheels

MacPherson struts
Semi-trailing arms, coil-
spring/damper units, hydrop
neumatic self-levelling,
electronic damper control
Disc, servo assisted; ABS

ZF recirculating ball, power
assisted
8.0 x 17 forged
235/45 ZR 17

Steel monocoque
2761
1470/1495
4720
1751
1412
1720
80

250 (limited)
6.3
15.5

3/92
120,000

V8 engines replaced the
bigger sixes from 1992,
with a broader BMW grille
as the external indication

E34: 5 SERIES DERIVATIVES

Specifications	518i	518g	525td	525tds	525iX
Engine					
Engine type	Inline 4-cylinder petrol	Inline 4-cylinder / natural gas	Inline 6-cylinder turbo diesel	Inline 6-cylinder intercooled turbo diesel	Inline 6-cylinder petrol
Capacity, cc	1796	1796	2443/2498	2498	2494
Max power, bhp @ rpm	113@5500	115@5500 (petrol); 101(natural gas)	115@4800	143@4800	192@5900
Max torque, Nm @ rpm	162@4250	168@3900 (petrol); 142 (natural gas)	222@1900	260@2200	251@4500
Transmission					
Manual transmission	5-speed	5-speed	5-speed	5-speed	5-speed
Automatic	ZF 4-speed	Not available	ZF 4-speed	ZF 4-speed	ZF 5-speed
Drive	Rear wheels	Rear wheels	Rear wheels	Rear wheels	All 4 wheels via central differential
Chassis					
Wheels/Tyres	195/65 HR 15	195/65 HR 15	195/65 HR 15	205/65 VR 15	225/55 VR 15
Body					
Kerb weight, kg	1400	1545	1485	1500	1610
Performance					
Max speed, km/h	190	192 (gas: 183)	190	205	215
0-100km/h	12.5	13.2 (gas: 16.2)	13.5	12.0	10.5
Fuel consumption , lit/100 km	11.0	8.6 (gas 5.6)	10.0	9.5	13.0
Marketing					
Launch date	9/89	12/95	11/87	9/91	9/91
Pricing, DM	43,500 (1993)	57,000	41,000	49,900	65,750

Specifications	520i (1990 on)	525i (1990 on)	530i (1992 on)	540i
Engine				
Cylinders	Inline 6-cylinder	Inline 6-cylinder	90-degree V8	90-degree V8
Capacity, cc	1991	2494	2997	3982
Valves	Dohc 24	Dohc 24	Dohc per bank, 32V	Dohc per bank, 32V
Fuelling	Bosch Motronic electronic	Bosch Motronic electronic fuel injection	Bosch Motronic electronic fuel injection	Bosch Motronic electronic fuel injection
fuel injection				
Max power, bhp @ rpm	150@5900	192@5900	218@5800	286@5800
Max torque, Nm @ rpm	190@4300	251@4500	290@4500	400@4500
Transmission				
Manual transmission	5-speed	5-speed	5-speed	5-speed
Automatic	ZF 4-speed (1992 on: 5-speed)	ZF 4-speed (1992 on: 5-speed)	ZF 5-speed	ZF 5-speed
Drive	Rear wheels	Rear wheels	Rear wheels	Rear wheels
Chassis				
Front suspension	MacPherson struts	MacPherson struts	MacPherson struts	MacPherson struts
Rear suspension	Semi-trailing arms, coil-spring/damper units	Semi-trailing arms, coil-spring/damper units	Semi-trailing arms, coil-spring/damper units; hydropneumatic self-levelling	Semi-trailing arms, coil-spring/damper units; hydropneumatic self-levelling
Braking	Disc, servo assisted; ABS	Disc, servo assisted; ABS	Disc, servo assisted; ABS	Disc, servo assisted; ABS
Steering	ZF recirculating ball, power assisted	ZF recirculating ball, power assisted	ZF recirculating ball, power assisted	ZF recirculating ball, power assisted
Wheels	6.0 x 15	6.0 x 15	7.0 x 15	7.0 x 15
Tyres	195/65 HR 15	195/65 VR 15	225/60 ZR 15	225/60 ZR 15
Body				
Length, mm	4720	4720	4720	4720
Width, mm	1751	1751	1751	1751
Height, mm	1412	1412	1412	1412
Kerb weight, kg	1475	1475	1610	1650
Performance				
Max speed, km/h	205	225	230	240
0-100km/h	11.5	9.0	8.0	7.5
Fuel consumption , lit/100 km	12.0	12.5	12.5	14.5
Marketing				
Launch date	5/90	5/90	7/92	7/92
Pricing, DM	42,600	51,600	69,500	82,000

BMW Grafik Design VT–13

"It was an unqualified success, not just as a car which was universally liked and easily sold, but as the model which saw BMW level-pegging with Mercedes-Benz. And as such it enjoys a very special place in BMW history"

Driveline variations included a four-wheel drive system (far left) common to the 3 Series, labelled 525iX; the 2.5 litre turbo diesel was offered with or without intercooler; both sold strongly.

its proximity in power to the M5 had led the importers to drop the beloved M-car from the US catalogue. There was some solace when BMW compensated by producing a limited run of 200 540i Sport special editions with the suspension and cosmetic trimmings of the M5 but the V8 engine of the 540; some of these had the desirable six-speed manual transmission.

The second iteration of the M5, from 1992 to the end of the 5 Series production run in 1995, was more impressive still. Expanded to 3.8 litres and 340 bhp, it was available as a Touring, too: both models were astonishingly fast and well behaved, but neither made it to the United States.

One last venture for this 5 Series came right at the end when the dual-fuel 518g Touring, running on either compressed natural gas or pump petrol, was developed. It cost more than the standard 518, had inferior performance on gas, and was dropped after fewer than 300 had found buyers.

Gas cars apart, there was plenty of life left in the E34 5 Series when it was replaced by the deceptively similar-looking E39 in September 1995: over 1.3 million had been made, 123,000 of them Tourings, 200,000 of them diesels and 11,000 of them M5s. It was an unqualified success, not just as a car which was universally liked and easily sold, but as the model which saw BMW level-pegging with Mercedes-Benz. And as such it enjoys a very special place in BMW history.

E34 SEDAN / TOURING

Specifications	Sedan	Touring
Type		
Wheelbase, mm	2760	2760
Track F/R, mm	1470/1495	1470/1495
Length, mm	4720	4720
Width, mm	1750	1750
Height, mm	1410	1420
Kerb weight, kg	–	Sedan +55-85 kg
Fuel tank capacity, lit	80	80
Marketing		
Launch date	1/88	9/91
Pricing, DM	–	Sedan +4,000 – 5,000

"The second iteration of the M5 was more impressive still. Expanded to 3.8 litres and 340 bhp, it was available as a Touring, too: both models were astonishingly fast and well behaved, but neither made it to the United States"

E34 THIRD 5 SERIES SEDAN PRODUCTION

Production History:	In production: 1987-96							Total produced 1,182,942				
model	518i	520i	525i	525iX	530i	535i	540i	M5	524td/ 525td	525tds	total for year	SKD
1987		90	68		76	1,845			57		2,136	
1988		50,814	45,060		12,279	27,766		331	14,188		150,438	1,050
1989	2,601	67,120	70,076		6,894	22,456		2,339	22,062		193,548	8,245
1990	8,969	75,064	69,967		1,030	12,772		3,022	21288	5	192,117	8,407
1991	7,343	71,375	61,122	556		5,652		2,153	13250	7,641	169,092	6618
1992	6,735	42,737	44,776	2,223	3,347	58	1,800	1,782	1	27,460	130,919	2,814
1993	8,368	25,576	32,300	945	13,531		9,960	773	6196	16,123	113,772	5,370
1994	5,523	28,784	33,686	701	9,085		6,857	483	5505	19,371	109,995	5,832
1995	6,741	22,263	27,905	358	4,280		4,027	215	2,855	9,851	78,495	4,086
1996	2	3	1		1		1				8	
totals	46,282	383,826	384,961	4,783	50,523	70,549	22,645	11,098	85,402	80,451		42,422
										grand total	1,140,520	
										grand total inc SKD	1,182,942	

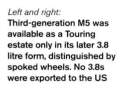

Left and right:
Third-generation M5 was available as a Touring estate only in its later 3.8 litre form, distinguished by spoked wheels. No 3.8s were exported to the US

Left:
M5 engine attained further heights of power and potency, finally reaching 3.8 litres and 340 horsepower. Like the exterior, the M5's cabin was underplayed and classy

THIRD 5 SERIES E34 TOURING PRODUCTION

Production History:	In production: 1990-96						Total produced 123,813			
model	518i Touring	520i Touring	525i Touring	525iX Touring	530i Touring	540i Touring	525td Touring	525tds Touring	total for year	SKD
1990		1							1	
1991		544	1,051	18				116	1,729	
1992	1	9,374	11,713	2,165	881		1	9,758	33,893	
1993	1,977	5,377	3,761	897	2,729	398	1,700	9,340	26,179	
1994	1,992	5,454	4,581	736	919	1,200	1,709	9,854	26,445	
1995	1,916	6,460	4,835	637	612	709	1,137	9,806	26,112	
1996	1,037	3,295	1,373	130	125	152	230	3,064	9,406	
totals	6,923	30,505	27,314	4,583	5,266	2,459	4,777	41,938		
								grand total	123,765	
								grand total inc SKD	123,813	
								derivative totals: sedan	1,182,942	
								Touring	123,813	
								Series total	1,306,755	

Z1

8 Series (E31)

Two extravagant dead-ends

Grand 850i coupé and novel-construction Z1 both fail to catch on

The whisper just prior to the unveiling of the BMW 850i in September 1989 was that the design had been kept on ice for some time before BMW had decided to press the 'go' button: the story was that there had been indecision on what, if anything, should replace the long-running 6 Series coupé, whose sales had been holding up better than expected. When the car's shape was finally shown it became clear that those rumours could indeed have been true: the 850's exaggerated wedge profile was reminiscent of another era, its toy-like BMW grille and pop-up lights recalled the Turbo concept of 1972 and its poor packaging had strong echoes of the Jaguar XJS of the mid 1970s.

A rolling showcase for BMW's technological skills, the 1989 850i sits with its illustratrious forbears. For BMW enthusiasts it failed to produce the same nagic

Just like Jaguar, BMW had been seduced by the smoothness and power of its five-litre V12 engine and had resolved to create the ultimate in luxury coupé refinement – and in precisely the same way as the British company BMW had ended up with a large (4.8 metre) and heavy (1800 kg) car with a cramped cabin and a poor boot.

Unlike Jaguar, however, BMW had poured its entire technical expertise into the big coupé. The car that resulted was a rolling showcase for everything advanced, complex or clever: the new multi-link rear suspension had passive rear-steer, later upgraded to active rear axle kinematics, BMW's take on four wheel steering; there was electronic damper control, ASC+T traction control, multiplex wiring, Servotronic steering, a

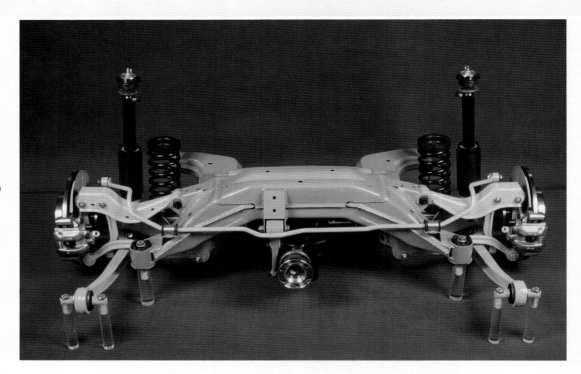

V12-engined 850i introduced a whole range of new technologies, including integral rear axle with active kinematics for rear steering (right); cabin was well designed but very cramped in relation to the car's bulky exterior

water-repellent windscreen and the first six-speed manual gearbox on a production car. Particularly intriguing were the electric windows in the frameless doors: to ensure good sealing at the very high speeds of which the 300 bhp 850i was capable, the window glass rose up a couple of millimetres to press tight against the seal once the door had been closed. The instant the handle was touched to re-open the door, the glass would twitch downwards again to free the glass from the seal. This system became commonplace on BMW products later in the 1990s, but in 1989 it counted as a real technical highlight.

Unfortunately, as with many very complicated cars, the driving experience at the wheel of the 850 did not live up to the promise spelt out by its specification. The later 850 CSi was a more focused sporting model with a 5.6 litre version of the V12 giving 381 bhp: distinguished by a deeper front spoiler and larger and wider rear wheels, it was built by BMW Motorsport GmbH and was one of the first cars to feature dynamic stability control: even so, it failed to hit the mark with customers. Luxury-oriented individuals would choose the Mercedes SL, sport-minded customers the Porsche 911. No one, it seemed, wanted to compromise on the 850.

Installing the lighter V8 engine – again from the 7 Series – made the car less expensive and less weighty to drive, but it was still no sports car.

It soldiered on for 10 years in all: two thirds of the eventual production run of 30,000 were sold in the first three years, leaving Dingolfing producing an average of fewer than five a day until it disappeared, unloved, in 1999. But if the record of other older BMWs is anything to go by, the 850's rarity, originality and engineering significance could eventually find it friends in the collectors' community.

As a model line the 850 was a dead-end. The original intention had been to produce a car to replace the respected 6 Series; the 850 instead jumped a class higher by virtue of its bulky V12 engine, but it did provide a handy laboratory of technologies – the integral rear axle is an example – to enrich future BMW model generations.

The Z1 is an example of a very different process at work, though it, too, did also lead to ultimate failure and loss of both cash and corporate pride, albeit at a somewhat lower level.

The car owes its origins to a research project into alternative materials carried out by BMW in the mid 1980s. BMW was investigating the feasibility of vehicles with plastic body panels attached to a galvanised steel chassis and sub-structure and had built a small two-seater sports roadster as a concept demonstrator for internal use. This prototype unfortunately – or perhaps deliberately – was scooped by a leading

V12 and, later V8 engine gave 8 Series gran turismo rather than supercar performance; final 5.6 litre V12 in manual-only CSi version with much stronger sporting focus gave 381 bhp

E31 8 SERIES

Specifications	840Ci	850Ci	850CSi
Engine			
Type	90-degree V8	60-degree V12	60-degree V12
Bore & stroke, mm	89 x 80 (1996 on: 92 x 82.7)	84 x 75 (1994 on: 85 x 79)	86 x 80
Capacity, cc	3982 (1996 on: 4398)	4988 (1994 on: 5379)	5576
Valves	32	24	24
Valve actuation	Dohc per bank; Vanos variable valve timing	Sohc per bank	Sohc per bank
Compression ratio	10.0:1	8.8:1 (1994 on: 10.0:1)	9.8:1
Fuelling	Bosch Motronic engine management	Dual Bosch Motronic engine management	Dual Bosch Motronic engine management
Max power, bhp @ rpm	286@5800 (1996 on: 5700)	300@5200 (1994 on: 326@5200)	381@6300
Max torque, Nm @ rpm	400@4500 (1996 on: 420@3900)	450@4100 (1994 on: 490@3900)	550@4000
Transmission			
Manual transmission	Getrag, 6-speed	6-speed	6-speed
Automatic	ZF 5-speed	ZF 4-speed or 5-speed; Steptronic from 1995	Not available
Drive	Rear wheels	Rear wheels	Rear wheels
Chassis			
Front suspension	MacPherson struts, lower wishbones	MacPherson struts, lower wishbones	MacPherson struts, lower wishbones
Rear suspension	Multi-link axle, coil springs, self-levelling, electronic damper control	Multi-link axle, coil springs, self-levelling, electronic damper control; active rear-axle kinematics	Multi-link axle, coil springs, self-levelling, electronic damper control
Braking	Disc, servo assistance, ABS	Disc, servo assistance, ABS	Disc, servo assistance, ABS
Steering	Recirculating ball, power assisted	Recirculating ball, power assisted	Recirculating ball, power assisted
Wheels front + rear	7.5 x 16	7.5 x 16	8.0 x 17 + 9.0 x 18
Tyres front + rear	235/50 ZRR 16	235/50 ZRR 16	235/45 ZRR 17 + 265/40 ZR 18
Body			
Structure	Steel monocoque	Steel monocoque	Steel monocoque
Wheelbase, mm	2684	2684	2684
Track F/R, mm	1554/1562	1554/1562	1554/1562
Length, mm	4780	4780	4780
Width, mm	1855	1855	1855
Height, mm	1340	1340	1340
Kerb weight, kg	1780	1780	1780
Fuel tank capacity, lit	90	90	90
Performance			
Max speed, km/h	250 (limited)	250 (limited)	250 (limited)
0-100 km/h, sec	7.4	6.8	6.0
Fuel consumption , lit/100km	11.4	13.0	12.8
Marketing			
Launch date	9/93	5/90	8/92
Pricing, DM	129,000	135,000	180,000

8 SERIES: E31 PRODUCTION

Production History:	In production: 1989-99				Total produced 30,621	
model	830i	840i	850i/ CSi	total for year	SKD	
1989			47	47		
1990			6,704	6,704	12	
1991			9,505	9,505	8	
1992	18		2,427	2,445	4	
1993		1,190	1,905	3,095		
1994		2,066	764	2,830		
1995		1,493	684	2,177		
1996		1,109	356	1,465		
1997		1,140	218	1,358		
1998		552	111	663		
1999		253	55	308		
totals	18	7,803	22,776			
			grand total	30,597		
			grand total inc SKD	30,621		

Steel chassied, plastic bodied Z1 roadster was a new concept for both BMW and the buying public; doors slid down into deep sills for access to interior

"The Z1 has all the ingredients of a future classic: it has a high-class brand name, it is rare, it is novel to look at and reasonably entertaining to drive and, perhaps vitally, it was a failure first time round"

magazine while out on test, and intense speculation followed that BMW was re-entering the sports car market.

Perhaps flattered by this very excited speculation, BMW sprung a big surprise at the 1987 Frankfurt motor show when it wheeled on a fully finished example of the car, which it labelled the Z1 – Z standing for Zukunft, or future. The Z1 was a research vehicle, said BMW, but it might be possible to build it in very small numbers. The press and public reaction was immediate and enthusiastic: the smart little roadster had novel drop-down doors which disappeared down into the substantial sills of the steel chassis, and the 2.5 litre 325i six-cylinder engine up front promised entertaining performance. The car could even be driven with the doors retracted, BMW said.

Almost instantly, some 5,000 buyers ordered Z1s, without even knowing its price or likely performance figures: BMW decided it would triple its production rate to save the customers

from having to wait too long. And that is where things began to go wrong.

As soon as the price was announced – DM 80,000, later raised to 89,000 – interest collapsed and it emerged that most of the supposed customers had been speculators hoping to make a five-figure profit on a high-profile car in short supply. Even before the production cars finally appeared in the spring of 1989 the speculators had been discounting the cars they had ordered: the situation was confused and chaotic.

A further blow to the Z1's already damaged credibility came when people drove the car. Everyone admired the Z1's originality and style, its workmanship and of course its party-trick doors, but for many the driving experience failed to thrill in the way they had expected. The car felt underpowered for a sports roadster, especially as the six-cylinder engine lacked low-down torque and had to fight against a kerb weight of 1290 kg – 100 kg more than the 3 Series saloon with

Specifications	Z1
Engine	
Type	Inline 6-cylinder
Bore & stroke, mm	84 x 75
Capacity, cc	2494
Valves	12
Valve actuation	Sohc
Compression ratio	8.8:1
Fuelling	Bosch Motronic electronic fuel injection
Max power, bhp @ rpm	170@5800
Max torque, Nm @ rpm	222@4300
Transmission	
Manual transmission	5-speed
Automatic	Not available
Drive	Rear wheels
Chassis	
Front suspension	MacPherson struts
Rear suspension	Trailing arms, diagonal links, transverse upper links, coil springs
Braking	Disc, power assisted, ABS
Steering	Rack and pinion, power assisted
Wheels	7.5 x 16
Tyres	225/45 ZR16
Body	
Structure	Steel monocoque chassis frame, bonded composite floor, composite exterior body panels
Wheelbase, mm	2450
Track F/R, mm	1456/1470
Length, mm	3925
Width, mm	1690
Height, mm	1248
Kerb weight, kg	1290
Fuel tank capacity, lit	57
Performance	
Max speed, km/h	220
0-100km/h, sec	9.0
Fuel consumption , lit/100 km	11.0
Marketing	
Launch date	3/89
Pricing, DM	80,000

"The Z1 was rejected by the sportscar establishment but found itself a niche among people wishing to make a design statement or those who enjoyed a gentle drive on a summer weekend"

Right and below:
A Z1 with its composite body panels removed. The car could be driven in this condition as the bodywork was unstressed

the same power unit.

The result was that the Z1 was roundly rejected by the sportscar establishment. Its price was way over the top and its performance was not even up to the level of competitors at two-thirds the cost. Instead, the Z1 found itself a niche among people wishing to make a design statement or those who enjoyed a gentle drive on a summer weekend. BMW resolved to cut its losses and keep manufacture going until the stocks of components had been used up.

The last of the 8,000 rolled off the line in June 1991 and was driven straight into the company museum – a sad end for an imaginative, but hopelessly expensive project. Nevertheless, the Z1 has all the ingredients of a future classic: it has a high-class brand name, it is rare, it is novel to look at and reasonably entertaining to drive and, perhaps vitally, it was a failure first time round.

Z1 PRODUCTION

Production History:	In production: 1988-1991 Total produced 8,000		
model	**Z1**	**total for year**	
1988	58	58	
1989	2,400	2,400	
1990	4,091	4,091	
1991	1,451	1,451	
total	**8,000**	**8,000**	

Technology
leadership

Speaking volumes

New style and five body types bring big-time sales to third 3 Series

Third 3 Series (E36)

→ 1990 – 1999
→ Larger and more comfortable
→ Stylish shape influenced by 5 Series
→ 4-door saloon, Touring, Cabrio
→ New Coupé version a strong seller
→ M3 now with six-cylinder engine
→ M3 lightweight extremely rare
→ Biggest selling BMW in history

With the highly successful launches of the new-look 7 and 5 Series in 1986 and 1988, a pattern in BMW's model strategy was becoming clear. Within each family there would be a major change – a change that would often push the boundaries of initial consumer acceptance – but for the next generation the change would be much more cautious, simply refining the lines of the incumbent model.

The big change for the 5 and the 7 had happened: now, as the '80s drew to a close, it was the turn of the 3 Series. The change proved to be bigger than anyone had expected: not only did the new 3 take on a more rounded, streamlined shape instead of the dated, boxy profile it had inhabited for almost a decade; it dared go one further and change the grille and headlights – the very face of BMW.

Few were concerned that the BMW double-kidney grille had been smoothed out and swept back: the larger cars already did that to a certain degree. The contentious issue was the new headlight design, which some complained had robbed the car of its familiar BMW 'eyes'. What the design team had done was to fair in the four lights behind transparent rectangular covers, but with the circular lights clearly visible through the covers – and in so doing they had significantly improved the car's drag coefficient as well as modernised its look.

The car was longer, taller and wider than the outgoing model, and a 130 mm stretch to the wheelbase translated into better rear seat space, though the 3 Series would never be counted roomy in this respect. Significantly, the new saloon was only offered as a four-door: astutely, the role of the two-door would be taken two years later by a more focused Coupé derivative.

The launch range – which went into production at both Munich and Regensburg right away – comprised a familiar line-up of engines, ranging from the four-cylinder 316i to the 325i

Third-generation 3 Series expanded into additional body styles: Coupé and Touring joined saloon and Cabrio.

189

The larger-capacity six-cylinder engines turned the third-generation 3 Series into rapid sports saloons

"The Coupé was redesigned from scratch by Claus Luthe, who was so concerned to achieve the perfect proportions that he changed every single panel. Not even the lights were shared with the saloon"

straight six. Underneath came a much bigger change: the switch away from the traditional semi trailing arm rear suspension to a more complex – but also more effective and more space-efficient – multi-link arrangement inspired by the Z1 roadster. This was in itself unusual – to launch a key chassis change on the smallest and least expensive car in the portfolio – though a more elaborate version of the axle had been shown on the low-volume 850i and within five years both the 7 Series and the 5 would be running the new layout, known either as the Z axle (from Z for Zentrum, or centre) or Integral axle.

Among the claimed advantages for the axle were greater stability in sidewinds, neutral responses with no self-steering effects if, for instance, a wheel encounters a bump or pothole while cornering, and much better immunity from torque reversal effects when lifting off the throttle in the middle of a bend.

By and large the system did work well: the

new 3 Series rode less stiffly than the old one, its steering was noticeably more direct and more fun, and the car cornered eagerly and predictably. The engines, too, were pleasing, and the new, rather lower driving position felt more intimate and more sporty. But there was a complaint, and a surprising one at that: the quality of the interior fittings, especially the dashboard and its ill-fitting glovebox, was not up to the usual high BMW standards – suddenly there seemed to be a lot of plastic around, and for the first time commentators became aware that this was a car produced in high volumes. The seats, too, felt somewhat thin and cramped in the rear, but there was no doubting the quality of the driving experience. The 3 Series had regained the fun factor that many versions of the outgoing series had lost.

A 325td with 115 bhp was added in 1991 and complemented by a 143 bhp intercooled variant two years later. By now the Coupé had

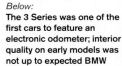

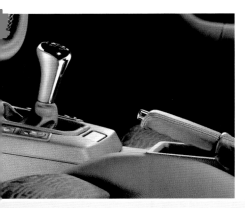

Below:
The 3 Series was one of the first cars to feature an electronic odometer; interior quality on early models was not up to expected BMW standards

Above:
New-shape 3 Series Saloon was not universally accepted at first, but quickly gained friends once its driving qualities had been appreciated

appeared: with typical BMW thoroughness it had been redesigned from scratch by Claus Luthe, who was so concerned to achieve the perfect proportions that he changed every single panel – not even the headlights or tail-lights were shared. At the time Luthe said he had given the Coupé a deliberately notchback look to provide echoes of the sporty 2002 and first 3 Series. Underneath, the Coupé had stiffened suspension and used either the 320i or 325i sixes. Later, the 16-valve, four-cylinder 316iS was added and the 325i was replaced by the 328i with the new all-aluminium M52 2.8 litre six with VANOS variable valve timing. A feature of the Coupé taken directly from the 850i was the system of frameless doors where the side windows rise to ensure a good seal after the door has been closed.

The Coupé soon established a pattern of strong sales at approximately one-third of the saloon's volume: the best seller was generally the 140 bhp 318iS, whereas with the saloon it was

the lower-powered 318i.

Summer 1993 saw the sales debut of the Cabriolet, which again was substantially re-engineered with a different bonnet and the windscreen pillars set further back in the interests of a more harmonious profile. Two engine versions appeared first: 318iS and 325i, later 328i. Listed options included an aluminium hardtop and an active rollover protection system which deployed twin hoops set behind the rear head restraints if an inversion appeared imminent.

The Touring was slow to arrive, finally making its bow in March 1995 with a choice of two petrol and two diesel engines. Clearly favouring style over sheer carrying capacity, it nevertheless had a far better load space – thanks largely to the clever compactness of the Z axle beneath the floor – and cargo space with the seats up was almost double that of the old Touring. Sales were steady rather than spectacular at around 30,000 units a year.

More equipment, including a passenger's airbag, became standard across all models in 1995, and not long after it had been dropped in the 325i the 2.5 litre engine was back in a car labelled 323i, though with a higher rear axle ratio for improved economy. This was the first time (apart from the 1979 545i turbo) that BMW had played tricks with designations, but it would not be the last. A minor facelift for the 1997 model year saw a stronger grille, side indicator repeaters and a high-level brake light; the boot handle became body colour at the same time.

The M3 story is rather simpler – that is if any car with a three-litre, 24-valve engine with twin overhead camshafts and continuously variable valve timing can be called simple. The move to a six-cylinder engine and three litres marked a definite step-up in mission for the M3: so did the cylinder head, which was the first to use BMW's double VANOS system that adjusted both inlet and exhaust camshafts, rather than just the inlet,

For the first time BMW featured a stand-alone Coupé body for the 3 Series. The look is similar to the saloon but every single panel is different; even the rear lights are unique to the Coupé

Specifications	316i	318i	318iS	320i	325i
Engine					
Engine type	Inline 4-cylinder	Inline 4-cylinder	Inline 4-cylinder	Inline 6-cylinder	Inline 6-cylinder
Bore & stroke, mm	84 x 72	84 x 81	84 x 81	80 x 66	84 x 75
Capacity, cc	1596	1796	1796	1991	2494
Valves	8	8	16	24	24
Valve actuation	Sohc	Sohc	Dohc	Dohc	Dohc
Compression ratio	9.0:1	8.8:1	9.0:1	11.1:1	10.5:1
Fuelling	Bosch Motronic fuel injection	Bosch Motronic fuel injection	Bosch Motronic fuel injection	Bosch Motronic fuel injection	Bosch Motronic fuel injection
Max power, bhp @ rpm	100@5500	113@5500	140@6000	150@5900	192@5900
Max torque, Nm @ rpm	141@4250	162@4250	175@4500	190@4200	245@4200
Transmission					
Manual transmission	5-speed	5-speed	5-speed	5-speed	5-speed
Automatic	4-speed optional	4-speed optional	4-speed optional	ZF 5-speed optional	ZF 5-speed optional
Drive	Rear wheels	Rear wheels	Rear wheels	Rear wheels	Rear wheels
Chassis					
Front suspension	MacPherson struts, lower wishbones	MacPherson struts, lower wishbones	MacPherson struts, lower wishbones	MacPherson struts, lower wishbones	MacPherson struts, lower wishbones
Rear suspension	Trailing arms, upper lateral control arm, lower lateral control links, coils springs, dampers	Trailing arms, upper lateral control arm, lower lateral control links, coils springs, dampers	Trailing arms, upper lateral control arm, lower lateral control links, coils springs, dampers	Trailing arms, upper lateral control arm, lower lateral control links, coils springs, dampers	Trailing arms, upper lateral control arm, lower lateral control links, coils springs, dampers
Braking	Disc/drum (all-disc from 1996); servo-assisted, ABS	Disc/drum (all-disc from 1996); servo-assisted, ABS	Disc; servo-assisted, ABS	Disc; servo-assisted, ABS	Disc; servo-assisted, ABS
Steering	Rack and pinion, power assisted	Rack and pinion, power assisted	Rack and pinion, power assisted	Rack and pinion, power assisted	Rack and pinion, power assisted
Wheels	6.5 x 15	6.5 x 15	7.0 x 15	6.5 x 15	7.0 x 15
Tyres	185/65 HR15	185/65 HR15	205/60 VR15	205/60 VR15	205/60 ZR15
Body					
Structure	Steel monocoque	Steel monocoque	Steel monocoque	Steel monocoque	Steel monocoque
Wheelbase, mm	2700	2700	2700	2700	2700
Track F/R, mm	1420/1430	1420/1430	1420/1430	1410/1420	1410/1420
Length, mm	4435	4435	4435	4435	4435
Width, mm	1700	1700	1700	1700	1700
Height, mm	1395	1395	1395	1395	1395
Kerb weight, kg	1185	1205	1240	1315	1330
Fuel tank capacity, lit	65	65	65	65	65
Performance					
Max speed, km/h	191	198	213	214	233
0-100km/h, sec	13.1	11.5	10.2	9.8	8.0
Fuel consumption , lit/100 km	7.9	8.3	8.3	8.8	8.8
Marketing					
Launch date	12/90	10/90	12/91	10/90	11/90
Pricing, DM	30,800	34,800	42,000	40,000	49,000

"For the M3 BMW again resisted the temptation to apply spoilers and other aerodynamic aids, but to the surprise of many a four-door saloon M3 had been added soon after the original Coupé and Cabrio"

and continuously rather than in two distinct phases. The benefit was felt in terms of low-down torque as well as the ability to prevent the power falling off towards peak revs. In the first iteration of this M3 the S50 engine gave 286 bhp at 7000 rpm; summer 1995 saw capacity taken out to 3.2 litres, compression raised to 11.3 to one, and power shoot up to 321 bhp at a dizzy 7400 rpm. At the same time BMW took the opportunity to slot in a six-speed transmission offering SMG sequential operation as an option.

Performance, needless to say, was spectacular, and changes to the chassis reflected the massively increased speed on tap – though BMW again sensibly resisted the temptation to apply spoilers and other aerodynamic aids. To the surprise of many, a four-door saloon M3 had been added soon after the original Coupé and Cabrio, and a homologation run of 350 special M3 GTs, finished in green and with substantial front and rear spoilers, had been completed for racing. For the United States the M3 was different again, using a special version of the three-litre engine detuned to 240 bhp

Considered the most exotic M3 of all,

The Cabriolet was costly but practical and popular: its windscreen position was changed from that of the Coupé's to improve the model's profile; M3 Cabriolet (left) offered a dramatic performance increase

E36 DERIVATIVES

Specifications	318tds	325td	325tds	323i	328i
Engine					
Engine type	Inline 4-cylinder intercooled turbo diesel	Inline 4-cylinder turbo diesel	Inline 4-cylinder intercooled turbo diesel	Inline 6-cylinder	Inline 6-cylinder
Capacity, cc	1665	2497	2497	2494	2793
Valves	8	12	12	Dohc 24, VANOS variable valve timing	Dohc 24, VANOS variable valve timing
Fuelling	Electronically controlled diesel injection	Electronically controlled diesel injection	Electronically controlled diesel injection	Siemens electronic fuel injection	Siemens electronic fuel injection
Max power, bhp @ rpm	90@4400	115@4800	143@4800	170@5500	193@5300
Max torque, Nm @ rpm	190@2200	222@1900	260@1900	245@3950	280@3950
Transmission					
Manual transmission	5-speed	5-speed	5-speed	5-speed	5-speed
Automatic	Not available	4-speed auto optional	ZF 5-speed auto optional	ZF 5-speed auto optional	ZF 5-speed auto optional
Drive	Rear wheels	Rear wheels	Rear wheels	Rear wheels	Rear wheels
Chassis					
Front suspension	MacPherson struts, lower wishbones	MacPherson struts, lower wishbones	MacPherson struts, lower wishbones	MacPherson struts, lower wishbones	MacPherson struts, lower wishbones
Rear suspension	Trailing arms, upper lateral control arm, lower lateral control links, coils springs, dampers	Trailing arms, upper lateral control arm, lower lateral control links, coils springs, dampers	Trailing arms, upper lateral control arm, lower lateral control links, coils springs, dampers	Trailing arms, upper lateral control arm, lower lateral control links, coils springs, dampers	Trailing arms, upper lateral control arm, lower lateral control links, coils springs, dampers
Braking	Disc; servo-assisted, ABS	Disc; servo-assisted, ABS	Disc; servo-assisted, ABS	Disc; servo-assisted, ABS	Disc; servo-assisted, ABS
Steering	Rack and pinion, power assisted	Rack and pinion, power assisted	Rack and pinion, power assisted	Rack and pinion, power assisted	Rack and pinion, power assisted
Wheels	6.5 x 15	6.5 x 15	6.5 x 15	6.5 x 15	7.0 x 15
Tyres	185/65 HR15	185/65 HR15	185/65 HR15	185/65 HR15	205/60 WR15
Body					
Length, mm	4435	4435	4435	4435	4435
Width, mm	1700	1700	1700	1700	1700
Height, mm	1395	1395	1395	1395	1395
Kerb weight, kg	1265	1335	1350	1310	1320
Performance					
Max speed, km/h	182	198	210	227	236
0-100km/h, sec	14.4	12.0	10.0	8.0	7.3
Fuel consumption , lit/100 km	6.0	6.9	6.9	9.0	9.2
Marketing					
Launch date	4/94	6/91	6/93	5/95	6/94
Pricing, DM	39,900	43,000	48,000	51,000	56,000

Specifications	2-door sedan	4-door sedan	Cabriolet	Touring
Dimensions				
Wheelbase, mm	2700	2700	2700	2700
Track F/R, mm	1407/1415	1407/1415	1418/1431	1418/1431
Length, mm	4433	4433	4433	4433
Width, mm	1710	1698	1645	1645
Height, mm	1366	1393	1350	1391
Kerb weight, kg	–	2-door + 25kg	2-door + 130 kg	2-door + 100 kg
Fuel tank capacity	55 (1987 on: 64)	55 (1987 on: 62)	62	55
Marketing				
Launch date	10/82	10/82	3/86	8/87
Pricing, DM	–	2-door + DM3000	2-door + DM8,500	2-door + DM500

"Clearly favouring style over sheer carrying capacity, the Touring nevertheless had far better load space – thanks largely to the clever compactness of the Z axle beneath the floor"

Above and right:
The Touring sold as much on style and status as it did on space. By the time of the second-generation Touring BMW had learnt more about estate-car practicality and provided more cargo space. The compact new Z axle suspension helped too

Three styles: Second-generation M3 was available in saloon as well as Coupé and Cabrio versions. The four-door enjoyed only limited success

E36
E36 M3

Specifications	M3 (1992-95)	M3 (1995-99)
Engine		
Engine type	Inline 6-cylinder	Inline 6-cylinder
Bore & stroke, mm	86 x 85.8	86.4 x 91
Capacity, cc	2990	3201
Valves	24	24
Valve actuation	Dohc, double VANOS variable valve timing	Dohc, double VANOS variable valve timing
Compression ratio	10.8:1	11.3:1
Fuelling	Bosch Motronic fuel injection	Bosch Motronic fuel injection
Max power, bhp @ rpm	286@7000	321@7400
Max torque, Nm @ rpm	320@3600	350@3250
Transmission		
Manual transmission	5-speed	6-speed (optional: sequential)
Automatic	Not available	Not available
Drive	Rear wheels	Rear wheels
Chassis		
Front suspension	MacPherson struts, lower wishbones	MacPherson struts, lower wishbones
Rear suspension	Trailing arms, upper lateral control arm, lower lateral control links, coils springs, dampers	Trailing arms, upper lateral control arm, lower lateral control links, coils springs, dampers
Braking	Disc; servo-assisted, Teves ABS	Disc; servo-assisted, Teves ABS, Cornering Brake Control
Steering	Rack and pinion, power assisted	Rack and pinion, power assisted
Wheels	7.0 x 15	7.5 x 17
Tyres front + rear	205/60 ZR15	225/45 ZR17 + 245/40 ZR17
Body		
Structure	Steel monocoque, aluminium bonnet	Steel monocoque, aluminium bonnet
Wheelbase, mm	2700	2700
Track F/R, mm	1420/1445	1420/1445
Length, mm	4435	4435
Width, mm	1710	1710
Height, mm	1335	1335
Kerb weight, kg	1460	1440
Fuel tank capacity, lit	65	65
Performance		
Max speed, km/h	250 (limited)	250 (limited)
0-100km/h, sec	6.0	5.5
Fuel consumption , lit/100 km	9.1	9.1
Marketing		
Launch date	9/92	7/95
Pricing, DM	80,000	88,500

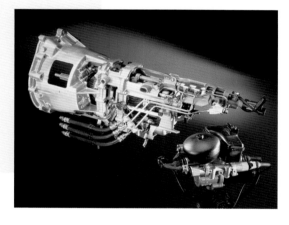

Engine became a six-cylinder, 24-valve powerhouse, giving M3 performance to rival serious big-name sports cars. Capacity was upped to 3.2 litres in 1995, and sequential transmission option added. The speedometer reading translates to 155 mph

however, is the lightweight. Offered essentially as the basis for a racing car, this stripped-out version saved up to 150 kg by jettisoning the air conditioning, sound insulation, stereo, toolkit, spare wheel and other non-essentials; the speed limiter in the central electronic processor was removed, and the car was supplied with further tuning hardware in the boot. Only 120 were produced during the course of 1995, most of which went to the USA; interestingly, the electric windows had to be retained as the motors were needed to ensure proper sealing of the glass against the door surround.

Again following a familiar pattern, the phasing out of the E36 3 Series began at the end of 1998 when the new E46 took over from the saloon. More than 1.5 million had been made, many of them in remote factories such as South Africa and the United States, and production of the Touring, Coupé and Cabriolet models continued until their E46 replacements too were ready to launch. The Compact, effectively a hybrid

of E36 and E30 components (see chapter 20), would last through into the new millennium. Yet again, the 3 series had beaten all the records, but – again at the risk of repeating the pattern – the new one was to do better still and beat its predecessor's totals after only six years on sale.

THIRD 3 SERIES: SEDAN PRODUCTION

Production History:	In production: 1990-99					Total produced 1,552,567							
model	316i	318i	318iS	318tds	320i	325i	325td	325tds	323i	328i	M3	total for year	SKD
1990	4	4,213			117	4,001						8,335	
1991	48,986	92,416	6		62,287	50,914	4,989					259,598	3,175
1992	63,152	86,755	6,589		44,040	32,358	19,679					252,573	15,856
1993	60,877	62,820	11,288		28,265	30,205	14,320	9,175				216,950	19,214
1994	41,524	40,968	16,700	6,669	24,684	26,058	9,096	18,509	1	31	288	184,528	21,536
1995	37,735	38,389	12,658	20,423	20,998	13,930	3,725	11,249	5,191	14,039	1,282	179,619	24,984
1996	31,134	34,378	9,380	10,629	13,304		1,828	6,485	9,042	23,144	3,639	142,963	22,308
1997	28,299	43,477	6,007	9,503	13,656		1,482	6,403	11,626	19,843	4,740	145,036	6,264
1998	8,127	17,596	1,901	1,296	2,852		130	966	3,711	9,951	2,486	49,016	612
totals	319,838	421,012	64,529	48,520	210,203	157,466	55,249	52,787	29,571	67,008	12,435		113,949
										grand total		1,438,618	
										grand total inc SKD		1,552,567	

THIRD 3 SERIES: TOURING PRODUCTION

Production History:	In production: 1994-99			Total produced 130,611				
model	316i Touring	318i Touring	320i Touring	323i Touring	328i Touring	318tds Touring	325tds Touring	total for year
1994			49		18	1	1	69
1995		3,954	10,215	186	4,302	6,901	2,106	27,664
1996	14	11,377	5,429	1,909	3,007	7,669	4,055	33,460
1997	7,601	8,500	4,522	2,881	1,827	5,707	3,432	34,470
1998	7,181	6,711	3,306	2,777	1,241	3,640	2,004	26,860
1999	2,570	2,001	1,116	682	223	1,058	438	8,088
totals	17,366	32,543	24,637	8,435	10,618	24,976	12,036	
							grand total	130,611

THIRD 3 SERIES COUPÉ / CABRIO PRODUCTION

Production History:	In production: 1991-99					Total produced 652,922						
model	316i Coupé	318iS Coupé	320i Coupé	323i Coupé	325i/328i Coupé	M3	318i/S Cabrio	320i Cabrio	325i Cabrio	328i Cabrio	M3 Cabrio	total for year
1991		40	103		2,614							2,757
1992		38,183	24,349		31,351	470		1	20			94,374
1993	6,854	35,429	15,680		21,916	6,080	14	600	16,931			103,504
1994	16,631	25,346	13,296	1	19,138	9,289	10,844	7,128	15,184		7	116,864
1995	10,911	17,976	8,378	3,922	18,387	9,828	11,709	6,895	6,670	52	9,401	104,129
1996	6,926	13,132	4,578	5,301	14,300	6,896	10,827	5,335		38	13,229	80,562
1997	5,696	9,971	3,772	7,544	9,813	5,873	7,668	5,003		3,543	13,480	72,363
1998	3,589	6,337	1,412	7,732	6,168	4,422	4,404	3,356		5,987	8,606	52,013
1999	407	2,358		2,184	990	2,919	4,223	2,247		5,910	5,118	26,356
totals	51,014	148,772	71,568	26,684	124,677	45,777	49,689	30,565	38,805	15,530	49,841	
										grand total		652,922
										Derivative Totals: Sedan		1,552,567
										Cabrio		184,430
										Touring		130,611
										Coupé		468,492
										Series total		2,336,100

Cautious evolution

Replacement for the dynamic 7 Series is disappointingly low-key in style

Third 7 Series (E38)

- → 1994 – 2001
- → Conservative style
- → 6, 8 and 12-cylinder engines
- → World's first V8 diesel
- → New rear suspension
- → Further advances in electronics
- → Majored on comfort and refinement

After the major advance of the 1986 7 Series, it felt disappointing to see BMW backtracking on its forward-looking design stance and coming up with an extremely conservative evolution of the model which had brought about such a shift in the public perception of the BMW brand. This indeed appeared to be the company's progressive-then-cautious policy in action.

But, luckily for BMW, it was a time when Mercedes was on the back foot: it was going through all sorts of internal upheavals and the massive and unpopular slab-sided 140-series S-Class was still causing headaches for the Stuttgart company. So, by happy coincidence, the launch of the very low-key, slim and neat new 7 Series was timed just right to capitalise on the disaffection for the brutal-looking Stuttgarter.

Third 7 Series was a cautious evolution of the more radical second generation but served BMW well at a time when a strong family identity was needed. This example wears the optional M Sport pack

In place of the undulating curves of the previous car the new 7 Series looked wide, low and very flat: from some angles it was hard to judge what size or class of vehicle it was. In terms of presence it had very little but, as we have seen, that could have been a good thing, especially in Germany, when times were hard and wealthy owners did not want to make an insensitive statement at a time when investment programmes were being cut back and workers were losing their jobs.

In many senses it represented a further refinement of the E32, though the switch to the multi-link integral rear axle was an important technical step. The wheels grew to 15-inch, adding to the impression of shallowness of the body – though in fact it was taller, wider, and longer than the old car. There was a long wheelbase variant, too, with the internal designation of E38/2.

Myriad controls and tiny buttons graced the otherwise well laid out interior: new was the multifunctional steering wheel, from which systems such as the telephone and the air conditioning could be operated; on some versions the steering wheel could be heated.

The third-generation 7 Series introduced built-in satellite navigation: the screen looks crude by today's standards. The ultra-smooth V12 engine had by now grown to 5.4 litres

One of the best features of the new 7 were the front seats, which had an extra hinge-point halfway up the backrest to provide multi-adjustable support and excellent comfort. In fact, comfort was the dominant theme of the new car: thanks to the new, rather softer, suspension and optional electronic damper control the ride was very smooth indeed and road noise well isolated. The V8 engines in the 730i and 740i, carried over from the old car, played through five-speed automatics, were remarkably smooth and silent, too. It seemed as if BMW was out to challenge the refinement achieved by Lexus.

If there was a fault it was that the engines were lacking in flexibility, needing to be revved hard for overtaking acceleration, and that the light power steering and soft ride robbed the driver of road feel and, ultimately, driving enjoyment.

Gradually, BMW began adding engine permutations. In the autumn of 1994 came the 750i V12, now enlarged to 5.4 litres and 326

E38: DIMENSIONS

Specifications	4-door standard wheelbase	4-door long wheelbase	Protection (armoured)
Dimensions			
Wheelbase, mm	2930	3070	2930
Track F/R, mm	1550/1570	1550/1570	1550/1570
Length, mm	4985	5125	4985
Width, mm	1860	1860	1860
Height, mm	1430	1430	1430
Kerb weight, kg	–	standard + 25-40kg	standard + 210kg
Fuel tank capacity, lit	85	95	95
Marketing			
Launch date	9/95	9/95	3/2000
Pricing, DM	–	standard + DM10,000	standard + DM79,100

The 1994 7 Series was the first big BMW with multi-link rear suspension, giving a notably smoother ride

E38: 7 SERIES

Specifications	728i	730i	735i	740i	750i
Engine					
Engine type	Inline 6-cylinder	90-degree V8	90-degree V8	90-degree V8	60-degree V12
Bore & stroke, mm	84 x 84	84 x 67.6	84 x 72.9	89 x 80 (From 1996: 92 x 82.7)	85 x 79
Capacity, cc	2793	2997	3498	3982 (From 1996: 4398)	5379
Valves	24	32	32	32	24
Valve actuation	Dohc; Vanos variable valve timing (from 1998: double Vanos)	Dohc per bank	Dohc per bank, Vanos variable valve timing	Dohc per bank, (From 1996: Vanos variable valve timing)	Sohc per bank
Compression ratio	10.2:1	10.5:1	10.1:1	10.1:1	10.1:1
Fuelling	Siemens electronic fuel injection	Bosch Motronic electronic fuel injection	Bosch Motronic electronic fuel injection	Bosch Motronic electronic fuel injection	Dual Bosch Motronic electronic fuel injection
Max power, bhp @ rpm	193@5300	218@5800	235@5700	286@5800	326@5000
Max torque, Nm @ rpm	280@3950	290@4500	320@3300	400@4500 (From 1996: 420@3900)	490@3900
Transmission					
Manual transmission	Not available	5-speed	5-speed	6-speed	Not available
Automatic	ZF 5-speed	ZF 5-speed	ZF 5-speed	ZF 5-speed	ZF 5-speed
Drive	Rear wheels	Rear wheels	Rear wheels	Rear wheels	Rear wheels
Chassis					
Front suspension	MacPherson strut, lower wishbones	MacPherson strut, lower wishbones	MacPherson strut, lower wishbones	MacPherson strut, lower wishbones	MacPherson strut, lower wishbones
Rear suspension	Four-link axle with twin transverse upper links, twin lower control arms, coil-spring/damper units; EDC and ride height levelling optional	Four-link axle with twin transverse upper links, twin lower control arms, coil-spring/damper units; EDC and ride height levelling optional	Four-link axle with twin transverse upper links, twin lower control arms, coil-spring/damper units; EDC and ride height levelling optional	Four-link axle with twin transverse upper links, twin lower control arms, coil-spring/damper units; EDC and ride height levelling optional	Four-link axle with twin transverse upper links, twin lower control arms, coil-spring/damper units; EDC and ride height levelling
Braking	Disc, servo assisted, ABS	Disc, servo assisted, ABS	Disc, servo assisted, ABS	Disc, servo assisted, ABS	Disc, servo assisted, ABS
Steering	Recirculating ball, power assisted	Recirculating ball, power assisted	Recirculating ball, power assisted	Recirculating ball, power assisted	Recirculating ball, power assisted
Wheels	7.0 x 16	7.5 x 16	7.5 x 16	7.5 x 16	7.5 x 16
Tyres	215/65 WR 16	215/65 WR 16	236/60 WR 16	235/60 WR 16	235/60 WR 16
Body					
Structure	Steel monocoque	Steel monocoque	Steel monocoque	Steel monocoque	Steel monocoque
Wheelbase, mm	2930	2930	2930	2930	2930
Track F/R, mm	1550/1570	1550/1570	1550/1570	1550/1570	1550/1570
Length, mm	4985	4985	4985	4985	4985
Width, mm	1860	1860	1860	1860	1860
Height, mm	1435	1435	1435	1435	1435
Kerb weight, kg	1710	1725	1745	1800	1995
Fuel tank capacity, lit	85	85	85	85	95
Performance					
Max speed, km/h	228	235	240	250	250
0-100km/h	8.6	8.3	7.6	6.6	6.6
Fuel consumption , lit/100 km	10.3	10.8	13.9	14.4	15.7
Marketing					
Launch date	9/95	4/94	3/96	4/94	10/94
Pricing (std wheelbase), DM	83,000	92,000	95,500	110,000	148,000

	725tds	730d	740d
	Inline 6-cylinder intercooled turbodiesel	Inline 6-cylinder intercooled direct injection turbodiesel	90-degree V8 intercooled direct injection turbodiesel
	80 x 82.8	84 x 88.8	84 x 88
	2497	2926	3902
	12	24	32
	sohc,	Dohc	Dohc,
	22::1	18.0:1	18.0:1
	Digital electonic diesel fuel injection	Bosch DDE common rail electronic diesel injection; variable nozzle Garrett turbocharger	Bosch DDE common rail electronic diesel injection; twin variable nozzle Garrett turbochargers; twin intercoolers
	143@4600	184@4000 (From 2000:193)	245@4000
	280@2200	411@2000 (From 2000: 430)	560@1750
	5-speed	Not available	Not available
	ZF 5-speed	ZF 5-speed	ZF 5-speed
	Rear wheels	Rear wheels	Rear wheels
	MacPherson strut, lower wishbones	MacPherson strut, lower wishbones	MacPherson strut, lower wishbones
	Four-link axle with twin transverse upper links, twin lower control arms, coil-spring/damper units; EDC and ride height levelling optional	Four-link axle with twin transverse upper links, twin lower control arms, coil-spring/damper units; EDC and ride height levelling optional	Four-link axle with twin transverse upper links, twin lower control arms, coil-spring/damper units; EDC and ride height levelling optional
	Disc, servo assisted, ABS	Disc, servo assisted, ABS	Disc, servo assisted, ABS
	Recirculating ball, power assisted	Recirculating ball, power assisted	Recirculating ball, power assisted
	7.5 x 16	7.5 x 16	7.5 x 15
	215/65 WR 16	215/65 WR 16	235/60 WR 16
	Steel monocoque	Steel monocoque	Steel monocoque
	2930	2930	2930
	1550/1570	1550/1570	1550/1570
	4985	4985	4985
	1860	1860	1860
	1435	1435	1435
	1710	1830	1960
	85	85	85
	206	220	242
	11.4	8.7	8.4
	9.7	8.7	9.8
	3/96	9/98	5/99
	80,000	96,700	130,000

bhp, while at the opposite end of the scale the six-cylinder 728i, launched in September the following year, went on to become the dominant best seller of the range. BMW was the first company to put a diesel engine into a prestige car with the 725 tds in 1996; two years later came the groundbreaking direct-injection three-litre six in the 730d, which edged steadily closer to 200 bhp with successive upgrades. However, the really big sensation was the world's first eight-cylinder diesel for true luxury car performance and refinement.

Four litres in capacity, with twin overhead camshafts, 32 valves , twin common rail injection systems, twin variable geometry turbochargers and twin intercoolers, the big diesel pumped out 245 bhp at 4000 rpm; still more impressive was its monster torque output of 560 Nm at just 1750 rpm. These figures combined to make a very quick car indeed, yet one which would exceed 240 km/h yet average better than 10 litres per 100 km in the European combined driving cycle. For the first time, a diesel car was as quick as its petrol equivalent and so close on ultimate refinement that few could tell the difference.

BMW's petrol-power was not standing still, however. In response to feedback from customers the two V8s had been enlarged by half a litre and had been given VANOS variable valve timing to improve flexibility, while the 2.8 litre six gained double VANOS (operating on both camshafts) to further boost low-revs response. A mild facelift at the same time saw narrower headlights with shaping along their bases, clear indicator lenses front, rear and on the sides, and a chrome strip above the rear number plate.

A third fuel was added to the 7 series'

Interior offered every conceivable luxury, including adjustable rear seats. Smooth and powerful M67 diesel V8 in 740d was the first in the luxury class and equalled petrol power for speed and refinement

"Comfort was the dominant theme of the new car: thanks to the new, rather softer, suspension and optional electronic damper control the rise was very smooth indeed and road noise was well isolated. It seemed as if BMW was out to challenge the refinement achieved by Lexus"

capabilities, albeit on an experimental basis, when BMW build a fleet of hydrogen-powered 750s, just as it had done with the previous 750i. This time, however, the car boasted good power (204 bhp), and could hit a top speed of 226 km/h and accelerate to 100 km/h in 9.6 seconds.

Befitting its status as the flagship model of the company, the 7 Series was available in three different wheelbases, with three different levels of armoured protection, with double glazing and with a whole host of entertainment and comfort systems for those in the rear seat.

And that effectively sums up this particular 7 Series: a car to relax in and appreciate from the back seat, not so much from directly behind the steering wheel. It may not have moved the game on in terms of external design or driver appeal in the way the E32 did, but it did move BMW closer to the middle ground as far as the conventional values of comfort, convenience and conformity are concerned.

July 2001: the last 740i leaves the production line, followed by its very different replacement

THIRD E SERIES: E38 PRODUCTION

Production History:	In production: 1993 – 2001					Total produced 327,599				
model	728i	730i	735i	740i	750i	725tds	730d	740d	total for year	SKD
1993		22		25	3				50	
1994		10,895		18,829	1,351				31,075	24
1995	3,836	10,823	70	26,745	7,652	18			49,144	888
1996	8,920	346	6,531	26,070	3,453	4,837			50,157	264
1997	9,044		6,526	26,505	3,901	2,920			48,896	180
1998	9,201		5,440	25,174	3,703	1,190	1833	22	46,563	
1999	5,328		4,361	22,250	2,462	82	4010	1,525	40,018	
2000	5,516		3,598	22,097	2,048	6	4238	1,477	38,980	
2001	3,918		1,679	12,438	644		2255	426	21,360	
totals	45,763	22,086	28,205	180,133	25,217	9,053	12,336	3,450		1,356
								grand total	326,243	
								grand total inc SKD	327,599	

Z3 roadster and coupé (E36-7)

- → 1995 – 2002
- → First BMW roadster since legendary 507
- → First BMW not made in Germany
- → Built exclusively in Spartanburg, US
- → Used 3 Series hardware
- → Potent M Roadster with 321 bhp
- → Controversially styled Z Coupé
- → Best model is 2.8 roadster

Going global

BMW moves to the US to build sports cars and sport utilities

BMW has not always been a global company, but it has always thought globally. Even in the early days after the restructuring, when 1500s and 2002s were selling like hot cakes through BMW dealers in West Germany, chairman Eberhard von Kuenheim was urging his sales organisation to look further afield. Before long, the company began setting up its own sales companies in key markets, even if it meant – as it did in the US – having to say goodbye to a tried and trusted importer.

The emotive styling of the Z3 was always a talking point, but the arrival of the Coupé in 1998 really divided opinion. Here, both are in potent 321 bhp M form

In other countries, often those with import restrictions, BMW organised satellite operations where local companies would assemble cars from CKD or SKD (completely knocked down or slightly knocked down) kits shipped out from the Munich factory. Many thousands of cars were built in Portugal, Uruguay, Thailand and India in this way: South Africa, through an organisation BMW inherited when it bought the Glas company, had always been one of the leading assemblers of BMWs, and indeed shipped considerable numbers to the United States.

The logical extension of this, reasoned von Kuenheim in 1989, was to build the cars where the main demand was – and for BMW, like many luxury car makers, this was in the US. Additionally, by setting up in the dollar area BMW would be

gaining a certain amount of protection against currency fluctuations: German industry chiefs remember all too well the times when a strong Mark and a weak dollar made everything from Porsches to Passats impossibly expensive the other side of the Atlantic.

This was the thinking that eventually resulted in a cluster of top BMW executives gathering in a field alongside an Interstate in South Carolina in 1992 to lay the foundation stone of what was to become BMW's Spartanburg plant, its first fully-independent facility outside Germany and Austria, where the Steyr engine factory had been established in the 1980s. Within three years Spartanburg was up and running and building 3 Series models for American customers, for when BMW launches a new manufacturing facility it always builds a familiar model there first, just to confirm internal procedures are working smoothly. With quality paramount, a new car in a new plant poses too many unknown quantities – that is why the new 1 series is being made in Regensburg and not at the new Leipzig plant.

Towards the end of 1995, with top-quality 3 Series models already coming off the line, it was time for the American associates to begin ramping up their exciting new product, the Z3 sports car. It was a major responsibility, for Spartanburg was to be the sole source of the Z3 worldwide; besides, as a keenly priced two-seater roadster, the model was very important for the domestic US market.

Spartanburg operatives found much that was familiar when they took their first training courses on the Z3, for the sports car was designed around the mechanical elements of the E36 3 Series. This meant MacPherson strut front suspension, the well-proven semi-trailing arm arrangement at the rear, and two four-cylinder engines out of the 3 Series catalogue. Everyone knew, however, that under the massive, all-opening bonnet of the Z3 there was room for the company's staple six-cylinder units – though no-one at this stage could have imagined that the massively potent 321 bhp powerhouse from the M3 could also be shoehorned in.

Stylistically, the Z3 was a romantic throwback into an earlier age of curvaceous roadsters expressing their power through their proportions and their stance on the road. So there was first and foremost a long bonnet tapering towards a small double-kidney grille in the front: either side of the bonnet were what appeared to be slatted air outlet grilles, clearly harking back to the brand hero, the 507. From the snug cockpit rearwards it was less muscular, with a short, pert boot with little clear character apart from a BMW roundel in the centre. But just in case anyone was unsure about the Z3's identity, BMW roundels also appeared on the bonnet, on each of the fake air outlets on the car's flanks, on the steering wheel and on all four road wheels.

The first test cars which set out from Spartanburg in the hands of the world's automobile journalists were 140 bhp, 1.9 litre editions: they were pleasant enough to drive,

Left:
BMW chairman Bernd Pischetsrieder opened the US manufacturing operation on September 8th 1997

Top and above:
Spartanburg, South Carolina was the sole source of the Z3. This was the first time a BMW model had not been built in Germany. Later, the plant would be doubled in capacity and the X5 sport activity vehicle added

"Just in case anyone was still unsure about the Z3's identity, BMW roundels appeared on the bonnet, boot lid, on each of the fake air outlets on the car's flanks, on the steering wheel and on all four road wheels"

The Z3 roadster took most of its engineering from the 3 Series, but the use of the old-generation rear suspension limited its appeal for keen drivers

E36-7 Z3 SERIES

Specifications	Z3 1.8	Z3 1.9	Z3 2.0i/2.2i	Z3 2.5	Z3 2.8i/3.0i
Engine					
Engine type	Inline 4-cylinder	Inline 4-cylinder	Inline 6-cylinder	Inline 6 cylinder	Inline 6-cylinder
Bore & stroke, mm	84 x 81	85 x 83.5	80 x 66 (2000 on: 80 x 72)	84 x 75	84 x 84 (From 2000: 84 x 89.6)
Capacity, cc	1796	1895	1991 (from 2000: 2171)	2494	2793 (From 2000: 2979)
Valves	8	8	24	24	24
Valve actuation	Sohc	Sohc	Dohc, double Vanos variable valve timing	Dohc, double Vanos variable valve timing	Dohc, Vanos variable valve timing (Double Vanos from 1999)
Compression ratio	9.7:1	10.0:1	11.0:1	10.5:1	10.2:1
Fuelling	Electronic fuel injection	Bosch Motronic Electronic fuel injection	Siemenselectronic fuel injection	Siemenselectronic fuel injection	Bosch Motronic Electronic fuel injection
Max power, bhp @ rpm	116@5500	140@6000	150@5900 (from 2000: 170@6250)	170@5500	192@5300 (from 1999: 193@5500; from 2000: 231@5900)
Max torque, Nm @ rpm	168@3900	180@4300	190@3500 (from 2000: 210)	245@3500	275@3950 (from 2000: 300)
Transmission					
Manual transmission	5-speed	5-speed	5-speed	5-speed	5-speed
Automatic	Not available	4-speed	4-speed	4-speed	4-speed
Drive	Rear wheels	Rear wheels	Rear wheels	Rear Wheels	Rear wheels
Chassis					
Front suspension	MacPherson strut, lower wishbones	MacPherson struts, lower wishbones	MacPherson struts, lower wishbones	MacPherson struts, lower wishbones	MacPherson struts, lower wishbones
Rear suspension	Semi-trailing arms, minibloc coil springs	Semi-trailing arms, minibloc coil springs	Semi-trailing arms, minibloc coil springs	Semi-trailing arms, minibloc coil springs	Semi-trailing arms, minibloc coil springs
Braking	Disc, servo assisted, ABS	Disc, servo assisted, ABS	Disc, servo assisted, ABS	Disc, servo assisted, ABS	Disc, servo assisted, ABS
Steering	Rack and pinion, power assisted	Rack and pinion, power assisted	Rack and pinion, power assisted	Rack and pinion, power assisted	Rack and pinion, power assisted
Wheels	6.5 x 15	6.5 x 15	7.0 x 16	7.0 x 16	7.0 x 16
Tyres	205/60 HR 15	205/60 VR 15	225/50 VR 16	225/50 VR 16	225/50 ZR 16
Body					
Structure	Steel monocoque	Steel monocoque	Steel monocoque	Steel monocoque	Steel monocoque
Wheelbase, mm	2445	2445	2445	2445	2445
Track F/R, mm	1410/1425	1410/1425	1413/1494	1410/1490	1415/1495
Length, mm	4025	4025	4050	4050	4025
Width, mm	1690	1690	1740	1740	1740
Height, mm	1290	1290	1293	1290	1290
Kerb weight, kg	1160	1225	1270	1270	1300
Fuel tank capacity, lit	51	51	51	51	51
Performance					
Max speed, km/h	194	205	210	210	218 (From 2000: 240)
0-100km/h	10.5	9.5	8.9	7.5	7.1 (from 2000: 6.0)
Fuel consumption , lit/100km	8.4	9.6	10.8	10.0	11.5
Marketing					
Launch date	9/95	9/95	4/99	1998	3/96
Pricing, Dm	43,700	48,700	54,050	–	61,300

Z3 Coupé 2.8/3.0	M Roadster	M Coupé
Inline 6-cylinder	Inline 6-cylinder	Inline 6-cylinder
84 x 84	86.4 x 91	86.4 x 91
(From 2000: 84 x 89.6)	(from 2001: 91 x 87)	(from 2001: 91 x 87)
2793 (From 2000: 2979)	3201 (from 2001: 3246)	3201 (from 2001: 3246)
24	24	24
Dohc, double Vanos variable valve timing	Dohc, double Vanos variable valve timing	Dohc, double Vanos variable valve timing
10.2:1	11.3:1	11.3:1
Bosch Motronic Electronic fuel injection	Siemens electronic fuel injection	Siemens electronic fuel injection
193@5500; (from 2000: 231@5900)	321@7400 (from 2001: 325)	321@7400 (from 2001: 325)
300@3950	350@3250	350@3250
5-speed	5-speed	5-speed
4-speed	Not avaible	Not available
Rear wheels	Rear wheels	Rear wheels
MacPherson struts, lower wishbones	MacPherson struts, lower wishbones	MacPherson struts, lower wishbones
Semi-trailing arms, minibloc coil springs	Semi-trailing arms, minibloc coil springs	Semi-trailing arms, minibloc coil springs
Disc, servo assisted, ABS	Disc, servo assisted, ABS	Disc, servo assisted, ABS
Rack and pinion, power assisted	Rack and pinion, power assisted	Rack and pinion, power assisted
7.0 x 16	7.5 x 17/ 9.0 x 17	7.5 x 17/ 9.0 x 17
225/50 ZR 16	225/45 ZR17 / 245/40 ZR 17	225/45 ZR17 / 245/40 ZR 17
Steel monocoque	Steel monocoque	Steel monocoque
2445	2459	2459
1415/1495	1422/1492	1422/1492
4025	4025	4025
1740	1740	1740
1290	1266	1266
1300	1350	1375
51	51	51
231 (From 2000: 250)	250 (limited)	250 (limited)
6.3 (from 2000: 6.0)	5.4	5.4
11.3	12.3	12.3
9/98	3/97	9/98
64,000	91,500	95,000

Top:
US-built Z3 leads a cavalcade with roadster ancestors at Spartanburg

Above and centre:
In action the early Z3s did not match the very high expectations enthusiasts had built up Facelifted Z3 bodywork had fatter rear wheel arches and BMW trademark raised indicators on resculpted rear light units

Plain M3 Roadster (left) had slatted side air vents. M models (right) had a more elegant chrome moulding.

"Soon BMW responded to criticisms of weak performance by installing the 2.8 litre six: its 190-plus bhp were to make it the best of all the engines in the Z3"

without having the agility or feeling of zippiness of, say, the Mazda MX5. But despite the slightly lukewarm reaction of a press saying that it was not quick enough to be a proper sports car, the Z3 sold well at first: everyone wanted to be seen in one, and the semi-retro look seemed to have gone down well. Soon, BMW obliged its critics by installing the 2.8 litre six in January 1997: its VANOS-assisted flexibility and smooth 190-plus bhp were to make it the best of all the engines in the Z3. Unusually, along with the engine came bodywork differences centred around the 70 mm increase in rear track: not only were the wheels wider, at 7J x 16, but the whole rear bodywork was beefed up to give a much more solid look.

What no one had expected, however, was for BMW to install the mighty 3.2 litre powerhouse from the M3 in the Z3. Normally, such outrageous

projects are the challenge of tuning firms like Alpina, Schnitzer or Hartge – but this was an official BMW job. The so-called Z3 M Roadster looked suitably intimidating, too, with its fat wheels and four massive exhausts curling up from under the rear apron. The air vents on the car's sides were stylishly redesigned, too, and the interior used much more leather, generally of a gaudy red or blue. It was entertaining to drive, as any car of only 1,350 kg with 321 bhp would be; it had quicker steering, made nice noises and impressed onlookers, but ultimately it was not as satisfying as its specification promised, and the feeling was that the chassis was not really up to the standard of the engine.

The second shock came when BMW suddenly put people's aesthetic standards to the test with the M Coupé, a stubby two-seater

Massive attack: quadruple
exhausts signalled the
presence of the M
powerhouse up front.
Coupé's styling caused shock
and argument

M roadster provided rapid
open-road progress but
Coupé version had tauter
feel on poor roads; pricier
M versions gained
colourful leather
upholstery, even on the
dashboard

"The Z3, for all the 300,000 customers it pulled in over its seven-year existence, never really fulfilled the dynamic expectations everyone had of a BMW sports car. The high praise heaped on its successor shows just how good the Z3 should have been"

coupé built off the roadster platform. The proportions were unusual, with the glass house pushed right back and the huge rear wheels appearing to consume all the space between the driver's door and the back bumper. Some people loved it, but many felt precisely the opposite: what was not in doubt was the fact that the Coupé drove much better than the roadster, with a much tauter feel to its chassis in particular.

Roadster and Coupé went through various engine permutations in the three more years before the Z4 took over as BMW's resident roadster; both were at their best with the 2.8 litre six, the more up-market Coupé never being available with four-cylinder power. The Z3, for all the 300,000 customers it pulled in over its seven-year existence, never really fulfilled the dynamic expectations everyone had of a BMW sports car. This, as BMW also found out to its embarrassment with the first Compact, was largely down to the cost-saving employment of a legacy suspension layout in a car in purporting to be the ultimate driving machine. BMW would never do this again, and the high praise heaped on its successor, the Z4, shows just how good the Z3 should have been.

Z3: E36 PRODUCTION

Production History:	In production: 1995-2003						Total produced 294,537				
model	Z3 1.8	Z3 1.9	Z3 2.0	Z3 2.2	Z3 2.8	Z3 3.0	Z3 3.2M	Z3 Coupé 2.8	Z3 Coupé 3.0	Z3 Coupé 3.2M	total for year
1995	1,248	818									2,066
1996	11,890	32,716			1,427		60				46,093
1997	10,384	27,137			21,302		2,013	4		19	60,859
1998	7,830	15,392	9		20,006		5,468	160		2475	51,340
1999	7,234	1,902	8,908		21,375	12	4,191	3,451	4	1831	48,908
2000	7,385		5,699	2,081	8,779	9,969	1,714	3,282	1,383	881	41,173
2001	7,609			16326		6,240	1,496	774	1,775	767	34,987
2002	2,511			2,645		2,566	380		691	318	9,111
totals	56,091	77,965	14,616	21,052	72,889	18,787	15,322	7,671	3,853	6,291	
									grand total		294,537
							Derivative totals: cabrio				268,620
									coupé		16,806
									Series total		285,426

3 Series Compact (E36-5)

→ 1994 – 2000
→ Shortened hatchback derivative of 3 Series
→ Introduced to compete with VW Golf
→ Suspension and interior from previous 3 Series
→ Launched with 1.6 litre four
→ Later 323i six is rewarding to drive

New man at the top

Smooth change of chairman and dramatic Rover takeover as Compact launches

Watching the sales charts closely, senior BMW executives led by Eberhard von Kuenheim had been keeping an especially close eye on the performance of the then-new 1991 Volkswagen Golf Mk III. The new VW had generally been given a rough ride in the press, criticised for its stodgy styling, its meagre equipment and its leaden performance. These lower models were of no concern to the BMW board, but there was one version which, if it proved to be the beginning of a trend, merited monitoring.

The fact that Volkswagen had invested heavily in an advanced 2.8 litre six-cylinder engine for the Golf meant just one thing: VW intended to inch its staple product steadily up market in speed, status and power, and to use its good name to try to get a slice of the premium market for medium cars – something which could threaten the comfortable margins BMW was earning. After some discussion BMW decided the best form of defence was attack, and resolved to launch a BMW into the Golf sector. The company figured that, faced with the choice of either a VW or a BMW at similar prices, enough buyers would go for the more prestigious name of BMW to make the project worthwhile; still more buyers might be tempted by the BMW's rear wheel drive, even at that

time a unique feature in that part of the market.

The function of the smaller BMW was not just to be cheaper: it would be more fun, too. At the back of everyone's mind was a sentimental return to the spirit of the 2002, which even then was being regularly cited as a kind of golden age for BMW: the new car could be small, light, simple and, above all, a BMW and thus great to drive.

The car which emerged under the name Compact in September 1993 promised to be all of those things. However, the recipe of taking a current 3 Series and chopping 22 cm off the boot to create a hatchback rear resulted in a car which, when it first broke cover, looked all out of proportion; worse, the interior was clearly making use of old BMW components, such as the dashboard from the previous 3 Series, even

The sharply cut off tail of the Compact came as a shock to many people, but this entry-level model line brought large numbers of new customers into the BMW brand, 65 per cent of whom went on to buy another BMW

221

"At the back of everyone's mind was a sentimental return to the spirit of the 2002, which even then was being regularly cited as a kind of golden age for BMW"

incorporating old-fashioned push-pull switches which hadn't been around for some time. Suspicions that this was an uncharacteristic cut-price job were heightened by a technical specification which showed the obsolete semi trailing arm rear suspension, also from the previous model line; the initial engine, too, was the lowest 8-valve 1.6 litre in the BMW line-up.

Once over the shock of the abbreviated shape and the chopped off tail, the Compact did indeed seem quite a fun idea. The driving experience, on the other hand, barely scraped over the BMW quality threshold. The engine was reasonably smooth and sounded lively, though in reality it had to be pushed hard to make quick progress; the handling and steering were reasonable enough, but this was clearly no thoroughbred. Nevertheless, its appeal was plain

for people who wanted to step up to BMW ownership but were not particularly bothered about which BMW.

Ironically, just weeks after the Compact entered the showrooms, another, much more major move took place, something which, on the admission of a senior BMW official at the time, would have made the whole Compact idea pointless. Having conceived the Compact in order to establish a defensive position on the fringes of the volume car sector, BMW then bought Britain's Rover group – with the express strategic intention of competing in the volume market with a second brand name. "We wouldn't have done the Compact at all if we'd known we were buying Rover," said the official.

The Rover purchase was masterminded by Bernd Pischetsrieder who, after having been

Colour choice was not a BMW strong suit when it tried to appeal to a younger market: Open Air version (far right) had a full length fabric sunroof

named as the designated successor to von Kuenheim some years before, had taken over the top job in May of the previous year. An enthusiast for British marques – he was the nephew of Sir Alec Issigonis, designer of the 1959 Mini – he could see the sense of preserving the status of BMW by keeping it out of the grubby competition in the big-numbers sectors.

Rover or no Rover, the Compact family steadily acquired larger engines, including a 1.7 litre diesel in the 318 tds and a 1.9 litre 16-valve, which gave a useful slice of extra power and was the first compact to use the ti designation. Autumn 1997 saw what proved to be the most entertaining of the Compacts, the 323ti with the 2.5 litre six-cylinder engine, complete with VANOS variable valve timing and an output of 170 horsepower. This was certainly a move in the direction of the 2002 Tii, but by now the

Compact was becoming quite pricey: the 323ti sold for the same price as the 320i saloon and not much less than the Coupé, both of which had the much superior Z-axle rear suspension.

BMW was never allowed to forget that it had asked its customers to accept second best with the Compact and its cast-off suspension and dashboard. The suspicion was around that this was verging on a cynical exploitation of the magnetism of the BMW badge. Sales of the model began to weaken after the first couple of years and for the final two and a half years of the car's life its prices were not raised one Pfennig – a sure sign of a car that is in trouble. It was a mistake that BMW would never make again – even when, much to everyone's astonishment, it launched a new Compact in 2001 after a gap of over a year.

E36: 3 SERIES COMPACTS

Specifications	316i	318ti	318tds	323ti

Engine				
Engine type	Inline 4-cylinder	Inline 4-cylinder	Inline 4-cylinder intercooled turbo diesel	Inline 6-cylinder
Bore & stroke, mm	84 x 72 (1999 on: 85 x 83.5)	84 x 72 (1999 on: 85 x 83.5)	80 x 82.2	84 x 75
Capacity, cc	1596 (1999 on: 1895)	1596 (1999 on: 1895)	1665	2494
Valves	8	16	8	24
Valve actuation	Sohc	Dohc	Sohc	Dohc VANOS
Compression ratio	9.7:1	10.0:1	22.0:1	10.5:1
Fuelling	Bosch Motronic fuel injection	Bosch Motronic fuel injection	Bosch digital diesel fuel injection	Siemens fuel injection
Max power, bhp @ rpm	102@5500 (1999 on: 105@5300)	140@6000	90@4400	170@5500
Max torque, Nm @ rpm	150@4250 (1999 on: 165@2500)	175@4500 (1999 on: 18.3@4300)	190@2000	245@3950
Transmission				
Manual transmission	5-speed	5-speed	5-speed	5-speed
Automatic	GM 4-speed	GM 4-speed	GM 4-speed	ZF 4-speed
Drive	Rear wheels	Rear wheels	Rear wheels	Rear wheels
Chassis				
Front suspension	MacPherson struts	MacPherson struts	MacPherson struts	MacPherson struts
Rear suspension	Semi-trailing arms, minibloc coil springs	Semi-trailing arms, minibloc coil springs	Semi-trailing arms, minibloc coil springs	Semi-trailing arms, minibloc coil springs
Braking	Disc/drum, servo assisted, ABS	Disc, servo assisted, ABS	Disc, servo assisted, ABS	Disc, servo assisted, ABS
Steering	Rack and pinion, power assisted	Rack and pinion, power assisted	Rack and pinion, power assisted	Rack and pinion, power assisted
Wheels	6.5 x 15	6.5 x 15	6.0 x 15	7.0 x 15
Tyres	185/65 HR15	205/60 VR15	185/65 HR15	225/50 WR15
Body				
Structure	Steel monocoque	Steel monocoque	Steel monocoque	Steel monocoque
Wheelbase, mm	2700	2700	2700	2700
Track F/R, mm	1400/1425	1400/1425	1400/1425	1413/1413
Length, mm	4210	4210	4210	4210
Width, mm	1698	1698	1698	1698
Height, mm	1393	1393	1393	1393
Kerb weight, kg	1175	1200	1175	1255
Fuel tank capacity, lit	55	55	55	55
Performance				
Max speed, km/h	188 (1999 on: 190)	209	188 (1999 on: 190)	230
0-100km/h, sec	12.3 (1999 on: 11.9)	9.9	12.3 (1999 on: 11.9)	7.8
Fuel consumption , lit/100km	7.6	7.9	7.6	9.3
Marketing				
Launch date	4/93	9/94	4/93	9/97
Pricing, DM	33,600	38,700	33,600	47,900

Pressure from customers and media encouraged BMW to fit the smooth, lively 2.5 litre six to the Compact in 1993. The 323ti became a rewarding driver's car, with distant echoes of the 2002 tii

E36
FIRST COMPACT E36 PRODUCTION

Production History:	In production: 1993 – 2000				Total produced 396,122	
model	316i Compact	318td Compact	318iS Compact	318ti Compact	323ti Compact	total for year
1993	120					120
1994	53,267	39	10,384			63,690
1995	50,905	7385	31,134	60		89,484
1996	33,624	7445	22	18,868		59,959
1997	36,388	6,723		18,261	3,562	64,934
1998	27,257	5,749		12,954	6,820	52,780
1999	27,997	5,104		4,090	3,340	40,531
2000	17,644	3,358		2,189	1,433	24,624
totals	**247,202**	**35,803**	**41,540**	**56,422**	**15,155**	
					grand total	**396,122**

04

Diversification
and disaster

Rover takeover

→ Deal announced Jan 1994
→ Secret negotiations
→ Prompted by needs for economies of scale
→ Land Rover seen as high potential brand
→ Secret talks with Rolls-Royce too

The Rover romance

BMW stuns the world by buying Britain's multi-marque group

The BMW board of management came to the conclusion in the late 1980s that its brand was near the limits of its market stretch. Its performance over the previous two decades was admired by car buyers and by investors alike. Production, sales and profits grew steadily and consistently, but there were sectors of the market where it would be inappropriate to sell models with BMW badges. It was an issue for tomorrow rather than today. Over the long term, though, it would become a problem and it would need a solution.

January 31 1994: BMW chief executive Bernd Pischetsrieder shakes hands on the Rover acquisition with Dick Evans, CEO of British Aerospace. The deal would rock BMW's mangement structure

Despite the solid growth, the group remained small by international standards. It sold half a million cars a year at a time when two million was considered a minimum level for economies of scale and General Motors and Ford each sold well over six million vehicles a year. As a group, BMW needed higher sales volumes each year in order to spread its engineering and manufacturing costs, but it had to achieve them without damaging the reputation it had carefully cultivated for the BMW brand itself. That suggested BMW would have to participate in the wave of motor industry consolidation, a development that was already making big companies even bigger. As that continued, BMW would shrink in relative terms, however much it

continued to grow organically.

For the decision-makers in Munich, there was another critical unknown: what was their great rival Mercedes-Benz in Stuttgart up to? The two had developed in uncanny lockstep through the great post-war car boom around the world. Both had become rich and famous. If BMW had a small saloon, Mercedes needed one. If Mercedes sold a roadster, BMW clearly had to as well. Both were in the process of building their first factories in the United States. Neither company could ignore what the other did.

The bombshell dropped by Mercedes chairman Helmut Werner in January 1993 caught everyone by surprise. Declaring that Mercedes products were over-priced and over-

"To achieve its strategic targets, BMW had already concluded that it had to embark on a policy of acquisition for the first time. It had the cash reserves to support any such action. What it needed were available targets"

engineered, Werner promised an efficiency and expansion drive that would transform the nature and scale of the group over the following years. He said Mercedes would launch more sports cars and coupes as well as a small car (which became the A-class), a sport-utility (M-class) and a people-carrier (V-class). This revolutionary stuff had obvious implications for BMW.

Organic growth was all very well, and would continue to serve BMW well. But the Mercedes announcement, coupled with BMW's own thinking, dictated a change of pace. To achieve its strategic targets, BMW's directors had already concluded that it had to embark on a policy of acquisition for the first time. It had the cash reserves to support any such action. What it needed were available targets. It would be ready to act when the opportunities arose.

The idea was that BMW would evolve from its mono-marque culture into a group with a portfolio of nameplates. It would effectively be a prestige version of a concept perfected by General Motors in the United States in the 1920s – a car for every purse and purpose. The difference was that BMW would compete in only the top sector of each market category. In particular, BMW chairman Eberhard von Kuenheim and technical director Wolfgang Reitzle felt the group needed a very high-end luxury marque like Rolls-Royce, an off-road maker such as Land Rover and some

compact front-wheel-drives like those made by Rover. Each marque would complement BMW's own range of rear-wheel-drive saloons, estates, coupes, convertibles and sports cars.

The first pieces of the strategy were put in place at the start of the 1990s, when Vickers, the British engineering group, secretly began to tout its twin Rolls-Royce and Bentley marques around the world's top car makers. Vickers had a lot of interest, but found no takers, in large measure because the would-be buyers knew a great deal of expensive restructuring would be required at Rolls-Royce's Crewe factory. In addition, it was a period of great uncertainty concerning the future of limousine makes like Rolls-Royce and Bentley. Economies around the world made the opening years of the 1990s a very difficult time to sell any cars, let alone exclusive models with numbing price tags.

Officially, Rolls-Royce and Bentley were not for sale at that stage; that came in the autumn of 1997. BMW was much more interested in the marques than it was prepared to acknowledge, however. Its offer to buy a 20 per cent share in Rolls-Royce and Bentley was rejected by Vickers, which was interested only in a full sale. Instead, BMW quietly began to make its latest technology and testing facilities available to Rolls-Royce, which had been starved of cash and resources for the previous two decades. No one outside the

Austin Mini Super de Luxe, 1964: BMW had already identified the iconic Mini as a brand with great future potential

Second-generation Range Rover was announced after BMW purchased Rover but the contract to use BMW diesel engines had been concluded before the acquisition. Land Rover was seen by BMW as an important brand, while Rover promised opportunities as a volume range

two companies knew about the work at the time. Indeed, Rolls-Royce went to enormous lengths to keep the business secret. The world found out about it only after BMW's chairman at the time, Dr Bernd Pischetsrieder, authorised a leak to the effect that it was happening. It was a 'hands off' warning to other car makers in case they became too interested in Rolls-Royce over the following few years. Just to reinforce the claim, when Bentley displayed a concept car called Java at the Geneva motor show in 1994, BMW quietly let it be known that it was based on the engineering and technology of the 5 Series. Rolls-Royce and Bentley were clearly being pulled ever more closely into the BMW orbit at that time.

By the end of the year, BMW had seemingly landed its catch. It beat Mercedes-Benz in a competition to provide engines for a new generation of Rolls-Royce and Bentley then being planned. The result was that the Silver Seraph was powered by a BMW V12 engine when it was launched in 1998, and the Arnage had a BMW twin-turbo V8. It was a controversial choice, because Rolls-Royce directors believed

the Mercedes option was preferable. When its advice was vetoed by the board of Vickers, its parent company, Rolls-Royce chief executive Peter Ward resigned. BMW therefore looked a shoe-in for that moment in the future when Vickers finally decided to rid itself of Rolls-Royce. The final outcome four years later did not work out how BMW planned, however.

By the start of 1994, though, BMW had engineered the coup that put in place most of its planned multi-brand strategy. In one of the greatest surprises the motor industry had then seen, BMW announced on January 31st that it had bought Britain's Rover Group. The move gave BMW control of, among others, the Rover, MG, Mini and, most importantly, Land Rover marques. It was another controversial development because, by buying British Aerospace's 80 per cent share in Rover, BMW effectively kicked out Honda, which owned the remaining 20 per cent. Without Honda, the Rover group would have expired long before. It seemed a less than gracious way to treat a company that had provided technical support to Rover over the previous 15 years.

"BMW had cause to celebrate 1994. The Rover purchase was considered a triumph at the time because it gave BMW its real prize, Land Rover, for little more than it would have cost to develop just one four-wheel drive model of its own"

George Simpson, chairman of Rover and deputy chief executive of British Aerospace negotiated the BMW purchase. He was despatched to Tokyo to discuss the deal with Nobuhiko Kawamoto, the president of Honda, which owned 20 per cent. Kawamoto refused to see him

The controversy did not end there. The episode during which BMW owned Rover came close to threatening the very future of the BMW group itself. Perhaps BMW officials did not study the history of the Rover group closely enough. If they had, they would have known that the group had an unhappy knack of bringing ruin to all those who tried to control it.

The group known as Rover at the time of the BMW purchase dates back to 1877 and some Starley and Sutton bicycles. The firm made its first Rover car in 1904, at roughly the same time as a wave of other fledgling car companies were getting started in Britain. Plenty of them failed over the following few years. Over the next nine decades, particularly from the early 1950s, most of what remained of those pioneering British car companies gradually came under control of the group that became Rover.

The cornerstone of the group was established in 1952 by the merger of the firms founded by two of Britain's best-known industrialists of the inter-war years, Herbert Austin and William Morris. By a curious coincidence, the 1920s Austin Seven provided BMW's start as a car maker. BMW was an aircraft engine and motorcycle maker that in 1928 bought the Eisenach Vehicle Factory. With it came a licence to build the Austin Seven in Germany under the name of Dixi.

One half of what became British Motor Corporation, or BMC, was Austin, founded in 1905 and based at Longbridge, south-west of Birmingham. The other half was the Nuffield Organisation, which was created in the inter-war years following Morris's purchase of Riley and

Wolseley and the establishment of the sporty MG (for Morris Garages) marque. Nuffield's centre of gravity was the old Morris works at Cowley on the edge of Oxford. Longbridge and Cowley came to feature prominently in the BMW story.

The merger turned BMC into the largest vehicle maker in the world outside the United States. But it was almost a merger in name only. A person worked for Austin or Morris, but not for BMC. There was precious little attempt to bring together the two old rivals, each of which identified the other as a competitor in the same category as Ford, Vauxhall, Hillman and Standard. It was perhaps a prelude to BMW's own failed industrial integration with Rover in the 1990s. In 1966, BMC bought the ailing Jaguar and Daimler business from the Docker family to form British Motor Holdings.

While all that was going on, the old-established commercial vehicle firm of Leyland returned to car making with the 1961 purchase of Standard-Triumph. Six years later, it bought Rover and its Land Rover subsidiary, which was founded in 1948.

One year later, in 1968, Leyland became the senior partner in the merger with BLMH that created British Leyland Motor Corporation. This was the firm that was known variously over the following years as British Leyland, BL and Rover Group. Thus, over a period of only 16 years, most of Britain's remaining independent car firms were swept into a sprawling conglomerate that comprised nameplates as diverse as Austin-Healey, Austin, Daimler, Jaguar, Land Rover, Leyland, Morris, MG, Riley, Rover, Triumph and Wolseley.

It was all too unwieldy ever to work properly. In addition to competing nameplates, British Leyland employed too many people in too many factories. It had a history of dreadful labour relations, poor quality and uncompetitive productivity. The group produced the occasional product gems – the Mini and 1100 series – but its models were often fundamentally flawed. Buyers around the world were underwhelmed. The industrial and commercial failure of Britain's biggest motor manufacturer led to its virtual nationalisation in 1975. By that time, British Leyland had lost its market lead in the UK to Ford.

The Conservative government that was elected in 1979 had a programme of privatisation at the heart of its agenda. Michael Edwardes, a feisty South African then in charge of the group, and his successor, Graham Day, a Canadian, were given the authority to close or sell what they considered necessary. Jaguar and the Unipart component businesses were privatised, with Ford subsequently buying Jaguar. The Leyland commercial vehicle business went to Daf. Some famous motoring names reached the end of the road, among them Austin, Morris and Triumph. Austin-Healey, Riley, Standard and Wolseley had motored into the sunset several years before.

What remained by the mid-1980s, then, was the Rover Group, which comprised only the Rover, Land Rover and MG marques. It was the country's last indigenous car maker of any size, the Rootes brothers having sold their Hillman-Humber-Sunbeam-Singer group to Chrysler in the 1960s. Rover was smaller and healthier than it was a decade earlier, but it was still a charge on the state. That was resolved in 1988. In a sudden move prompted solely by political expediency, Prime Minister Margaret Thatcher sold an 80 per cent shareholding in Rover to British Aerospace. The cost was a mere £150 million, for which, it subsequently emerged, BAe received secret government sweeteners of £44 million.

Having a defence contractor and builder of civilian airliners in charge of a mainstream car maker made no industrial or commercial sense. The aircraft and automotive industries speak different languages. Cars are sold in hundred of thousands, aircraft in hundreds. Cars are bought by people, aircraft by governments and airlines.

Car unit costs are denominated in thousands, those of aircraft in millions or billions. If the necessary investments in the motor industry are sky-high, those in the aircraft industry are stratospheric. The only commercial synergy, and it would have been a small one, would be if BAe sealed a deal for Hawk trainer aircraft by throwing in a couple of hundred Land Rover Defenders – and a Range Rover or two for the air chief marshal.

The sale of BAe's shareholding in Rover to BMW less than six years later essentially proved the frailty of the logic behind it in the first place.

Rover would not have survived the whole period without Honda. While the Japanese company bought the remaining 20 per cent in Rover at the time of the privatisation, its real contribution stemmed from a 1979 agreement to supply technology to the struggling British car maker. It resulted initially in the quick introduction of the Triumph Acclaim – a Civic-based saloon assembled in England – and later in the Honda-based 200, 400, 600 and 800. The episode served Rover exceptionally well at a period when it was at its most vulnerable. It also helped Honda with insights into the European market as it geared up to manufacture cars at its newly established factory in Swindon. When BMW bought BAe's Rover shareholding, Honda was forced to devise a completely different strategy for its Swindon plant. The initial one had been costed on the basis of collaboration with Rover on engine supply, body stampings and shared components.

The future of Rover was picked over during the final months of 1993, but its fate was decided in only a few days in late January 1994. BAe's financial troubles in the early 1990s meant it needed to cash in on its Rover asset. Honda was invited to increase its shareholding, but it was not prepared to be bumped into a quick decision and was not interested in taking its share beyond 47.5 per cent. That was not, and is not, the Japanese way of doing business. Unlike BAe, Honda was in no hurry.

It knew about BMW's interest in Rover, but did not grasp its determination. On January 26th, the BAe board of directors was presented with an offer of £800 million for its 80 per cent

holding in Rover by Dr Hagen Luderitz, BMW's corporate planning director. Considering the financial plight of BAe, and what it had paid for its shareholding little more than five years earlier, its board was ready to grab the deal. As a Rover shareholder with a proposal of its own in the pending file, though, Honda had to be asked whether it wanted to reconsider. The following day, George Simpson, chairman of Rover and deputy chief executive of BAe, was despatched to Tokyo to discuss the matter with Nobuhiko Kawamoto, the president of Honda. It was not a happy encounter for either side. Simpson never got to see Kawamoto, whose colleagues informed the BAe representative that Honda was not prepared to increase its offer.

Honda felt betrayed. It had been treated in a cavalier manner, in spite of its support for Rover through a series of crises. Its anger, though, was not directed at Rover, or even at BMW. It was towards British Aerospace. Honda eventually sold its 20 per cent share to BMW.

BMW had cause to celebrate in 1994. The Rover purchase was considered a triumph at the time because it gave BMW its real prize, Land Rover, for little more than it would have cost to develop just one four-wheel-drive model of its own. It had MG, which was still remembered around the world as one of the great sports car brands. Pischetsrieder talked fondly of his admiration for old Rileys. It thought Rover could be developed as a luxury brand to complement the more sporty BMW. It already had plans to transform the ancient Mini model into a separate Mini brand. Separately, BMW believed it had out-manoeuvred all other possible purchasers for that moment when Rolls-Royce and Bentley were eventually put up for sale.

The developments turned Pischetsrieder into the motor industry's hero of the moment. A manufacturing specialist who was little known outside BMW until he was made chairman the previous May, Pischetsrieder combined an affable nature with quick, bold decisions and clear strategic vision. As events unfolded over the remainder of the decade, however, a different image of Pischetsrieder began to emerge.

The power to win

Formula One constructor McLaren chooses BMW V12 to propel the world's fastest road car

It was not just because of his personal links with BMW that McLaren's Gordon Murray chose BMW to provide the engine for the F1, the British racing car constructor's ambitious project to develop the ultimate roadgoing sports car.

Murray, who designed the Brabham grand prix cars which took the 1983 World Championship courtesy of BMW turbo engines, already enjoyed a good relationship with BMW's racing engineers. But for the F1 road car, where every horsepower and every gramme of weight were just as crucial as on the Formula One circuit, it wasn't enough just to rely on past contacts: Murray and his team systematically analysed every high powered engine available or potentially available, and only then did the choice come back to BMW.

The demands were enormous. Murray had calculated that he needed in excess of 600 bhp in order to achieve the required maximum speed of 370-plus km/h; the engine had to be light, it had to be strong as it would be used to transmit chassis and cornering loads, and it had to be extremely flexible, with instant pick-up at any speed. This completely ruled out turbocharging, which had been the easy route to the superficially

impressive 480-550 bhp outputs of existing supercars such as the Ferrari F40, Jaguar XJ220 and the short-lived quad-turbo Bugatti EB110.

Only a large-capacity V12 would be suitable, reasoned Murray, and the five-litre BMW M70, as used in the 7 Series, was the one which best fitted the bill and had the greatest potential for development.

Murray and his team were soon busy exploring design concepts, the most radical of which was chosen. This placed the driver in the centre line of the car, with a passenger either side set slightly to the rear; luggage space, normally non-existent in supercars of this calibre, was provided in the flanks of the car between the butterfly-style doors and the rear wheel arches. In terms of packaging, Murray's car was little short of brilliant: all the elements were packed into a smooth body, styled by Peter Stevens, formerly of Lotus, which measured just 4290 mm in length

Alien encounter: McLaren chose BMW V12 power for its F1 project to build the ultimate supercar. Only 100 were built

and, crucially to Murray's priorities for handling, just 1820 mm in width. The Jaguar XJ220 was a giant by contrast, at almost five metres in length and 2.2 metres wide.

On the engine front BMW Motorsport specialists thoroughly reworked what they by now had designated the S70. The most fundamental changes were an expansion to 6.1 litres and the move to four-valve cylinder heads and twin chain-driven overhead camshafts per bank, with steplessly variable timing for the inlet camshaft. Later, roadgoing BMWs would reflect this layout.

The induction system moved to a cylinder-by-cylinder layout, with each having its own throttle butterfly and injector; all these were fed by a specially-fabricated carbon-fibre airbox in the centre of the vee. The exhaust system grouped

"On the engine front BMW Motorsport specialists thoroughly reworked the V12 they had by now redesignated S70. The most fundamental changes were the move to 6.1 litre and four-valve heads, with steplessly variable timing for the inlet valves. Later, roadgoing BMWs would reflect this layout"

Gordon Murray's ingenious design for the F1 supercar placed the driver centrally for optimum handling: within a short overall length Murray packaged the mighty BMW V12 engine, three occupants

four clusters of three equal-length manifold pipes, each group feeding a separate catalyst, while internally some parts such as the cam carriers moved from aluminium to magnesium in the interests of saving eight.

The result was a sensational 627 bhp at 7400 rpm, with a massive 617 Nm of torque available all the way from 4000 to 7000 rpm. This was fed through to a six-speed transverse transmission and a triple-plate carbon clutch to the limited slip differential and thence to the rear wheels. No form of traction control was fitted, so good was the grip provided by the McLaren chassis; on Murray's insistence, the F1's brakes had neither ABS nor servo assistance. The steering was unassisted, to, Murray believing drivers should experience exact forces applied to the wheels with no loss of road feel.

McLAREN F1

Specifications	McLaren F1	McLaren F1 GTR
Engine		
Engine type	60-degree V12	60-degree V12
Bore & stroke, mm	86 x 87	86 x 86
Capacity, cc	6064	5991
Valves	48	48
Valve actuation	Dohc per bank	Dohc per bank
Compression ratio	10.5:1	11:1
Fuelling	Bosch lectronic fuel injection	Electronic fuel injection
Max power, bhp @ rpm	627@7500	608@7000
Max torque, Nm @ rpm	617@4000	687@5500
Transmission		
Manual transmission	Transverse 6-speed	Transverse 6-speed
Automatic	Not available	Not available
Drive	Rear wheels	Rear wheels
Chassis		
Front suspension	Double wishbones, inboard-mounted coil-spring/damper units operated via pushrods	Double wishbones, inboard-mounted coil-spring/damper units operated via pushrods
Rear suspension	Double wishbones, inboard-mounted coil-spring/damper units operated via pushrods	Double wishbones, inboard-mounted coil-spring/damper units operated via pushrods
Braking	Disc, unassisted; no ABS	Disc, unassisted; no ABS
Steering	Rack and pinion, unassisted	Rack and pinion, unassisted
Wheels front + rear	9.0 x 17 + 11.5 x 17	11.0 x 17 + 13.0 x 17
Tyres front + rear	235/45 ZR 17 + 315/45 ZR 17	235/45 ZR 17 + 315/45 ZR 17
Body		
Structure	Carbon fibre composite monocoque and outer panels	Carbon fibre composite monocoque and outer panels
Wheelbase, mm	2720	2720
Track F/R, mm	1570/1470	1600/1560
Length, mm	4290	4920
Width, mm	1820	1920
Height, mm	1140	1120
Kerb weight, kg	1140	950
Fuel tank capacity, lit	90	100
Performance		
Max speed, km/h	350	350
0-100km/h	3.2	-
Fuel consumption , lit/100km	21.0	21.0
Marketing		
Launch date	5/92	11/96
Pricing, (£)	630,000	–

Following the unveiling of the car in Monte Carlo in May 1992 and subsequent magazine reports, these unassisted systems proved to be just about the only point of criticism on a vehicle which had writers struggling to outdo each other with superlatives and hyperbolae. Britain's *Autocar,* the only publication granted permission to do acceleration figures, clocked the F1 to 60 mph (97 km/h) in 3.2 seconds and to 199mph (320 km/h) in a mind-boggling 28 seconds, declaring it the finest driving machine yet built for the public road. "It possesses more performance than all of the cars racing at Le Mans this year," continued the magazine, estimating its top speed at 236mph (380 km/h) and concluding that it was likely to stand as the fastest road car in the whole history of the automobile.

Those figures may of course be eventually exceeded by the 1001 bhp Bugatti Veyron, but the Autocar observation about Le Mans proved uncannily accurate: the following year McLaren F1 GTRs in the hands of private owners swept the board, finishing first, third, fourth, fifth and 13th. Not only was this the best-ever result for one marque in a single year, it was the first time in the history of the event that a new marque had won first time out.

The 1995 Le Mans cars differed subtly from the road models: they were the most powerful of all, with 680 bhp from their S70/2 GTR LM engines at 7800 rpm; they had an 8500 rpm rev limit and used straight-cut gears. The body carried a simple spoiler at the rear to increase downforce. To commemorate the famous victory McLaren built what must be the most exclusive run of limited edition cars ever: five Papaya

Making history: the McLaren F1 crosses the line to win the 1995 Le Mans 24 Hours. By winning first time out, with other McLaren F1s in 3rd, 4th, 5th and 13th places, Mclaren established a new record. Left: Dieter Quester drives the spectacular McLaren F1 GTR Le Mans at the 2004 Goodwood Festival of Speed

"The following year, McLaren F1 GTRs in the hands of private owners swept the board at Le Mans, finishing first, third, fourth, fifth and 13th. It was the first time in the history of the event that a new marque had won first time out"

orange (in honour of Bruce McLaren's racing colours) F1 LMs, with only the minimum modifications to the GTR to make them legal for road use.

The following year the Le Mans regulations changed, with cars limited to 600 bhp: McLaren's response was to trim the F1's weight by 100 kg (a remarkable feat, considering how meticulously it had been engineered); using the latest S70/3 iteration of the BMWE engine it finished fourth at Le Mans. Then final derivative, the GTR97, saw further weight reductions to 915 kg, despite newly extended front and rear bodywork to increase downforce: even with the 600 bhp limit in place these long-tail cars were up to five seconds a lap quicker than the originals.

The GTR97 in turn gave rise to the final road

car, the long-tailed F1 GT. Only three of these long-bodied, low-drag F1s were built, bringing to a close a saga where, perhaps for the only time in history, the world's finest engine builder joined forces with the most brilliant brains and the top name in Formula One to create an absolute best, money-no-object ultimate road car. The tax-paid price tag of about a million dollars was certainly a reflection of the astonishing ingenuity of the engineering, as well as the 1.5 man-years expended on the crafting of each car (a Nissan Micra takes less than seven hours); whether it was all worth it, and whether McLaren would have sold more than the 100 it did had the general economic situation been better – these are questions that may never be answered.

23

Fourth 5 Series (E39)

→ 1995 – 2003
→ Evolution of E34 styling theme
→ Longer, wider, taller but lighter
→ First car with aluminium suspension
→ State of the art diesel engines
→ M5 V8 breaks 400 bhp barrier
→ Distinctive 'light ring' headlights on facelift models
→ Multiple award winner
→ 1.5 million built by end of 2003

Business as usual

The rows about Rover hogged the headlines, but BMW itself kept on launching brilliant cars

The fourth-generation 5 Series that appeared in the autumn of 1995 was rolling proof of BMW's two steps forward, one step back philosophy of design. The previous model had pushed the 5 some way in a more adventurous visual direction; this car merely tidied up the theme, smartened up the contours and was happy to allow the engineering to do the rest. A sense of continuity was important at this stage as BMW had encountering a lot of criticism for its involvement with Rover and it needed to show that as far as BMW-brand cars were concerned it was business – excellent business – as usual.

The smooth, classy look of the fourth-generation 5 Series helped build a strong brand identity across all BMW model lines. Light guide rings developed by Hella for facelift model gave the range a strong visual signature, especially at night

As with so many of BMW's small-step updates, this E39 was initially hard to tell at a glance from its predecessor; soon, however, the subtle differences started to become more apparent, the new look began to seem more attractive, to fit in seamlessly with its 3 and 7 companions, and the model went on to become an outstanding success.

So successful, in fact, that by the end of 2003, with the Touring still in production for a couple of months more, close on 1.5 million examples had been built and sold. More remarkably, the 5 Series continued winning awards from influential magazines all over the word throughout its eight-year production life:

such awards nearly always go to the latest release in each sector, and it must have been a particular pleasure in Munich to see their contender beat two successive generations of Mercedes' E-Class and come a very close second to the latest E – with a design that was approaching nine years since its launch.

It is not easy to single out any individual quality which made this fourth-generation 5 Series such a success: it was perhaps the model's smooth, mature shape, its beautifully-honed engineering, its finely-judged chassis, its immaculately assembled interior – a combination of the disciplines at which BMW invariably excels, but crystallised together in a particularly happy

E39

E39: 5SERIES

Specifications	520i	523i/525i	528i	530i	535i
Engine					
Engine type	Inline 6-cylinder	Inline 6-cylinder	Inline 6-cylinder	Inline 6-cylinder	90-degree V8
Bore & stroke, mm	80 x 66 (from 2001: 80 x 72)	84 x 75	84 x 84	84 x 89.6	84 x 78.9
Capacity, cc	1991 (from 2001: 2171)	2494	2793	2979	3498
Valves	24	24	24	24	32
Valve actuation	Dohc, Vanos variable valve timing (from 1998: double Vanos)	Dohc, Vanos variable valve timing (from 1998: double Vanos)	Dohc, Vanos variable valve timing (from 1998: double Vanos)	Dohc, Vanos variable valve timing (from 1998: double Vanos)	Dohc per bank (from 1998: Vanos variable valve timing)
Compression ratio	11:1	10.5:1	10.2:1	10.2:1	10.0:1
Fuelling	Electronic fuel injection	Electronic fuel injection	Siemens electronic fuel injection	Electronic fuel injection	Bosch Motronic electronic fuel injection
Max power, bhp @ rpm	150@5900 (from 2001: 170@6100)	170@5500	193@5300	231@5900	235@5800 (from 1998: 245@5800)
Max torque, Nm @ rpm	190@4200 (from 2001: 210@3500)	245@3950 (from 1998: 525i, 3500)	280@3950	300@3500	330@3300 (from 1998: 345@3800)
Transmission					
Manual transmission	5-speed	5-speed	5-speed	5-speed	5-speed
Automatic	ZF 5-speed (from 1998: Steptronic sequential option)	ZF 5-speed (from 1998: Steptronic sequential option)	ZF 5-speed (from 1998: Steptronic sequential option)	ZF 5-speed (from 1998: Steptronic sequential option)	ZF 5-speed (from 1998: Steptronic sequential option)
Drive	Rear wheels, ASC+T traction control	Rear wheels, ASC+T traction control	Rear wheels, ASC+T traction control	Rear wheels, ASC+T traction control	Rear wheels, ASC+T traction control
Chassis					
Front suspension	Double-pivot MacPherson struts, lower wishbones, coil springs	Double-pivot MacPherson struts, lower wishbones, coil springs	Double-pivot MacPherson struts, lower wishbones, coil springs	Double-pivot MacPherson struts, lower wishbones, coil springs	Double-pivot MacPherson struts, lower wishbones, coil springs
Rear suspension	Multi-link axle with trailing arms, twin transverse upper links, lower control arms, coil-springs	Multi-link axle with trailing arms, twin transverse upper links, lower control arms, coil-springs	Multi-link axle with trailing arms, twin transverse upper links, lower control arms, coil-springs	Multi-link axle with trailing arms, twin transverse upper links, lower control arms, coil-springs	Multi-link axle with trailing arms, twin transverse upper links, lower control arms, coil-springs
Braking	Disc, servo assisted, ABS	Disc, servo assisted, ABS	Disc, servo assisted, ABS	Disc, servo assisted, ABS	Disc, servo assisted, ABS
Steering	Rack and pinion, power assisted	Rack and pinion, power assisted	Rack and pinion, power assisted	Rack and pinion, power assisted	Recirculating ball, power assisted
Wheels	6.5 x 15	6.5 x 15	7.0 x 15	7.0 x 16	7.0 x 16
Tyres	1205/65 VR 15	205/65 VR 15	225/60 WR 15	225/55 R 16	225/55 R 16
Body					
Structure	Steel monocoque, front and rear subframes, light-alloy suspension	Steel monocoque, front and rear subframes, light-alloy suspension	Steel monocoque, front and rear subframes, light-alloy suspension	Steel monocoque, front and rear subframes, light-alloy suspension	Steel monocoque, front and rear subframes, light-alloy suspension
Wheelbase, mm	2830	2830	2830	2830	2830
Track F/R, mm	1515/1530	1515/1530	1515/1530	1515/1530	1515/1530
Length, mm	4775	4775	4775	4775	4775
Width, mm	1800	1800	1800	1800	1800
Height, mm	1430	1430	1430	1430	1430
Kerb weight, kg	1410 (from 2001: 1495)	1420	1440	1540	1610
Fuel tank capacity, lit	70	70	70	70	70
Performance					
Max speed, km/h	220	228	236	250	250
0-100km/h, sec	10.2	8.5	7.5	7.1	7.0 (from 1998: 6.9)
Fuel consumption, lit/100 km	10.6	10.6	10.8	9.3	13.2
Marketing					
Launch date	1/96	12/95	12/95	3/96	6/96
Pricing, DM	54,500	58,800	65,000	–	76,000

540i

90-degree V8
92 x 82.7
4398
32
Dohc per bank (from 1998:
Vanos variable valve timing)

10.0:1
Bosch Motronic electronic
fuel injection
286@5700
(from 1998: 5500)
420@3900
(from 1998: 440@3600)

6-speed
ZF 5-speed (from 1998:
Steptronic sequential option)
Rear wheels, ASC+T traction
control

Double-pivot MacPherson
struts, lower wishbones, coil
springs
Multi-link axle with trailing
arms, twin transverse upper
links, lower control arms, coil-
springs
Disc, servo assisted, ABS
Recirculating ball, power
assisted
7.0 x 16
225/55 R 16

Steel monocoque, front and
rear subframes, light-alloy
suspension
2830
1515/1530
4775
1800
1430
1630
70

250
6.2
13.7

6/96
88,000

Chassis of E39 5 Series incorporated important innovations such as weight-saving aluminium suspension, with sophisticated Z axle multi-link design at the rear

combination. Whichever powertrain, whichever body shape, whichever trim grade – they all seemed to work in a smooth, harmonious and agreeable manner.

The smoothened body shape, which blended naturally with its 3 Series and 7 Series brothers, was larger in every dimension than the outgoing car, yet careful computer-aided design had ensured the bare shell was 50 per cent stiffer for its weight than its predecessor; also helping to save weight were aluminium suspension systems front and rear, as well as lighter driveline components. The weight saving over the equivalent steel components was estimated at 36 per cent.

Important, too, was the move to the same multi-link axle rear layout which had given such a useful improvement to the 7 Series; the six-

cylinder cars switched to rack and pinion steering but for reasons of space and weight the V8s retained the traditional recirculating ball layout. Three petrol and one diesel engine were initially offered, starting with the confusingly-badged 523i, which in fact had the 2.5 litre, 170 bhp M52 engine with single VANOS variable valve timing. Next up was the 528i on 193 bhp, while the 525tds gave 143 bhp; soon afterwards came the 520i, a genuine two-litre on 150 bhp, and the two V8 models, the 535i (235 bhp) and 540i with a full 286 bhp. The V8s had six-speed gearboxes, air suspension at the rear, and were distinguished externally by chromed vertical bars in the BMW grilles.

The 523i and, especially, the 528i got off to a strong sales start; in the spring of 1997 Touring models were added, with the same engine

BMW's six-cylinder direct-injection diesel marked a watershed in buyer attitudes to diesel: for the first time a diesel could be as powerful, flexible, smooth and as refined as the equivalent petrol unit. 4.4 litre M52 V8 in 540i was the luxury option (bottom)

choices as the saloon: this time the 525tds was much the stronger seller. The Touring body, like the saloon's, was a logical development of the old model's: the separately opening rear window (which by now had even been copied by Renault) was retained and made easier to use, a slide-out load platform was listed as an option and, later, a powered tailgate open/close function, activated by the key sender or a button on the tailgate rim, was introduced.

There was much excitement at the Geneva show in March 1998 when BMW unveiled the new M5. It was more powerfully styled than its predecessor, with a deeper front moulding and airflow management under the chassis, the air exiting at the rear in a diffuser-like structure dominated by large quadruple exhausts aimed upwards like missile launchers. These gave a strong clue to the main highlight under the bonnet, where the brand new S68 five-litre V8 resided, boasting the then-astonishing power output of 400 bhp. A notable innovation was dual mapping for the engine: the sport/standard switch on the dashboard could be pressed to toggle between rapid throttle response for hard driving and a gentler response for town work. The

M5 also introduce a novel electronic rev counter which took account of a cold engine and illuminated a ring of red LEDs to show the lower rev limit which should be applied until the engine and its fluids had reached full working temperature. As the engine warmed, the red line crept up.

The M5 impressed all with its astonishing pace, its civilised manners and its throaty engine sound when pushed hard. The price was high but once again BMW had upped the ante with its performance saloon: just over 20,000 were built. Yet, appealing though the M5 unquestionably was, BMW was soon to come up with a different development of much greater commercial significance. Most leading carmakers had by this stage been working on direct-injection diesels, which can be up to 20 per cent more efficient than the older swirl chamber type. Volkswagen in particular had cashed in heavily with its broad range of TDI diesels.

However, BMW's take on the direct-injection diesel blew all the others into the weeds. First put out as the 530d, the state-of-the-art straight six-cylinder, 24-valve common rail M57 had not only unprecedented power (193 bhp) and torque, but

New Touring was again an intelligent update of the previous generation: the more compact rear suspension allowed an improved load bay. Aluminium was used extensively in suspension and chassis to save weight

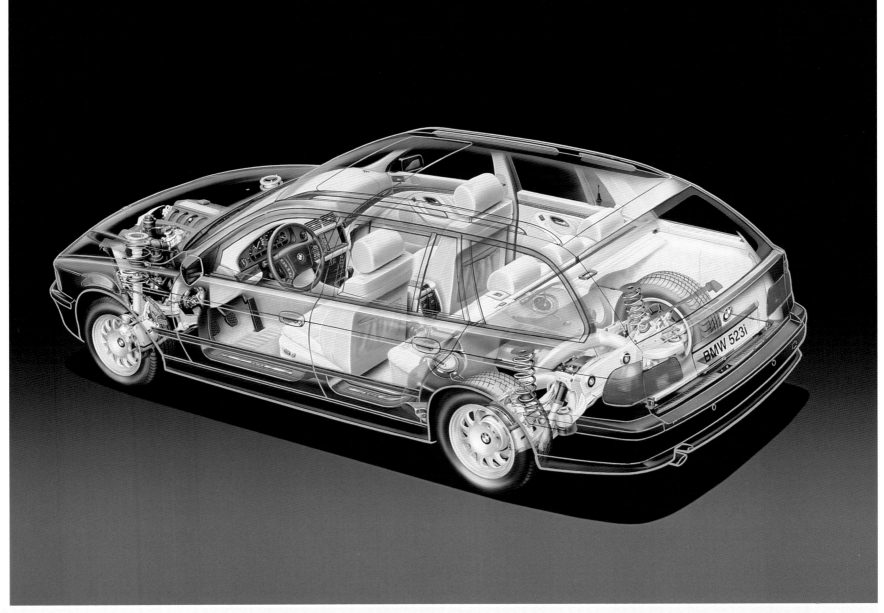

"Appealing though the M5 unquestionably was, BMW was soon to come up with a different development of much greater commercial signficance – the three-litre six cylinder diesel"

BMW Touring estate design majored on style rather than the ultimate in space. Contemporary Mercedes models did just the opposite. Facelift in 2001 added the distictive light rings (below) which proved a major incentive to buyers

astonishing smoothness and refinement too. In all parameters except outright straightline power it was a match for the equivalent petrol, yet it consumed 30 per cent less fuel and had better torque at low rpm. Diesel had really arrived in the luxury class and there was no longer any excuse for prejudice. It was a significant moment indeed.

The arrival of the key new diesels in 1998 – a 525d and a four-cylinder 520d were added soon afterwards – coincided with changes in the petrol engines which saw all the units gain double VANOS variable valve timing, the 520i grow to 2.2 litres and 170 bhp, the 523i relabelled 525i and the 528i become the 530i which, with 231 bhp, was now effectively just as powerful as the 535i V8. Five-speed Steptronic automatic was now the transmission option on all models. The cars all had the same pleasing air of mechanical perfection to them, but the sixes continued to be more enjoyable to handle on account of their more precise rack and pinion steering.

Specifications	520d	525tds	525d	530d
Engine				
Type	Inline 4-cylinder direct injection turbo diesel	Inline 6-cylinder turbo diesel	Inline 6-cylinder direct injection common rail turbo diesel	Inline 6-cylinder direct injection common rail turbo diesel
Capacity, cc	1951	2497	2497	2926
Valves	16	12	24	24
Fuelling	Digital diesel direct injection, turbocharger, intercooler	Digital diesel injection, turbocharger, intercooler	Digital diesel direct common rail injection, variable geometry turbocharger, intercooler	Digital diesel direct common rail injection, variable geometry turbocharger, intercooler
Max power, bhp @ rpm	136@4000	143@4800	163@4000	193@4000
Max torque, Nm @ rpm	280@1750	260@2200	350@2000	410@1750
Transmission				
Manual transmission	5-speed	5-speed	5-speed	5-speed
Automatic	Not available	ZF 5-speed	ZF 5-speed	ZF 5-speed
Drive	Rear wheels, ASC+T traction control	Rear wheels, ASC+T traction control	Rear wheels, ASC+T traction control	Rear wheels, ASC+T traction control
Chassis				
Front suspension	Double-pivot MacPherson struts, lower wishbones, coil springs	Double-pivot MacPherson struts, lower wishbones, coil springs	Double-pivot MacPherson struts, lower wishbones, coil springs	Double-pivot MacPherson struts, lower wishbones, coil springs
Rear suspension	Multi-link axle with trailing arms, twin transverse upper links, lower control arms, coil-springs	Multi-link axle with trailing arms, twin transverse upper links, lower control arms, coil-springs	Multi-link axle with trailing arms, twin transverse upper links, lower control arms, coil-springs	Multi-link axle with trailing arms, twin transverse upper links, lower control arms, coil-springs
Braking	Disc, servo assisted, ABS	Disc, servo assisted, ABS	Disc, servo assisted, ABS	Disc, servo assisted, ABS
Steering	Rack and pinion, power assisted	Rack and pinion, power assisted	Rack and pinion, power assisted	Rack and pinion, power assisted
Wheels	6.5 x 15	6.5 x 15	7.0 x 15	7.0 x 16
Tyres	205/65 VR 15	205/65 VR 15	225/60 R 15	225/55 R 16
Body				
Length, mm	4775	4775	4775	4775
Width, mm	1800	1800	1800	1800
Height, mm	1440	1440	1440	1440
Kerb weight, kg	1490	1480	1595	1625
Performance				
Max speed, km/h	206	211	219	230
0-100km/h, sec	10.6	10.4	8.9	7.8
Fuel consumption , lit/100km	6.1	8.3	7.1	7.5
Marketing				
Launch date	1/2000	1/96	1/2000	1/2000
Pricing, DM	59,800	57,000	64,000	68,000

E39
E39 SERIES: M5

Specifications	M5
Engine	
Engine type	90-degree V8
Bore & stroke, mm	94 x 89
Capacity, cc	4941
Valves	32
Valve actuation	Dohc per bank; double Vanos variable valve timing
Compression ratio	11:1
Fuelling	BMW electronic fuel injection; electronic control of individual butterflies
Max power, bhp @ rpm	400@6600
Max torque, Nm @ rpm	500@3800
Transmission	
Manual transmission	6-speed
Automatic	Not available
Drive	Rear wheels, DSC driving dynamic control
Chassis	
Front suspension	Double-pivot MacPherson struts, lower wishbones, coil springs
Rear suspension	Multi-link axle with trailing arms, twin transverse upper links, lower control arms, coil-springs
Braking	Disc, servo assisted, ABS, cornering brake control
Steering	Recirculating ball, power assisted
Wheels front + rear	8.0 x 18 + 9.0 x 18
Tyres front + rear	245/40 R18 + 275/35 R 18
Body	
Structure	Steel monocoque, front and rear subframes, light-alloy suspension
Wheelbase, mm	2830
Track F/R, mm	1515/1525
Length, mm	4785
Width, mm	1800
Height, mm	1440
Kerb weight, kg	1720
Fuel tank capacity, lit	70
Performance	
Max speed, km/h	250
0-100km/h, sec	5.3
Fuel consumption , lit/100km	13.9
Marketing	
Launch date	9/98
Pricing, DM	140,000

At the same time came a minor facelift which acquired a prominence out of all proportion to its technical magnitude. The chrome strip around the BMW grilles was widened, the rear lights adopted LED technology and the front foglights went from rectangular to round. But the change that everyone noticed came at night, when the four distinctive light rings round the headlights were illuminated. This simple change gave the 5 Series a highly individual nocturnal signature, reinforcing the typically BMW face; it would be later adopted on the top 7 Series.

The E39 saloon bowed out in the summer of 2003, at the height of its powers and with 1.2 million having found buyers. Its clean, smoothly-groomed looks and immaculately-honed engineering proved to be reassuringly right for a time when BMW was facing uncertainty over Rover and needed continuity in its own products. Critically, its success proved that BMW could keep its eye on its own brand ball even while it was having to manage a deteriorating relationship with what would soon become known as the English Patient.

M5 rev counter had a moveable red line which indicated a lower rev limit when the engine was cold. The red line rose as the engine reached working temperature

The M5 reached new heights of performance in the E39, hitting the 400 bhp mark with its five-litre V8. Dual engine maps allowed the driver to choose the throttle response profile; rear axle incorporated intelligent electronics

FOURTH 5 SERIES E39: SEDAN PRODUCTION

Production History:	In production: 1995 – 2003						Total produced 1,221,833						
model	520i	523i	525i	528i	530i	535i	540i	M5	520d	525td/tds/d	530d	total for year	SKD
1995	37	4,632		4,143		2	50			60			8,924
1996	35,296	45,227		63,553		3,470	12,170			29,099		188,815	1,212
1997	42,029	40,399		61,095		5,086	14,703	1		28,738		192,051	3,372
1998	38,375	38,845		56,264		4,618	14,120	678		22,475	4,859	180,234	864
1999	22,035	30,028		44,484		3,177	10,871	5,425	13	8,483	28,967	153,483	2,460
2000	19,047	14,196	14,661	28,340	13,286	2,086	9,870	5,824	7,810	10,308	23,342	148,770	2,796
2001	19,728		35,757		36,087	946	9,460	4,630	6,336	14,509	22,411	149,864	2,964
2002	15,279		29,813		33,205	613	6,689	2,412	4,070	13,548	19,514	125,143	2,716
2003	6,699		16,019		16,371	137	3,306	1,512	1,493	5,245	6,483	57,265	900
totals	198,525	173,327	96,250	257,879	98,949	20,135	81,239	20,482	19,722	132,465	105,576		17,284

grand total	1,204,549
grand total inc SKD	1,221,833
Derivative totals: sedan	1,221,833
Touring	266,226
Series total	1,488,059

FOURTH 5 SERIES TOURING PRODUCTION

Production History:	In production: 1996 – 2004						Total produced 266,226			
model	520i	523i	525i	528i	530i	540i	520d	525tds/d	530d	totals for year
1996	11	7		59		11		57		145
1997	6,675	7,774		9,681		1,675		11,973		37,778
1998	6,330	9,739		8,238		2,375		8,932	2,612	38,226
1999	5,207	7,947		9,545	1	2,050	7	3,578	14,009	42,344
2000	4,734	3,702	3,555	2,721	1,740	1,266	2,742	6,002	14,006	40,468
2001	5,537		7,909		3,896	1,009	3,220	9,036	13,569	44,176
2002	4,002		6,575		2,553	828	1,933	8,629	13,039	37,559
2003	2,555		4,135		1,205	341	1,197	7,182	8,915	25,530
totals	35,051	29,169	22,174	30,244	9,395	9,555	9,099	55,389	66,150	

grand total	266,226

Perfect pitch

BMW gives the new 3 Series the corporate face of the 5 and 7 Series

Fourth 3 Series (E46)

→ Launched in 1998
→ Cautious evolution of older model
→ Five body styles
→ Favoured comfort over sports handling
→ Update with firmer steering and suspension
→ Coupé M3 sets new dynamic standards
→ World debut of innovative Valvetronic engine principle

It was simply a matter of time before BMW's smallest, but also most commercially important, range fell into line to adopt the new, smoother and friendlier corporate face. It was early 1998 and the company needed to be sure of its image and project a confident message that all was well at BMW Towers, even if the business with Rover appeared to be in a shambles.

The shiny new E46 3 Series was just the car for the job. Unveiled at the Geneva show in March 1998, it was perfectly pitched: smooth, fresh and modern enough to draw in new customers and inspire existing owners to upgrade to the new generation, but in no way risking any radical features or sudden changes that might put off even the most conservative of customers.

The investment in the new model generation was DM 4 bn, said BMW, claiming the new car would offer a wide range of luxury features which had hitherto been reserved for top-segment ranges such as the 7 Series. As examples, BMW gave satellite navigation, cruise control, the multi-function steering wheel and DSC dynamic stability control.

The new car closely echoed the style and poise of the old one, but came across as visibly smarter, smoother and neater. The BMW grille, for instance, was integrated into the bonnet, just as on the bigger 5 and 7 Series, and the 'wave' shape of the lower edge of the headlights gave a hint of BMW's traditional four-headlight face and counted as a distinctive identification point. The way the wheelarches closely hugged the tyres, the way the panels fitted with millimetre perfection, the way the new door handles pulled out with a well-machined precision – all contributed to a powerful impression of classiness and quality.

The new car was longer and wider than the old, principally in order to address constant complaints about the 3 Series being too cramped in the rear. The main mechanical elements were carried over, suitably updated, with the front MacPherson strut arrangements now featuring forged aluminium lower links. Two additional engines filled out the carried over complement:

As with the previous generation, the Coupé version of the 3 Series had completely different bodywork to the saloon. Only the door handles and the BMW badges were shared

E46: 3 SERIES

Specifications	316i	318i	320i	320d	323i
Engine					
Engine type	Inline 4-cylinder	Inline 4-cylinder	Inline 6-cylinder	Inline 4-cylinder direct injection turbodiesel	Inline 6-cylinder
Bore & stroke, mm	85 x 83.5	85 x 83.5	80 x 66 (from 2000: 80 x 72)	84 x 88(from 2001: 84 x 90)	84 x 75
Capacity, cc	1895	1895	1991 (from 2000: 2171)	1951 (from 2001: 1995)	2494
Valves	8	8	24	16	24
Valve actuation	Sohc	Sohc	Dohc, double Vanos variable valve timing	Dohc	Dohc, double Vanos variable valve timing
Compression ratio	9.7:1	9.7:1	11.0:1 (from 2000: 10.7:1)	19.0:1 (from 2001: 17.0:1)	10.5:1
Fuelling	Siemens fuel injection	Siemens fuel injection	Siemens fuel injection	Digital diesel injection; turbocharger, intercooler (from 2001: common rail)	Siemens fuel injection
Max power, bhp @ rpm	105@5300	118@5500	150@5900 (from 2000: 170@6100)	136@4000 (from 2001: 150)	170@5500
Max torque, Nm @ rpm	165@2500	180@3900	190@3500 (from 2000: 210)	280@1750 (from 2001: 330@2000))	245@3500
Transmission					
Manual transmission	5-speed	5-speed	5-speed	5-speed	5-speed
Automatic	GM 4-speed	GM 4-speed	ZF 5-speed	ZF 5-speed	ZF 5-speed
Drive	Rear wheels	Rear wheels	Rear wheels	Rear wheels	Rear wheels
Chassis					
Front suspension	MacPherson strut, lower wishbones	MacPherson struts, lower wishbones	MacPherson struts, lower wishbones	MacPherson struts, lower wishbones	MacPherson struts, lower wishbones
Rear suspension	Multi-link axle with trailing arms, twin transverse upper links, lower control arms, coil-springs	Multi-link axle with trailing arms, twin transverse upper links, lower control arms, coil-springs	Multi-link axle with trailing arms, twin transverse upper links, lower control arms, coil-springs	Multi-link axle with trailing arms, twin transverse upper links, lower control arms, coil-springs	Multi-link axle with trailing arms, twin transverse upper links, lower control arms, coil-springs
Braking	Disc, servo assisted, ABS	Disc, servo assisted, ABS	Disc, servo assisted, ABS	Disc, servo assisted, ABS	Disc, servo assisted, ABS
Steering	Rack and pinion, power assisted	Rack and pinion, power assisted	Rack and pinion, power assisted	Rack and pinion, power assisted	Rack and pinion, power assisted
Wheels	6.5 x 15	6.5 x 15	6.5 x 15	6.5 x 15	6.5 x 15
Tyres	195/65 HR 15	195/65 HR 15	195/65 HR 15	195/65 HR 15	195/65 HR 15
Body					
Structure	Steel monocoque; rear subframe	Steel monocoque; rear subframe	Steel monocoque; rear subframe	Steel monocoque; rear subframe	Steel monocoque; rear subframe
Wheelbase, mm	2725	2725	2725	2725	2725
Track F/R, mm	1480/1490	1480/1490	1480/1490	1480/1490	1480/1490
Length, mm	4470	4470	4470	4470	4470
Width, mm	1740	1740	1740	1740	1740
Height, mm	1420	1420	1420	1420	1420
Kerb weight, kg	1285	1285	1365	1375	1370
Fuel tank capacity, lit	63	63	63	63	63
Performance					
Max speed, km/h	200	206	219 (from 2000: 226)	207 (from 2001: 216)	231
0-100km/h, sec	12.4	10.4	9.9 (from 2000: 8.3)	9.9 (from 2001: 8.9)	8.0
Fuel consumption , lit/100km	9.0	8.6	9.0 (from 2000: 9.3)	6.1	9.8
Marketing					
Launch date	12/97	3/98	3/98	3/98	3/98
Pricing, DM	42,400	45,400	53,700	48,400	56,600

328i

Inline 6-cylinder

84 x 84

2793
24
Dohc, double Vanos variable
valve timing
10:2:1
Siemens fuel injection

193@5500

280@3500

5-speed
ZF 5-speed
Rear wheels

MacPherson struts, lower
wishbones
Multi-link axle with trailing
arms, twin transverse upper
links, lower control arms,
coil-springs
Disc, servo assisted, ABS
Rack and pinion, power
assisted
7.0 x 16
205/55 WR 16

Steel monocoque;
rear subframe
2725
1480/1490
4470
1740
1420
1395
63

240
7.0
9.8

4/98
61,700

the 1.9 litre petrol with twin balancer shafts, as fitted to the Z3, and the new 320d direct-injection diesel, which was to prove immensely significant as the best-selling power unit of the whole line-up. Production started simultaneously in four factories – Munich, Regensburg and Dingolfing in Germany, and Rosslyn, South Africa – showing the massive importance of the new model: in some plants the new car ran on the same lines as the still-current Touring and Coupé versions of the old model. Customer response was rapid: between May and December 1998 more than 170,000 had been built: the following year, with both the Coupé and

the Touring having joined the range, the total was almost a third of a million.

The Coupé, which carried the name Ci, was again an all-new body, longer and wider than the saloon: only the door handles and the BMW badges were common to the four-door. Four engines were initially offered: the four-cylinder 318Ci, with the 118 bhp M43 four-cylinder, the six-cylinder 150 bhp 320Ci, 170 bhp 323i – actually a 2.5 litre – and the top 328Ci on 193 bhp. Prices ran at about DM 2,000 more than the corresponding saloon: the premium for the Touring, launched later that same year, was

New generation 3 Series emerged with cleaner, smoother lines giving a classier image but still preserving the familiar proportions

E46

E46 3 SERIES FROM 2001

Specifications	316i	318i	318d	325i/Xi	330i/Xi
Engine					
Engine type	Inline 4-cylinder with Valvetronic	Inline 4-cylinder with Valvetronic	Inline 4-cylinder direct injection common rail turbo diesel	Inline 6-cylinder	Inline 6-cylinder
Capacity, cc	1796	1995	1995	2494	2979
Valves	Dohc 16, Valvetronic fully variable valve timing and lift	Dohc 16, Valvetronic fully variable valve timing and lift	Dohc 16	Dohc, double Vanos variable valve timing	Dohc, double Vanos variable valve timing
Fuelling	Bosch electronic fuel injection	Bosch electronic fuel injection	Common rail diesel injection; turbocharger, intercooler	Siemens electronic fuel injection	Siemens electronic fuel injection
Max power, bhp @ rpm	115@5500	143@6000	115@ 4000	192@6000	231@5900
Max torque, Nm @ rpm	175@3750	200@3900	280@2000	245@3500	300@3500
Transmission					
Manual transmission	5-speed	5-speed	5-speed	5-speed	5-speed
Automatic	GM 4-speed	GM 4-speed	GM 4-speed	ZF 5-speed	ZF 5-speed
Drive	Rear wheels	Rear wheels	Rear wheels	Rear wheels (Xi: four wheel drive via central differential)	Rear wheels (Xi: four wheel drive via central differential)
Chassis					
Front suspension	MacPherson strut, lower wishbones	MacPherson struts, lower wishbones	MacPherson struts, lower wishbones	MacPherson struts, lower wishbones	MacPherson struts, lower wishbones
Rear suspension	Multi-link axle with trailing arms, twin transverse upper links, lower control arms, coil-springs	Multi-link axle with trailing arms, twin transverse upper links, lower control arms, coil-springs	Multi-link axle with trailing arms, twin transverse upper links, lower control arms, coil-springs	Multi-link axle with trailing arms, twin transverse upper links, lower control arms, coil-springs	Multi-link axle with trailing arms, twin transverse upper links, lower control arms, coil-springs
Braking	Disc, servo assisted, ABS	Disc, servo assisted, ABS	Disc, servo assisted, ABS	Disc, servo assisted, ABS	Disc, servo assisted, ABS
Steering	Rack and pinion, power assisted	Rack and pinion, power assisted	Rack and pinion, power assisted	Rack and pinion, power assisted	Rack and pinion, power assisted
Wheels	6.5 x 15	6.5 x 15	6.5 x 15	7.0 x 16	7.0 x 17
Tyres	195/65 HR 15	195/65 HR 15	195/65 R 15	205/55 R 16	205/50 R 17
Body					
Length, mm	4470	4470	4470	4470	4470
Width, mm	1740	1740	1740	1740	1740
Height, mm	1415	1415	1415	1415	1415
Kerb weight, kg	1285	1285	1395	1410	1430
Performance					
Max speed, km/h	206	218	205	240	250
0-100km/h, sec	10.9	10.4	10.6	7.2	6.5
Fuel consumption , lit/100km	7.1	7.9	5.6	9.6	9.6
Marketing					
Launch date	4/2001	4/2001	3/2004	7/2000	6/2000
Pricing, DM	42,700	45,700	–	58,600 (Xi + 4,500)	65,300 (Xi + 4,500)

E30: DERIVATIVES DIMENSIONS

330d/Xd

Inline 6-cylinder direct injection common rail turbo diesel
2926
Dohc 24

Digital diesel common rail injection, variable geometry turbocharger, intercooler
184@4000
390@1750

5-speed
ZF 5-speed
Rear wheels (Xi: four wheel drive via central differential)

MacPherson struts, lower wishbones
Multi-link axle with trailing arms, twin transverse upper links, lower control arms, coil-springs
Disc, servo assisted, ABS
Rack and pinion, power assisted
7.0 x 17
205/50 R 17

4470
1740
1415
1520

227
7.8
7.2

10/99
–

Specifications	Sedan	Coupé	Cabriolet	Touring
Dimensions				
Wheelbase, mm	2725	2725	2725	2725
Track F/R, mm	1480/1490	1470/1480	1470/1485	1480/1490
Length, mm	4470	4490	4490	4480
Width, mm	1740	1755	1755	1740
Height, mm	1420	1370	1370	1410
Kerb weight, kg	–	–	Sedan +DM130	Sedan +DM70
Fuel tank capacity, lit	65	65	65	65
Marketing				
Launch date	3/98	3/99	3/2000	10/99
Pricing, DM	–	Sedan +DM2,000	Sedan +DM6,200	Sedan +DM2,800

Touring estate version carefully cultivated the discreet upper-class style of the larger 5 Series; the interior shared the same elegant, ergonomic design as all the 3 Series

E46

E46: M3

Specifications	M3	M3 CSL
Engine		
Engine type	Inline 6-cylinder	Inline 6-cylinder
Bore & stroke, mm	87 x 91	87 x 91
Capacity, cc	3245	3245
Valves	24	24
Valve actuation	Dohc, double Vanos variable valve timing	Dohc, double Vanos variable valve timing
Compression ratio	11.3:1	11.5:1
Fuelling	Bosch Motronic fuel injection	Bosch Motronic fuel injection
Max power, bhp @ rpm	343@7900	360@7900
Max torque, Nm @ rpm	365@4900	370@4900
Transmission		
Manual transmission	Getrag 6-speed	Getrag 6-speed sequential manual
Automatic	SMG sequential manual optional	Not available
Drive	Rear wheels; limited slip differential, DSC driving dynamic control	Rear wheels; limited slip differential, DSC driving dynamic control
Chassis		
Front suspension	MacPherson struts, lower wishbones	MacPherson struts, lower wishbones
Rear suspension	Multi-link axle with trailing arms, twin transverse upper links, lower control arms, coil-springs	Multi-link axle with trailing arms, twin transverse upper links, lower control arms, coil-springs
Braking	Disc servo assisted, ABS	Disc servo assisted, ABS
Steering	Rack and pinion, power assisted	Rack and pinion, power assisted
Wheels front + rear	8.0 x 18 + 9.0 x 18	8.5 x 19 + 9.5 x 19
Tyres front + rear	225/45 ZR 18 + 255/40 ZR 18	235/35 ZR 19 + 265/30 ZR 19
Body		
Structure	Steel monocoque; rear subframe, aluminium suspension and bonnet	Steel monocoque; rear subframe; aluminium suspension, bonnet, boot floor; other composite panels
Wheelbase, mm	2730	2729
Track F/R, mm	1510/1525	1518/1525
Length, mm	4490	4492
Width, mm	1780	1780
Height, mm	1370	1365
Kerb weight, kg	1495	1385
Fuel tank capacity, lit	63	63
Performance		
Max speed, km/h	250 (limited)	250 (limited)
0-100km/h, sec	5.2	4.9
Fuel consumption, lit/100km	12.7	13.1
Marketing		
Launch date	3/2000	3/2003
Pricing (Coupé)	DM 100,000	€85,000

Discreet side air vents and
not-so-discreet quadruple
exhaust outlets have become
the calling-cards of BMW M
models. Cabriolet and Coupé
were the only E46 body styles
offered with the 3.6 litre M
engine

fractionally more. The Touring, again larger in all dimensions than its forbear, had engine choices focused more on utility, with a 318i, 320d, 320i and 328i. Several of the features of the already successful 5 Series Touring, such as the separately opening rear window, were picked up by the smaller car, and the model was enthusiastically received for its style and its driving refinement, if not its roominess.

At the same time the by now celebrated three-litre direct injection diesel engine was slotted into the E46 to create the 330d. It proved to be a car with a simply astonishing combination of factors never hitherto associated with diesels – speed, acceleration, power, response, refinement – allied to excellent fuel economy, even by the elevated standards of a diesel car. Many magazines pronounced it the best diesel car ever.

However, the press's praise for the 3 Series did not extend to every aspect of the model. One of the most immediate complaints was that it lacked the sporty feel everyone expected from a BMW: the suspension was too soft and imprecise, the power steering too light and unresponsive, and road feel worryingly absent. At first BMW appeared to dismiss these complaints but had in fact taken them on board; with the added impetus of the new management – Joachim Milberg had taken over after Pischetsrieder's expulsion at the dramatic board meeting in February 1999 – a programme of measures was put through in order to sharpen up the car's dynamic act.

The changes would first be seen on the new Compact, an introduction which took most commentators by surprise in spring 2001, and would make all 3 Series much more enjoyable to drive.

Meanwhile, however, at the turn of the Millennium, Detroit showgoers had witnessed the world debut of the 3 Series Cabriolet in 323Ci form, later to be joined by a 330Ci, the first application of the new M54 three-litre six that would soon be rolled out into all the body shapes apart from the Compact. The Cabriolet embodied all the key features of its predecessor – electric hood, flush-fitting metal tonneau cover, four full seats – but added refinements such as a glass rear window, standard flip-up rollover

protection and seat belts integrated into the front seats to provide better belt paths and to simplify access to the rear. The rear deck line was given a sharper trailing edge, adding to the open car's visual identity.

A raft of changes affect all the models in June 2002 and, paralleling the experience with the 5 Series, caused some confusion among consumers. The 320i became a 2.2 litre, with 170 bhp, but retained the same designation; the 323i, which had always been a 2.5 litre, took on the 325i label and rose to 192 bhp, while the 330i gained an electronic 'drive by wire' throttle and the option of four-wheel-drive, courtesy of the X5's parts bin, was made available on saloon and Touring versions of the 330i, 330d and 325i. As before, the 4x4 models were suffixed X and the additional cost was a substantial DM 4,500.

Mindful of its reputation as a world leader in engine technologies, BMW was ready to launch the first of its next-generation petrol engines in the spring of 2001. Manufactured, like all BMW petrol four-cylinder units, at the purpose-built Hamms Hall plant in the English Midlands, the N40 1.6 litre Valvetronic broke new ground as the first production engine to do away with

Engine innovation: BMW Valvetronic in 318i (right) was the world's first to do away with throttle butterfly, while the four-cylinder turbo diesel (far right) in the 320d proved a runaway success, giving up to 150 bhp

"The press's praise for the new 3 Series did not extend to every aspect of the model. One of the most immediate complaints was that it lacked the sporty feel everyone was expecting a BMW to provide"

throttle butterfly valves and instead use variable valve lift to control engine output. By eliminating the pumping losses caused by the traditional throttles, BMW claimed to improve power by 21 per cent, torque by 11 per cent and economy also by 11 per cent: as proof of the pudding, the Valvetronic engine gave 115 bhp, compared with the standard unit's 105.

The surprise was not that BMW chose the Compact in which to launch the Valvetronic engine, but that it decided to revive the Compact at all. The original had sold reasonably well to start with, but its use of outdated components had hurt BMW's image, sales had faded fast and it was dropped with no word of a replacement. Yet in its defence thee original 1994 Compact had brought many new buyers into the BMW fold: two out of every three Compact owners had not bought a BMW before and 65 per cent of them went on to buy another car in the range. So with Rover now disposed of and the MINI not yet

on the market, BMW needed a lead-in model to attract converts – and a fresh Compact was a convenient answer. This time, however, BMW made sure it was the equal of the regular 3 Series in terms of its chassis, its interior and its dynamics; the exterior, chopped 220mm shorter than the saloon's, was restyled with separate round lights cut into holes in the bonnet, Alfa GTV style, and somewhat gaudy rear lights reminiscent of the Lexus IS 200. It made sense to launch the model with an innovative small-capacity engine majoring on economy, but to catch the more serious enthusiast a 325ti was included in the initial line-up, too. Soon, a 318ti, with a two-litre, 143 bhp Valvetronic engine was added, as was a 320td diesel.

The two-litre, four-cylinder M47 diesel had been dramatically uprated with the adoption of state of the art second-generation common rail technology, with a variable geometry turbocharger, 1600 bar injection pressure and

The facelift package for the 3 Series in late 2001 gave a new shape to the headlights and placed the indicators behind clear glass covers. Coupés were given a different headlamp shaping

electronic management of all key parameters. The result was a sparkling 150 bhp and 330 Nm of torque, coupled with remarkable 5.5 litre consumption: that engine has since been developed yet further for the 1 Series, where it gives 163 bhp.

Both Valvetronic engines found their way into the revised mainstream 3 Series models in late 2001, along with chassis changes such as quicker steering and firmer suspension aimed at sharpening up the handling; shortly afterwards came a minor exterior facelift these improvements consisting of a wider kidney grille leading to a new bonnet with more of a central bulge, clear glass covering the curvier headlights and indicators, clear-glass indicators at the rear and teardrop repeater lights each side. The Coupé's lights changed to a different pattern, and

it received LED tail lights, with two-stage brake-light illumination reserved for the US market where, unlike Europe, it is allowed under motor vehicle regulations. Transmission options expanded, too, with six-speed manuals available on 2.5 litre models and the new SSG sport sequential – allowing launch control for rapid starts – on both 325i and 330i.

The most exotic member of every 3 Series generation has always been the M3, and by common consent the E46 iteration, with its 3.2 litres, 343 bhp and six-speed sequential transmission option, represents an all-time high. Lowered suspension, a deeper frontal air dam, and side air vents kept the external modifications discreet but still allowed it to be distinguished from the standard 330Ci Coupé: from the rear the fatter tyres and M signature quadruple

Past classic, future classic: BMW revived the famous CSL designation from the 1970s for the special lightweight version of the M3 in 2003. The 100 kg weight saving, allied with increased engine output, made for a highly focused performance coupé that could match a Porsche 911. Here, the 2003 car sits alongside its 1973 mentor

E46

FOURTH 3-SERIES: E46 SEDAN PRODUCTION

Production History:			In production: 1998-2005			Total produced 1,704,043						
model	**316i**	**318i**	**318d**	**320d**	**320i**	**323i**	**325Xi**	**328i**	**330Xi**	**330d**	**total for year**	**SKD**
1997		232		93	38	46		224			633	
1998	3,187	72,493		37,489	21,750	29,944		31,783			196,646	1,440
1999	47,030	67,745		68,206	44,925	48,550		31,501	18	3,871	311,846	4,512
2000	40,311	58,355	6	69,893	37,742	24,601	24,720	10,812	21,087	18,005	305,532	8,856
2001	28,109	41,323	3,627	86,605	32,340		60,465		29,918	18,349	300,736	9,792
2002	42,787	32,050	9,496	65,442	25,869		72,857		29,807	15,538	293,846	9,696
2003	37,570	22,390	8,961	58,684	21,143		71,289		21,113	11,198	252,348	8,160
totals	**198,994**	**294,588**	**22,090**	**386,412**	**183,807**	**103,141**	**229,331**	**74,320**	**101,943**	**66,961**		**42,456**
										grand total	**1,661,587**	
										grand total inc SKD	**1,704,043**	
										Derivative totals: sedan	**1,704,043**	
										Cabrio	**190,597**	
										Touring	**324,817**	
										Coupé	**356,083**	
										Compact	**166,364**	
										Series total	**2,687,431**	

FOURTH 3-SERIES: E46 TOURING PRODUCTION

Production History:			In production: 1998-2006			Total produced 324,817				
model	**316i Touring**	**318i Touring**	**318d Touring**	**320d Touring**	**320i Touring**	**323i Touring**	**5i/iX Touring**	**328i Touring**	**330Xi Touring**	**330d Touring**	**total for year**
1998		9		1	2	1		23		5	41
1999		6,149		4,239	1,551	28		2,719	9	52	14,747
2000		12,737	6	27,407	5,693	3,628	3,415	1,900	3,048	7,634	65,468
2001	10	12,461	4	36,643	7,463		8,365		4,389	12,408	81,743
2002	3,558	12,365	4,115	36,981	5,639		9,096		3,561	10,544	85,859
2003	5,407	10,313	5,910	34,331	4,249		6,348		1,989	8,412	76,959
totals	**8,975**	**54,034**	**10,035**	**139,602**	**24,597**	**3,657**	**27,224**	**4,642**	**12,996**	**39,055**	
										grand total	**324,817**

FOURTH 3-SERIES: E46 COUPÉ/CABRIO PRODUCTION

Production History:			In production: 1998-2006			Total produced 546,680							
model	**316Ci Coupé**	**318Ci Coupé**	**320Ci Coupé**	**325Ci Coupé**	**330Ci Coupé**	**M3**	**320Cd Coupé**	**330Cd Coupé**	**320Ci Cabrio**	**323Ci/325Ci Cabrio**	**330Ci Cabrio**	**M3 Cabrio**	**total for year**
1998				76	125					2			203
1999	231	5,955	8,417	24,253	22,195	29				160			61,240
2000	730	19,184	10,979	23,537	23,065	1,216			2,582	20,760	11,221	84	113,358
2001	657	14,208	11,629	18,779	20,144	11,197			11,256	17,225	18,640	4,097	127,832
2002	904	12,387	7,846	16,232	18,415	15,665		18	14,355	14,443	18,467	8,089	126,821
2003	638	9,129	6,399	14,032	13,174	12,490	4,788	7,360	13,491	12,843	16,101	6,781	117,226
totals	**3,160**	**60,863**	**45,270**	**96,909**	**97,118**	**40,597**	**4,788**	**7,378**	**41,684**	**65,433**	**64,429**	**19,051**	
												grand total	**546,680**

E46

E46: SERIES 3 COMPACT

Specifications	316ti Compact	318ti Compact	320td Compact	325ti Compact
Engine				
Type	Inline 4-cylinder with Valvetronic	Inline 4-cylinder with Valvetronic	Inline 4-cylinder direct injection turbodiesel	Inline 6-cylinder
Capacity, cc	1796	1995	1995	2494
Valves	Dohc 16, Valvetronic fully variable valve timing and lift	Dohc 16, Valvetronic fully variable valve timing and lift	Digital diesel injection; turbocharger, intercooler	Dohc, double Vanos variable valve timing
Fuelling	Bosch electronic fuel injection	Bosch electronic fuel injection	Digital diesel injection; turbocharger, intercooler	Siemens electronic fuel injection
Max power, bhp @ rpm	116@5500	143@6000	136@4000	192@6000
Max torque, Nm @ rpm	180@3500	200@3900	280@1750	245@3500
Transmission				
Manual transmission	5-speed	5-speed	5-speed	5-speed
Automatic	5-speed	5-speed	Not available	5-speed
Drive	Rear wheels	Rear wheels	Rear wheels	Rear wheels
Chassis				
Front suspension	MacPherson strut, lower wishbones	MacPherson strut, lower wishbones	MacPherson strut, lower wishbones	MacPherson strut, lower wishbones
Rear suspension	Multi-link axle with trailing arms, twin transverse upper links, lower control arms, coil-springs	Multi-link axle with trailing arms, twin transverse upper links, lower control arms, coil-springs	Multi-link axle with trailing arms, twin transverse upper links, lower control arms, coil-springs	Multi-link axle with trailing arms, twin transverse upper links, lower control arms, coil-springs
Braking	Disc, servo assisted, ABS	Disc, servo assisted, ABS	Disc, servo assisted, ABS	Disc, servo assisted, ABS
Steering	Rack and pinion, power assisted	Rack and pinion, power assisted	Rack and pinion, power assisted	Rack and pinion, power assisted
Wheels	6.5 x 15	6.5 x 15	6.5 x 15	7.0 x 16
Tyres	195/65 R 15	195/65 R 15	195/65 R 15	205/55 R16
Body				
Length, mm	4260	4260	4260	4260
Width, mm	1750	1750	1750	1750
Height, mm	1410	1410	1410	1410
Kerb weight, kg	1300	1300	1395	1405
Performance				
Max speed, km/h	201	214	214	235
0-100km/h, sec	10.9	9.3	8.9	7.1
Fuel consumption , lit/100km	6.9	7.2	5.5	8.9
Marketing				
Launch date	3/2001	9/2001	9/2001	3/2001
Pricing, DM	39,899	–	–	56,132

exhausts were quicker to give the game away. Like the larger M5, the M3 had numerous electronic systems to take care of stability, traction and control responses: unlike the M5, however, the M3's steering was short on feel at low speeds – just about the only flaw in a car which everyone agreed had astonishing dynamics yet which seated four in comfort and was smooth and easy to drive around town.

What is likely to be the final chapter in the M3 saga came in 2003 when the CSL version was presented, first as a concept at the Geneva show, then as a limited series production vehicle. Recalling the epic 3.0 'Batmobile' CSL in name only, the lightweight M3 saved 110 kg through the use of aluminium and composite panels for the bonnet, boot, doors and roof: many comfort features such as the air conditioning were thrown out in the interests of lightness, and the engine

received a further boost in power (to 360 bhp) and torque. The result was a highly-focused sports coupé with a harder edge, a much higher price than the standard M3 and a select few contented enthusiasts.

The E46 3 Series will go down in BMW history not merely as one of the company's most statistically successful models but also as the model which best encapsulated the evolving philosophy of the marque. This 3 Series was the final piece in a jigsaw puzzle of models which interlocked seamlessly in terms of style, of engineering, of driving feel, and even of quality and performance. BMW had ushered in an age of car buying where, in contrast to the 'one size fits all' approach of clothes shopping, one style of car fitted everyone and the buyer would simply chose the size – 3, 5 or 7 – to match his or her budget.

The Compact was unexpectedly reintroduced in 2001 to attract a younger audience into the BMW brand. This time BMW ensured it had the same chassis specifications as the equivalent saloons

SERIES 3: COMPACT PRODUCTION

Production History:		In production: 2001 on			Total produced 166,364		
model	316ti	318ti	318td	320td	320ti	325ti	total for year
2001	29,394	4,670		8,105	3	5,577	47,749
2002	32,247	11,179	6	17,008		3,058	63,498
2003	25,547	7,944	6,868	13,150		1,608	55,117
totals	87,188	23,793	6,874	38,263	3	10,243	
						grand total	166,364

25

Crossing continents

America provides inspiration for the world's first Sports Activity Vehicle, the X5

X5 (E53) 1999 on

→ BMW's sporty take on the SUV theme
→ Declared the best-handling sports utility
→ All-independent suspension
→ Car-like ride and steering
→ Engines up to 4.8 litres

When BMW launched the X5 to the world's press it did so on US Interstate freeways, on small American back-roads and on twisty mountain sectors. And in a large, steep-sided disused quarry made muddy by the passage of countless excavators, bulldozers and recreational Jeeps. And, remarkably, on a race track – a real race track used by 400 km/h sports racing cars in the American Le Mans series.

No other automaker would have dared launch an SUV on a high-speed racing circuit. But then BMW was determined that its X5 was not like any other SUV: it was an entirely different class of car, said BMW: it was a sports *activity* vehicle. The rest of the world, however, didn't really understand the difference and happily lumped it together with the Range Rover, the Jeep Grand Cherokee and the Mercedes-Benz M-Class, the car whose success had prompted BMW into thinking it needed to respond.

In the early 1990s, before BMW bought Rover in order to get hold of Land Rover, the idea of an off-roader bearing the blue and white roundel was unthinkable. A taut-handling, executive sedan to chug across ploughed fields and scale rock-strewn hillsides – it seemed faintly ludicrous, not to mention technically unfeasible.

But then to 1970s eyes the prospect of BMW being big in diesels must have seemed equally laughable, as might the concept of a BMW family estate car in the 1980s. But all these once-unlikely things have since come to pass, with BMW succeeding in applying its own corporate slant on the product definition to ensure the result sat securely within the values of speed, agility, quality and driving enjoyment that constitute its brand pillars.

Nevertheless, to produce an able off-road climber also capable of honouring these values was a much tougher task, for everyone knew that there was no way that a truck-like SUV with traditionally clunky four-wheel-drive hardware could be made to ride smoothly, let alone steer or handle in the way a BMW customer would expect. Instead, BMW approached the problem from the

Taking the rough with the smooth: BMW X5 aimed to be the first off-roader with car-like steering, handling and ride

Three-litre diesel engine (top) has been much the most popular choice in Europe, while 347 bhp output of the mighty 4.6iS V8 (left) gives a top speed of 240 km/h

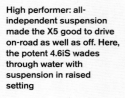

High performer: all-independent suspension made the X5 good to drive on-road as well as off. Here, the potent 4.6iS wades through water with suspension in raised setting

opposite angle, figuring out how a car that was good on the paved road – where, after all, it would spend nine tenths of its active life – could be made to perform well off the highway, too.

The solution proved to be an all-new vehicle based loosely on the platform of the 5 Series, using running gear based equally loosely on that of the 7 Series. Engines would be drawn from the 5 Series palette, transmissions, too, and large wheels and tyres, together with air spring struts, would take care of ground clearance issues.

Having ruled out the old-fashioned separate chassis and heavy, rigid axles, the next notion BMW threw out was the cumbersome second gearbox associated with traditional off-roaders. The main function of this had always been to provide a high degree of engine braking for slow descents down steep and slippery slopes, and in a rare example of technology transfer from Rover into BMW, Land Rover had contributed its Hill Descent Control which used the ABS circuitry to keep the vehicle stable at a slow walking pace whatever the steepness of the incline.

Specifications	X5 3.0i	X5 3.0d	X5 4.4i	X5 4.6i	X5 4.8i
Engine					
Type	Inline 6-cylinder	Inline 6-cylinder direct injection common rail turbo diesel	90-degree V8	90-degree V8	90-degree V8
Bore & stroke, mm	84 x 89.6	84 x 88	92 x 82.7	93 x 85	93 x 88.3
Capacity, cc	2979	2926	4398	4619	4799
Valves	24	24	32	32	32
Valve actuation	Dohc, double Vanos variable valve timing	Dohc	Dohc per bank, double Vanos variable valve timing	Dohc per bank, double Vanos variable valve timing; Valvetronic variable valve lift	Dohc per bank, double Vanos variable valve timing; Valvetronic variable valve lift
Compression ratio	10.2:1	18:1	10.2:1	10.2:1	11:1
Fuelling	Siemens electronic fuel injection	Digital diesel common rail injection, variable geometry turbocharger, intercooler	Bosch Motronic electronic fuel injection	Bosch Motronic electronic fuel injection	Bosch Motronic electronic fuel injection
Max power, bhp @ rpm	231@5900	184@4000	286@5400	347@5700	360@6200
Max torque, Nm @ rpm	300@3500	390@1750	440@3600	480@3700	490@3600
Transmission					
Manual transmission	5-speed	5-speed	Not available	Not available	Not available
Automatic	5-speed	ZF 5-speed	5-speed	5-speed	6-speed
Drive	All 4 wheels via centre differential	All 4 wheels via centre differential	All 4 wheels via electronic centre differential	All 4 wheels via electronic centre multiplate clutch	All 4 wheels via electronic centre multiplate clutch
Chassis					
Front suspension	MacPherson struts, coil springs, diagonal links	MacPherson struts, coil springs, diagonal links	MacPherson struts, coil springs, diagonal links	MacPherson struts, coil springs, diagonal links	MacPherson struts, coil springs, diagonal links
Rear suspension	Multi-link axle with trailing links, transverse links and diagonal links; coil springs. Air springs optional	Multi-link axle with trailing links, transverse links and diagonal links; coil springs. Air springs optional	Multi-link axle with trailing links, transverse links and diagonal links; coil springs. Air springs optional	Multi-link axle with trailing links, transverse links and diagonal links; coil springs. Air springs optional	Multi-link axle with trailing links, transverse links and diagonal links; coil springs. Air springs optional
Braking	Discs, servo assisted, with ABS, CBC and Hill Descent Control	Discs, servo assisted, with ABS, CBC and Hill Descent Control	Discs, servo assisted, with ABS, CBC and Hill Descent Control	Discs, servo assisted, with ABS, CBC and Hill Descent Control	Discs, servo assisted, with ABS, CBC and Hill Descent Control
Steering	Rack and pinion, power assisted	Rack and pinion, power assisted	Rack and pinion, power assisted	Rack and pinion, power assisted	Rack and pinion, power assisted
Wheels	7.5 x 17	7.5 x 17	7.5 x 17 (Sport package 9.0 x 19 + 10.0 x 19)	9.0 x 19 + 10.0 x 19	9.2 x 20 + 10.0 x 20
Tyres	235/65 HR 17	235/65 HR 17	235/65 HR 17 (Sport package 225/50 VR 19 + 285/45 VR 19)	225/50 VR 19 + 285/45 VR 19	275/40 R 20 + 315/35 R 20
Body					
Structure	Steel monocoque	Steel monocoque	Steel monocoque	Steel monocoque	Steel monocoque
Wheelbase, mm	2820	2820	2820	2820	2820
Track F/R, mm	1576/1576	1576/1576	1576/1576	1576/1576	1576/1576
Length, mm	4667	4667	4667	4667	4667
Width, mm	1872	1872	1872	1872	1872
Height, mm	1715	1715	1715	1707	1707
Kerb weight, kg	1990	2095	2095	2105	2200
Fuel tank capacity, lit	92	92	92	92	92
Performance					
Max speed, km/h	202	180	207 (Sport pack 230)	240	246
0-100km/h, sec	8.5	10.0	7.5	6.5	6.1
Fuel consumption , lit/100km	13.4	9.7	14.6	14.9	13.5
Marketing					
Launch date	1/2000	4/2001	1/99	1/2001	3/2004
Pricing (Europe, 3/2000), DM	80,000	80,400	111,000	150,600	€81,600

2004 model year X5 4.8iS features was an enlarged version of the Valvetronic V8 from the 7 Series and is the most powerful X5 to date

"True to BMW's purpose, the most immediately impressive thing about the X5 was the way it drove. The steering was positive and accurate, like no other SUV's"

The ABS circuits, together with the traction control system, could also replace two other items of 4x4 hardware: the differential locks in the front and rear axles. Already, the engineering was looking simpler, even if the electronics were becoming more complex. Before long, chassis mules of what would become the X5 were being tested, clothed in adapted 5 Series Touring bodies for disguise.

Manufacture at BMW's Spartanburg, South Carolina factory was already part of the plan: production of the Z3 sports car occupied only a tiny portion of the site and it was a simple – if costly – matter to double capacity to accommodate the X5. Pre-production X5s began coming off the line in the middle of 1999: the first proper production example was immediately given to a US cancer charity and auctioned on eBay for $159,000 – three times its list price. The BMW sports activity vehicle had revealed itself as tall, wide and stylish, recognisably a BMW but with disproportionately huge wheels and tyres; under the bonnet was a 4.4 litre V8, with the promise of three-litre petrol and diesel inline sixes to come, while inside the smoothly styled cabin was space for five, but no more.

True to BMW's promise, the most immediately

impressive thing about the X5 was the way it drove. The steering was positive and accurate, like no other SUV, the ride was smooth, sidewind stability was good and, most reassuringly of all, it did not feel like it would topple over when thrown into a turn. That is why BMW encouraged the report-writers to hurtle it around the race track. Off road, the X5 performed well enough, but certainly not up to Land Rover standards.

The rest of the X5 story is pretty straightforward, the 4.4 litre V8 engine being complemented by 3.0 litre petrol and diesel options for the vehicle's debut in Europe. The V8 yielded ever-larger derivatives, culminating in 2004's 360 bhp 4.8 litre, capable of 246 km/h – but even this pales into insignificance compared with the mighty X5 Le Mans built by BMW as a concept car for the 2000 Geneva show. Strictly not for sale, the Le Mans got its name from its engine – BMW's 24-hours winning six-litre V12, all 700 bhp of it. The idea behind the car, said BMW, was to explore the outer limits of what a four-wheel drive vehicle can do. The Le Mans succeeded in lapping the fearsome Nurburgring faster than a Ferrari 360 Stradale, Porsche 911 Turbo and Lamborghini Murcielago – which clearly indicates those limits are indeed pretty extreme.

The X5 successfully challenged established SUV favourites to bring high standards of road behaviour to the class

X5 SERIES: E53

Production History: In production: 1999-2006 Total produced 316,557				
model	X5 3.0i	X5 3.0d	X5 4.4i	total for year
1999	38		2,769	2,807
2000	22,855	57	22,095	45,007
2001	46,882	11,885	28,700	87,467
2002	48,196	30,036	5,408	83,640
2003	47,328	41,294	9,014	97,636
totals	165,299	83,272	67,986	
			grand total	316,557

A brand too far

BMW boss's public outburst as impatience with Rover boils over

Rover showdown

→ Successful debut of Rover 75
→ Pischetsrieder critises UK workforce
→ Sales targets failed
→ Rover 75 well received
→ Precipitated BMW's worst crisis since 1959
→ Export strategy backfired

The public debut of the Rover 75 scheduled for October 1998 promised to be a watershed for BMW ownership of the Rover Group. A number of new Rover, Land Rover and MG models were launched following BMW's surprise purchase in January 1994 but they were inherited projects initiated before the change of ownership. The 75 was different: it was a model conceived and developed wholly under BMW's watch.

What's more, the new parent's huge investments meant the 75 was the first Rover group model in decades that was properly funded. Up to the take-over, the shaky financial state of Rover (and BL and British Leyland before it) meant it was obliged to compromise on whatever it did. The 75, then, was the first true indicator of BMW's vision of what a thoroughly modern, well-financed Rover should be.

Everyone interested in cars, from customers to Rover's rivals, wanted to know more about the 75. Mostly, they hoped for the best, because Rover, one of the firms that virtually defined the executive car category during the 1960s and 1970s, had a peripheral role in the market by that stage. The aspirant, wealthy British families who once bought Rovers, Triumphs and Wolseleys had switched their allegiances to Audi, BMW, Mercedes and Volvo.

Walter Hasselkus, who took over as Rover chief executive following the resignation of John Towers, talked up the expectations. He spent the run-up to the 75's launch assuring the outside world that BMW knew far better than Ford, the owner of Jaguar, how to make a premium British saloon. It hardly seemed possible, as at that stage Jaguar was a success and Rover definitely was not. The parallel was chosen because Jaguar was also scheduled to unveil a new model at the 1998 British International Motor Show. The cars were not quite the same – Jaguar's S-Type proved to be bigger and more expensive than the 75 – but the two firms were old rivals and the show was staged at the National Exhibition Centre, located between the motor cities of Coventry and Birmingham, turning the twin unveilings into a local derby.

The interest focused on how a German group

The Rover 75, the only model developed entirely under BMW's ownership, was a high quality car which reflected BMW's aspirations for the Rover brand. However, on the day of the 75's unveiling BMW's boss hit out at the UK operation's inefficiency

"Walter Hasselkus spent the run-up to the 75's launch assuring the outside world that BMW knew far better than Ford, the owner of Jaguar, how to make a premium British saloon. It hardly seemed possible, as at that stage Jaguar was a success and Rover definitely was not"

BMW chairman Bernd Pischetsrieder told Rover employees investment would be cancelled unless productivity improved

would interpret the values of an archetypal British luxury car. It would be a challenge, because during the wilderness years of British Aerospace ownership, Rover attempted to recapture some of its post-war social cachet by billing itself as a 'British BMW'. Now the world had to come to terms with the reality of a British Rover from BMW.

The immediate reaction after the 75 unveiling on the morning of the motor show press preview day was positive. The car looked classy the way a Rover should, it was distinctive, and it clearly wasn't a BMW (or a Jaguar). No one outside the company at that stage knew what the newcomer would be like to drive or how well made and reliable it would be. The consensus, though, seemed to be that the project could be a success.

The 75 looked good, and it was a product of one of the world's most admired automotive engineering groups. That itself was a sign that the dark days of unreliable and unremarkable Rovers were over. After all the years of turmoil and uncertainty, the mood on the Rover stand was one of quiet optimism – euphoria even.

It completely vanished a few hours later as the morning's chilled champagne was replaced by cold tea.

Bernd Pischetsrieder, the BMW chairman, chose a press conference that afternoon to spell out his company's concerns about the state of Rover, and in particular the poor productivity of the giant Longbridge car plant. Unless employees shaped up, Pischetsrieder said, BMW would cancel its planned investment at Longbridge. Worse, Longbridge could even be closed completely. Suddenly, the 75 was like a new bride reduced to tears as a brawl broke out at her wedding reception. Not surprisingly, the headlines the following morning focused on the punch-up rather than the beautiful bride: BMW's worries about Rover were real enough, but it was not the most sensible moment to air them.

The episode became the catalyst for plenty of reappraisal of BMW's progress with its Rover turn-round. It had achieved a tremendous amount, but it increasingly looked as though resolving Rover's deep-seated problems would require more effort and money than could be

Rover 75 delivered a high-class driving experience thanks to an adapted version of BMW's 5 Series platform and the Z axle rear suspension; diesel engines came from BMW, too

justified. Pischetsrieder's belated big stick approach masked deep divisions among BMW managers and shareholders about the right tactics and strategy for Rover. They were profound, as events over the following few months proved. Less than four months later, Pischetsrieder was gone, and so were Wolfgang Reitzle, BMW's engineering director, and Hasselkus, Rover's chief executive. By May 2000, BMW had reversed completely out of its Rover responsibilities and the U-turn was accompanied by the departures of three other members of BMW's board of management.

BMW was an orderly, stable and successful car maker for nearly three decades up to the Rover episode. In only seven years, Rover managed to precipitate the worst crisis at BMW since its near collapse of late 1959.

With the benefit of hindsight, it is clear that BMW's attitude to Rover was far too benign in the early stages. Nationality and history played their part. The new German owner, mindful that Rover, Land Rover and MG were precious icons in a country that had been its enemy during the century's two great conflicts, was desperate not to appear triumphalist. In its determination to act sensitively, BMW allowed Rover to carry on running its own business for too long. Pischetsrieder became Rover chairman, but John Towers remained in position as day-to-day chief executive. There was no great exodus of Rover personnel, and no great influx of BMW people to replace them. Ultimately, Rover had to answer to BMW, but the company was still largely in charge of its own destiny. The main difference was that, for the first time in aeons, it could rely on a substantial revenue source to get the job done properly.

It could not last. The history of the motor industry is marked by more failures than successes when it comes to mergers and take – overs. The job of integrating a new company into an existing structure always takes far more time and money than anyone involved believes. BMW's stewardship of Rover fell into that category. Gradually, BMW came to the realisation that its hands-off approach was not working. Rover losses in 1995 almost doubled over the

Rover 600 (right) and 200 series were typical of the Honda-based legacy products BMW inherited. The link with Honda had helped Rover regain reliability and consumer confidence

Land Rover Freelander (left) was launched under BMW's watch, but development had begun before the takeover

previous year, and there seemed little prospect of any improvement over the coming years.

BMW decided it had to shift up a gear. Pischetsrieder was replaced as Rover chairman in September 1995 by Wolfgang Reitzle, the engineering guru responsible for BMW's strong product line-up. He immediately took a more active role in everything that went on in Rover. He was more critical and interventionist than his predecessor, and established a structure in which Nick Stephenson, Rover's new engineering director, reported to BMW. Importantly, Reitzle represented a change of emphasis at Rover. While he saw great potential for the Land Rover marque, he had little faith in the future of Rover and was ambivalent about MG.

Few were surprised when Towers, the chief executive, decided the following May to quit. He was accompanied by John Russell, Rover's sales and marketing director, who was replaced by Tom Purves, a former Rolls-Royce apprentice who by

that stage was chief executive of BMW's sales subsidiary in the UK.

BMW said it tried to recruit a suitable local executive to replace Towers, but in September announced the appointment of one of its own career executives. German-born Walter Hasselkus was the next best thing to a Briton, however. During a stint as head of BMW (GB) in the 1980s, Hasselkus acquired the 'Sir Walter' nickname on account of his Anglophile nature. He joined Rover as chief executive after a period in charge of the group's motorcycle operations.

At last, BMW began to take more control of Rover. Some of the drama of that period was revealed in a BBC television series aired in early 1997. *When Rover met BMW* provided a very public insight into the take-over, its aftermath and the tensions involved when cultures clashed.

What was not in doubt was BMW's financial commitment to the Rover Group. Despite handing over £1 billion ($1.5 billion) to British Aerospace and Honda for the privilege of owning Rover in 1994, BMW then set about righting one of its worst wrongs – a chronic lack of investment in new products and manufacturing facilities. Over the following five years, BMW allocated an average of just over £500 million ($800 million) a year in investments in Rover. They included commitments to modernise the factory at Oxford (formerly known as Cowley) to make the new 75, a stamping facility at Solihull and an all-new factory at HammsHall to produce four-cylinder engines for BMW and Rover models. There were plans in the pending file to develop a truly modern Mini and to manufacture it at Longbridge. In addition, Reitzle instigated the development of a new generation of Range Rovers – models that, as events turned out, became part of the Land Rover package bought by Ford in 2000.

Arguably, it was still not enough to overcome the historical handicap of under-investment. During the five years under BAe control, for example, Rover received average investments each year of £200 million ($330 million). They were trifling sums that were wholly inadequate if the shareholders expected Rover to regain competitiveness.

It is a tribute to many Rover personnel that the whole enterprise had not simply ground to a halt. They managed to launch the Honda-based 600 saloon in April 1993, a new version of the Range Rover eight months after the BMW take-over, and the all-new MG F roadster in the spring of 1995. The MG was an indication of the constraints faced by the company, because its development costs, and its profits, were shared with Mayflower, the engineering group that supplied its body shell. Without Mayflower, the MG would not have been possible.

At the time of the take-over, Land Rover engineers had begun development work on a smaller addition to the range to rival the Toyota RAV4. Known as CB40, it went on sale as the Freelander in autumn 1997. In another indication of the constraints under which the group worked, the Freelander was developed only for Europe. It seemed an incomprehensible decision at the time, because Land Rover proudly boasts that it sells in virtually every country of the world and had recently started selling vehicles in the United States once more. It was a question of money. The United States is comfortably the largest market in the world for sport-utility vehicles, but to make Freelander comply with the country's safety and emissions legislation would have broken the budget. Only with BMW backing did Freelander make it to America, four years after its debut.

In all other respects, though, Rover's products were barely competitive. The Mini and Rover 100 (formerly Metro) were already ancient but still part of the line-up. The Land Rover Defender was a decade old by 1994. The Honda Legend-based Rover 800, which dated from 1986, disappeared from the showrooms only with the launch of the 75. The Rover 200 and Rover 400 – also Honda-based and the group's highest volumes models – and the Land Rover Discovery first went on sale in 1989. A decade would elapse before they were replaced.

As a group, Rover sold roughly 400,000 to 500,000 vehicles a year during the period of BMW ownership. But to produce them, BMW was burdened by the fixed costs associated with four factories: Longbridge and Oxford to make the cars, Solihull to make Land Rovers, and a stamping plant at Swindon. By modern standards, it was at least two factories too many, which was

"BMW was an orderly, stable and successful car maker for nearly three decades up to the Rover episode. In only seven years, Rover managed to precipitate the worst crisis at BMW since its near collapse in 1959"

"BMW shareholders, long accustomed to regular dividends and steady gains in the value of their holdings, seriously questioned the wisdom of the Rover purchase in the first place"

one of the reasons BMW began to talk in terms of raising Rover Group's annual sales to 750,000. It was wishful thinking.

Rover made no real progress in achieving those higher sales numbers BMW dreamed about. Indeed, it began to lose ground in its home market as BMW initiated a strategic switch to exports. The real handicap, though, was BMW's delusion about the sales potential of Rover as an upmarket brand. Simply saying it was and imposing higher prices did not turn Rover into one in the minds of car buyers. They knew that Rovers were intrinsically no better than Fords or Renaults, and were all too frequently worse. The newish Rover 600 was reasonably successful, but BMW tried to charge Mondeo prices for the Escort-sized 200 and 400, which were already old by car industry standards. Buyers saw through the ruse and refused to buy unless the cars were discounted. This was an alien concept to BMW, whose mystique (and consequently high prices) was achieved by constantly keeping supply in arrears of demand. In the volume car sector in which Rover really competed, as distinct from the prestige car niche in which BMW

thought it ought to be, it would never work

The delusion was one of several Rover decisions that came to haunt BMW. By giving priority to the development of the Rover 75, BMW believed it would set new customer expectations for all future Rover models. The success of the 75 flagship, it was argued, would have a trickle-down effect on subsequent smaller models. But the 25 and 45, which is what the 200 and 400 became in autumn 1999, were patently little more than modified versions of the Hondas they originally were. They had none of the 75's evident BMW engineering integrity.

Whatever the success of the 75, though, it was a pricey model with limited potential to make much difference to overall Rover sales volumes. To achieve the level of annual sales needed by Rover would have required proper, ground-up replacements for the 25 and 45. Those launches never came. Looking back, then, it is possible to argue that BMW was wrong to give priority to a high-end model when new mainstream cars could have provided the volume it needed.

The other flaw turned out to be BMW's decision to emphasise exports. Rover and its

Walter Hasselkus (right) was a popular CEO of Rover and known as 'Sir Walter' because of his English manner

John Towers (far right): resigned from Rover CEO post when BMW began to take closer control of day-to-day operations

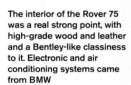

The interior of the Rover 75 was a real strong point, with high-grade wood and leather and a Bentley-like classiness to it. Electronic and air conditioning systems came from BMW

predecessor companies never met much success when trying to sell cars outside its home market. No matter how much better Rovers were by the 1990s, sales resistance in the rest of Europe and other parts of the world stemmed from the poor quality and unreliable delivery dates of earlier times. Rover achieved reasonable sales in France and Italy, and Land Rover was a big exporter, but for years the group's export level hovered around the 40 per cent mark. It was nowhere near enough for a group like BMW with global ambitions. Gradually, Rover sales outside the UK climbed on the strength of BMW's reputation and its distribution network, reaching nearly 60 per cent by the late 1990s.

Unfortunately, the export push coincided with a financial crisis involving sterling. The UK currency soared in value as soon as it left the European Exchange Rate Mechanism in early 1995. BMW's forward planning was done on the basis of an exchange rate of around DM 2.60/£1, but the company suddenly faced the prospect of a DM 3.0 sterling exchange. Fortunately, BMW had bought its sterling requirements in advance at a lower rate, and was therefore cushioned for a period from the day-to-day effect of its climb in value. By the middle of

1998, though, its reserves of hedged currency were running out. Every million pounds of investment ear-marked for its UK subsidiary suddenly cost BMW a lot more German Marks to buy. The outlook became so bad that BMW suspended some of its planned investments, including on the new generation Mini.

The currency swing was equally felt in Rover's sales operations. The strong pound drove up its prices outside the UK, while handing a commercial advantage to European companies like Renault and Peugeot that sold their cars in the UK. Rover was handicapped in export markets and lost sales at home.

The whole Rover scenario – continuing financial losses, stagnant sales, poor productivity and the even bigger drain on BMW reserves caused by sterling's strength – gradually brought matters to a head as the 75 was prepared for its unveiling at the NEC. BMW shareholders, long accustomed to regular dividends and steady gains in the value of their holdings, seriously began to question the wisdom of the Rover purchase in the first place. No one was more aware of that than Bernd Pischetsrieder when he unexpectedly let fly about Rover's business performance a few hours later.

The English Patient

BMW loses six top managers, sells Land Rover, lets Rover go for £10

The Longbridge efficiency and investment controversy that disrupted the Rover 75 coming-out party in October 1998 was a rare instance of internal BMW divisions erupting in public. It was increasingly difficult to keep a lid on the dissent within BMW concerning Rover. The English Patient, as Rover became known in Germany after a film of the time, was a serious burden on the group, but it was one with which BMW managers and shareholders were not qualified to deal.

Up to that point, BMW gave the impression that all was right with its world, a little like one of its magnificent 7 Series saloons powering effortlessly along the Autobahn. The long-term goals were clear to everyone, from sweeper to shareholder. If changes had to be made along the way, they were carefully considered internally and communicated efficiently to the public. Nothing was left to chance. Recruiting people from outside the group was rare because young talents were nurtured to become middle managers, then senior managers and directors. That meant everyone was steeped in the BMW way of doing business. The formula worked exceptionally well once the 1959 crisis was over. BMW grew and prospered, and its global reputation soared. Buyers who once thought only

in terms of Mercedes-Benz had to consider BMW as well.

The group was so successful for so long that its training manual contained nothing about the possibility of failure. Whether it was complacency or arrogance, the purchase of Rover raised that need. Neither did BMW have much experience of the joint ventures or take overs that swept through the international motor industry. Even by the early 21st century, the small petrol engine collaboration with Peugeot-Citroen scheduled for 2005 was the exception rather than the rule. There was BMW's purchase of the ailing Glas car making firm in Dingolfing in 1966, but that was more like a cosy Bavarian arrangement between old colleagues. Otherwise, BMW's expansion over the years was essentially organic.

Development of the third-generation Range Rover was authorised by Wolfgang Reitzle whilst at BMW; later, Reitzle was able to launch the model after first he and then Land Rover had moved to Ford

279

Wolfgang Reitzle was the inspiration behind the Range Rover's high standards when he was at BMW; after leaving BMW he joined Ford which bought Land Rover off BMW, allowing him to complete the launch of the product he had always promoted

Top:
Ford CEO Jac Nasser hired Reitzle to run Ford's premium brands; within a year the American multinational had bought Land Rover off BMW

Above:
Professor Joachim Milberg (standing): taking over BMW hot-seat after Pischetsrieder's departure, he resolved to support Rover – until the price became too high. On his right is Helmet Panke, who was to succeed him as BMW CEO

The company was, therefore, in many ways unprepared for the Rover acquisition. What could it possibly know of managing take overs? Yet the development took BMW into manufacturing in a country that does not share the Bavarian work ethic, its engineering integrity or its quality standards. It required BMW to deal with people who were not schooled in its business methods and moved BMW into categories of the car market about which it had no knowledge. What is more, it brought together a group that for years knew nothing but success with one that was schooled in penny-pinching contraction. Both sides were keen to make the take-over work, but it is now clear that the chasm was too great to jump.

The multi-brand vision behind the acquisition of the Rover group was in place at the time of the Rover 75 launch. BMW insisted it would continue to develop Land Rover, Rover and MG to complement the core BMW range. Mini was destined to be resurrected in 2001 as a brand in its own right. And, following a separate 1998 agreement, Rolls-Royce would join the BMW family at the start of 2003. This multi-brand approach remained the official strategy right up to the moment in March 2000 when BMW executed its shock U-turn.

Not everyone within BMW was convinced it would work, however, and the dissent centred on Wolfgang Reitzle, the board member responsible for new product development. He also served as chairman of the Rover Group until shortly after

the appointment of Walter Hasselkus as chief executive in September 1996. After his stint in Britain, Reitzle returned to BMW headquarters in Munich with his theories about multi-branding reinforced.

Long before the purchase of the Rover Group, Reitzle had identified Land Rover as a suitable complement to BMW. As far as Reitzle was concerned, Land Rover's future was secure. He also favoured the creation of a 21st century interpretation of the iconic Mini. MG was too small to be relevant, though the mid-engined MG F, launched in spring 1995, was a minor success. But with so much else to do, would it be sensible to nurture MG in the same way that BMW planned to do with Land Rover? BMW knew how to design roadsters. Besides, MG had perhaps reached its sell-by date. Buyers of a certain age with an interest in motoring history fondly recalled all the MG sports cars of the 1930s and the post-war era, but the brand was later devalued by badge engineering abuse. By the 1990s, thirtysomethings who wanted affordable roadsters turned to Alfa Romeo, Lotus, Mazda and Toyota.

Reitzle's main reservations revolved around the Rover nameplate. If the decision had been his, BMW would probably have ditched Rover long before, and the sprawling, decrepit Longbridge factory along with it. Such actions were probably impossible because of the enormous political, social and economic

implications in Britain. Nevertheless, Reitzle knew that the Rover brand's market appeal was not strong enough, and that, as a manufacturing group, Rover had far more capacity than it required. And yet here was BMW about to pour more good money after bad. Plenty of people in Munich agreed with the Reitzle thesis. They included some influential shareholders.

Even as 1998 drew to a close, the multi-brand theory still looked plausible on paper. As the months went by, though, it became increasingly evident that it did not work in practice. It could be made to, but the question being asked was whether the management effort and money was worthwhile. After heavy investment buying and modernising Rover, BMW was preparing to invest an additional £1.7 billion ($2.45 billion) in order to modernise the appallingly neglected Longbridge factory in order to bring the new Mini and R30 (the 25/45 replacement) to market.

The investment depended on an agreement with the unions over new working practices and a contribution by the British government to support the development with selective regional development aid. After all, BMW argued, it demonstrated a commitment to manufacturing in Britain just as much as Ford and General Motors, which had previously received regional development aid. Longbridge aid totalling £150 million ($215 million) was eventually agreed following a bout of nasty political infighting. But national government approval was one thing. The grant had to be signed off by the European Commission, which still sat on the issue when BMW pulled the plug on Rover.

What BMW shareholders received in return for this mountainous financial commitment to Rover was a series of heavy losses by the British group, culminating in a £650 million ($940 million) deficit in 1998. Hasselkus, the Rover chairman and chief executive, did the honourable thing by resigning. He did so on the day that the unions and BMW agreed to new work practices for Longbridge, thus clearing the way for the big investment. Those events temporarily deflected the heat from his boss, Bernd Pischetsrieder, the principal architect of the Rover strategy. Hasselkus was replaced by Werner Saemann, a

technology specialist who was little known outside BMW.

The impact of Rover's troubles and losses, and the absence of any immediate solutions to the problems, had disastrous consequences on the values of investors' holdings, and on the size of their dividend cheques. The action that was supposed to secure the long-term future of the BMW group was in danger of ruining it.

The Rover brand was at the core of the multi-brand failure. Land Rover, with a recently launched revamped Discovery, was improving, though the product quality levels emerging from the Solihull factory remained unacceptable. MG sales were steady, even if the numbers were too small to make much material difference. Mini and Rolls-Royce were at that stage unknowns. However, it was a period when they were costing the parent group a lot of money in research and development without producing anything in return. Through all this, worldwide sales of BMW branded vehicles steadily increased in the familiar pattern.

The Rover flaw remained paramount. Old prejudices take a long time to alter, as the Volkswagen group discovered when it tried to push Audi upmarket. Only after a couple of decades did car buyers begin to think of Audis in the same class as BMWs and Mercedes-Benz. And they simply did not believe the BMW assertion that a Rover was a worthy premium car alternative to a Jaguar, or to a Volvo or to an Audi. Given more time (and money), the Rover 75 might have started to change public perceptions. So might the stillborn smaller R30, but BMW did not have time, especially when the 75 took many months longer than forecast to get into full production.

The denouement came at a long and tense meeting of the BMW board of management in February 1999. With the health of the English Patient deteriorating, Pischetsrieder, the surgeon who masterminded its purchase in the first place (and that of Rolls-Royce), tendered his resignation. It was immediately accepted by the supervisory board. To the outside world, which at that stage knew nothing of the events unfolding behind closed doors, Reitzle would have been the natural replacement. Having earlier lost out on the chairmanship to Pischetsrieder, he wanted

the role and was patently qualified to do it. It is not the way it happened.

It is still not clear why Reitzle also resigned that day. It may have been implacable opposition by Eberhard von Kuenheim, the chairman of the supervisory board and close confidant of the Quandt family, the key BMW shareholders. It may have been opposition by employee representatives on the supervisory board. It may have been on account of Reitzle's known determination to rid BMW of the Rover brand. Whatever the true cause, the new chairman was a former academic at Munich Technical University who had joined BMW less than six years earlier.

Joachim Milberg was a quiet manufacturing professor whose role was to rebuild consensus at BMW. There would be no change of direction concerning the Rover Group, he declared, though one of his first actions was to give BMW executives direct, day-to-day control over everything that happened in the British firm. Rover's days of autonomy were over, which was arguably what should have happened in the first place.

Milberg declared shortly after his appointment: "The multi-brand strategy that was pursued was right in principle. The type of group leadership, however, proved to be wrong." He then added: "Our strategy is the strategy of the entire (his emphasis) BMW board of management. And since this is demonstrated by all of us, you will not see any of us developing and announcing his own strategies."

It seemed curious even at the time. There would be no change of direction concerning the multi-brand strategy. But in order to determine that, BMW had within the space of only two months lost three of its top directors, Pischetsrieder, Reitzle and Hasselkus. Worse, Reitzle was quickly recruited by Ford president Jacques Nasser to run a new project he was putting together. Ford already owned Aston Martin, Jaguar and Lincoln. In April 1999, it bought the car-making part of Volvo. Just over a year after that, Ford added Land Rover. All of them were pulled together to form Premier Automotive Group, whose primary role was to challenge BMW and Mercedes-Benz on behalf of Ford. Reitzle was to be its boss.

"The one-sided nature of the agreement was a clear indication of how desperate BMW was by this stage to close the Rover episode. For only £10, Phoenix bought the Longbridge site, the rights to existing Rover and MG cars, thousands of unsold vehicles, and working capital of £500 million"

Back at BMW, it was business as usual after the February 1999 blood-letting, at least on the face of things. The new team on the bridge declared it had not, and would not, be driven from the multi-brand course drawn up at the time of the Rover acquisition. Its main task was to get the Rover 75 to market. The car had been scheduled to go on sale in January of that year, but manufacturing and quality problems determined BMW to delay the launch for six months. That turned the renovated Oxford plant into another drain on BMW cash as it sat idle while problems were resolved. However, the 75 received a very positive reception from the press and public when it did go on sale that summer. Subsequent ownership reports indicated that quality was good too. Perhaps BMW could build a "better Jaguar", as Hasselkus promised.

But concerns among BMW shareholders about the Rover Group did not go away. The share price remained in the doldrums in spite of all the reassurances from BMW board members. The open speculation about BMW's real intention, as distinct from the one professed in public, was sufficiently powerful for a relatively little known private equity company in London to request a meeting with BMW management.

Jon Moulton and Eric Walters, the founders of Alchemy Partners, were looking for a substantial new project following their turn-round of the FADs chain of do-it-yourself stores in Britain. Rover seemed to fit the bill. Their first meeting with Helmut Panke, the BMW finance director, and Hagen Luederitz, the strategy director, took place at BMW's headquarters in Munich in October, 1999. While the initial encounter did not look promising, the meetings continued on a regular basis over the following few months. Gradually, both sides came to the realisation that a Rover deal was possible. Importantly for BMW, any sale would provide it with an acceptable exit strategy from the Rover millstone. It was at least

an attractive alternative to continuing to pour money into Rover, given that BMW did not want to go down in history as the group that killed the last vestiges of the motor industry in Britain.

Through the rest of 1999 and into the first months of the new millennium, BMW maintained the façade that Rover was safe. That did not prevent it from sounding out most of the world's largest automotive groups in order to determine whether it had any other options. BMW did not take long to establish that Alchemy would be the only bidder at any secret auction.

At the end of February 2000, on the eve of the annual motor show in Geneva, chairman Milberg once more restated his company's position: "BMW is stronger than ever before. And proceeding from this excellent position we will continue the process of restructuring the Rover brand consistently and in line with our targets." He dismissed all the rumours about any change of direction for Rover, and about the need for BMW to seek a merger or acquisition partner because of the drain caused by Rover on the group. "The only strategy can be to make Rover a strong and powerful brand," he added.

It is hard to understand why Milberg and his colleagues felt they could be so unequivocal about the future of Rover when they knew what was going on behind closed doors. Something a little more circumspect might have been in order in the light of BMW's confirmation on March 16, 2000, that all the speculation was true – it had agreed to sell the car-manufacturing side of Rover and the Longbridge factory complex. The buyer was to be Alchemy, which immediately began six weeks of due diligence. Two days later, it emerged that BMW had agreed to sell the Land Rover sport-utility business to Ford.

BMW would make the new Mini at Oxford instead, and it would continue the construction of the Hamms Hall engine factory, which was to open in 2001. In other respects, the Alchemy and Ford developments were broadly in line with all the rumours, but the sudden reality of them after all the flat denials sent shockwaves through the United Kingdom. Politicians in Westminster, civil servants in Whitehall and car workers in the English Midlands were not the only ones wrong-footed. The volte face immediately led to three

more top-level resignations from the BMW board of management. Carl-Peter Forster, the head of manufacturing; Wolfgang Ziebart, the head of engineering; and Henrich Heitmann, the head of sales and marketing, effectively became further victims of BMW's ill-fated experiment in multi-branding. Each had been in office for little more than 13 months following the previous boardroom coup.

For BMW, a solution to the unfortunate episode of Rover ownership was in sight, however. In March 2000, the Ford purchase of Land Rover went through for £1.8 billion ($2.9 billion) and, ironically, allowed Reitzle to finish development of the beloved Range Rover he had initiated whilst at BMW. What the Alchemy due diligence team discovered was sufficient to put it off for good. It abandoned its scheme to turn Longbridge and the Rover passenger car range into a slimmed-down MG Car Company. The news suited Longbridge employees and the Midlands business community, which from the start regarded Alchemy as asset strippers. By that time, they had backed an alternative plan for Rover that, they believed, would preserve more jobs and offer a better long term future for Rover.

With Alchemy out of the picture, BMW had to listen more seriously to the counter-proposals by the Phoenix consortium. The Phoenix group comprised four Midlands businessmen with long associations with Rover: John Towers, the former chief executive; Nick Stephenson, the former engineering director; Rover car dealer John Edwards and his financial director, Peter Beale. They quickly put Phoenix together in response to fears about what the Alchemy plan might do to manufacturing in the Midlands. For Longbridge workers, and for the thousands of others who were employed by companies that depended on Longbridge, the Phoenix four would ensure their future. For BMW, Phoenix would provide an acceptable exit strategy. The two sides had to agree.

The one-sided nature of the agreement was a clear indication of how desperate BMW was by that stage to close the Rover episode. For only £10 ($16), Phoenix bought the Longbridge site, the rights to continue to sell existing Rover and MG passenger cars, thousands of unsold

vehicles, and working capital of around £500 million ($800 million). BMW bore the cost of moving Rover 75 production from Oxford to Longbridge. Also included was ownership of the MG nameplate (and Austin, Morris and Wolseley) and the free use of the Rover name for as long as it remained under Phoenix control. If Phoenix at some stage sells the car business, the Rover brand reverts to BMW. Intriguingly, BMW also retained ownership of the dormant Triumph and Riley brands.

For BMW, the nightmare was over. It had discharged its Rover Group responsibilities and could continue in a modified direction. It soon became clear that more BMW-brand models would be introduced to compensate for the volume loss, including the smaller 1 Series and X3 sport-activity vehicle. At the same time, the new generation MINI would over the years evolve into a broader, more rounded range of models. And, at the top of the group portfolio, there would be Rolls-Royce.

As a group, BMW was soon in the fast lane once more, even if, as a brand, it was never out of it. Memories of the Rover Group experiment fade with each passing year. The longer MG Rover remains an independent business, the better it will be for BMW. Whatever happens to MG Rover in the future, BMW will not now be tarnished by any suggestions that it failed in its duty to Rover and the car industry in Britain. It was, though, all a monumentally undignified and unproductive episode in BMW history.

28

Back to the future

Retro-styled Z8 was the last word in exclusivity but it didn't quite hit the spot

Z8 (E52)

- → 1999 – 2003
- → Elegant and exclusive sports roadster
- → Production version of 1997 Z07 concept
- → Aluminium spaceframe construction
- → 400 bhp engine from M5
- → Used in James Bond film
- → High price restricted sales
- → Desirable collector's car

It was not just the Japanese crowds but the whole world which was stunned when BMW pulled back the covers from its Z07 concept car at the 1997 Tokyo motor show. What was revealed was not the avant-garde supercar that had been widely expected, nor a futuristic luxury sedan: instead, it was an instantly evocative flashback to the glories of the 1950s, to the era of high-powered wind-in-the-hair sports roadsters, the romance of the open road before rules and regulations killed all the fun.

And the car buffs in the crowd immediately said just one thing: BMW 507. From its low, split-grille nose to its air outlets behind the front wheels and its flowing rear wing line the Z07 concept – was its name deliberately so close? – was pure 507 – and to anchor the 1950s impression the wire-spoke steering wheel, the driver's head fairing and the elegantly tapered tail were authentic Jaguar D-Type.

Designers Chris Bangle and Henrik Fisker had produced a much-praised and skilful tribute to an honoured ancestor. But would a committedly future-oriented BMW really consider series production for a design as openly retro as this?

After the Z07 made a second show appearance – at Detroit in January 1998 – the answer seemed more clearly yes, and following a relentless campaign in the specialist car magazines around the world the real-world Z07 was revealed at the 1999 Frankfurt show as the Z8. It looked remarkably similar to the concept, minus the more extreme features such as the driver's fairing.

But though it looked like a piece of naked nostalgia, the Z8 was brim full of modern engineering beneath its time-warp skin and behind its vintage-look dashboard with its central instruments and wire-spoke wheel. The E-Type-like rear bumper contained aerials for the hi-fi and telephone; tiny xenon headlights peeped through old-style streamlined plexiglass covers on the front wings. The structure, for a start, was an advanced space frame construction from

Despite its retro looks the Z8 was a thoroughly modern sports car underneath, with the acclaimed 400 bhp V8 engine from the M5 and state-of the art chassis systems

E52: Z8

Specifications	Z8 roadster

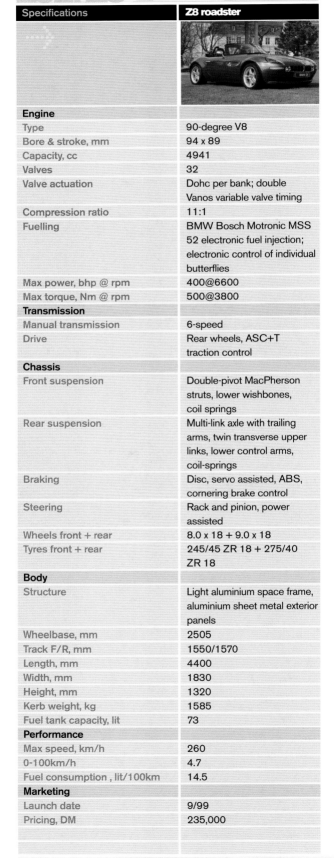

Engine	
Type	90-degree V8
Bore & stroke, mm	94 x 89
Capacity, cc	4941
Valves	32
Valve actuation	Dohc per bank; double Vanos variable valve timing
Compression ratio	11:1
Fuelling	BMW Bosch Motronic MSS 52 electronic fuel injection; electronic control of individual butterflies
Max power, bhp @ rpm	400@6600
Max torque, Nm @ rpm	500@3800
Transmission	
Manual transmission	6-speed
Drive	Rear wheels, ASC+T traction control
Chassis	
Front suspension	Double-pivot MacPherson struts, lower wishbones, coil springs
Rear suspension	Multi-link axle with trailing arms, twin transverse upper links, lower control arms, coil-springs
Braking	Disc, servo assisted, ABS, cornering brake control
Steering	Rack and pinion, power assisted
Wheels front + rear	8.0 x 18 + 9.0 x 18
Tyres front + rear	245/45 ZR 18 + 275/40 ZR 18
Body	
Structure	Light aluminium space frame, aluminium sheet metal exterior panels
Wheelbase, mm	2505
Track F/R, mm	1550/1570
Length, mm	4400
Width, mm	1830
Height, mm	1320
Kerb weight, kg	1585
Fuel tank capacity, lit	73
Performance	
Max speed, km/h	260
0-100km/h	4.7
Fuel consumption , lit/100km	14.5
Marketing	
Launch date	9/99
Pricing, DM	235,000

extruded aluminium sections chosen for their lightness, strength and good performance in an impact; the suspension followed current BMW principles of MacPherson struts and lower wishbones at the front and a sophisticated five-link set-up at the rear – except that wherever possible it was made of aluminium too. The brake system came from the V12-engined 750i, while the steering was rack and pinion – the first time BMW had used departed from recirculating ball on a V8-engined car.

That V8 was something special, too: it came from the M5, and used not just double VANOS variable valve timing but also a complex system of individual throttle butterfly valves to ensure perfect fuelling for each cylinder. In the interests of achieving a 50/50 weight distribution the engine was placed as far back as possible, sitting almost against the firewall. The lubrication system was upgraded to one with one pressure and two scavenge pumps, triggered when the chassis' dynamic stability sensors detected sufficient lateral acceleration to cause oil surge; in other respects the 400 bhp drivetrain was the same as in the M5, linked to a six-speed manual gearbox. An automatic option was talked about but never delivered.

Considering the aluminium structure, body and suspension and the compact two-seater body, the Z8's 1585 kg weight came as something of a surprise. The engineers blamed it on the amount of luxury equipment demanded on a high price sports car, but it was still 135 kg less than the M5 and acceleration was prodigious, 100 km/h coming up in 4.7 seconds. The maximum speed would have been around 290 km/h had it not been for the fitment of an electronic limiter, hinted BMW. Even so, the Z8 was not the sensational drive that its looks, its format and its M5 power had led enthusiasts to hope for: it made great noises and really looked the part but it did not sway many hard-line Porsche devotees.

One of the main issues was the price, which, at DM 235,000, was right up there with the top 911s and AMG's Mercedes SL and way beyond anything from Jaguar. Some explanation lay in the fact that the Z8 was produced on a special prototype-build line in Munich, largely by hand: the talk was that it took 10 times as many man-hours to finish as a 3 Series saloon.

One driver who very publicly took to the Z8

was Pierce Brosnan as James Bond in The world is not enough. But despite the endorsement of Hollywood the Z8 never really had the scent of success to it, and production ceased in 2003 after 5703 had been made. In being admired rather than desired and in falling short of expectations BMW's modern-retro V8 roadster ironically suffered a similar fate to the 1956 BMW 507 it was so obviously modelled on.

BMW said at the time that the Z8 was a car "designed for connoisseurs, its blend of aesthetic design and dynamic performance born of BMW's desire to show how the 1956 BMW 507 might have developed had it been an integral part of the BMW range in the intervening period." Only one twentieth as many 507s were made, but, just like its mentor, the Z8 is sure to be just as desirable in years to come.

Tokyo show, October 1999: Henrik Fisker and Chris Bangle's Z07 design study suggested a new direction for BMW. The production Z8 would closely follow the original concept

Experience gained with the aluminium spaceframe construction of the Z8 would prove invaluable in the manufacture of the Rolls-Royce Phantom in 2003. Pricing well into the Porsche 911 bracket kept sales slow

"Though it looked like a piece of naked nostalgia, the Z8 was brim full of modern engineering beneath its time-warp skin and behind the central instruments of its vintage-look dashboard"

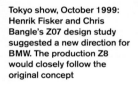

E52: Z8

Production History:	In production: 1999-2003 Total produced: 5,703	
model	Z8	total for year
1999	69	69
2000	1,928	1,928
2001	2,302	2,302
2002	926	926
2003	478	478
totals	5,703	
	grand total	5,703

The Grand Prix adventure

BMW commits to success in Formula One and at Le Mans

After excelling in most motorsport disciplines since the early 1960s, BMW had two major challenges unfulfilled by the end of the '70s – Grand Prix racing and tackling the Le Mans endurance racing challenge with an in-house sports car. Several car makers have paid the price for misguided F1 adventures, before and since, from Aston Martin and Peugeot to Lamborghini, but BMW was committed to winning.

BMW's delay in mounting a Grand Prix challenge until the early 1980s reflects the innate caution of its board about committing to the highest-cost, highest-risk, and highest-profile division of the sport. Veteran Munich motorsport guru Alex von Falkenhausen's legacy, after retiring in 1975, was to propose a flat-eight F1 power plant and keep the topic alive in BMW's executive offices. Bavarian pride helped swing the boardroom argument towards the Grand Prix grid after Jochen Neerpasch, the motorsport manager who orchestrated so many successes, unwisely agreed to build an F1 engine for the French Talbot organisation.

Neerpasch, later to move to arch rivals Mercedes, left at the end of 1979 and his successor Dieter Stappert received executive backing for BMW's assault on the summit of

motorsport. With Brabham as the chosen partner and chassis builder, BMW Motorsport's facilities in Munich's Preussenstrasse provided base camp for this ambitious climb.

True to its motorsport traditions BMW took the production-related route, nominating the iron-block of a mainstream four-cylinder road car engine as the basis for a unique programme.

The 'mighty atom' F1 units used blocks which had been through 100,000 kilometres (62,500 miles) of 'maturing' or simulated testing to show up strengths and weaknesses in preparation for the often literally explosive high-pressure nature of turbocharging small engines.

Renault had pioneered turbochargers in F1 from 1979 onwards with its V6 counterpart, forcing BMW to enter the power stakes. BMW racing legend reveals that the M12/13 engines

Le Mans, June 1999: BMW emerges victorious after 24 hours of hard-fought racing

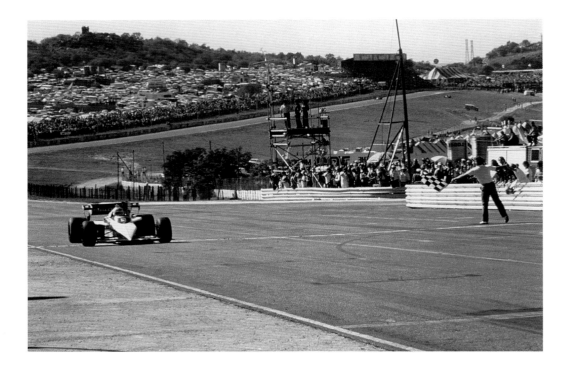

would go from the planning stages to running in the back of a Brabham in just 630 days.

The racing power output would also escalate from 550 in 1980 to nearer 1,000 horsepower by the time the engine ceased to be a factory engine at the end of 1986. A massive output for any engine, but stunning for a stock block four-cylinder.

En route to the 1983 world title for Brazilian Nelson Piquet, and an eventual nine BMW-propelled Grand Prix victories, the power and glory theme embraced 'grenade' qualifying engines generating a genuinely awesome 1,200 horsepower.

The grenade tag came courtesy of these engines being run on ultra high boost for three or four crack qualifying laps before they threatened to self destruct. Special synthetic fuel, supplied by BASF and later banned by the sport's authorities, provided another element in that unique combination.

Piquet, who likened the rocket-like throttle response to turning on a light bulb, was also quoted as saying his job involved aiming the '83 title-winning, needle-nosed BT52 Brabham down the middle of the track and "constant prayer." Piquet and fellow drivers including Italian Ricardo Patrese used a cockpit-mounted boost control to crank up the turbo boost to 5.5 bar.

BMW's explosive engine was the first to exploit electronic engine management control units (now standard in humble family saloons) and power unit mapping. The company's hugely influential engine guru Paul Rosche confided that the sense of track-side theatre was heightened by selecting from a felt-lined box of electronic chip units.

Dictating different power outputs and engine characteristics, they carried the names of reviled national leaders, including the Colonel Gaddafi chip after the Libyan leader, and also the Hitler chip. With its arrow-like aerodynamics and lack of sidepods the slimline BT52 was clocked at 340km/h (212mph) and registered a blistering 0 to 160km/h in 4.8 seconds.

The relationship between BMW and Brabham, then run by Bernie Ecclestone, was not always harmonious, particularly at the onset of the campaign. During the 1982 debut year, there

Nelson Piquet wins the F1 world championship in South Africa in 1983 with BMW turbo power. The designer of his Brabham BT52, Gordon Murray, would go on to build the BMW-powered McLaren F1 road car in 1994

The Formula One engine of the 1980s was based on a BMW road-car block and eventually achieved over 1200 horsepower in qualifying trim. BMW preferred engines from used cars with 100,000 km on the clock

was a fragmented approach with Brabham hedging its bets and often falling back on the 3-litre, normally-aspirated DFV Cosworth. Such was the lack of consistent faith in the project from Ecclestone that an ultimatum was issued during the summer by the BMW board threatening to dissolve the partnership.

Ecclestone claimed that Piquet was unenthusiastic about the rapidly developing, but fragile engine, while in fact the Brazilian apparently urged the team owner to persist and ultimately exploit its potential.

At times it was a roller-coaster ride as typified by the largely unexpected maiden victory in the 1982 Montreal Canadian Grand Prix. This contrasted with failing to qualify one week earlier in Detroit, in the backyard of Ford, whom BMW dearly wanted to unseat in F1.

If BMW and Rosche kept the programme's momentum intact, the other prime mover was the Bohemian alternative designer at Brabham, Gordon Murray.

The lanky South African applied a great deal of lateral thinking to the cars carrying BMW's engines and claimed later that the 1984 title should have been also be won.

Despite seizing nine pole positions, the Brabham-BMW BT52 regularly suffered from turbo-related failure, which Murray claimed was down to the poor quality of the Garrett turbocharger, substituted for the previous KKK device.

It was Murray who later designed the McLaren F1 GT V12 which maintained the long-term road and track links with BMW. He also derived immense pride from Piquet clinching the 1983 world title at the South African's home race at Kyalami, although Patrese was gifted that deciding event.

The F1 turbo engine continued in various official BMW guises until the end of 1986 when another piece of synchronicity saw future BMW F1 motorsport manager Gerhard Berger, of Austria, score the company's ninth and last turbo engine victory for Benetton in Mexico.

Le Mans continues as a blue riband night and day endurance race, surrounded by unmatched heritage and legend, which was the reason for BMW's determination to add a victory there to its

"BMW's explosive 1980s Formula One engine was the first to exploit electronic engine management control (now standard on every family saloon) and power unit mapping"

The JJ Lehto/Steve Soper
BMW at the Sears Point
Raceway, California, in 1999

"BMW's Le Mans win came at the peak of recent factory involvement, both in terms of quantity and quality, where there were works Mercedes, Nissans, Toyotas and Audis doing battle"

The winning BMW V12 LM of
Yannick Dalmas,
Jo Winkelhock and Pierluigi
Martini crosses the Le Mans
finishing line in 1999

portfolio of triumphs. Whereas it played a
supporting role to the McLaren Le Mans debut
victory of 1995, the connection with Williams
Grand Prix Engineering (announced in late
1997) had BMW's corporate ambitions writ
large on the agenda.

BMW established a specialist Le Mans
prototype racing unit, near Oxford, adjacent to
Williams F1 operation. The UK location was
potentially a sensitive domestic issue and to
offset German press hostility, the mechanical and
electronic heart and lungs of the project
remained in Munich where the 6-litre V12 racing
engine and transmission were designed and built.

The white, open-topped roadster had an
inauspicious debut at Le Mans in 1998, with
recurring wheel bearing problems leading to the
cars being withdrawn during the race.

Twelve months later, a likely 1-2 victory was
thwarted when flying Finn J J Lehto flew into the
barriers on the Sunday morning when dominating
the race. This allowed the slower of the two
works Schnitzer cars, driven by Frenchman

Yannick Dalmas, German Jo Winkelhock and
Italian Pierluigi Martini, to emerge victorious.

That win came arguably at the peak of recent
Le Mans factory involvement, both in terms of
quantity and quality, when there were works
Mercedes, Nissans, Toyotas and Audis doing battle.

In a race which consists of a series of sprints,
divided up by pit stops, BMW's relatively frugal
fuel economy, tyre and most importantly brake
pad wear paid dividends as fewer visits were paid
to the team of mechanics.

After scaling the F1 heights (returning to its
treacherous slopes in 2000), and earning a Le
Mans win, BMW was left to consider challenging
for the last major gold standard prize, the
Indianapolis 500.

BMW, by virtue of its Spartanburg factory in
South Carolina, is an American manufacturer
and winning at the hallowed circuit would
provide a valuable promotional tool, just as it did
for Mercedes.

The Indy 500 provides the jewel in the Indy
Racing League's slightly tarnished crown, in a US

domestic series where only oval speed bowls are used, and BMW decided to delay competing in the race.

Two years before winning Le Mans, and after internal corporate soul-searching on a epic scale, BMW entered a long-term partnership with Williams to return to F1.

Stalwart Rosche had been allowed to keep BMW's Grand Prix pulse running with an secret research and development team called E-90 which had built a stillborn V12, 3.5-litre F1 engine over 1993 and 1994.

This was the third time that Frank Williams had proposed an F1 link between BMW and his racing organisation and while Sir Frank remains fiercely protective of his company's independence, the team is officially badged BMW Williams, carrying Munich's corporate colours.

Rather than repeat the troublesome public proving of the BMW-powered Brabham nearly 20 years earlier, an exhaustive track testing programme ran through 1999 on board a Williams FW20. Despite concerns that the BMW V12 was bulky and heavy, its arrival and BMW's return to F1 was far more seamless than many Grand Prix debuts.

Ralf Schumacher and young Englishman Jensen Button collected 36 points between them, finishing the comeback season in fifth and eighth places respectively in the drivers' world rankings.

This equated to third in the constructors' league with Schumacher scoring an outstanding third place on the car's Australian Grand Prix debut, adding similar podium positions in Belgium and Italy.

By the end of the following year, the Anglo-German alliance closed the gap on McLaren Mercedes to retain third place in the constructors' table while Schumacher moved up to fourth driver, winning in San Marino, Canada and Germany.

Juan-Pablo Montoya played his fiery part in the growing influence of BMW Williams with a first Grand Prix triumph at Monza as he collected 31 points.

In 2002 Montoya powered into third in the drivers' series, eight points ahead of Schumacher to push the team ahead of McLaren-Mercedes at

the end of the year, but still light years behind Ferrari. Too often, less than perfect tactics got in the way while the cars' Michelin tyres lacked the consistency and early race effectiveness of Ferrari's Bridgestones.

BMW and Williams could and should have lifted the F1 constructors' trophy in 2003 but, instead, a roller-coaster, intercontinental 16-race sequence started and ended with dips. The 2004 car was ready in time for the opening race in Australia but BMW Motorsport director Mario Theissen conceded that "the team's kick-off is too weak". The FW25 Williams chassis took too long to balance, which was frustrating for the Munich management whose BMW P83 engine generated over 900 horsepower and was reliable, with only two retirements related to the power unit.

Although some candid concerns were expressed in public, particularly by motorsport manager Gerhard Berger, the problems did not degenerate into internecine warfare and solutions were found by analysis and hard work.

BMW and Williams confessed to the flaws which blunted their 2003 challenges but another set of circumstances, ostensibly beyond their control, arguably had an impact on them losing the drivers' and constructors' titles.

After Williams' one-two German Grand Prix dominance round Hockenheim, Bridgestone demanded a review of Williams' Michelin tyres, claiming they were applying more than the legal maximum 270mm tread with on to the road. The challenge was made at the behest of then struggling Ferrari.

Michelin's tyre construction was essentially no different from that used for three years but the review was distracting as BMW Williams and Ferrari regrouped for the final three races. There were also several spats between the drivers and the team, and there was constant tension between Ralf Schumacher and volatile Colombian, Juan-Pablo Montoya.

After a car to pits shouting match during the French Grand Prix, when Schumacher second-guessed him in terms of pit stop sequence, Montoya signed with McLaren-Mercedes, racing and corporate arch rivals. This resulted in the incongruous spectacle of McLaren announcing

Bottom:
Ralf Schumacher in the early BMW Williams FW23
Below:
BMW Williams star Juan-Pablo Montoya after winning the 2003 Monaco Grand Prix

before the end of 2003 that Montoya would be defecting in 2005.

It was a setback but BMW Williams, who sacrificed a four-point constructors' title lead entering the last two races, emerged with some pride intact.

Their cars completed 1,800 laps, ahead of Ferrari and McLaren, and were the only team to score two one-two finishes, at the European (Nurburgring) and French Grand Prix.

Formula 1 involvement was once likened to that of a small space programme in terms of the scale of budget, the high level of technology personnel skills, plus constant pressure to drive the programme forward.

The BMW Williams' UK headquarters employs 475 staff who are electronically linked to the 220 located at the Munich Euro industry engine development and production unit. F1 requires a large team to support the drivers: during the 2003 season, the BMW Williams F1 team numbered 100 each race weekend. A separate test team, averaging 60 personnel, covered 54,604 kilometres (33,930 miles) development running on nine European tracks

over 107 days involving six drivers.

In 2003 some 200,000 chassis components were produced for the FW25, and more than 200 engines supplied by Munich for the 16 races, with 10 power units used each Grand Prix weekend. This scale of resources and cost was reduced in 2004 with more restricted testing and only one engine per car allowed at each Grand Prix.

BMW's holistic approach to motorsport extends to driver development, channelled largely through the Formula BMW junior single seater championships, which in Germany permits drivers from the age of 15.

One of them is Nico Rosberg, son of former Williams world champion Keke, who has been through F1 team testing.

Also gaining a testing ride in a 900 horsepower Williams-BMW was "Nelshino" Piquet, F3 racing son of Nelson, the first and only BMW-powered F1 world champion. They were joined by Asia Pacific Formula BMW champion Ho-Pin Tung, the first Chinese driver to drive an F1 car and a shrewd marketing move in a rapidly expanding car market as Shanghai prepared to host a Grand Prix in September 2004.

05

The global
grand plan

Little car, big hit

After a troubled gestation period, BMW's born-again MINI is an astonishing success

MINI (R50-R53)

→ Launched in 2001
→ First premium supermini
→ BMW group's first front-drive car
→ 1.6 litre engines
→ Supercharged MINI Cooper S
→ Convertibles launched 2004
→ Diesel engine from Toyota
→ Far exceeded sales expectations
→ Unexpected hit in US
→ Built in Oxford, UK

The BMW group MINI, like its 1959 mentor from Austin-Morris, is not so much a car as a social phenomenon. But for all the astonishing sales glory that it is now basking in – a success which took even BMW's meticulously thorough planners by surprise – it was not always an easy project for BMW to handle: it went through seven designers and four changes of programme director, and at times its very existence was threatened.

By mid 2004, the Oxford factory was working round the clock to build enough MINIs to satisfy demand from worldwide markets – literally Australia to Alaska, Tokyo to Trieste. Designed for a capacity of 100,000 cars a year, the plant is running at nearly double that – and still the customers can't get enough. Dealers are having to put eager buyers on waiting lists with six or eight months' worth of names already on them, something unheard of in the small-car sector.

Many factors have helped the MINI become the phenomenon it now is. Mini has always been a very emotive word in the automotive lexicon: for most people it is associated with the excitement and independence of their first car, the fun of great handling, the anti-establishment buzz of driving something small and cheeky; for others it taps into rallying and the thrills of the racetrack.

BMW's acute awareness of the power of the Mini name was one of the main reasons it bought Rover in 1994.

Ultimately, however, it was the strength of BMW, both in the trust that it enjoys and in the engineering resources it can muster, that enabled the born-again MINI to take off like it did. The MINI's funky design immediately appealed to younger buyers; its eager, go-kart like handling straightaway sold it to sporty drivers, the supercharged Cooper S attracted the attention of the serious hard-driving enthusiast and, more recently, the Convertible has drawn in the open-air set. And, last but not least, the reassurance of the BMW brand behind the whole venture has encouraged a lot of older people, who would normally walk away from such a dramatic design, to sign up for one: the MINI may be spontaneous

Performance profile: the MINI Cooper S, MINI One and MINI Cooper have all dramatically exceeded BMW's sales expectations

"The thoroughness of the engineering was something new for the small-car segment. There had never been a premium supermini before, so the MINI's use of an intricate multi-link rear axle causes much interest. At a time when most volume car makers were struggling to take cost and content out of their small cars, BMW appeared to be busy putting it in"

and fun, but it is a serious quality product from a quality organisation.

The tremendous diversity of the MINI's clientele is the result of a well-judged product, clever marketing and the enormous reservoir of popular goodwill towards the Mini idea. But it wasn't always so: in fact, the development programme was riven with dissent and division at many stages in its five-year history – and the fact that the history lasted five years rather than the more usual three speaks for itself.

Ideas on how to replace the original Mini had always been kicked around within the many successive incarnations of the company that was once BMC, but there was never the courage, let alone the budget, to face up to the need to replace the corporate icon. But with the takeover by BMW – whose then chairman, Bernd Pischetsrieder, is the nephew of Sir Alec Issigonis, brains behind the original Mini – interest quickened and a project team was formed three months after BMW had become

owners. Many different design teams submitted proposals, including independents, and BMW's own Designworks studio in California. Some were truly radical – one, intended to reflect the revolutionary nature of the 1959 car, even had an underfloor engine. Others were more cautious, more retro. Eventually, a compromise between several proposals was chosen and attributed to Frank Stevenson, the American who is now chief designer at Ferrari; two Englishmen penned the complex and unconventional interior.

The engineering story became increasingly fractious as control of the programme swung back and forth between England and Germany as responsibilities were shifted and programme managers replaced. The car that emerged was perhaps less technically ground-breaking than some of the engineers had hoped, but to anyone outside the programme it seemed extraordinarily sophisticated for such a small car.

The thoroughness of the engineering was something new for the small car segment. There

Following the private showing of the MINI concept to journalists at the Frankfurt IAA in 1999, BMW supplied these first official photographs

had never been a premium supermini before, so the MINI's use of an intricate multi-link rear axle caused much interest, as did its comprehensive safety package taking in six airbags, ABS brakes, cornering brake control and tyre pressure monitoring. At a time when most volume carmakers were struggling to take cost and content out of their small cars, BMW appeared to be busy putting it in. Other examples were the radical dashboard, one of the most complex sub-assemblies ever put into a small car, and the frameless doors which, just like BMW's own coupés, have electric windows which drop down a fraction to allow the glass to clear the seal. The bonnet, too, was a very complex creation: the whole front of the car hinges up in a single piece to give excellent engine access, but positioning has to be sub-millimetre accurate to blend in smoothly with the rest of the body.

The overriding impression was one of solidity and integrity, both in design and construction: the materials and the workmanship were of an altogether higher order than had ever been seen in a car of this size.

Two versions were offered when the MINI went on sale in July 2001: the MINI One, with a 90 bhp version of the 1.6-litre engine supplied by the BMW-Chrysler Tritec joint venture in Brazil, and the MINI Cooper, with 115 bhp. Yet as soon as the prices were announced the analysts began reaching for their calculators and spreadsheets: with a starting figure of just over £10,000 – in 2001, equivalent to €16,500 – many experts wondered whether BMW could possibly be making any money on the MINI. The puzzle was all the greater given the fact that because of the MINI's famous second colour on its roof the cars had to go through the paint shop twice – this was just one of the factors with threatened to limit the factory's output to not

much more than 100,000 cars a year. This, reasoned some commentators, would prevent BMW getting the economies of scale enjoyed by other carmakers with production volumes of half a million or more the business model for the MINI looked questionable indeed.

But what those analysts had not reckoned with was the sheer enthusiasm that swamped the MINI dealer network when it opened for business on launch day. Customers were so taken with the multitude of option packages offered with the cars that they spent as heavily on extras as they did on the car itself. Alloy wheels, roof decals, flags, stripes, mirrors, grilles, instruments, lights, stereos – all were available in such a wide variety of shapes, sizes and colours that customers were able to personalise an already intensely personal car in a way that

MINI One is the entry point to the BMW group ranges and accounts for one fifth of MINI sales

simply was not possible with any other small car.

It helped a lot, too, that MINIs were not sold off the showroom floor from stock – there has never been any stock. Instead, customers became much more involved in the process of choosing the exact features they wanted, the precise specification of every tiny detail. In this, MINI echoed the practice of the BMW mother brand, where every car is built to order – and, inevitably, the customer ends up spending more. The typical MINI customer – if such a person can possibly exist among such a broad spectrum of people – could spend €15,000 on a MINI One and a further €3,000 on extras.

This figure is far higher than the industry average and, as any auto sector economist knows, manufacturers make far better margins on extras and accessories than on the car itself. Pricier versions, even the MINI Cooper with its premium of just €1,500 over the basic model – earn good returns, too. Soon it became clear that, to excited reviews from the automotive and style press, the MINI Cooper was taking almost two thirds of all sales: even more remarkable was the sudden impact of the MINI derivative most eagerly awaited of all – the Cooper S.

The MINI Cooper S benefited from the addition of a supercharger to its engine – still the 1.6 litre Tritec unit – boosting power to 163 bhp, later to rise to 170; this, along with a six-speed gearbox, stiffer suspension and even bigger tyres, turned it into such a serious performance machine that even Porsche drivers were tempted to make the swap. The S won unanimous praise in the press, and soon another profitable line was opened up with the inclusion of John Cooper 'Works' tuning packages in the options list. This meant a further improvement in MINI's revenue earned per car. Together, the Cooper and Cooper S accounted for 75 per cent of MINI sales in 2003, the remainder going to the MINI One in its petrol and – courtesy of Toyota as engine supplier – diesel forms.

In 2004 MINI again hit the headlines, this time with its Convertible, A full four-seater with an electric hood, the open MINI retails at some €3,500 above the fixed-head car's price: again, it has won praise as a properly engineered quality vehicle in an area of the market where

New MINI Cooper S leads classic Mini in the mountains above Monte Carlo

"The supercharged MINI Cooper S had a six-speed gearbox, stiffer suspension and even bigger tyres, turning it into a serious performance machine that even Porsche drivers were tempted by"

R50 MINI

Specifications	One	Mini One D	Mini Cooper	Mini Cooper S

Engine				
Engine type	Inline 4-cylinder	Inline 4 cylinder direct injection turbo diesel	Inline 4-cylinder	Inline 4-cylinder, supercharged
Bore & stroke, mm	77 x 85.8	73 x 81.5	77 x 85.8	77 x 85.8
Capacity, cc	1598	1364	1598	1598
Valves	16	16	16	16
Valve actuation	Sohc	Sohc	Sohc	Sohc
Compression ratio	10.6:1	18:1	10.6:1	8.3:1
Fuelling	Siemens EMS2000 electronic fuel injection	Bosch EDC15 common rail diesel injection	Siemens EMS2000 electronic fuel injection	Siemens EMS2000 electronic fuel injection; Roots-type supercharger, intercooler
Max power, bhp @ rpm	90@5500	75@4000	115@6000	163@6000; (7/04:170@6000)
Max torque, Nm @ rpm	140@3000	180@2000	150@4500	210@4000 (7/04:220@4000)
Transmission				
Manual transmission	5-speed	6-speed	5-speed	6-speed
Automatic	CVT Steptronic	Not available	CVT Steptronic	Not available
Drive	Front wheels; ASC+T traction control optional, CBC	Front wheels; ASC+T traction control, CBC	Front wheels; ASC+T traction control optional, CBC	Front wheels; ASC+T traction control, CBC
Chassis				
Front suspension	Single-joint MacPherson strut	Single-joint MacPherson strut	Single-joint MacPherson strut	Single-joint MacPherson strut
Rear suspension	Z-axle with longitudinal arms, centrally pivoted track control arms, coil springs	Z-axle with longitudinal arms, centrally pivoted track control arms, coil springs	Z-axle with longitudinal arms, centrally pivoted track control arms, coil springs	Z-axle with longitudinal arms, centrally pivoted track control arms, coil springs
Braking	Discs, servo assisted, ABS	Discs, servo assisted, ABS	Discs, servo assisted, ABS	Discs, servo assisted, ABS
Steering	Rack and pinion, electro-hydraulic power assistance	Rack and pinion, electro-hydraulic power assistance	Rack and pinion, electro-hydraulic power assistance	Rack and pinion, electro-hydraulic power assistance
Wheels	5.5 x 15	5.5 x 15	5.5 x 15	6.5 x 16
Tyres	175/65 R 15	175/65 R 15	175/65 R 15	195/55 R 16
Body				
Structure	Steel monocoque	Steel monocoque	Steel monocoque	Steel monocoque
Wheelbase, mm	2467	2467	2467	2467
Track F/R, mm	1458/1466	1458/1466	1458/1466	1458/1466
Length, mm	3626	3626	3626	3626
Width, mm	1688	1688	1688	1688
Height, mm	1416	1416	1416	1416
Kerb weight, kg	1040 (Cabrio 1240)	1175	1050 (Cabrio 1250)	1140 (Cabrio 1315)
Fuel tank capacity, lit	50	50	50	50
Performance				
Max speed, km/h	181 (Cabrio 175)	166	200 (Cabrio 193)	218; 7/04 on: 222 (Cabrio 215)
0-100km/h, sec	10.9 (Cabrio 11.8)	13.8	9.1 (Cabrio 9.8)	7.4; 7/04 on: 7.2 (Cabrio 7.4)
Fuel consumption , lit/100km	6.8 (Cabrio 7.2)	4.8	6.9 (Cabrio 7.3)	8.4; 7/04 on: 8.6 (Cabrio 8.8)
Marketing				
Launch date	7/2001 (Cabrio 6/2004)	5/2003	7/2001 (Cabrio 6/2004)	5/2002 (Cabrio 9/2004)
Pricing, euro	14,700 (Cabrio 18,300)	16,200	16,600 (Cabrio 20,000)	20,400 (Cabrio 24,000)

convertibles tend to be either expensive or poorly put together.

Central to MINI's success have been innovative and frequently award winning advertising campaigns in its many markets, coupled with inventive websites and imaginative promotions such as the MINI circus at the 2004 British International Motor Show.

But despite all the fun and the apparent frivolity the MINI remains a very serious car, not just in its engineering – as BMW's first front wheel drive design – but also in its market intent. For all its troubled beginnings it emerged a remarkably trouble-free final product and one which was astutely judged to hit the consumers' sentimental sweet spot and bring in the young and enthusiastic customers for whom a BMW was too expensive, too big or too redolent of business. Its success has been studied intently by the rest of the auto industry, but as yet no one else has come up with a concept that's quite as much fun or which exerts such a strong emotional pull.

MINI Convertible is a full four-seater with an electric roof: this example is a Cooper S with the optional Chrono instrument pack

MINI 'Works' tuning packages offer still more performance, even for Cooper S

BMW turned to Toyota for a state of the art turbo diesel engine for the MINI

Proof of concept

BMW show-cars preview new styles or future technologies to prepare public opinion

BMW's relationship with concept cars has always been on-off – and generally more off than on. In a company which prided itself on getting with the job of building high-quality road cars for customers to buy, drive and enjoy, it was rarely a priority to waste valuable resources on styling exercises which gave no more than a few moments of corporate glory at a motor show before being wheeled into the company museum or, worse, the crusher.

The early exception was the 1972 BMW Turbo, built specially to make the most of the world's attention being on Munich for the Olympic Games. That car was not only inspiring and uplifting for BMW's own morale, but it proved profoundly influential in determining future BMW designs as well as those of other manufacturers. More recently, the show cars have been coming thick and fast, not just to display engine solutions – like the E1 electric of 1991 – but also to bring new ways of thinking, new vocabularies of design, into the public domain.

That, many would argue, is precisely what a concept car should do: stimulate debate, throw new ideas into the ring to test public and professional reaction, and put down a marker for where the company intends to be in the future. So when, three decades later, BMW unveiled the smart open-topped shape of the small CS1 at the 2002 Geneva show, it was a clear signal staking out the territory to be annexed by the

upcoming BMW 1 Series range two years later.

The same can happen with engineering concepts as well as design ideas: the 1999 Z9 gran turismo, for instance, previewed the V8 diesel engine that was to make such an impact in the luxury class in the following years. And take the Z14 of 1999, exploring the concept of a light motorcycle with the safety and weather protection of a car: the public reaction was positive, and it became the C1 commuter bike.

But not every concept is there for style or substance: indeed, some volunteer the difficult task of displaying electronic and materials developments, systems for which direct in-vehicle experience is the only truly informative introduction. Almost all of the vehicles on these pages owe their origin to one of BMW's greatest inventions: Technik GmbH, a self-contained cross between a think tank and a skunk works (secret location where a car manufacturer develops design ideas), which was deliberately located at arm's length from BMW's administrative and engineering centres. Technik GmbH comes up with the wildest of ideas in order to try out its new techniques: the Z1 sports car, for instance, began life as a test-bed for new and advanced plastics materials. And the iDrive centralised control system arose out of a programme to study the human-machine interface.

Mercifully, not every concept ends up on the production line. Many, such as the Z22 and Z18, have sacrificed beauty in the name of function or experimentation. But each somehow leaves its trace on future mainstream products. The ideas may seem unconventional or uncomfortable at the time they are first shown, but new concepts need careful introduction into the consciousness of car buyers if they are to have a smooth ride into the everyday arena. Almost every feature on a modern BMW can be traced back to a concept car of some description – proof indeed that the system works.

BMW Turbo, 1972
Styled by BMW design director Paul Bracq and built to gain maximum exposure at the 1972 Olympic Games in Munich, the BMW Turbo was part design exercise, part rolling testbed for innovative technologies, and part the corporate boast of a newly-confident company seeking to make its mark on the establishment

The low, flat and wide theme of Bracq's mid-engined coupé layout set the tone for many future BMWs – the 850i and Z1 are immediate examples that spring to mind – and was the direct template around which the M1 was conceived. Its mid-mounted 200 bhp turbo engine soon found its way into the front of the 2002, and its space-age cockpit and gullwing doors found imitators for years afterwards

BMW Z18

Looking for all the world like an amputated army Jeep, the Z18 was based on the running gear of the then-new X5 sport utility and was intended to explore the concept of an enduro (desert racer). Despite a 4.4 litre V8 engine it found little sympathy in any quarter and, to no one's regret, proved to be a dead end

BMW Z11, 1991

The early 1990s was a time when fuel shortages and tightening emissions regulations forced builders of predominantly luxury cars, such as BMW, to reassess their priorities and invest serious sums in research into alternative forms of propulsion. And with California threatening to make zero emissions vehicles a part of every carmaker's catalogue, electric power was a top priority. The E1, part of the Z11 urban car programme, was battery powered; the later and larger E2, shown in the USA, made use of a BMW motorcycle engine. Later still, the more stylish Z13 picked up where the E2 left off

BMW Z14

Worried for many years that commuters were being put off motorcycles by the prospect of getting cold, wet or, worse still, injured in an accident, BMW proposed the Z14 – a light motorcycle with a roof, seat belts and a place to stow your briefcase. It even had a windscreen wiper and a mobile phone socket. Positive comments encouraged BMW to build it for real as the C1 (above) but it failed to catch on with its target market. To blame were its top-heavy feel and the fact that many countries obliged riders to wear helmets when BMW insisted it was as safe as a small car even for the unhelmeted user

BMW Z22

A classic instance of brains rather than beauty, the Z22 of the late 1990s was stuffed full of computers to handle everything from starting and stopping to steering and navigation, gearchanging and parking. It was built – out of exotic carbon fibre and high-ticket alloys, of course – to test out what BMW calls Mechatronics, the art of getting electronics to command mechanical systems. Drive-by-wire is the vogue word for its steering and braking, both of which involve no direct mechanical connection between the controls and the components they are controlling

BMW Z07

Star of the 1999 Tokyo motor show, the Z09 was the very direct precursor of the Z8 luxury sports car. An unashamedly nostalgic tribute to the 1950s 507 roadster, which for many is the all-time icon of the BMW brand, the Z07 came at a time when retro was just beginning to go back out of fashion, Nevertheless, the production Z8 which followed was an accomplished design full of exquisite details, nostalgic or not

BMW Z9

This, as far as anyone at modern-day BMW is concerned, is the big one. Unwrapped at the 1999 Frankfurt show, it was the manifesto, no less, for the new age of automotive design being ushered in by new design director Chris Bangle. Here was a complete suite of fresh and challenging ideas which were baffling when first shown but which now make more sense in the context of actual cars on real roads

Clearly evident in the long and low shape of the Z9 is the template for the 645 Ci Coupé, especially in the shaping around the nose, the exaggerated bustle at the back and, to a lesser extent, in the complex surfacing of the car's flanks, described by Bangle as flame surfacing. Under the long bonnet sat the world's first eight-cylinder diesel engine, while pressing a button to raise the gullwing door revealed not just sumptuous seating for four but also a serious bid to break the mould of interior design – especially as far as control operation was concerned. The Z9 had a

dashboard of exaggerated simplicity – just a starter button and the light switch interrupted its broad surface. Everything was handled by what Bangle called the Intuitive Interaction Concept, a menu-based switching system which led to a simplified version in the subsequent open-topped version of the Z9 (above) shown a year later in Paris. Bangle's intention had been to simplify the 50-odd switches found in a top-of-the-line luxury car, but the eventual production system, premiered in the 2001 7 Series as iDrive, turned out to be anything but intuitive

> "The 1999 Z9 was the manifesto for the new age of automotive design being ushered in by new design director Chris Bangle. Here was a complete suite of fresh and challenging ideas"

BMW X Coupé *(above)*
Presented at the 2001 Detroit auto show, the X Coupé caused more controversy than all BMW's previous concepts combined – some achievement considering the stir still surrounding 1999's Z9 gran turismo. If Chris Bangle's intention was to shock, then the X Coupé could not have succeeded better. The Z9 in its coupé and convertible forms was by comparison easy to understand: it was clearly an elegant grand tourer, even if many of the details seemed out of place or incomprehensible. But the X Coupé was something else: it was hard to understand what type of vehicle it was trying to be, let alone try to grasp the subtleties – if indeed there were any – of its design language.

The most striking aspect of the design was its scale: it had some of the proportions of a smaller coupé – in its cabin shape, for example --

but was grossly inflated in every other dimension. The wheels were huge, the body sides a weird amalgam of curves and planes intersecting one another at seemingly random angles and positions.

As if that was not enough, the whole car was asymmetric, too. The huge one-piece rear cover hinged backwards, the skewed rear window extending much further forward on the right hand side so that its forward edge met the trailing edge of the passenger door. On the left there was a conventional B-pillar and driver's door, and the left wheelarch remained in position when the rear cover was opened. Onlookers struggled to understand it at the time, Bangle insisting that people's shock and incomprehension showed how fixed their ideas had become. One day, perhaps, we will understand what it was all about

"The X Coupé caused more controversy than all BMW's previous concepts combined"

BMW xActivity *(below)*
Arriving exactly two years after the X Coupé, the xActivity concept came as something of a relief. It was clearly identifiable as an ambassador for the forthcoming smaller off-roader from BMW, now of course in production as the X3. The SUV (BMW would insist it was an SAV, or sports activity, not utility, vehicle) proportions were clearly there, even if Bangle's flowery language spoke of 'frame structure convertibles' and the synthesising of the excitement of an open car and the ruggedness of an SAV.

The most noticeable feature of the xActivity is its roof construction, where long single rails run from the screen to the base of the tailgate area. There are no B- or C-pillars, and on the concept the roof is left completely open apart from a crossmember in line with the rear doors. Conveniently, little was said about covering the vast roof aperture in cold or wet weather. The xActivity was notable, too, for flagging up some of the distorted, angular style elements later featured on the production X3, and for its unusual colour scheme. This was described by BMW as bronze moss, which changed between bronze, green and blue-grey, depending on the light, ostensibly reflecting the xActivity's versatility

BMW CS1

Described by BMW as offering "a first glimpse of the design philosophy which might characterise the exterior of a 'small' BMW in future", the neat and attractive CS1 convertible proved to be a very accurate foretaste of the eventual 1 Series of 2004. Unlike previous BMW design studies, it struck an immediate chord with onlookers: instead of puzzled head-scratching the immediate reaction was that this was a real car that one could relate to, get into and drive off. Coming just two years before the launch of the volume small car line, its job was not to make bold philosophical statements or change the course of design thought: its task was the much easier one of promoting a forthcoming product rather than making an intellectual or aesthetic point.

The study is subtle in how it marries the classical proportions of a four-seater convertible with the familiar feeling of BMW design cues such as the double-kidney grilles, yet it takes each of these elements a careful step forward. Inside, where there is human contact with the vehicle, the design is deliberately delicate and light; where the car has to communicate with the road the form is much firmer and more powerful, symbolised by wide-set wheels, subtly flared arches and owl-eye headlight looking powerfully at the road ahead.

Establishment challenges

Chris Bangle launches the era of confrontational design with the fourth-generation 7 Series

In decades to come, the fourth generation of BMW's 7 Series may come to be seen as the design which changed our thinking about the way large luxury cars should look, the way they should be controlled, and the way they drive.

Such was the shock value of the new style and the new technology, however, that immediately following the car's summer 2001 launch it was difficult to focus on precisely what the new 7 had achieved and how this might eventually affect all the cars we drive. Only one thing could be said for certain: this car had an excellent chassis and driveline and had made notable advances in refinement, ride comfort and handling.

The fact that not everyone realised this was significant, too. Those who first tried the car were so mesmerised by the onslaught of new technologies and different ways of controlling once-familiar systems that they felt alienated and out of their depth, despite many years of experience with all manner of new vehicles. Even seasoned auto journalists on the press launch were treated to individual in-car briefings by specially trained personnel whose task it was to explain the myriad functions needed to operate the car. The briefings lasted a good 10 minutes, and even then the drivers were not really sure of all the procedures. It was a classic case of

techno-fear gripping and paralysing the mind – like an elderly person unfamiliar with information technology being given a computer and asked to send an email for the first time.

There was no ignition switch, handbrake or gearlever; the seat switches had a dozen small buttons and so many different modes that it was hard even to get comfortable behind the electrically adjusted wheel. But what symbolised the whole problem most graphically was the iDrive controller, a large shiny metal knob mounted on the centre console between the front seats. This appeared to have more to do with working a computer program than the

The bold, imposing design direction taken by the new 7 Series came as a big shock after the low-key style of the outgoing model. This is the 745i, much the biggest selling of the five engine choices

E65: 7 SERIES

Specifications	730i	735i	745i	760i	730d
Engine					
Engine type	Inline 6-cylinder	90-degree V8	90-degree V8	60-degree V12 direct injection	Inline 6-cylinder direct injection turbo diesel
Bore & stroke, mm	84 x 89.6	84 x 81.2	92 x 82.7	89 x 80	84 x 90
Capacity, cc	2979	3600	4398	5972	2993
Valves	24	32	32	48	24
Valve actuation	Dohc, double Vanos variable valve timing	Dohc, double Vanos variable valve timing, Valvetronic variable valve lift	Dohc, double Vanos variable valve timing, Valvetronic variable valve lift	Dohc, double Vanos variable valve timing, Valvetronic variable valve lift	Dohc
Compression ratio	10.2:1	10.5:1	10.5:1	11.3:1	17:1
Fuelling	Siemens MS45 electronic fuel injection	ME9 Electronic fuel injection	ME9 Electronic fuel injection	ME9 Electronic fuel injection	Bosch DDE 5 common rail diesel direct injection; variable geometry turbocharger, intercooler
Max power, bhp @ rpm	231@5900	272@6200	333@6100	445@6o00	218@4000
Max torque, Nm @ rpm	300@3500	360@3700	450@3600	600@3950	500@2000
Transmission					
Manual transmission	Not available	Not available	Not available	Not available	Not available
Automatic	ZF 6-speed 6HP26 Steptronic	ZF 6-speed 6HP26 Steptronic	ZF 6-speed 6HP26 Steptronic	ZF 6-speed 6HP26 Steptronic	ZF 6-speed 6HP26 Steptronic
Drive	Rear wheels; ASC	Rear wheels; ASC	Rear wheels; ASC	Rear wheels; ASC	Rear wheels; ASC
Chassis					
Front suspension	Double-pivot MacPherson strut, lower wishbones	Double-pivot MacPherson strut, lower wishbones	Double-pivot MacPherson strut, lower wishbones	Double-pivot MacPherson strut, lower wishbones	Double-pivot MacPherson strut, lower wishbones
Rear suspension	Integral IV multi-link axle with twin transverse links, trailing arms ands tie bars, coil springs; Dynamic Drive active anti-roll bars	Integral IV multi-link axle with twin transverse links, trailing arms ands tie bars, coil springs; Dynamic Drive active anti-roll bars	Integral IV multi-link axle with twin transverse links, trailing arms ands tie bars, coil springs; Dynamic Drive active anti-roll bars	Integral IV multi-link axle with twin transverse links, trailing arms ands tie bars, coil springs; Dynamic Drive active anti-roll bars	Integral IV multi-link axle with twin transverse links, trailing arms ands tie bars, coil springs; Dynamic Drive active anti-roll bars
Braking	Disc, servo assisted; ABS, Cornering Brake Control	Disc, servo assisted; ABS, Cornering Brake Control	Disc, servo assisted; ABS, Cornering Brake Control	Disc, servo assisted; ABS, Cornering Brake Control	Disc, servo assisted; ABS, Cornering Brake Control
Steering	Rack and pinion Servotronic, power assisted	Rack and pinion Servotronic, power assisted	Rack and pinion Servotronic, power assisted	Rack and pinion Servotronic, power assisted	Rack and pinion Servotronic, power assisted
Wheels	8.0 x 17	8.0 x 17	8.0 x 17	8.0 x 18	8.0 x 17
Tyres	245/55 R17	245/55 R17	245/55 R17	245/50 R18	245/55 R17
Body					
Structure	Steel monocoque, aluminium subframes and suspension	Steel monocoque, aluminium subframes and suspension	Steel monocoque, aluminium subframes and suspension	Steel monocoque, aluminium subframes and suspension	Steel monocoque, aluminium subframes and suspension
Wheelbase, mm	2990 (L: 3130)	2990 (L: 3130)	2990 (L: 3130)	2990 (L: 3130)§	2990 (L: 3130)
Track F/R, mm	1586/1590	1586/1590	1586/1590	1586/1590	1586/1590
Length, mm	5029 (L: 5269)	5029 (L: 5269)	5029 (L: 5269)	5029 (L: 5269)	5029 (L: 5269)
Width, mm	1902	1902	1902	1902	1902
Height, mm	1492	1492	1492	1492	1492
Kerb weight, kg	1935	1935	1945	2090	1935
Fuel tank capacity, lit	88	88	88	88	88
Performance					
Max speed, km/h	237	250	250	250	227
0-100km/h, sec	8.1	7.6	6.3	5.5	8.8
Fuel consumption , lit/100km	106	10.7	10.9	13.4	8.5
Marketing					
Launch date	9/2002	9/2001	9/2001	9/2002	9/2002
Pricing, €	61,500	64,000	71,000	111,900	59,500

740d

90-degree V8 direct injection
turbo diesel
84 x 81.2
3600
32
Dohc

18:1
Bosch DDE5 common rail
diesel direct injection; twin
variable geometry
turbochargers, intercooler
258@4000
600@1900

Not available
ZF 6-speed 6HP26
Steptronic
Rear wheels; ASC

Double-pivot MacPherson
strut, lower wishbones
Integral IV multi-link axle with
twin transverse links, trailing
arms ands tie bars, coil
springs; Dynamic Drive active
anti-roll bars
Disc, servo assisted; ABS,
Cornering Brake Control
Rack and pinion Servotronic,
power assisted
8.0 x 17
245/55 R17

Steel monocoque, aluminium
subframes and suspension
2990 (L: 3130)
1586/1590
5029 (L: 5269)
1902
1492
1935
88

250
7.4
9.7

9/2002
77,200

Unmistakable: Chris Bangle's design for the 7 Series is unlike anything else on the road. Rear-end bustle has caused particular controversy

"The iDrive controller, a large shiny metal knob mounted on the centre console between the front seats, appeared to have more to do with working a computer program than the familiar act of driving a car"

familiar mechanical act of driving a car: by moving the knob in one of its eight directions the user could access a whole menu of on-screen options relating to a particular aspect of the car such as navigation, air conditioning, suspension or in-car entertainment. None of these options was essential to starting or driving the car, but the general reaction was one of panic and BMW's repeated claims that this was a quantum leap for control ergonomics were dismissed as laughable.

There was in any case already a raging controversy over the Bangle-inspired looks of the new car. Few had a good word to say: instead, the style had been tactfully described as 'striking', 'imposing' or 'full of presence'. And presence it certainly had: in the metal the new car looked larger and more imposing still, with deep, weighty

sides, a high, block-like tail and severe-looking brows over its wide headlights. It felt large, too, but once under way and out of congested conditions it underwent a transformation. The big limousine not only rode with remarkable smoothness but it also handled twisty roads with even more remarkable composure – excellent body control and very little roll on bends – in a way that big luxury cars had never done before.

BMW's twin secrets were continuous electronic control of the dampers, simpler versions of which had been seen before on several other luxury cars, and a key innovation – Dynamic Drive. This did something chassis engineers had been wanting to do for years: to be able to control the stiffness of the anti-roll bars in real time, from instant to instant. BMW

The 760i features the world's first direct-injection V12 engine for supreme refinement; this is the L version with 140 mm extra wheelbase for still greater rear seat comfort

"The big limousine not only rode with remarkable smoothness but it also handled twisty roads with even more remarkable composure – in a way that big luxury cars had never done before"

reasoned that if it could in effect disconnect the anti-roll bar whenever it was not needed it would no longer have to strike such a compromise between ride comfort and body control. The switch to rack and pinion steering made a big difference to accuracy and feel at the wheel rim, too.

The initial powertrains were of a similarly high order. Valvetronic technology had now been applied to the large V8s, giving not only continuous adjustment of cam phasing but of valve lift too, doing away with the throttle butterfly valve and eliminating pumping losses from the engine – another long-held dream of thermodynamics engineers. The improvement in efficiency was clear to see: the 745i engine, with a full 333 bhp, barely consumed any more fuel than the non-Valvetronic 3.5 litre in the old 272 bhp 735i. Both engines fed their power through another world first – the six-speed automatic from ZF. The result was uncanny smoothness from both engine and transmission but also quick and decisive power whenever it was needed.

Nevertheless, despite its excellent dynamic performance the 7 Series was constantly criticised in the press for the complexity of its on-board systems – not just electronic systems such as navigation and internet access, which people expect to be complicated – but also essentials such as adjusting the seats, setting the parking brake and programming the several extra customisable buttons on the steering wheel. There was even talk at an early stage that BMW had got cold feet about the whole iDrive system

and was preparing to launch a parallel version with conventional control systems. That never happened, but Helmut Panke, by now CEO of the group following Professor Milberg's early stepping down in 2002, went on record in 2004 as admitting that the company did not do enough to explain these complex new systems and got a bad press as a result.

Further engine derivatives followed the initial 735i and 745i, and within the space of a year the six-cylinder 730i and 730d and the V8-engined 740d had arrived: each used substantially the same engine as in the previous series, updated to the latest specifications and emissions norms and integrated with the new six-speed transmission. The big step ahead came with what until the return of Rolls-Royce in 2003 would be the flagship of the whole BMW group, the V12-engined 760i.

The 760i broke new engineering ground: its six-litre V12 engine was the first in the world to feature direct injection which, in combination with BMW's complete suite of double VANOS and Valvetronic technologies, helped it to outputs of 445 bhp at 6000 rpm and no less than 600 Nm torque at 3950 rpm, with 500 Nm available all the way from 1500 rpm. Thanks to that substantial torque BMW was able to specify very tall overall gearing: at 160 km/h the V12 was turning over at just 2500 rpm. This in turn helped it to an overall consumption figure of 13.4 lit/100 km – an impressive result for a large two-tonne car capable of reaching 100 km/h from rest in 5.5 seconds and 200 km/h in 17.

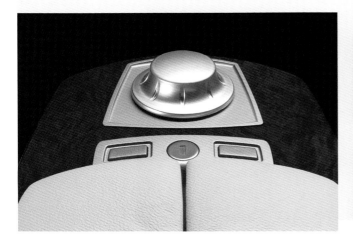

The 7 Series' iDrive controller looks after a multitude of functions, moving in eight directions, while options are highlighted on display screen (left), showing navigation system. Early users found the system intimidating

"to the student of consumer behaviour and business strategy this 7 Series may come to represent the point where the engineers got the upper hand and imposed complexity-no-object solutions with little regard for the end user"

The V12 models are identified externally, as has become the BMW tradition, by wider kidney grilles at the front: on the 760i there are also chrome strips in the bumpers and chrome trim running the length of the roof, and 18-inch star-spoke light alloy wheels.

In spring 2003 a sports chassis pack was made available on six- and eight-cylinder models: this upgraded the wheels to huge 19-inch V-spoke items, with 245/45 R19 tyres on 9J rims at the front and 275/40 R19s on 10J rims at the rear. Ride height was reduced by 20 mm at the front and 10 mm at the rear, spring, damper and anti-roll bar settings were modified and a sports steering wheel fitted.

An important future development instigated by the 7 Series is that of hydrogen power. Previous generations of 7 Series have been used by BMW to develop internal combustion engines running on this zero-CO_2 dream fuel – a fleet of fifteen 750h prototypes was built for the company's Clean Energy World Tour, which began in Berlin in 2000. The new 760 takes that process a step further: the V12 is a dual-fuel unit running on either petrol or hydrogen, and BMW has stated that it will become part of the commercially-available range during the lifecycle of this model.

When they come to look back on the era which this Bangle-inspired 7 Series opened up, corporate historians are likely to arrive at very different conclusions to those of the more technical chroniclers of engineering developments. To an engineer this 7 Series was like birthday and Christmas rolled into one: it launched so many exciting and original ideas, and its software-based control systems opened up seemingly limitless possibilities for computer-style upgrades and enhancements. Here, they exclaimed, was the flexible, fully configurable future of the motor car.

But to the student of consumer behaviour and business strategy the E65 may come to represent the point where the engineers got the upper hand and imposed complexity-no-object solutions with little regard for the end user. This, allied with the model's insensitively grandiose styling, brings uncomfortable parallels with Mercedes-Benz's gargantuan W140 S-Class of 1991. The vast, slab-sided limousine, more battleship than flagship, had been developed at huge cost by engineers given carte blanche to implement the best possible solutions: when the design was roundly rejected by consumers, handing 7 Series sales to BMW on a silver platter, Daimler-Benz shocked itself, Germany and the world by plunging into loss and was forced to completely rethink the way it ran its business and developed its cars.

While the 7 Series never threatened to be such a sales disaster, it has become one of the rare BMWs where dealers have felt the need to offer rebates or reductions. The message was not lost on BMW managers: subsequent models have backtracked noticeably on non user-friendly control systems.

State of the art direct-injection diesel V8 (left) is linked to six-speed automatic transmission – a world first

The production-ready V12 (right) takes advantage of direct injection technology to run efficiently on both zero emission hydrogen and conventional petrol. BMW has promised this engine for commercial sale within the lifecycle of this 7 Series

E65: 7 SERIES PRODUCTION

Production History:	In production: 1900-1900				Total produced 119750	
model	735i	745i	730d	740d	760i/Li	total for year
2001	4094	8535				12629
2002	12815	42495	4201	692	166	60369
2003	4885	28343	7305	1057	5162	46752
totals	21794	79373	11506	1749	5328	
					grand total	119,750

Fifth 5 Series (E60/61)

→ Launched in 2003
→ New styling theme better accepted
→ Intelligent lightweight construction
→ Aluminium suspension
→ World first active front steering
→ Head-up display optional
→ Six-speed transmissions
→ Improved iDrive controller
→ M5 with 507 bhp V10

Five times five

The fifth generation of BMW's core model takes on the new look – and gets it right

Replacing the most successful and perhaps best-loved 5 series in BMW's history, the planned 2003 E60 had a lot to live up to. BMW's engineering reputation meant that its customers quite naturally expected significant technical advances from each new model, yet there was some anxiety that, as had so clearly happened with the 2001 7 Series, a whole avalanche of innovations might be presented in such a complex manner that users would not be able to benefit from them or, worse, would be put off the product altogether.

There was also considerable concern, volubly expressed in the specialist press, that the new 5 Series would end up being a down-sized 7 Series not only in its engineering hardware (which was fine) but also in its iDrive control interface, which was frankly hated, and in its heavyweight looks, which were disliked with an equal intensity. The prospect of such features would go against the whole ethos of a satisfying driver-oriented sports saloon, it was argued, and BMW would be betraying its brand values if it embarked on such a course.

In the event there was audible relief when the new 5 Series was announced in February 2003. Yes, it did have certain echoes of the 7 Series to it, but the overall feel was much smaller and more

sporty, and with none of the 7's slab-sided heaviness. The low nose and swept-back headlights even recalled the Z4 sports car, and though there was still what the Americans called a Bangle butt at the rear it looked less like an afterthought than it did on the bigger car.

Inside, the dreaded iDrive was, as promised, present, but BMW insisted it had listened to the critics and had rationalised the system's functions to make it more user-friendly. Enthusiasts were pleased to find a normal handbrake and a conventional centre-mounted gearshift rather than the fiddly wheel- and column-mounted controls on the large car, and the whole stance of the new model seemed to suggest it would be simpler, handier and more manageable.

Old and young: first and fifth generation 5 Series line up. Both ranges share a 525i and 520i

E60: 5 SERIES

Specifications	520i	525i	530i	545i	525d
Engine					
Engine type	Inline 6-cylinder	Inline 6-cylinder	Inline 6-cylinder	90-degree V8	Inline 6-cylinder
Bore & stroke, mm	80 x 72	84 x 75	84 x 89.6	92 x 82.7	80 x 83
Capacity, cc	2171	2495	2979	4398	2497
Valves	24	24	24	32	24
Valve actuation	Dohc, double Vanos variable valve timing	Dohc, double Vanos variable valve timing	Dohc, double Vanos variable valve timing	Dohc, double Vanos variable valve timing; Valvetronic	Dohc
Compression ratio	10.8:1	10.5:1	10.2:1	10:1	22:1
Fuelling	Siemens MS45 electronic fuel injection	Siemens MS45 electronic fuel injection	Siemens MS45 electronic fuel injection	Bosch Motronic electronic fuel injection	Bosch DDE 5 common rail diesel direct injection; variable geometry turbocharger; intercooler
Max power, bhp @ rpm	170@6100	192@6000	231@5900	333@6100	177@4000
Max torque, Nm @ rpm	210@3500	245@3500	300@3500	450@3600	400@2000
Transmission					
Manual transmission	6-speed	6-speed	6-speed	6-speed	6-speed
Automatic	ZF 6-speed Steptronic	ZF 6-speed Steptronic	ZF 6-speed Steptronic	ZF 6-speed Steptronic	ZF 6-speed Steptronic
Drive	Rear wheels, ASC, DTC	Rear wheels, ASC, DTC	Rear wheels, ASC, DTC	Rear wheels, ASC, DTC	Rear wheels, ASC, DTC
Chassis					
Front suspension	Double-pivot MacPherson strut, lower wishbones	Double-pivot MacPherson strut, lower wishbones	Double-pivot MacPherson strut, lower wishbones	Double-pivot MacPherson strut, lower wishbones	Double-pivot MacPherson strut, lower wishbones
Rear suspension	Integral IV multi-link axle with twin transverse links, trailing arms, tie bars, coil springs; optional Dynamic Drive	Integral IV multi-link axle with twin transverse links, trailing arms, tie bars, coil springs; optional Dynamic Drive; Touring: self-levelling standard	Integral IV multi-link axle with twin transverse links, trailing arms, tie bars, coil springs; optional Dynamic Drive; Touring: self-levelling standard	Integral IV multi-link axle with twin transverse links, trailing arms, tie bars, coil springs; optional Dynamic Drive	Integral IV multi-link axle with twin transverse links, trailing arms, tie bars, coil springs; optional Dynamic Drive; Touring: self-levelling standard
Braking	Disc, servo assisted; ABS, Cornering Brake Control	Disc, servo assisted; ABS, Cornering Brake Control	Disc, servo assisted; ABS, Cornering Brake Control	Disc, servo assisted; ABS, Cornering Brake Control	Disc, servo assisted; ABS, Cornering Brake Control
Steering	Rack and pinion, power assisted; Optional variable ratio Active Front Steering	Rack and pinion, power assisted; Optional variable ratio Active Front Steering	Rack and pinion, power assisted; Optional variable ratio Active Front Steering	Rack and pinion, power assisted; Optional variable ratio Active Front Steering	Rack and pinion, power assisted; Optional variable ratio Active Front Steering
Wheels	7.0 x 16	7.0 x 16	7.0 x 16	7.0 x 17	7.0 x 16
Tyres	225/55 R16; optional Tyre Defect Indicator	225/55 R16; optional Tyre Defect Indicator	225/55 R16; optional Tyre Defect Indicator	225/50 R17; optional Tyre Defect Indicator	225/55 R16; optional Tyre Defect Indicator
Body					
Structure	Steel/aluminium monocoque; aluminium subframes and suspension	Steel/aluminium monocoque; aluminium subframes and suspension	Steel/aluminium monocoque; aluminium subframes and suspension	Steel/aluminium monocoque; aluminium subframes and suspension	Steel/aluminium monocoque; aluminium subframes and suspension
Wheelbase, mm	2888	2888	2888	2888	2888
Track F/R, mm	1558/1582	1558/1582	1558/1582	1558/1582	1558/1582
Length, mm	4841	4841 (Touring: 4843)	4841	4841 (Touring: 4843)	4841 (Touring: 4480)
Width, mm	1846	1846	1846	1846	1846
Height, mm	1468	1468 (Touring: 1490)	1468 (Touring: 1490)	1468 (Touring: 1490)	1468 (Touring: 1490)
Kerb weight, kg	1560	1560 (Touring: 1655)	1570	1640 (Touring: 1795)	1660 (Touring: 1750)
Fuel tank capacity, lit	70	70	70	70	70
Performance					
Max speed, km/h	230	238	250	250	226
0-100km/h, sec	9.0	7.9	6.9	5.8	8.3
Fuel consumption , lit/100km	9.0	9.4	9.5	10.6	7.0
Marketing					
Launch date	7/2003	10/2003	7/2003	10/2003	10/2003
Pricing, €	35,500	38,000	41,100	58,000	38,550

530d	535d

Inline 6-cylinder direct injection turbo diesel	Inline 6-cylinder direct injection two-stage turbo diesel
84 x 90	84 x 90
2993	2993
24	24
Dohc	Dohc
17:1	16.5:1
Bosch DDE 5 common rail diesel direct injection; variable geometry turbocharger, intercooler	Bosch DDE 5 common rail diesel direct injection; dual variable geometry turbochargers, intercooler
218@4000	272@4400
500@2000	560@2000
6-speed	6-speed
ZF 6-speed Steptronic	ZF 6-speed Steptronic
Rear wheels, ASC, DTC	Rear wheels, ASC, DTC
Double-pivot MacPherson strut, lower wishbones	Double-pivot MacPherson strut, lower wishbones
Integral IV multi-link axle with twin transverse links, trailing arms, tie bars, coil springs; optional Dynamic Drive; Touring: self-levelling standard	Integral IV multi-link axle with twin transverse links, trailing arms, tie bars, coil springs; optional Dynamic Drive;
Disc, servo assisted; ABS, Cornering Brake Control	Disc, servo assisted; ABS, Cornering Brake Control
Rack and pinion, power assisted; Optional variable ratio Active Front Steering	Rack and pinion, power assisted; Optional variable ratio Active Front Steering
7.0 x 16	7.0 x 16
225/55 R16; optional Tyre Defect Indicator	225/55 R16; optional Tyre Defect Indicator
Steel/aluminium monocoque; aluminium subframes and suspension	Steel/aluminium monocoque; aluminium subframes and suspension
2888	2888
1558/1582	1558/1582
4841 (Touring: 4480)	4841
1846	1846
1468 (Touring: 1490)	1468
1670 (touring: 1760)	1670
70	70
245	250
7.1	6.5
6.9	–
7/2003	7/2004

"There was audible relief when the new 5 Series was announced in February 2003. The overall feel was much smaller and more sporty, and with none of the 7's slab-sided heaviness"

Engineering innovations were expected, and delivered. The initial three-litre petrol and turbo diesel sixes were similar to those on the outgoing model but upgraded to 231 and 218 bhp respectively; transmissions were six-speed automatic or manual. In the pipeline for later in the year were a 525d with 177 bhp and a 333 bhp, V8-engined 545i – the diesel was a carry-over from the previous model but the V8 had acquired Valvetronic.

The body-chassis structure was innovative in the way that it strategically blended steel and aluminium to keep weight to a minimum and to ensure that the distribution was maintained at 50/50. In this process BMW deliberately kept the heavier materials towards the centre of the car to keep its yaw inertia to a minimum, a well-established practice in motorsport.

What was completely new in any branch of the car business was the concept of active steering. Developed in conjunction with ZF, the 5 Series optional AFS (Active Front Steering) ingeniously managed to change the ratio of the steering in relation to the speed of the vehicle. The idea was to have very quick steering at town speeds to minimise wheel movement for parking,

New-look 5 Series comes across as more sculptural and less severe than heavy 7 Series. Selective use of aluminium in body structure and suspension has saved weight and ensured ideal front-rear weight distribution

Complex xenon adaptive light units (above) anticipate where car will steer; twin light guide rings each side giving characteristic 5 Series signature

Equality in action: six-cylinder 3.0 diesel (bottom) is a close match for petrol unit of the same capacity (below), with little difference in performance or refinement; diesel wins on economy

manoeuvring and turning, but to move to a lower gearing for high speeds so that car was not too sensitive on the open road. Unlike the steer-by-wire systems that were at the research phase with other carmakers at the time, BMW's AFS kept a direct mechanical link between the steering wheel and the road at all times, the ratio change being effected seamlessly, under the control of the chassis electronics, by a planetary gear set between the column and the steering rack. It could change the ratio but not the amount of assistance fed into the system, though there was also the theoretical possibility of the car's dynamical stability system intervening in the steering to prevent a skid or to correct one that had already started.

Drivers testing cars with AFS fitted were surprised at the ease with which slalom tests could be negotiated: there was little of the usual wheel-twirling, the steering requiring only small, easy movements. On the open road the cars felt naturally very stable, too: it was when changing speed – say when entering a town from a fast open road – that some acclimatisation was needed.

The models were also offered with the option of Dynamic Drive, the 7 Series' system of active anti-roll bars, and other sophisticated chassis options such as a more sports-oriented form of traction control, making for a rewarding drive with either the petrol or diesel engine.

Further world firsts included a head-up display for important vehicle and journey information. This aircraft-derived technology made it possible to project navigation information, speed and control settings onto the windscreen but focused ahead of the car so the driver did not have to take their eyes off the road. The system could even display telephone text messages, though it always gave priority to warnings from any of the 300 safety-related issues on the car. All these preferences would be stored in the car's key, so that each user did not have to readjust the setting each time they took the wheel.

Improvements to the iDrive system for the 5 Series included a colour screen and the simplification of the control knob, which now only moved in four directions rather than eight. Significantly, on the 2004 1 Series, BMW made

iDrive an option rather than a standard fit.

March 2004 saw three important events in the 5 Series story – the announcement of the high-performance 535d with two-stage turbocharging, the launch of the Touring and the unveiling, also at the Geneva show, of the Concept M5. While the Touring was much as expected, with its estate-car rear favouring style and elegance rather than van-like cargo space, the Concept M5 immediately started the pulses racing.

Ever since its first incarnation in 1985, the BMW M5 had always occupied a privileged position in the car world as the hot-shot sports saloon to have. Each successive generation left competitors trailing in its wake: no one ever came within catching distance of the M5's combination of scorching performance linked to impeccable refinement, an astonishing ease of driving and – most important to buyers in this elite sector – a discreet exterior which does not scream speed or power.

Each successive generation of M5 raised the performance stakes: the previous E39 model upped the ante significantly in 1998 when it moved from BMW's classic straight six to a fire-breathing V8 of no less than 400 horsepower. Since then, BMW had gone back into Formula One, and the adoption of a Grand Prix-inspired V10 engine for the new-generation E60 M5 became an exciting possibility.

Translating Formula 1 technology directly into a road car, the V10 developed by BMW for the new M5 is five litres, redlined at 8250 rpm and gave a massive 507 bhp and 520 Nm of torque – enough to propel the car to 100 km/h in under five seconds and on to a regulated top speed of 250 km/h. Without the speed limiter, the car would have had a top speed of 330 km/h, said BMW. Such impressive levels of performance were made possible by specially modified high-pressure Bi-VANOS camshaft timing, low-mass valves and reciprocating components, individual

"The body-chassis structure was innovative in the way that it strategically blended steel and aluminium to keep weight to a minimum and to ensure that the distribution was maintained at 50/50"

The rear of the Touring estate offers a less unconventional style than the equivalent saloon

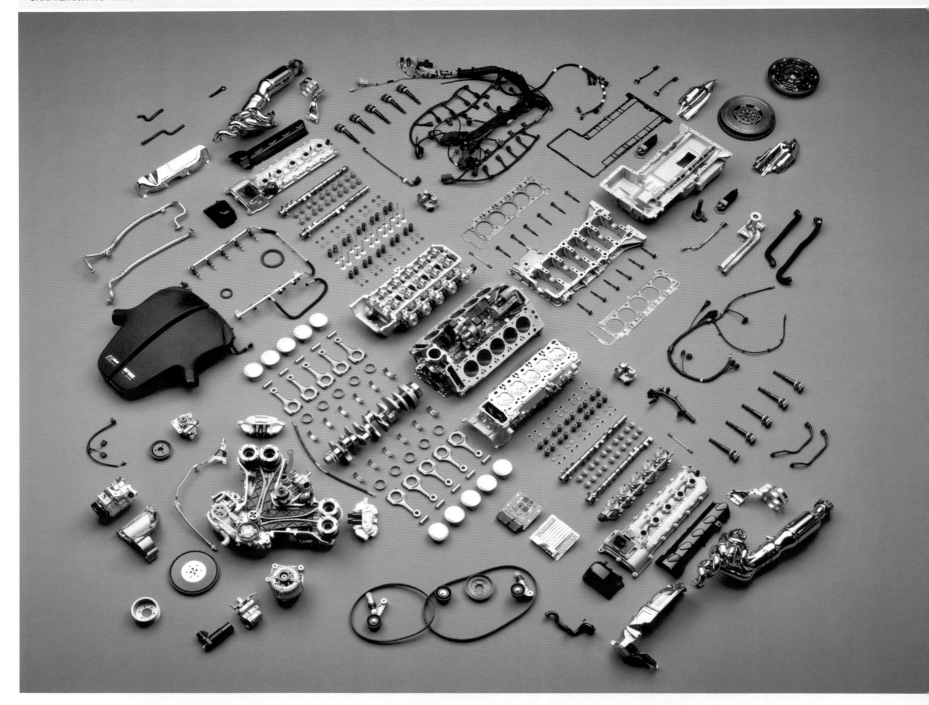

throttle butterflies and engine electronics derived from the BMW Williams F1 car. This was hailed by BMW as a major breakthrough, using ionic current technology to detect engine knock, cylinder misfirings and ignition misses and dealing with more than 50 inputs to calculate the optimum ignition point and cylinder fill for every revolution. The MS65 engine management module contained over 1,000 individual components to give it unparalleled package density: it had to carry out 200 million calculations per second.

The seven-speed sequential transmission was one of the most complicated ever conceived, too. It dramatically increased the number of shift modes available to the driver, with 11 programs to choose from. Five of these allowed the driver to adjust the speed and the responsiveness of the changes in manual mode; five more controlled shift speed in automatic, while the 11th was launch control for impressively rapid getaways from standstill. Further enhancements were made to the traction control, which became

a three-mode system, adding an MDynamic setting (similar to the Track mode in the M3 CSL) which allowed the car to reach much higher limits of traction and even allowed for some side slip and opposite lock on the part of the driver.

An MDrive button on the steering promised to make it much easier for the sporting driver to suddenly shift to a higher tempo: a push of this switch instantly activated all of the previously programmed-in sports engine, transmission, damper control, stability control, traction control, differential and even active seat control settings. A second push and the M5 would be back in cruising mode.

Visually, the BMW M5 stuck close to the Geneva show concept car and was differentiated from its 'standard' 5 Series brethren by the addition of modified front and rear air dams, side sills, side air vents and four exhaust tailpipes. Additionally, it had M alloy wheels of an exclusive design measuring 8.5J x 19 on the front and 9.5J x 19 on the rear, with 255 / 40 ZR 19 and 285 / 35 ZR 19 tyres respectively.

Specifications	M5
Engine	
Engine type	90 degree V10
Capacity, cc	5000
Valves	40
Valve actuation	Dohc, double Vanos variable valve timing
Max power, bhp @ rpm	507@6600
Max torque, Nm @ rpm	520@6100
Transmission	
Manual transmission	7-speed sequential manual
Drive	Rear wheels, ASC, DTC
Wheels front + rear	8.5 x 19 / 9.5 x 19
Tyres front + rear	255/40 ZR19 / 285/35 ZR19
Kerb weight, kg	1755
Fuel tank capacity, lit	
Performance	
Max speed, km/h	250 (331 if derestricted)
0-100km/h, sec	4.7
0-200km/h, sec	15.0

Work of many parts: the remarkable ten cylinder, 40-valve M5 engine dismantled for the camera (far left) and ready to fire up (left)

Geneva show, March 2004:
BMW Concept M5

The Concept M5 shown at Geneva in March 2004 whetted enthusiast's appetites with its high-revving V10 engine and discreetly powerful stance. The engine of the production version (right) five-litre engine was announced at 507 bhp – the most powerful BMW ever produced

Just prior to its launch the new M5 was said to be able to lap the fearsome Nordschleife of the Nurburgring in eight minutes – an unprecedentedly good time for a series production road car, and something that would have led the entire field in the German Grand Prix in the 1970s, in air-conditioned comfort and surrounded by full Dolby Pro Logic stereo sound.

It was certainly some achievement to develop a high-revving V10 engine with a lifetime's durability rather than just the 800 km of a grand prix weekend. The BMW V10 brought tremendous power, many engineering innovations and an impressive weight of just 250 kg – the same as the outgoing V8 with 20 per cent less power. And, observed BMW, it even complied with the EU4 and US LEV2 emissions limits.

Nevertheless, the very high performance provided by the 272 bhp, two-stage turbocharged three-litre 535d, while less overtly glamorous or exciting, was felt by many to be the development of the greatest long-term engineering significance. Its introduction was made all the more poignant by the announcement that semi-private rally-raid X5s that had finished fourth and eighth overall and cleaned up the diesel class in the gruelling Dakar rally the month before were secretly running those very same engines.

Production History:		In production: 2003 on			Total produced 113,561				
model	520i	525i	525d	530i	530d	545i	M5	total for year	
2003	19,219	17,164	27	35,038	36,751	5,321	41		
totals	19,219	17,164	27	35,038	36,751	5,321	41	113,561	
							grand total	113,561	

X3 (E83)

- → Launched 2003
- → Competitor to Jeep Cherokee and Land Rover Freelander
- → Market position below BMW X5
- → Cheaper than X5 but almost same size
- → Built by Magna Steyr, Austria
- → Introduced XDrive 4WD system

Z4 (E85)

- → Launched in 2003
- → Distinctive and attractive
- → New chassis design
- → Z axle rear suspension
- → 2.5 and 3.0 litre engines, later, 2.2
- → SMG sequential transmission optional
- → Built exclusively in Spartanburg

Second thoughts

New Z4 roadster raises BMW's sports car game; new X3 off-roader plugs a market gap

The Z4 was unquestionably the car the Z3 should have been all along. Right from its first day on the road it showed a sharp-handling chassis and keen engines, whereas the Z3 misfired in its early years with lacklustre dynamics and weak engines. Sharp in its styling, too, the Z4 showed none of the Z3's sentimentality towards the past, immediately giving it a more ambitious temperament.

The magazines immediately picked up on this. Whereas the Z3 had been thrown into the test ring with the Porsche Boxster and Mercedes SLK and was dealt such a knockout blow that it was never invited back, the new Z4 met the updated versions of those same competitors and emerged with honour – if not always the outright winner, then certainly with its pride intact and keen for a rematch.

What made the difference? A sceptic would suggest that it was because BMW had been

stung into taking the roadster market more seriously, hurt by the lukewarm press received by the Z3 and even more chastened by the implication that it had cynically saved money by using a previous-generation suspension system in the hope that the good name of BMW would see the car through to success.

A marketing specialist, on the other hand, might contend that with an emotive and upscale product such as a sports car it would have been better to launch a powerful one first, so as to

The Z4 showed that BMW could resist retro and design a roadster with true originality and flair

Thanks to a sophisticated chassis specification including the four-link rear axle, the Z4 proved much more rewarding to drive than its predecessor. One push of the Dynamic Drive Control button put all systems into sport mode

The Bangle team's design for the Z4 produced some exquisite details, including the wheel arches (bottom) and the set back indicator repeater behind the BMW badge (below). The flashing indicator illuminates the whole recess

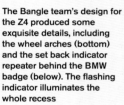

> "The Z4 was one of the most successful new-wave designs to emerge from the corporate studios. It had the authentic roadster profile, with a long bonnet, compact cockpit and short boot, but Bangle's highly sculptural surfacing gave it real character"

establish a reputation for performance rather than, as happened with the Z3, the unhelpful 'girlie-car' image fostered by the dull four-cylinder versions that monopolised the catalogues for the first two years. Had the 2.8 been in the launch line-up, the Z3 could have ended up with a much more favourable public profile.

Whatever the answers to these hypothetical questions might be, BMW appeared much wiser second time round and gave the Z4 completely fresh design and engineering and ensured that high-calibre models were the first to be released and set the tone for the rest of the range.

Clearly showing evidence of the new and radical design philosophy instilled by Chris Bangle following the 7 Series launch in 2001, the Z4 was one of the most successful new-wave designs to emerge from the corporate studios. It had the authentic roadster profile, for sure, with a long bonnet, compact cockpit and short boot, but Bangle's highly sculptural surfacing gave real character to the nose, with its twin BMW grilles neatly integrated, and to the tail with a pronounced lip in the centre to carry the third brake light. Yet the real strength came in the sides, where the design team contrived an

elegant scooped-out section running along the base of the door and tapering into the rear wheel arch: at its front end the scoop was stopped by a dramatic diagonal slash, a continuation of the screen pillar line, that bisected the recessed indicator carrying the BMW roundel. The effect was that the Z4 always looked interesting and animated, all its curves, contours and angles catching the light whatever the conditions.

The indicator itself was celebrated in several magazines as a thing of beauty in its own right. Set in a round recess, it would flash a star pattern into the hollow whenever it illuminated, further highlighting the contours of the car's side.

The launch engines were the 2.5 and 3.0 litre sixes of 192 and 231 bhp; the bigger unit came with a six-speed manual gearbox and both had the option of the M3-style SMG sequential box – again a sign of serious intent. So, too, was the suspension set-up, with the E46's multilink axle at the rear, lowered and widened, and a high proportion of lighter aluminium components. The model introduced a system called Dynamic Drive Control (DDC), which is not to be confused with Dynamic Drive on the 5 and 7 Series: DDC was operated by the sport button on the dash and when engaged told the electronics to give sharper response to the throttle, less assistance to the power steering and, on automatics or SMGs, put the transmission into sport mode.

But what made the Z4 work so well was that it did not ever feel as if it was the electronics that were controlling the car: it came across as a fun-loving pure sports car, with plenty of power even in 2.5 litre form. The interior was pleasing, too, with semi-circular instruments, a foldaway navigation monitor and tasteful use of metal-finish plastics. In many countries the Z4 was playfully advertised as The Fastest Soft-Top in the World: the hood would raise or lower in 10 seconds, which was indeed faster than any other convertible.

While the Z4 was a great critical success among both customers and commentators, the same does not hold true for the car launched just a few months after the roadster, namely the X3. The press, certainly, gave BMW an unaccustomed rough ride over several aspects of the X3's design, especially its relationship to the

E85: Z4

Specifications	Z4 2.2i	Z4 2.5i	Z4 3.0i
Engine			
Engine type	Inline 6-cylinder	Inline 6-cylinder	Inline 6-cylinder
Bore & stroke, mm	80 x 72	84 x 75	84 x 89.6
Capacity, cc	2171	2495	2979
Valves	24	24	24
Valve actuation	Dohc, double Vanos variable valve timing	Dohc, double Vanos variable valve timing	Dohc, double Vanos variable valve timing
Compression ratio	10.8:1	10.5:1	10.2:1
Fuelling	Siemens MS45 electronic fuel injection	Siemens MS45 electronic fuel injection	Siemens MS45 electronic fuel injection
Max power, bhp @ rpm	170@6100	192@6000	231@5900
Max torque, Nm @ rpm	210@3500	245@3500	300@3500
Transmission			
Manual transmission	5-speed	5-speed; 6-speed SMG optional	6-speed; SMG optional
Automatic	5-speed ZF 5HP19 Steptronic	5-speed ZF 5HP19 Steptronic	5-speed ZF 5HP19 Steptronic
Drive	Rear wheels	Rear wheels	Rear wheels
Chassis			
Front suspension	MacPherson struts, lower wishbones	MacPherson struts, lower wishbones	MacPherson struts, lower wishbones
Rear suspension	Multi-link axle with trailing arms, twin transverse upper links, lower control arms, coil-springs	Multi-link axle with trailing arms, twin transverse upper links, lower control arms, coil-springs	Multi-link axle with trailing arms, twin transverse upper links, lower control arms, coil-springs
Braking	Discs, servo assisted, ABS	Discs, servo assisted, ABS	Discs, servo assisted, ABS
Steering	Rack and pinion, electric power assistance	Rack and pinion, electric power assistance	Rack and pinion, electric power assistance
Wheels	7.0 x 16	7.0 x 16	8.0 x 17
Tyres	205/55 R16	225/50 R16	225/45 R17
Body			
Structure	Steel monocoque, aluminium bonnet	Steel monocoque, aluminium bonnet	Steel monocoque, aluminium bonnet
Wheelbase, mm	2495	2495	2495
Track F/R, mm	1473	1473	1473
Length, mm	1523	1523	1523
Width, mm	4091	4091	4091
Height, mm	1781	1781	1781
Kerb weight, kg	1335	1335	1335
Fuel tank capacity, lit	55	55	55
Performance			
Max speed, km/h	225	235	250
0-100km/h, sec	7.7	7.0	5.9
Fuel consumption , lit/100km	8.8	8.9	9.1
Marketing			
Launch date	3/2003	3/2003	3/2003
Pricing, €	29,900	32,500	38,500

highly successful X5, and even normally moderate reviewers wondered publicly whether BMW had done its sums right when it came to judging the car's suspension and ride.

The X3 seemed a logical enough idea as a premium-branded SUV to slot in below the X5, a vehicle which had been steadily moving up market. BMW certainly had the hardware for the job – good, powerful diesel engines, refined petrol engines and a strong set of suspension components, in particular the versatile Z axle for the rear. The company also had some experience, gained with the X5, in four-wheel-drive systems and in making cars with off-road capability handle well on normal roads too.

What BMW did not have was anywhere to build the proposed E83 model: all its plants around the world were running at, or beyond, capacity, and the avalanche of new models (Z4, 6 series, 1 Series, Rolls-Royce, MINI Convertible, and of course the X3 itself) threatened to make matters worse. BMW decided on a novel solution: to contract out the manufacture of the E83 to Magna Steyr in Graz, Austria, a company with much experience in high-quality manufacture of four-wheel-drive vehicles.

The January 2003 Detroit show provided a handy preview of the eventual design when BMW wheeled out its xActivity concept study, effectively an X3 without a fixed roof. The design study was greeted with equanimity rather than the outrage that had tended to accompany BMW styling reveals since the Bangle cultural revolution swept through the group's design operation. The early signs seemed good, yet the eventual result was judged by many to be

Z4 PRODUCTION

Production History: In production: from 2002 Total produced 67,851				
model	2.2	2.5	3.0	total for year
2002		882	9,864	10,746
2003	3,287	16,155	37,663	57,105
totals	3,287	17,037	47,527	
			grand total	67,851
			grand total inc SKD	67,851

Splashdown: The X3 Sports Activity Vehicle launched in September 2003 came uncomfortably close to the pricier X5 in terms of size and specification. The X3's style did not have the classy cleanness of the older X5

"The press gave BMW an unaccustomed rough ride over several aspects of the X3's design"

Top:
On the rough: the X3 showed itself a consummate performer and sharp handler, but its poor ride was a consistent complaint

E83: X3

Specifications	X3 2.5i	X3 3.0i
Engine		
Engine type	Inline 6-cylinder	Inline 6-cylinder
Bore & stroke, mm	84 x 75	84 x 89.6
Capacity, cc	2495	2979
Valves	24	24
Valve actuation	Dohc, double Vanos variable valve timing	Dohc, double Vanos variable valve timing
Compression ratio	10.5:1	10.2:1
Fuelling	Siemens MS45 electronic fuel injection	Siemens MS45 electronic fuel injection
Max power, bhp @ rpm	192@6000	231@5900
Max torque, Nm @ rpm	245@3500	300@3500
Transmission		
Manual transmission	6-speed	Not available
Automatic	ZF 5-speed Steptronic	ZF 5-speed Steptronic
Drive	xDrive four wheel drive via central multiplate clutch; traction control via DSC sensor system	xDrive four wheel drive via central multiplate clutch; traction control via DSC sensor system
Chassis		
Front suspension	Double-pivot MacPherson strut, lower wishbones	Double-pivot MacPherson strut, lower wishbones
Rear suspension	Integral IV multi-link axle with twin transverse links, trailing arms ands tie bars, coil springs; optional Dynamic Drive active anti-roll bars	Integral IV multi-link axle with twin transverse links, trailing arms ands tie bars, coil springs; optional Dynamic Drive active anti-roll bars
Braking	Disc, servo assisted; ABS, Cornering Brake Control; Hill Descent Control	Disc, servo assisted; ABS, Cornering Brake Control; Hill Descent Control
Steering	Rack and pinion, power assisted	Rack and pinion, power assisted
Wheels	8.0 x 17	8.0 x 17
Tyres	235/55 R 17	235/55 R 17
Body		
Structure	Steel monocoque, steel suspension	Steel monocoque, steel suspension
Wheelbase, mm	2795	2795
Track F/R, mm	1538/1556	1524/1542
Length, mm	4565)	4565
Width, mm	1853	1853
Height, mm	1674	1674
Kerb weight, kg	1815	1815
Fuel tank capacity, lit	67	67
Performance		
Max speed, km/h	208	210 (sport: 221)
0-100km/h, sec	8.9	8.1
Fuel consumption , lit/100km	11.2	12.1
Marketing		
Launch date	3/2004	3/2004
Pricing, €	31,800	40,300

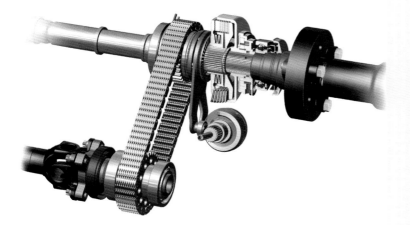

The X3 chassis brought new levels of on-road agility to four-wheel-drives thanks to its innovative multiplate centre clutch (detail) which could feed torque to either axle to counter understeer or oversteer

"For a company which got it so right with the X5, the X3 looked like something of a misjudgement -- not just in its appearance and its less than convincing cabin execution, but also, wholly out of character for BMW, in its chassis settings"

something of a disappointment.

The X3 had none of the classy elegance of its older brother: its sides looked flat and slabby, its rear treatment was fussy and complicated, as was the detailing around the headlights and the remodelled BMW grilles, and the attempt to reinterpret the famous Hofmeister kink in the rearmost pillar had made it look like a 1980s Toyota.

The X3's dimensions caused some head-scratching, too. The specification sheet revealed that it was a few centimetres shorter than the X5 buit offered more space in the boot as well as greater headroom for rear passengers. The X3's role in BMW's grand plan seemed uncertain. However, there was no room for doubt when it came to the X3's technical specification: two advanced six-cylinder engines of acknowledged excellence, the smoothest six-cylinder diesel on the market, a set of very good transmissions and XDrive, a new take on four-wheel-drive courtesy of a fast-responding multiplate centre clutch for distributing power between front and rear axles.

Yet, as *Car and Driver* observed, the X3 was a vehicle which was less appealing on the road than it seemed on paper. The XDrive centre clutch did indeed work as BMW claimed, feeding power across the axles so as to prevent the onset of either understeer or oversteer. This made the X3 a rapid drive on twisty roads where, in the words of the US publication, it had an uncanny ability to straighten out the bends. But C&D's editors, along with many other commentators, soon got tired of the new car because of its awful, bone-jarring ride. "Pack some aspirin" said one journal: others were less complimentary still, making it clear that even the non-sports suspension, with its higher-profile tyres, offered little improvement.

For a company which got it so right with the X5, the X3 looked like something of a misjudgement — not just in its appearance and its less than convincing cabin execution, but also, wholly out of character for BMW, in its chassis settings. The size issue was more understandable in the context of the X5's likely move up market to face the Range Rover, leaving the X3 to face the Discovery; what was not so easy to grasp was why BMW engineers seemed to put more effort into designing clever luggage rails and mountain bike racks rather than getting the X3's ride right.

BMW's factories were running at full capacity in the run-up to the X3's launch, so the manufacture of the new sport-utility had to be outsourced to specialists Magna Steyr in Austria

E83: X3 PRODUCTION

Production History:		In production: 2003 on				Total produced 8,770
model	X3 2.0d	X3 2.0i	X3 2.5i	X3 3.0i	X3 3.0d	total for year
2003	8	10	93	8,594	65	8,770
totals	8	10	93	8,594	65	
					grand total	8,770

Return of the Six

BMW brings back a classic nameplate wearing an avant-garde suit

Second 6 Series (E63)

- → Launched in 2003
- → First big coupé design since 1989
- → Influenced by Z9 concept car
- → Valvetronic V8 engines
- → World's lightest 6-cylinder in 630i
- → First magnesium engine
- → Convertible version in 2004
- → New standards of rollover protection
- → Intelligent lightweight construction

The revival of the 6 Series nameplate was always an emotive issue within BMW. The original model had been held in high regard right up to its replacement in 1989 by the 8 Series, a car which did not strike such a resonant chord among owners and enthusiasts.

Some said the 8 Series was overburdened with technology, others that it was too big and too expensive, too cramped, too divorced from the real world to be enjoyable to drive. One way or another, it became the mission of a born-again 6 Series to heal these wounds, to put right all the wrongs of the big, misunderstood 8 and to recapture the charisma of the 1977 classic.

While the pivotal Z9 large coupé concept produced for the 1999 Frankfurt show was greeted with puzzlement or even distaste by many onlookers, the design was clearly a blueprint for the forthcoming 8 Series replacement and the show car performed a valuable role in softening up public (and customer) opinion in advance of the 6 Series' planned on sale date in September 2003. The Z9 convertible study presented in Paris the following year backtracked on some of the wilder ideas of the gullwing-doored fixed head version and again gave strong clues as to what an open-topped 6 Series could look like.

The concepts did their job well, and so too in

a way did the 2001 7 Series: at the official debut of the 645Ci at the 2003 Frankfurt show, protests at the style of the new car were surprisingly muted. The design had an elegant sweep from the stylised BMW kidneys at the extreme front, through the broadening bonnet and over the windscreen and roof before meeting the kicked-up rear boot line. For many, the raised 'Bangle butt' boot, which again looked like an afterthought, was the only real point of objection in an otherwise harmonious and dynamic grand tourer shape: the pronounced inward slope of the cabin sides gave added forward thrust to the design and, as always, BMW had achieved a textbook-perfect

The 645Ci was launched in 2003 to considerable excitement about the revival of the 6 Series name: its new-era styling caused less of a rumpus than that of the 2001 7 Series

Classic and contemporary: will the 2003 6 Series also be regarded as such a fine design when it a quarter-century old?

fit between wheels, tyres and wheelarches.

Excitement about the 645's technical specification was modest only because the main elements in the Coupé's make-up had already been seen on the bigger 7 Series and the companion 5, which in chassis terms was a very close relative. From the larger car came the Engine of the Year Award-winning 4.4 litre Valvetronic V8, while the complete 5 Series rear subframe and multi-link suspension were grafted in on a platform shortened by just over 100 mm from the four-door's.

Picking from the chassis systems lists of both models as well as that of the Z4, the 645 standardised on the normal traction control and dynamic stability control functions, linking these with the one-push Driving Dynamics Control of the Z4, whose job it was to put all systems into sport mode; a key option was Dynamic Drive, the 7 Series' acclaimed active roll-bar system which ended the traditional conflict of interests between straightline ride comfort and cornering stability. Also on the options list was the innovative AFS

active steering first seen on the 5 Series earlier that year: promising an end to both over-sensitivity on the motorway and crossed arms when driving in town, AFS effectively added its own computed steering angle to that already applied by the driver. At low speeds it would add extra angle, so that the driver only had to turn the wheel about half a turn for full lock; at high speed the unit would slightly counter the driver's inputs to improve straightline stability. Active Steering, claimed BMW, offered the 6 Series Coupé driver "all of the advantages of an all-electronic steer-by-wire system with the precise feedback provided by mechanical steering."

Active Cruise Control was also offered, a radar-based system enabling the 645 to keep a constant distance (or time interval) behind the vehicle in front, no matter how much that vehicle speeded up or slowed down.

In the interests of saving weight and ensuring its preferred 50/50 loading between front and rear axles, BMW pursued what it called intelligent lightweight construction. Unlike the Audi A8 and

E63: NEW 6 SERIES

Specifications	630i Coupé	630i Cabriolet	645Ci Coupé	645Ci Cabriolet

Engine				
Engine type	Inline 6-cylinder	Inline 6-cylinder	90-degree V8	90-degree V8
Bore & stroke, mm	85 x 88	85 x 88	92 x 82.7	92 x 82.7
Capacity, cc	2977	2977	4398	4398
Valves	24	24	32	32
Valve actuation	Dohc, double Vanos variable valve timing, Valvetronic variable valve lift	Dohc, double Vanos variable valve timing, Valvetronic variable valve lift	Dohc, double Vanos variable valve timing, Valvetronic variable valve lift	Dohc, double Vanos variable valve timing, Valvetronic variable valve lift
Compression ratio		10.7 : 1	10.0:1	10.0:1
Fuelling	Bosch MS70 sequential multiport fuel injection	Bosch MS70 sequential multiport fuel injection	Bosch ME9.2.1 Electronic fuel injection	Bosch ME9.2.1 Electronic fuel injection
Max power, bhp @ rpm	258@6650	258@6650	333@6100	333@6100
Max torque, Nm @ rpm	300@2500	300@2500	450@3600	450@3600
Transmission				
Manual transmission	6-speed; optional SMG sequentlail	6-speed; optional SMG sequentlail	6-speed; optional SMG sequentlail	6-speed; optional SMG sequential
Automatic	ZF 6-speed 6HP26 Steptronic	ZF 6-speed 6HP26 Steptronic	ZF 6-speed 6HP26 Steptronic	ZF 6-speed 6HP26 Steptronic
Drive	Rear wheels; ASC	Rear wheels; ASC	Rear wheels; ASC	Rear wheels; ASC
Chassis				
Front suspension	Double-pivot MacPherson strut, lower wishbones	Double-pivot MacPherson strut, lower wishbones	Double-pivot MacPherson strut, lower wishbones	Double-pivot MacPherson strut, lower wishbones
Rear suspension	Integral IV multi-link axle with twin transverse links, trailing arms and tie bars, coil springs; optional Dynamic Drive active anti-roll bars	Integral IV multi-link axle with twin transverse links, trailing arms and tie bars, coil springs; optional Dynamic Drive active anti-roll bars	Integral IV multi-link axle with twin transverse links, trailing arms and tie bars, coil springs; optional Dynamic Drive active anti-roll bars	Integral IV multi-link axle with twin transverse links, trailing arms and tie bars, coil springs; optional Dynamic Drive active anti-roll bars
Braking	Disc, servo assisted; ABS, Cornering Brake Control	Disc, servo assisted; ABS, Cornering Brake Control	Disc, servo assisted; ABS, Cornering Brake Control	Disc, servo assisted; ABS, Cornering Brake Control
Steering	Rack and pinion Servotronic, power assisted; optional Active Steering	Rack and pinion Servotronic, power assisted; optional Active Steering	Rack and pinion Servotronic, power assisted; optional Active Steering	Rack and pinion Servotronic, power assisted; optional Active Steering
Wheels	8.0 x 17	8.0 x 17	8.0 x 18	8.0 x 18
Tyres	245/50 R17	245/50 R17	245/45 R18	245/45 R18
Body				
Structure	Steel monocoque; aluminium subframes, suspension, bonnet; composite boot lid	Steel monocoque; aluminium subframes, suspension, bonnet; composite boot lid	Steel monocoque; aluminium subframes, suspension, bonnet; composite boot lid	Steel monocoque; aluminium subframes, suspension, bonnet; composite boot lid
Wheelbase, mm	2780	2780	2780	2780
Track F/R, mm	1558/1592	1558/1592	1558/1592	1558/1592
Length, mm	4820	4820	4820	4820
Width, mm	1851	1851	1851	1851
Height, mm	1373	1373	1373	1373
Kerb weight, kg	1560	1685	1690	1815
Fuel tank capacity, lit	70	70	70	70
Performance				
Max speed, km/h	250	250	250	250
0-100km/h, sec	6.5	6.9	5.6	6.1
Fuel consumption , lit/100km	9.0	9.6	11.7	11.7
Marketing				
Launch date	9/2004	9/2004	9/2003	9/2003
Pricing, €	–	–	72,000	80,000

Bold BMW style may still divide opinions, but details such as rear light and side indicator repeater can be beautifully judged

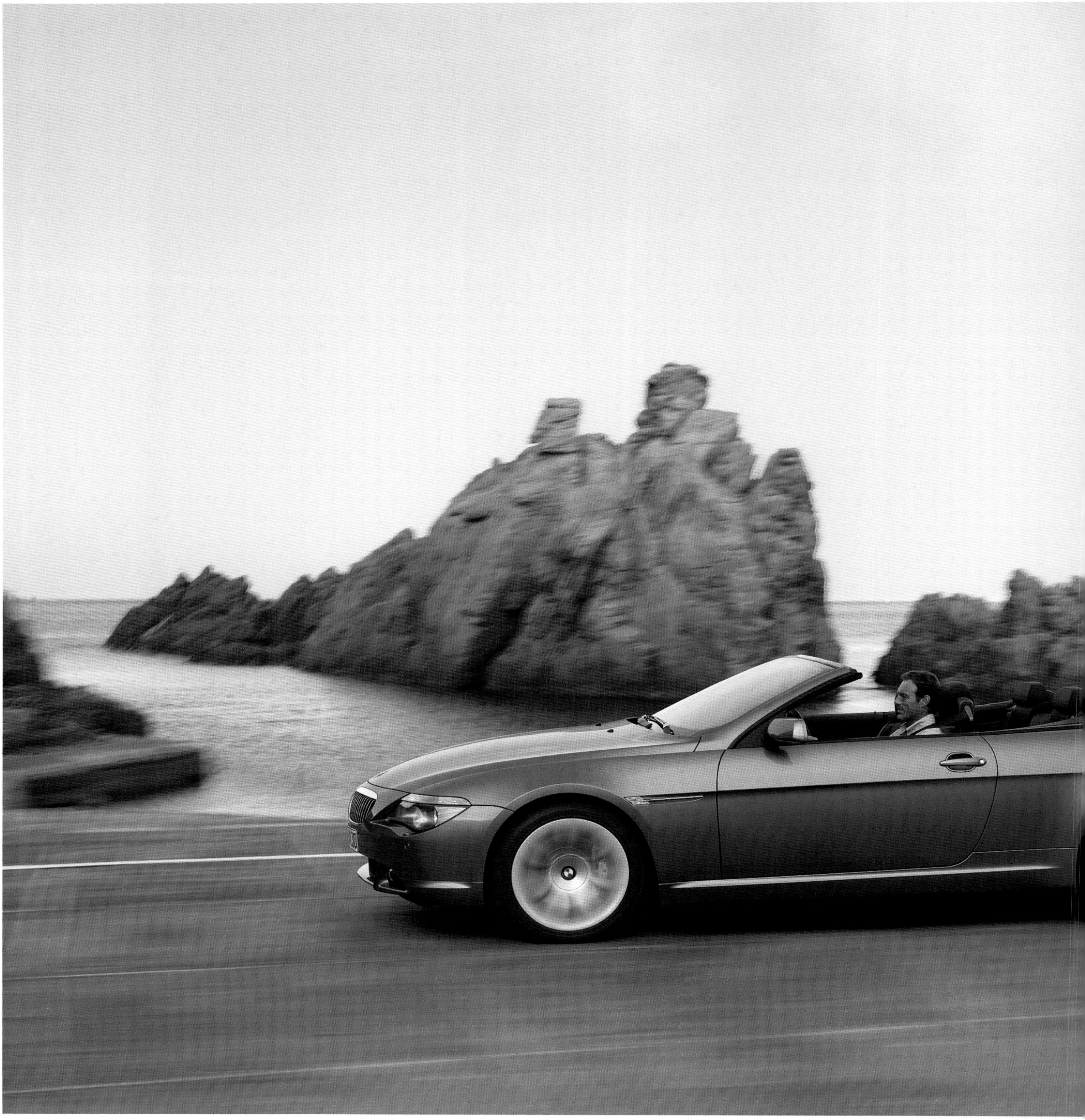

"The 6 Series design had an elegant sweep from the stylised BMW kidneys at the extreme front to the raised boot, which again looked like an afterthought. This was the only real point of objection in an otherwise harmonious and dynamic grand tourer shape"

The 645Ci Cabriolet adds a new style to the 6 Series portfolio: the original 1977 model was a coupé only

The 630i was the first car to receive BMW's advanced, new-generation R6 Valvetronic six-cylinder. The use of magnesium in the block made it the world's lightest six. Electric water pump (inset) used just one tenth the energy and was also a world first. Cylinder head (below) has magnesium cover

as without the glasshouse the waistline was more clearly defined and drew more attention to the horizontal. Extensive use was made of tailored and rolled steel blanks in the car's structure: the sills were double walled, extruded V-section aluminium bars gave protection in the doors, and IHU steel profiles from Thyssen-Krupp's New Steel Body project gave extra strength to the screen pillars for rollover protection. BMW claimed best-in-class strength and vibration reduction for its Convertible structure, which it said was as good in these respects as a two-seat roadster with a much smaller cabin aperture. Active protection measures, in addition to the normal suite of airbags, included pop-up roll hoops behind the rear passengers' head restraints, triggered by the Active Safety Electronics system.

Unusually, both versions of the 645 included a smooth underbody tray to improve aerodynamics and, again in pursuit of reduced drag, a novel flap arrangement behind the BMW grilles blanked off airflow until the engine management signalled that radiator cooling was required. A further intriguing touch on the Convertible was the rear roof compartment cover, moulded in a composite material: like the bumpers on the Z8 it housed the antenna for the radio and cell phone.

Inside, the two models featured similar equipment to both the 5 and 7 Series, though in terms of layout they were much closer to the smaller of these two cars and, much to the relief of enthusiasts, the conventional gear lever, handbrake and ignition key were retained. Two levels of second-generation iDrive were offered, the more sophisticated of the two offering the same eight axes of movement for the central knob as on the 7 Series. Additional options included the head-up display first seen on the 5 Series.

In the autumn of 2004 the 6 Series was the bringer of a further BMW innovation, whose huge importance will come to be realised in the years ahead. The newly announced 630i Coupé and Convertible featured a brand new three-litre straight six cylinder engine, the first six to incorporate Valvetronic and, thanks to extensive use of sophisticated digital design tools and magnesium in its construction, also the lightest

Jaguar XJ series, BMW retained steel for the basic structure of the 6 Series, using aluminium in strategic areas where weight could most usefully be saved. This philosophy called for aluminium to be used in the doors and bonnet, and composite plastic compounds for the front wings and the boot structure, complete with its characteristic hump. The suspension was virtually all-aluminium, as were the brakes apart from the grey cast iron coated contact surfaces of the four huge discs. Yet despite all these strenuous efforts to keep mass to a minimum, the 645Ci still ended up weighing 50 kg more than the equivalent 545i. This is a common phenomenon in the auto industry, where coupés also tend to be better equipped.

Though Los Angeles would have been a more appropriate venue in terms of weather and potential clients, it was Detroit in January 2004 which played host to the debut of the 645Ci Convertible. Essentially similar to the Coupé, the Convertible nevertheless had a lower, flatter look

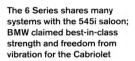
The 6 Series shares many systems with the 545i saloon; BMW claimed best-in-class strength and freedom from vibration for the Cabriolet

six-cylinder engine in the world at 161 kg.

The R6 was the first of a wholly new generation of engines, said BMW, with the existing M54 having reached the point where any further improvements would increase its weight. In 2004 the M54 was being used in almost every single BMW model line: the 3, 5 and 7 Series, the X3 and X5, and the Z4; only the Compact, the new 1 Series and the 6 Series did not use it – so the potential of the new engine would be huge. Six-cylinder engines represented over half of the power units built by BMW, said board member Dr Norbert Reithofer, underlining the significance of the R6.

The R6 marked numerous world firsts: it used magnesium for the outer casting of its main block (aluminium still has to be used for the cylinder liners and where there is contact with coolant) to save 57 percent in weight compared with grey-cast iron and 24 per cent compared to simple

aluminium; it was the first to use an electric rather than mechanical water pump, saving 1.8 kW, and it was the world's first six-cylinder Valvetronic, completing BMW's family of four, six, eight and 12-cylinder units with this innovative fuel-saving system.

Production History:		In production: 2003 on Total produced 4,311	
model	645Ci Cabrio	645Ci Coupé	total for year
2002	10	4,138	4,148
2003	5	158	163
totals	15	4,296	
		grand total	4,311

Top management

BMW acquires Rolls-Royce and reinterprets the 'world's best car' for the 21st century

Rolls-Royce Phantom (R-01)

- → Launched in 2003
- → Developed entirely within the BMW group
- → Aluminium space frame body made in Germany
- → Final assembly in Goodwood, England
- → Direct-injection V12 engine
- → 'Coach' rear doors
- → New standards of smoothness, silence
- → V16-engined 100EX show car

It was a daunting, yet thrilling challenge – precisely the kind of test any ambitious automotive engineer or designer would dream about taking on. The task was no less an assignment than to create a brand new Rolls-Royce: to construct the template which would launch the 'best car in the world' into the 21st century with a fresh dynasty of designs.

Not to scale: the Rolls-Royce Phantom is quite literally a massive presence on the road, dwarfing other cars. It was designed and built by the project team under BMW in less than five years

It was late summer 1998 and the messy business of the Rolls-Royce and Bentley sell-off had at last been sorted out. Volkswagen, which had bought the combined businesses from their former parent company, UK weapons manufacturer Vickers, would keep the Bentley brand, the Crewe factory, the worldwide dealer network and the customer database, also worldwide; BMW, for the tidy sum of £40 million, would acquire the right to use the Rolls-Royce name, the double-R symbol, and the Spirit of Ecstasy mascot. Nothing else – no cars, no designs, no factories or facilities; not even any client records or contact details. Rolls-Royce had nearly a century of history, yet BMW had bought no more than a name.

The deal had numerous consequences. Firstly, the two brands – though one hesitates to call them mere brands: they were more like institutions – would have to be separated. They

had been joined at the hip for almost half a century as cash-starved managements had skimped on product development by making Bentleys virtual carbon copies of their Rolls-Royce equivalents. Now the marques would have to forge separate identities, but it could not possibly happen straight away as the few cars that were still being produced all came from the same Crewe factory: the date of January 1st 2003 was set for BMW to assume formal ownership of the RR label. In the intervening period Rolls-Royces produced under VW ownership would be sold through the existing network: it was unrealistic to expect VW to invest in the Rolls-Royce brand if the marque was to pass to BMW in less than five years.

This gave BMW a firm but demanding timetable to work to. In little more than 50 months it had to be ready to launch not just an all-new product worthy of the sky-high expectations that

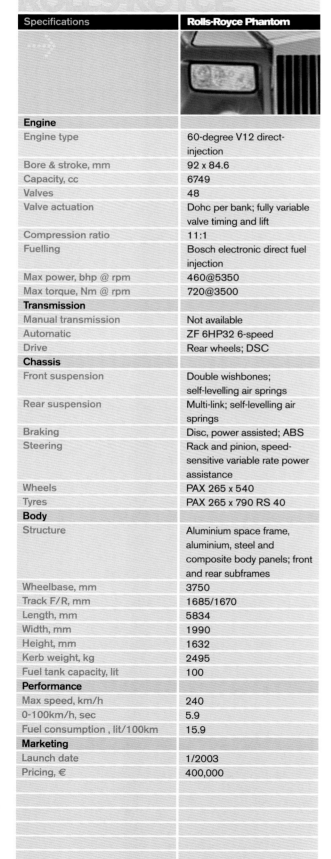

Specifications	Rolls-Royce Phantom
Engine	
Engine type	60-degree V12 direct-injection
Bore & stroke, mm	92 x 84.6
Capacity, cc	6749
Valves	48
Valve actuation	Dohc per bank; fully variable valve timing and lift
Compression ratio	11:1
Fuelling	Bosch electronic direct fuel injection
Max power, bhp @ rpm	460@5350
Max torque, Nm @ rpm	720@3500
Transmission	
Manual transmission	Not available
Automatic	ZF 6HP32 6-speed
Drive	Rear wheels; DSC
Chassis	
Front suspension	Double wishbones; self-levelling air springs
Rear suspension	Multi-link; self-levelling air springs
Braking	Disc, power assisted; ABS
Steering	Rack and pinion, speed-sensitive variable rate power assistance
Wheels	PAX 265 x 540
Tyres	PAX 265 x 790 RS 40
Body	
Structure	Aluminium space frame, aluminium, steel and composite body panels; front and rear subframes
Wheelbase, mm	3750
Track F/R, mm	1685/1670
Length, mm	5834
Width, mm	1990
Height, mm	1632
Kerb weight, kg	2495
Fuel tank capacity, lit	100
Performance	
Max speed, km/h	240
0-100km/h, sec	5.9
Fuel consumption , lit/100km	15.9
Marketing	
Launch date	1/2003
Pricing, €	400,000

were bound to arise; it also had to be ready with a complete manufacturing system, a sales organisation, an administrative structure. And, as of August 1998, the only thing that was definite was that 1/1/2003 date when the Rolls-Royce name would become BMW's to use. It was like coming up with a completely new heritage – within the space of less than five years.

Design and engineering teams were soon set up and work began on defining what sort of Rolls-Royce should be produced and how it should be engineered. The teams identified the Silver Cloud from the 1950s as being the archetypal Rolls-Royce in most potential customers' minds: the long, sweeping lines, the massive, upright temple-like grille, the thick rear pillars and the gracefully tapering tail were all seen as desirable Rolls-Royce characteristics. The teams quickly realised something else, too: there was no point relating to the engineering of the then-current Rolls-Royce models as – apart from their BMW-supplied engines and air conditioning – they were thoroughly outdated designs which because of lack of investment had stood technologically still while other car makers had advanced through several generations of ever-newer products.

This meant that the designers' sheets of paper and the engineers' CAD screens were totally blank: everyone had a completely free hand.

BMW officials found themselves with a near-sacred British icon on their hands but with little or no experience of operating at these lofty levels; the encounter with Rover, which was just about to explode into public dissent, was of little help in knowing how to handle Rolls-Royce. In any case, what BMW had in mind for the top marque was to set up a quasi-autonomous company that would be seen as independent and not sullied by visible connections with volume market vehicles, even BMW vehicles. This tallied conveniently with the famous maxim of Sir Henry Royce (the engineer in the Rolls and Royce duo) which BMW personnel were fond of quoting: "Strive for perfection in everything you do," urged the motto. "Take the best which exists and make it better: when it does not exist, design it."

Taking this advice to heart, the Rolls-Royce teams straightaway knew that there was no existing chassis or vehicle structure that was anywhere near good enough to be a potential Rolls-Royce, however much it could be improved: a totally fresh body and chassis design was therefore essential. Yet when it came to mechanical hardware there was much more in the cupboard to which the second of Royce's exhortations could legitimately be applied. BMW was a world-class designer and constructor of engines of the very highest calibre, including a highly praised V12 for McLaren; on chassis systems it was an acknowledged expert, especially when it came to the marrying of electronic and mechanical disciplines, and as a company it had a reputation for quality second only to that of its arch rival, Mercedes-Benz.

Thus it was that the Rolls-Royce project team made the key engineering and marketing decisions that would shape the new organisation's first product, codenamed R-01. The car had to be very big, and particularly very tall, to recapture the grandeur and the stately superiority enjoyed in their time by classic Rolls-Royce models such as the Silver Cloud and Phantom – and for a car of such size to be strong, safe and sufficiently powerful and economical it would have to have a radical, much lighter form of body construction. After some study, it was decided to employ an aluminium space frame structure with mainly aluminium outer panels: conveniently, this tied in with another programme BMW was embarking on, that to build the Z8 luxury sports car, also an aluminium space frame vehicle.

The choice of engine was an easier one. Twelve cylinders were essential for the requisite refinement, plenty of easily-accessible torque was more important than peak power, and the horrified reactions of Bentley drivers to the earlier turbocharged BMW V8 in the Mulsanne meant that any form of forced induction was out of the question. All this pointed to a large-capacity, low-revving V12, and BMW set about developing just such a unit to the very highest standards and with every sophistication in its already very fat patent book.

While the engineers were busy, so too were the property negotiators. Rolls-Royce needed a new home for everything it did: administration,

"The car had to be very big, and particularly very tall, to recapture the grandeur and the stately superiority enjoyed in their time by classic Rolls-Royce models such as the Silver Cloud and Phantom, the cars identified as being the archetypal Rolls-Royces"

Inspiration: the Silver Cloud (right) was remembered with particular affection by potential Rolls-Royce buyers. Its influence on the Phantom design can be seen in deep rear pillars and bold, upright grille

The Rolls-Royce factory at Goodwood in England performs final assembly on the aluminium space fame bodies shipped in from Germany. Leather and wood trim is hand crafted on site in Goodwood but most components are of German origin

"There has always been an element of corporate vanity in the desire to control firms that build cars for the super rich, and rarely have the returns from this notoriously fickle market allowed the companies to become as rich as their customers. But if anyone can make it work, it must be BMW"

sales, manufacturing, distribution, servicing. To everyone's surprise it was announced in May 2000 that Rolls-Royce would establish itself at Goodwood in southern England, on land owned by Lord March, the car-enthusiast aristocrat who had become a central figure in the historic racing car world with his annual Festival of Speed and Goodwood Revival meetings. The location was a surprising one for an assembly plant as the region had no industry whatsoever, though later Rolls-Royce was to attract craftsmen for its timber shops from the south coast boatbuilding yards in nearby Chichester and Portsmouth. The skills of sailmakers were found to be useful in the leather and upholstery shops too.

The factory itself had to be partially sunk in a hollow below ground level so as not to impinge on the rural skyline: the complex was designed by a top-level architectural firm and featured a living roof stocked with thousands of sedum plants, attractive with star-shaped flowers . Another notable feature was the use of the lake for cooling the air supply to the building.

The car that was finally revealed – with some ceremony, too – on January 1st 2003 stunned every onlooker and indeed everyone who subsequently picked up a newspaper or magazine report. Christened Phantom – officials

said it was Rolls-Royce's most cherished name – Ian Cameron's design caused gasps of amazement not just for its sheer size but also for the bold, not to say severe, reinterpretation of the Rolls-Royce theme for the 21st century. The car stood wide and tall, seemingly bigger than anything else on the road, and its huge, shiny Rolls-Royce grille was thrust forward in aggressive defiance of any concession to aerodynamics, looking like the Parthenon on the edge of the Acropolis. It was notable how many design cues had been picked up from the Silver Cloud: the tapered, boat-like tail, the very thick rear pillars offering privacy to the occupants, the spreading wake of the grille as it moved the length of the bonnet. A major break with tradition (or at least the last half-century of tradition) were the so-called 'coach' rear doors: hinged at the back, they allowed dignified movement for guests of all ages entering the spacious rear compartment. An intriguing exterior touch, and something in which the engineers expressed great pride, was the double-R logo in the centre of each wheel: these were weighted and set in a bearing so that the letters always remained upright.

In terms of engineering, Rolls-Royce announced the engine as a 6.75 litre direct injection V12, claiming that it was pure

coincidence that the capacity of the expanded BMW unit had ended up at precisely the size Rolls-Royce had been using for 30 years or more. The Phantom's interior was remarkable in how it managed to tactfully conceal its high technology: 21st century gadgetry could be working unseen behind exquisitely grained and inlaid wood panels of an antique façade. The instruments, traditionally few in number on a Rolls-Royce, included a speedometer but not a rev counter: instead, a power reserve gauge was provided, and so much surplus energy did the 460 bhp engine have that the needle rarely moved far from the 100 per cent mark.

On the more serious note of economics, the Phantom's space frame construction offered numerous advantages beyond those of lightweight and good crash performance. It is an easy structure to modify or adapt, providing a very real possibility of bodywork variations at low cost and in small or larger series. One example was given at the Geneva show in March 2004 when Rolls-Royce showed the

glamorous 100EX four-seater convertible concept, complete with V16 engine.

Rolls-Royce has always expressed confidence that the worldwide supply of wealthy individuals willing to spend €400,000 on a car will provide sufficient demand to keep its new factory busy at its maximum capacity of 20 cars a week. Order-take over the first 18 months was judged by some commentators to have been disappointing, but BMW is resolute that it is in this for the long term. Like Rolls-Royce power outputs in the past, BMW would not disclose the size of its investment in the company. There has always been an element of corporate vanity in the desire to control firms that build cars for the super rich, and rarely have the returns from this notoriously fickle market allowed the companies to become as rich as their customers. But if anyone can make it work, it must be BMW.

The 100EX Centenary Experimental Car shown In Geneva in March 2004 could point the way to a future Rolls-Royce convertible. The rear decking shows a marine influence, while the car's space frame construction makes body variations relatively easy to produce

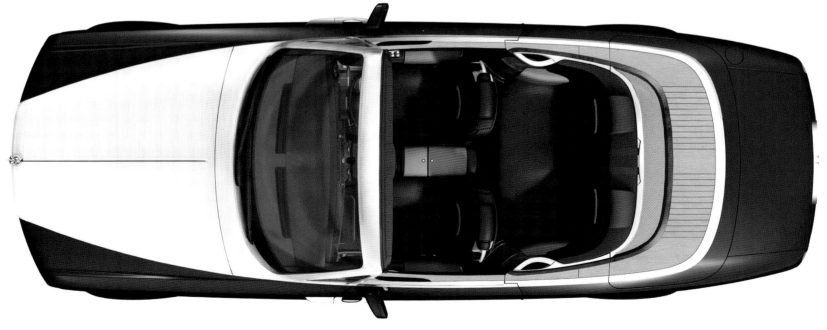

1-upmanship

BMW rounds out its range by returning to its small-car roots with the 1 Series

1 Series (E82)

→ Launched in 2004
→ First small BMW since
   '02 Series of 1966
→ Only rear-wheel drive car
   in small segment
→ Five-door hatch first to launch
→ Engines shared with 3 Series
→ Top model is 163 bhp diesel
→ Other body styles scheduled
→ Priced below 3 Series, level
   with Audi A3

When BMW disposed of Rover in the spring of 2000, it was relieved to be getting rid of the major headache of managing a chronically loss-making, time-consuming conglomerate. But it was also saying goodbye to the prospect of medium-sized volume models to bridge the considerable gap between the MINI, then at an advanced stage of development, and the lower rungs of the Compact and 3 Series ladder.

This posed the risk that, a few years down the line, contented MINI owners wishing to upgrade within the BMW family would find the size and price gap to the 3 Series too great and would be forced to defect to a competitor model such as the Audi A3 or Volkswagen Golf.

Leaving such a chasm in the product offering would not just risk losing upwardly mobile MINI customers: it would also be wasting an opportunity to draw in new customers from other brands. Even while the dust was still settling from the Rover pull-out, BMW officials were busy brushing off a different kind of dust – the deposit that had gathered on plans, discarded after the Rover acquisition, to study the feasibility of a new, smaller high performance model to revive the spirit of the 2002.

BMW's engineering chief Wolfgang Reitzle was said to be especially keen on the idea, but the plan was deferred and the Compact was

launched as a stopgap: after 1994, with Rover on board and supplying the feeder models, there would no longer be any need for a new small BMW, so the plan was quietly forgotten.

Six years later, after the exit from Rover, any engineering elements in the early '90s proposals would of course have long since been consigned to the museum or the crusher. However, the principle remained the same: a BMW offering in the Golf/Audi A3 sector would be the only rear wheel drive model in the segment and could exploit this advantage to draw in keen, and therefore frequently wealthier buyers, meaning that a healthy price premium could be charged.

Rear-wheel drive layout gives the 1 Series a very different profile to conventional lower-medium sized cars

E82: NEW 1 SERIES

Specifications	116i	120i	118d	120d
Engine				
Engine type	Inline 4-cylinder	Inline 4-cylinder	Inline 4-cylinder direct injection turbodiesel	Inline 4-cylinder direct injection turbodiesel
Bore & stroke, mm	72 x 84	90 x 84	90 x 84	90 x 84
Capacity, cc	1596	1995	1995	1995
Valves	16	16	16	16
Valve actuation	Dohc	Dohc; double Vanos, Valvetronic fully variable valve timing and lift	Dohc	Dohc
Compression ratio	10.2:1	10.5:1	17.2:1	17.0:1
Fuelling	Bosch electronic fuel injection	Bosch electronic fuel injection	Digital diesel injection; turbocharger, intercooler	Digital diesel injection; variable geometry turbocharger, intercooler
Max power, bhp @ rpm	115@6000	150@6200	122@4000	163@4000
Max torque, Nm @ rpm	150@4300	200@3600	280@2000	340@2000
Transmission				
Manual transmission	5-speed	6-speed	6-speed	6-speed
Automatic	Not available	6-speed		6-speed
Drive	Rear wheels	Rear wheels	Rear wheels	Rear wheels
Chassis				
Front suspension	Double-joint thrust-rod spring strut axle in aluminium	Double-joint thrust-rod spring strut axle in aluminium	Double-joint thrust-rod spring strut axle in aluminium	Double-joint thrust-rod spring strut axle in aluminium
Rear suspension	Independent 5-arm axle, steel-lightweight construction	Independent 5-arm axle, steel-lightweight construction	Independent 5-arm axle, steel-lightweight construction	Independent 5-arm axle, steel-lightweight construction
Braking	Discs, servo assisted, ABS, CBC	Discs, servo assisted, ABS, CBC	Discs, servo assisted, ABS, CBC	Discs, servo assisted, ABS, CBC
Steering	Rack and pinion, power assisted	Rack and pinion, power assisted	Rack and pinion, power assisted	Rack and pinion, power assisted
Wheels	6.0 x 16	6.5 x 16	6.0 x 16	6.5 x 16
Tyres	195/60 R 16	195/55 R 16	185/60 R 16	195/55 R 16
Body				
Structure	Steel monocoque	Steel monocoque	Steel monocoque	Steel monocoque
Wheelbase, mm	2660	2660	2660	2660
Track F/R, mm	1494/1507	1484/1497	1494/1507	1484/1484
Length, mm	4227	4227	4227	4227
Width, mm	1751	1751	1751	1751
Height, mm	1430	1430	1430	1430
Kerb weight, kg	1280	1336	1385	1415
Fuel tank capacity, lit	50	50	50	50
Performance				
Max speed, km/h	202	218	202	221
0-100km/h, sec	10.8	8.7	10.0	7.9
Fuel consumption , lit/100km	7.5	7.4	5.6	5.7
Marketing				
Launch date	9/2004	9/2004	11/2004	9/2004
Pricing, €	19,800	23,600	21,900	24,400

Relatively large grilles and headlights ensure a strong BMW identity on the company's first small car for 30 years

Unexpected: the five-door hatchback of the 1 series launch model is an entirely new shape for BMW. Later editions will include Coupé and Cabriolet

So it was not long before BMW officially announced its intention to launch a new, smaller model: the company even stated that it would be known as the 1 Series, contrary to the word on the industry grapevine which suggested that 2 Series would be chosen because of the emotional link with the fondly remembered '02 models of the late 1960s and early 1970s. BMW said that it needed a new plant to cater for the many new models due to come on stream; soon, Leipzig/Halle was chosen from a list of five sites, only three of which were in Germany. BMW practice is always to put new models into experienced plants, so the 1 Series was earmarked for Regensburg and €1 billion was put aside for the building of the fifth-generation 3 Series in Leipzig from 2005.

A strong hint as to the likely final look of the 1 Series came in March 2002 when BMW showed the CS1 design study at the Geneva motor show. The smart, gold-coloured four-seater convertible was well received and BMW dealers started

"In terms of style the 1 Series represented a moderate, rather than extreme, interpretation of BMW's new-era design philosophy"

receiving enquiries. First official details of the five-door hatchback version of the 1 Series were published in spring 2004: compared with potential competitors such as the VW Golf, Alfa Romeo 147 and Audi A3, the design showed very different proportions, with short front and rear overhangs, a long bonnet and a cabin that appeared to be pushed far back, a natural consequence of its rear-wheel drive configuration.

Engines, said the announcement, would comprise 1.6 and 2.0 litre petrol units and two different power ratings of a two-litre turbo diesel, while examination of the dimensions provided some interesting comparisons with current and historic BMW models. In the metal, the car looked surprisingly long, yet at 4227 mm from bumper to bumper it was 35 mm shorter than the Compact

which, in isolation, seemed shorter; the 3 Series saloon, a clear 244 mm longer, seemed much bigger, but it was a surprise to find the neat-looking 2002 in fact just 3 mm smaller.

In terms of style the 1 Series represented a moderate, rather than extreme, interpretation of BMW's new-era design philosophy. Its most distinctive features, apart from its high sides and long, low-roofed cabin, were its large BMW grilles, its wraparound headlights, and the twin creases running down the side. The upper crease, running just above the door handles, gave a clear demarcation between vertical and horizontal, with the lower one a gently curving scoop to give interesting surfacing to the car's sides, in the successful style of the Z4 roadster. The rear was perhaps less distinctive and, apart from the BMW roundel (which also acts as the

boot release) was uncomfortably similar to the Opel Astra.

The philosophy was explained by design project leader Kevin Rice as follows: "The key to the BMW 1 Series design was to redefine the benchmark with a unique premium product in its category. It communicates BMW's 'Driving Pleasure' philosophy with its proportions, surfaces and details, creating a dynamic statement. The car embodies the typical characteristics of a BMW, but in a smaller package that indicates its balance of practicality and sporting ability. The driving experience stands out in its class and we wanted the car's looks to do the same."

Generating that driving experience was the classic BMW layout of a front engine and rear-wheel drive, with independent suspension all round and the engine set well back in the chassis to ensure 50/50 weight distribution. To save weight most of the suspension components were made of aluminium and at the rear a five-link setup was selected as preferable to double wishbones; subframes at both ends helped isolate road noise. Dynamic stability control, with its subsidiary cornering brake control and dynamic traction control for sportier driving, were standard

on all versions. Yet despite the extensive use of light metal the most modest of 1 Series versions, the 116i, weighed over 1200 kg; 30 years ago, even the heaviest of the '02 series, the 2002 tii, weighed less than a tonne – a reflection of how much safer and how much better-equipped cars have become in the intervening period.

The four different engines appeared to be carefully targeted at different potential buyer groups. The 116i provided a tempting entry point to the BMW brand at just under €20,000: even then, it still had double Vanos variable valve timing for its 115 bhp engine, though it was alone in the launch range with a five-speed transmission. The diesel 118i, likewise, appeared designed to draw in sales from medium-powered diesel competitors, giving 122 bhp from its two-litre, direct injection engine and featuring a six-speed gearbox for a convincing 5.6 litre consumption figure. Next up in power and intended perhaps to attract buyers downsizing from larger cars came the 120i, its fully Valvetronic two-litre engine benefiting from improved manifolding and ECU technology to gain 5 bhp over its 135 in the larger 318i; this engine also featured balancer shafts for smooth running.

Unusually, the top engine in the launch line-up was a diesel. Thanks to an improved 1600-bar

Role model: the CS1 concept study of 2002 gave a strong indication of the look of the future 1 Series Cabriolet

pressure second-generation common rail injection system and variable nozzle turbocharger, the same basic engine as the 118i was lifted to no less than 163 bhp, with 340 Nm torque: in the 1415 kg vehicle it gave 100 km/h acceleration in 7.9 seconds and a maximum speed of 221 – better performance than many sports hatchbacks. The 120d was quieter than other diesels in the class, claimed BMW, because of the engine's four injection pulses per combustion stroke; balancer shafts were fitted to minimise vibration and in cold weather the glow plugs in the cylinders would be energised as soon as the driver opened the door, rather than having to wait for them to turn on the ignition.

Two interesting details characterised the electrical system. A sensor monitored the state of charge of the battery to ensure there would always be enough energy to restart the car, raising engine idle speed or shutting down non-essential loads if it detected a low level of charge. The light control module, finally, would monitor all the bulbs in the system and, should one fail, it could command a suitable substitute (such as a tail light when the indicator that side had failed) to take over until a new bulb had been fitted. The brake lights themselves marked a useful step forward in safety, incorporating brake force display to signal with an extra panel of brake lights when the ABS was activated or braking deceleration exceeded 5 ms^{-2}.

BMW itself was candid in admitting that because of its rear-wheel drive layout the 1 Series did not have as much boot space as comparable mainstream cars; however it could offer large-car sophistication rarely seen in the Golf class. Features such as xenon lights, parking sensors and automatic climate control were all in the specification, whether as standard equipment or options. Optional on all models was iDrive, which came with a folding colour screen and was listed as part of either the Professional or the Business satellite navigation packages at up to €3,000. This was the first time the cost of iDrive had been isolated in this way: on the 5, 6 and 7 Series it had always been standard.

By August 2004, seven weeks before the on-sale date, BMW had already received more than 10,000 orders for the initial five-door hatchback, and this model was just the first of several 1 Series body styles. Expected in 2005 and 2006 are a three door hatchback with a coupé flavour, a convertible and, just possibly, a version majoring on practicality. Each derivative is likely to repeat the same pattern of anticipation and demand, fuelling an expansion of this newly created premium small car sector by about 80 per cent by 2010. The history of other, larger segments supports this, and BMW, as the creator of the genre, is in pole position to benefit.

38

Full throttle into the future

Premium products in all market sectors build BMW a strong position for years to come

"We will keep our foot on the accelerator pedal, we will continue to forge ahead," declared BMW chief executive Dr Helmut Panke when announcing the group's results for 2003/4. "It's straight ahead – as usual."

But in the highly animated Panke's driving manual, acceleration does not just mean gently easing up to everyone else's speed, setting the cruise control and relaxing in the driver's seat as the kilometres clock up. For him, it's real foot-to-the-floor, take it to the red line M5 stuff, making the most of the clear road ahead to increase his lead over the rest of the field.

To the other competitors it must seem that BMW is on a different track altogether. If it's a racetrack it is a wide, smooth one, with fast, well-sighted bends, clearly-defined braking points, a few chicanes and eager, cheering crowds. No need for pit stops, safety cars or run-off areas here: everything's under control. If it's an Autobahn it is broad and straight and clear, and it certainly does not have any speed restrictions.

But the rest appear to be running on an entirely different road system, one that's full of potholes and bumps, road works, diversions and delays. Often, it's not even parallel. The signposts are not always easily visible, and all too often an attempt at a shortcut does no more than get you back to where you first started.

There would seem to be one set of rules for BMW (together with a select few including Porsche and perhaps Honda) and a different set for the rest; BMW having the skill to avoid the holes in the road that others drive straight into, BMW having the knack of choosing the clear route when all the others are jammed.

What, therefore, is so different about BMW? What has it done that is so special?

Eberhard von Kuenheim, BMW's chairman throughout its quarter-century of astonishing growth, denies with his characteristic modesty that there is any special secret. "We were just doing our duty," he says. What perhaps he could not see, simply because he was so close to it all and indeed was responsible for subconsciously creating it, was the special culture that marked BMW out as different. It is a question of attitude, of belief, of a commitment that goes beyond the bounds of the normal working day and extends into animated after-hours conversations in bars and restaurants.

That is the kind of energy that produces ideas, visions and a powerful feeling of direction and common purpose. It is the buzz that inspired the setting up of the FIZ engineering and research centre, BMW Technik GmbH and BMW M GmbH, formerly the Motorsport division – the three constantly-evolving organisations whose unstoppable stream of ideas and innovations have been crucial to building up BMW's huge technological momentum.

BMW is an organisation driven by engineering and ideals, not by delusions of world domination or extravagant lifestyles for its bosses. Cash does enter into the equation, but only in the sense that BMW has always been adept at obtaining very good prices for the kinds of products it likes to build. This win-win position, together with top-class management and rigorous but not restrictive internal procedures, has given the company an unbroken run of profit since the early 1960s, with only the few years of the Rover disaster taking the shine off its sparkling financial record.

But it was not always so. Weak management in the 1950s saw BMW fail to take advantage of the West German economic miracle that propelled other companies into permanent profits, and at the dramatic dénouement in 1959 BMW was a millimetre away from being auctioned off as bankrupt stock and turned into a Mercedes-Benz nut-and-bolt business. Then, an enlightened investor, Herbert Quandt, spotted the potential in BMW, developed a vision of how it could evolve in the future, and hired Eberhard von Kuenheim – who went on to become arguably the most successful auto industry boss in living memory – to put that vision into practice. Together, the two forged the foundations of modern-day BMW, the interlocking template of distinct body designs sharing a common pool of outstanding engines, a formula which provided not just impeccable technical integrity but a sound business base too. That base was secure enough to anchor the exhilarating but never reckless expansion of the 1970s and 1980s, culminating in the triumphant launch of German's first V12 engine for half a century.

Moreover, that base was solid enough not to be toppled by the only truly big mistake BMW made: the takeover of Rover in 1994. The original Touring, the Z1, the 850, the C1 scooter later on – these were all intelligent products that failed to strike lucky: Rover was a strategic disaster of an altogether higher order. The move on Rover, born not so much out of delusions of grandeur as out of BMW's misguided notion that it could not survive without the synergies of a volume business alongside it, was, ironically, the decision that could easily have pulled its house down. That it did not topple BMW must be put down to the innate strength of its management. Their only real failing was that they didn't know how to cope with failing: after three decades of straight profits, the concepts of inefficiency, adversity and incompetence simply weren't in the BMW brand book. BMW was rocked rather than brought down, losing some of its key managers out of principle rather than necessity. But, crucially, it showed the world that its attention had not been diverted and that, despite the recriminations surrounding the English Patient, as far as the core BMW brand was concerned it was business as usual. In fact, two of the most successful of all BMW designs – the E39 5 series and the E46 3 Series – were developed against the background of the darkest of the Rover dark days.

Less than a year after BMW had rid itself of Rover it was its old confident self again. No longer did it need cover-ups or double-speak to explain its actions; no longer did it have to deal with messy politics, and at last it could get back to the more comfortable territory of engineering. In June 2001 group chairman professor Joachim Milberg proudly announced a new product and marketing offensive aimed at increasing sales by one third and boosting turnover to 50 billion euro over the next ten years. This programme would cost €16 billion, said Milberg, with €10 billion of that being spent on the development of 20 new models and three new-generation engines during that period. It was one of the biggest investment programmes the company had ever announced and came as a defiant expression of independence and self-assurance aimed at those who had maintained BMW had been critically wounded by the Rover episode and was incapable of prospering on its own.

Milberg was clearly back on the gas, and his message was the most explicit full-throttle signal that anybody could possibly have given. Three years into his 10-year plan, BMW has already launched three wholly incremental model ranges – the X3, the 6 Series and, most recently, the 1 Series. The 7 and 5 Series have been renewed and the big-volume 3 Series – which represents over half BMW's business – will be replaced in 2005. This, coupled with the introduction of numerous derivatives such as the M3 CSL, means that BMW will have launched more in three years than it used to launch in a decade.

The heat is on. The development engineers are working overtime; the factory technicians are working round the clock. In 2003 they made a record number of cars: 928,000 BMWs, 175,000 Minis and 502 Rolls-Royces; 2004 looks like being even better, 2005 – when more 1 Series derivatives and the new core-model 3 Series come into play – even more so. Without any question, the BMW is not only firing on all cylinders but it is at the peak of its efficiency.

But just how long can it keep up this full-throttle blast? Is the engine being pushed so hard that it's at risk of overheating? And how long will the fuel in the tank last?

While BMW would not disagree that it is pushing hard and working fast, it would observe that the fuel in its tank is different to that which other carmakers are running on. BMW's fuel, it suggests, is renewable and therefore sustainable. Forecasts BMW quotes in support of its all-premium brand strategy – unique in the auto industry – point to a 50 per cent increase in the market for premium cars over the next decade, compared with just half that increase for volume-branded vehicles. BMW would be a direct beneficiary of this, though even with a one-third increase in its output it would see its share of the expanded premium market diluted slightly.

Historical evidence strongly supports BMW's contention. Since the late 1980s premium brands have steadily increased their share of successive segments of the market at the expense of volume producers. The process began – in Europe, at least – in the so-called E segment, which today is completely dominated by Mercedes-Benz, with the E-Class, BMW with its

5 Series, and the Audi A6. Twenty years ago, volume makers like Ford, General Motors, Renault, Citroen and Peugeot all had big sellers in this sector. In the USA there has been a parallel migration away from the big-volume domestic products like the Ford Taurus.

The process has steadily been repeated lower down the market in Europe. The top sellers in the next category down come from BMW, Mercedes and Audi: the Ford Mondeo, Renault Laguna and Opel Vectra are nowhere to be seen: 10 years ago, these were the dominant forces in the sector.

One rung further down, the model choice is more diverse but the trends towards what we could label premiumisation are equally clear. The Audi A3 has made a strong impact as a classier alternative to a VW Golf; the Mercedes A-Class has a superior badge to a Toyota Corolla or Peugeot 307, the Alfa 147 carries more status than a Ford Focus. This is the broad target area of the BMW 1 Series, though it will be something of a unique position with its rear-wheel drive and sportier flavour and is likely to draw in customers from all directions.

The success of the BMW-inspired MINI has already shown the potential for a high-quality, premium-badged small car: buyers are willing – eager, even – to pay extra for exclusivity in looks, in performance, in workmanship and in status. What the 1 Series lacks in terms of extreme stand-out MINI-type looks it more than makes up for with its engineering configuration. This alone is sure to be a major attraction for the performance-focused driver; others will be drawn to it simply because it is a BMW, once again demonstrating the power of the brand.

The big question, not just for the 1 Series but for BMW and indeed premium brands in general, must be this: how far can the premiumisation process go?

Taking the process to its logical conclusion, what happens when all the products in the sector are premium models? Will consumer preferences follow the fashion industry, where it is often impossible to sell clothes which do not carry a credible designer label? Or will a 'super-premium' brand push itself up above those that are merely premium and start the whole process over again

"The BMW's manager's only real failing was that they didn't know how to cope with failing: after three decades of straight profits, the concepts of inefficiency, adversity and incompetence simply weren't in the BMW brand book"

"Even without its blue and white badge a BMW would still be BMW. You can tell from the way it feels, the way it drives, the way it sounds, the way it responds. You can't say that about any other carmaker's products. That, at the end of the day, must be the most powerful selling point of all"

– just like when platinum credit cards took over from gold ones?

One immediate consequence of everyone being on an equal premium footing is that price competition – the very thing that premium branding is intended to make unnecessary – will begin to become a factor again and margins will become eroded. Perhaps then we will see the emergence of the automotive equivalent of the supermarkets' own-brand cornflakes, packaged in an unadorned white box and sold at half the price of the heavily promoted major-brand equivalent.

The auto industry has received its own warning about this phenomenon in recent years when the lower-priced Skoda models began steadily stealing sales from their Volkswagen equivalents, which share the same engineering underneath but which are promoted as high-quality, high-image products for a more discerning clientele. For the Volkswagen group this was a disturbing trend as the VW-brand products are designed to earn significantly higher margins.

The Skoda experience underlines a very important dictum in the marketing of premium products – not just cars, but any premium product. For a premium position to be sustainable over the long term, it must be backed by a genuine, lasting, credible benefit to the consumer. This could be in the form of a distinctive style, visibly better quality, a unique technical feature or consistently superior performance: the snob value of the label itself does not count as this can evaporate overnight, as Cadillac proved in the 1970s when it placed its grille on tinny little Chevrolets and convinced no one.

BMW has a huge advantage in all this as it is accepted everywhere without any hesitation as a genuine premium brand, up there with Mercedes-Benz, ahead of Audi, Jaguar, Lexus and Cadillac; wannabee premium producers such as Volvo, Alfa Romeo and Honda are not in the same league. BMW has the further advantage of a very strong brand image centred around powerful engines, responsive handling and a sporty temperament: quality and safety are of course taken for granted. The clear brand picture is especially useful when tackling new market segments: when BMW announced its intention to launch the premium sports utility which became the X5, potential buyers knew that the vehicle would be good to drive and set new dynamic standards for the class.

From MINI, through 1 Series to 7 Series and up to the absolute top-segment Rolls-Royce, and from the X3 and X5 via the Z4 to the 6 Series, it is tempting to think that BMW has all the bases covered. Indeed, it probably does: the only conspicuous absence is any form of multi-seater family transport – but BMW is sure to plug this gap with a model which, true to type, redefines expectations in the sector.

Once again, innovation will be the key to bringing the BMW driving experience to different people and different corners of the car market, whichever way technology and transportation evolve. The desire to own a BMW will be felt just as acutely in the expanding territories of China and the Far East as in car-saturated Europe, North America and Japan: BMW's strong brand identity will ensure it a distinctiveness and a cachet – and thus a profitable position – that only the select few enjoy.

Even without its blue and white badge a BMW would still be BMW. You can tell from the way it feels, the way it drives, the way it sounds, the way it responds. You can't say that about any other carmaker's products. That, at the end of the day, must be the most powerful selling point of all – and the surest pointer to a full-throttle future, without overheating.

Appendices

Appendix A: What the E numbers mean

Confused by BMW's numbering system? Each vehicle type or family is developed under a code number (E stands for *Entwicklung*, or development), and here is the list so far

Designation	Model	Years
Type 114	'02 Series	67-76*
Type 118	"Neue Klasse" 1500-1800 Series	62-70
Type 121	2000 saloons	66-70
E3	2500/2800 saloons, later versions	68-77
E9	2000-2800 coupés, later versions	68-74
E12	1st 5 Series	75-81
E21	1st 3 Series	76-83
E23	1st 7 Series	78-87
E24	1st 6 Series	77-89
E25	Turbo concept	72
E26	M1	78-81
E28	2nd 5 Series	82-88
E30	2nd 3 Series	84-92
E31	8 Series	91-97
E32	2nd 7 Series	86-94
E32/2	2nd 7 Series long wheelbase	87-94
E34	3rd 5 Series	89-95
E36	3rd 3 Series	92-99
E36/5	1st Compact	94-00
E36/7	Z3/M Roadster/M Coupé	95-02
E38	3rd 7 Series	94-01
E38/2	3rd 7 Series long wheelbase	94-01
E38/3	3rd 7 Series Protection	98-01
E38/L7	3rd 7 Series super long wheelbase	99-01
E39	4th 5 Series	96-04
E46	4th 3 Series	99 onwards
E46/5	2nd Compact	01 onwards
E52	Z8	00-03
E53	X5	99 onwards
E60	5th 5 Series	04 onwards
E61	5th 5 Series Touring	04 onwards
E63	2nd 6 Series	03 onwards
E65	4th 7 Series	01 onwards
E66	4th 7 Series long wheelbase	02 onwards
E67	4th 7 Series Protection	01 onwards
E68	4th 7 Series Hydrogen	Under development
E82	1 Series	04 onwards
E83	X3	03 onwards
E85	Z4	03 onwards
R50	MINI One/Cooper	01 onwards
R52	MINI Convertible	04 onwards
R53	MINI Cooper S	02 onwards
R-01	Rolls-Royce Phantom	03 onwards

*No formal designations existed before 1967

Appendix B: BMW engine codes

BMW employs a complex system of engine codes designating every variant and every application. Here we list the main basic engine types and their principal applications

Engine code	Cylinders	Valves	Capacity	Used in	Production years	Number made	Comments
M10	Inline 4	8	1499 – 1990	114, 118, E9, E12, E21, E28, E30	62-88	3,202,434	The mainstay four-cylinder for over 20 years, the engine that gave BMW its sporty reputation. First with fuel injection
M20	Inline 6	12	1990 – 2494	E12, E30, E30 (Z1), E34	77-91	2,317,907	Inline sohc small block six. Belt-driven overhead camshaft
M21	Inline 6	12	2443	E28, E34	83-91	254,684	BMW's first diesel, first-ever six-cylinder car diesel. Turbo version came first
M30	Inline 6	12	2693-3430	E3, E9, E12, E23, E24, E28, E32, E34	68-92	1,415,729	The original big six, developed from the M10. Chain-driven single overhead camshaft
M40	Inline 4	8	1596 – 1977	E30, E36	88-94	844,705	Successor to the M10. Belt-driven overhead camshaft
M41	Inline 4	8	1665	E36	95-00	42,007	Four-cylinder turbo diesel used in Compact and 3 Series
M42	Inline 4	16	1796	E30	90-91	269,744	Dohc 16-valve version of M40
M43	Inline 4	8	1596-1895	E36, E36 (Z3), E46	94-00	1,240,601	Upgrade of M43. Mainstay four cylinder for 3 Series
M44	Inline 4	16	1895	E36, E36 (Z3)	96-99	209,389	Dohc 16-valve version of M43
M47	Inline 4	16	1995	E46	00 onwards	695,957	Four cylinder direct-injection turbo diesel used in Compact, 3 Series and 1 series. Numerous upgrades, coded M47U
M50	Inline 6	24	1991	E34, E36	91-96	1,068,844	Dohc 24 valves. First modern small six.
M51	Inline 6	12	2494	E34, E36, E38, E39	93-99	231,520	Six-cylinder swirl-chamber diesel, turbo (M51T) or turbo intercooler (M51S)
M52	Inline 6	24	1991-2793	E36, E36 (Z3), E38, E39, E46	95-00	1,592,915	Dohc 24-valve six with single Vanos variable valve timing
M54	Inline 6	24	2171-2979	E36 (Z3), E39, E46, E60, E61, E65/E66, E83, E85	01 onwards	1,437,531	Dohc 24-valve six with double Vanos, successor to M52
M57	Inline 6	24	2926-2993	E39, E46, E60, E61, E65/E66, E83	00 onwards	433,151	Direct-injection common rail six-cylinder diesel. First universally accepted high performance diesel
M60	V8	32	2997-3982	E32, E34, E38	92-96	182,704	First BMW V8s, as fitted to E32
M62	V8	32	3498-4398	E38, E39	96-04	381,436	Upgraded V8s. Used by Morgan
M67	V8	32	3600	E38, E65	99 onwards	5,199	First diesel V8. New standards of smoothness, power
M70	V12	24	4988	E31, E32	88-94	68,780	First V12: 2 valves per cylinder
M73	V12	24	5379	E38	95-01		Enlarged version of M70
N40	Inline 4	16	1596-1895	E46	02 onwards	8,993	New-generation dohc 16-valve, used in 3 Series
N42	Inline 4	16	1796-1995	E46	01 onwards	344,360	New-generation dohc four cylinder with double Vanos and Valvetronic
N45	Inline 4	16	1596	E87	04 onwards	–	New-generation 1.6, dohc double Vanos
N46	Inline 4	16	1796-1995	E46, E87	04 onwards	–	1.8 to 2.0 litre dohc four cylinder with double Vanos and Valvetronic
N62	V8	32	3600-4799	E60, E61, E63, E64, E65/E66, E53	02 onwards	115,605	32 valve double Vanos Valvetronic V8. First seen on E65 7 Series
N73	V12	48	5972	E65/E66, R-01	03 onwards	5328	Direct injection V12 with double Vanos and Valvetronic, used in 760i and Rolls-Royce
S14	Inline 4	16	2302-2496	E30, M3	87-91	21,715	16-valve four cylinder, derived from S38
S38	Inline 6	24	3453-3535	E24, E34	87-92	20,547	Dohc 24 valve six, used in E34 M5
S39	Inline 6	24	3795	E34	92-95		Dohc 24 valve six, used in later E34 M5
S50	Inline 6	24	2990	E36, E36 Roadster/ Coupé)	92-00	19,780	Dohc 24-valve six on E36 M3. First BMW (M engine with Vanos
S52	Inline 6	24	3201	E36	95-99	49,355	Larger capacity version of S50. Double Vanos, individual throttle butterflies
S54	Inline 6	24	3246	E36 (M Roadster/ Coupé), E46	01 onwards	62,669	
S62	V8	32	4941	E39, E52	99-03	20,185	Dohc double Vanos. Used in E39 M5
S70	V12	24	5576	E31	93-97	1,313	24-valve V12 used in 850. Basis of 48-valve Vanos engine developed for McLaren
W10	Inline 4	16	1598	R50	01 onwards	295,186	Sohc 16 valve for MINI
W11	Inline 4	16	1598	R53	02 onwards	78,325	Supercharged version of 10 for MINI Cooper S
W17	Inline 4	16	1364	R50	03 onwards	13,314	1.4 litre direct injection turbo diesel supplied by Toyota for MINI One D
R6	Inline 6	24		E63	04 onwards	–	New generation lightweight Sixes with Valvetronic and magnesium block

All production figures are to the end of 2003. Source BMW

Appendix C: Currency conversions at the then-prevailing rate

year	German Mark (DM)	euro	US dollar	UK pounds
1971	100		27	11
	1,000		275	115
	10,000		2747	1148
1973	100		31	13
	1,000		312	133
	10,000		3120	1329
1975	100		36	16
	1,000		363	157
	10,000		3626	1574
1977	100		43	25
	1,000		426	250
	10,000		4263	2495
1979	100		55	27
	1,000		549	270
	10,000		5488	2704
1981	100		51	21
	1,000		506	213
	10,000		5063	2126
1983	100		42	26
	1,000		421	259
	10,000		4212	2595
1985	100		32	27
	1,000		315	275
	10,000		3152	2746
1987	100		52	35
	1,000		521	350
	10,000		5214	3499
1989	100		57	31
	1,000		567	311
	10,000		5669	3111
1991	100		67	35
	1,000		671	346
	10,000		6711	3455
1993	100		61	41
	1,000		611	407
	10,000		6109	4067
1995	100		64	41
	1,000		644	411
	10,000		6435	4115
1997	100		65	38
	1,000		649	385
	10,000		6489	3848
	100,000		64893	38475
1999	100	71	60	36
	1,000	710	601	362
	10,000	7098	6006	3620
	100,000	70976	60060	36198
2001	100	46	48	32
	1,000	458	484	323
	10,000	4579	4838	3229
	100,000	45788	48379	32293
2003	100	56	54	33
	1,000	562	536	333
	10,000	5624	5362	3331
	100,000	56240	53619	33314

Appendix D: Measurement conversions

speed

km/h	mph
50	31
100	62
150	93
175	109
200	124
225	140
250	155
275	171
300	186
325	202
350	218
375	233
400	249

fuel consumption

lit/100 km	mpg (US)	mpg (Imp)
5	47	57
6	39	47
7	34	40
8	29	35
9	26	31
10	24	28
11	21	26
12	20	24
13	18	22
14	17	20
15	16	19
16	15	18
17	14	17
18	13	16
19	12	15
20	12	14
21	11	13
22	11	13
23	10	12
24	10	12
25	9	11

distance (km-miles)

km	miles
1	0.6
50	31
100	62
150	93
200	124
250	155
300	186
350	217
400	248

distance (mm-inches)

mm	inches
50	2.0
60	2.4
70	2.8
80	3.1
90	3.5
100	3.9
500	19.7
1000	39.4
1500	59.1
1750	68.9
2000	78.7
2250	88.6
2500	98.4
2750	108.3
3000	118.1
3250	128.0
3500	137.8
3750	147.6
4000	157.5
4250	167.3
4500	177.2
4750	187.0
5000	196.9

mass

kg	pounds	Tons (US)	Tons (imp)
1	2	0.0	0.0
100	220	0.1	0.1
200	441	0.2	0.2
300	661	0.3	0.3
400	882	0.4	0.4
500	1102	0.6	0.5
600	1323	0.7	0.6
700	1543	0.8	0.7
800	1764	0.9	0.8
900	1984	1.0	0.9
1000	2205	1.1	1.0
1100	2425	1.2	1.1
1200	2646	1.3	1.2
1300	2866	1.4	1.3
1400	3086	1.5	1.4
1500	3307	1.7	1.5
1600	3527	1.8	1.6
1700	3748	1.9	1.7
1800	3968	2.0	1.8
1900	4189	2.1	1.9
2000	4409	2.2	2.0
2100	4630	2.3	2.1
2200	4850	2.4	2.2

capacity

cc	cu in
250	15.3
500	30.5
750	45.8
1000	61.0
1250	76.3
1500	91.5
1750	106.8
2000	122.0
2250	137.3
2500	152.5
2750	167.8
3000	183.0
3250	198.3
3500	213.5
3750	228.8
4000	244.0
4250	259.3
4500	274.5
4750	289.8
5000	305.0
5250	320.3

litres	US gal	Imp gal
30	7.9	6.6
40	10.6	8.8
50	13.2	11.0
60	15.9	13.2
70	18.5	15.4
80	21.1	17.6
90	23.8	19.8
100	26.4	22.0

Index

Acknowledgments

An ambitious project such as *The Complete Book of BMW* could not have been contemplated without the assurance of access to a truly exceptional library of photographs, a collection extensive enough to do justice to the hundreds of different cars detailed in these pages.

With only a handful of exceptions, all the photographs and illustrations in this book come from the collection of BMW Historisches Archiv at the company headquarters in Munich. My thanks go to BMW for kindly allowing us to reproduce these many splendid images, and to Ruth Standfuss for so ably tracking down the precise shots I required.

I am forever indebted to Richard Gaul, BMW's director of public relations, for his instrumental role in convincing his former chairman, Eberhard von Kuenheim, to agree to a rare interview specially for this book; I was honoured that Mr von Kuenheim was able to spare me several hours of his precious time.

My thanks, too, go to Kai Jacobsen at BMW Mobile Tradition for his assistance, and Chris Willows of BMW GB deserves my thanks, too, for his steadfast support for this book and for his encyclopaedic knowledge of all things BMW, especially motor sport.

The co-operation of two of my colleagues, Hugh Hunston and Richard Feast, on chapters 13 and 29, and on 21, 26 and 27 respectively, has been invaluable, and on a more practical level my son George has come up trumps in the huge task of finding, selecting and organising the hundreds of photographs on these pages.

The annual *Automobile Revue, Glass's Guide Car Check Book* and websites such as bmwworld.com have provided valuable guidance on several technical points, as have the pages of the *Financial Times, Automotive News Europe* and *FT Automotive World* on business issues. Many shelves full of heavyweight books have been consulted in my researches: among the most useful have been these:

Horst Mönnig: *The BMW story: a Company in its time*, Sidgwick and Jackson, for BMW AG, London, 1991

Halwart Schrader, Trans Ron Wakefield: *BMW: a History*, Osprey, London, 1979

Werner Oswald and Eberhard Kittler: *Alle BMW Automobile seit 1928*, 2nd edition, Motor Buch Verlag, Stuttgart, 2002

Richard Feast: *Kidnap of the Flying Lady: how Germany captured both Rolls-Royce and Bentley*, Motorbooks International, St Paul, MN, 2003

BMW M Power, published by BMW M GmbH, Munich, 1998

Ken Gross: *The Illustrated BMW Buyers' Guide*, 2nd edition, Motorbooks International, Osceola, WI, 1994

Fred Larimer: *BMW Buyers' Guide*, Motorbooks International, St Paul, MN, 2002

Laurence Meredith: *BMW 1975-2001 Model* by Model, Crowood Press, Marlborough, 2002

Eric Dymock: *BMW – a Celebration*, Pavilion Books, London, 1990

Martin Buckley and Nick Dimbleby: *BMW Cars*, MBI Publishing Company, St Paul, MN, 2001

BMW Coupés – a tradition of elegance, BMW AG profiles, IAA edition 2003, BMW Mobile Tradition, Munich, 2003

And finally there is one person without whom this book really would not have come about. Publisher Rob Golding devised the concept for this book – and I did not need much persuasion to take on the writing and research,. My thanks to him.

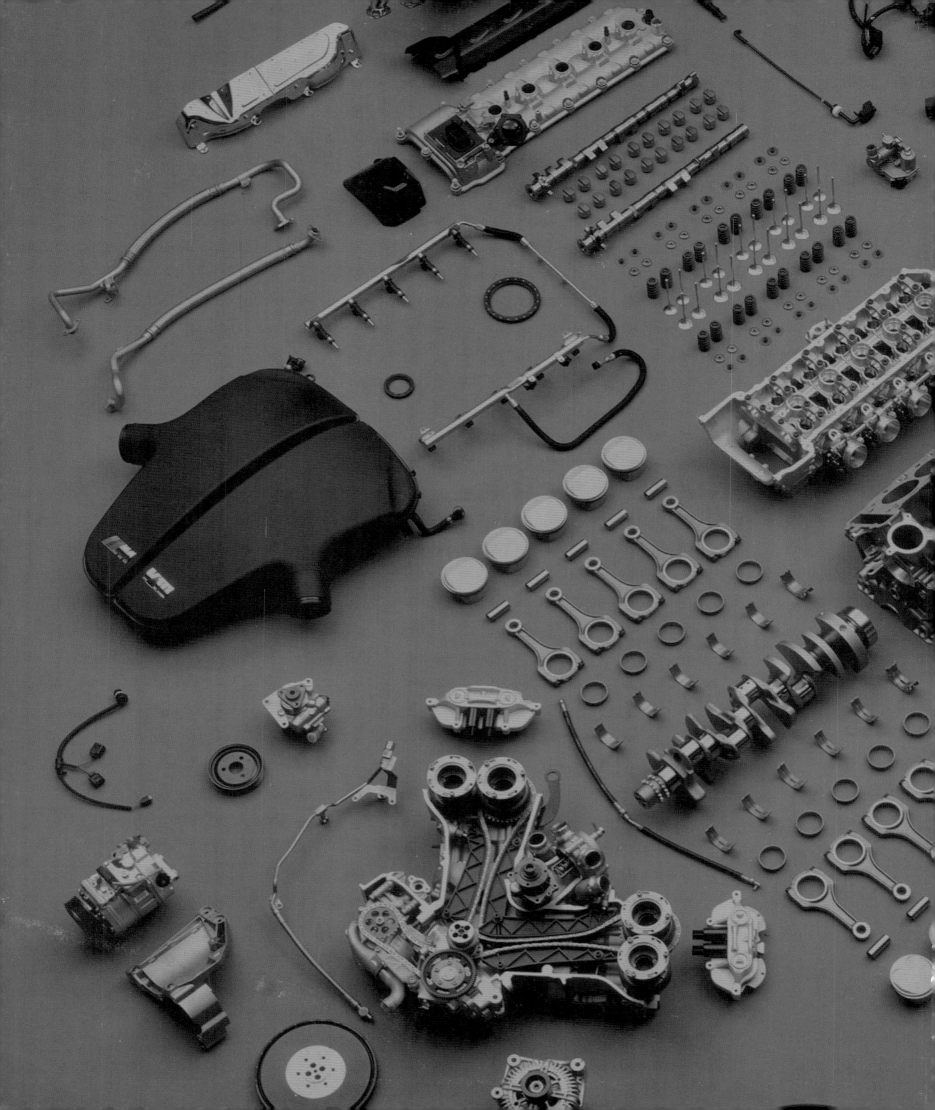